Knowledge,
Difference,
and Power

Knowledge, Difference, and Power

Essays Inspired by

Women's Ways of Knowing

Nancy Rule Goldberger

Jill Mattuck Tarule

Blythe McVicker Clinchy

Mary Field Belenky,

Editors

BASIC

BOOKS

A Member of the Perseus Books Group

Published by Basic Books,
A Member of the Perseus Books Group.

Designed by Elliott Beard

Library of Congress Cataloging-in-Publication Data

Knowledge, difference, and power: essays inspired by women's
ways of knowing/edited by Nancy Rule Goldberger. . . [et al.]—
1st ed.
    p. cm.
Includes index.
ISBN 0-465-09098-2 (cloth)
ISBN 0-465-03733-x (paper)
    1. Women—United States, Psychology. 2. Women—Educa-
tion—United States. 3. Self-actualization (Psychology) 4. Feminism—United States. 5. Knowledge, Theory of.   I. Goldberger,
Nancy Rule, 1935– .
HQ1206.W32 1996
305.4—dc20   96-21580
                                                           CIP

10 9 8 7 6 5 4

To William G. Perry Jr. and Carol Gilligan
who led the way

"It is wise to listen."
Heraclitus

CONTENTS

The Beginning of the Story

Collaboration and Separation

TEN YEARS AGO, my colleagues—Mary Belenky, Blythe Clinchy, Jill Tarule—and I introduced a theory of women's psychology, development, and ways of knowing in our coauthored book *Women's Ways of Knowing* (WWK). One by-product of *WWK's* publication and its subsequent positive reception was the interest in the nature of our collaboration it triggered: How did four people write together, think together? What about feelings of territoriality? Did we never disagree or get angry—or, heaven forbid, become competitive? Weren't the ideas *really* attributable to individuals? Who really wrote which chapter?

Indeed, as we four worked together, we marveled at how ideas grew as we talked and listened to one another. On our own, by ourselves, the ideas often seemed elusive. They sprang to life once we sat down to talk. In the writing of WWK, we were determined to speak in a single voice, an exercise that was difficult but in the end successful, we thought. Throughout the writing, we kept in mind the metaphor of a chorus of voices that was to sing the story we wanted to tell; there were to be no solos. Such a cooperative approach to inquiry and authorship was transformative for all of us. We began to refer to our method as "pajama-party model scholarship" to emphasize the fact that we worked by meeting and working in our homes days at a time, laughing, arguing, and eating together. When it came time to turn our manuscript over to the publisher, we anguished over how we could communicate the truly collaborative nature of our work in a linear culture that insists on reading the order of authorship as indicating the degree of contribution. The only solution (since the publisher did not think a circle of names would work) was to arrange our names alphabetically. Even so, "Belenky" became known to many as the author; the rest of us often disappeared into the "et al."

Following the publication of the book, separation anxiety set in as we returned to our old milieus and began, once again, to put our professional lives together outside the collaboration. Our sense of "we" became more diffuse as the years passed and we each developed new focuses and interests; our individual voices began to emerge. Even though we moved about giving talks and workshops about our collaborative work, most often we traveled and spoke *alone* to audiences. The use of "I" began to supplant the "we."

Mary, Blythe, Jill, and I did have chances, however, during the past decade to interact and continue to work collaboratively. One such important opportunity was the annual meeting of the National Conference on Education for Women's Development (a network of women researchers, administrators, teachers, and students), which our project had spawned in the mid-1980s. By coming together with others who had been influenced by our work, we reconnected and extended our study circle. Some members of the network are contributors to this book.

As the tenth anniversary of the publication of WWK approached, we four began to think about creating a new book to bring our own research up to date and provide a forum in which other scholars could discuss the relevance of our work to theirs. This time, however, we decided that individuals would speak in their own voices, narrating the story of the relation of the ways of knowing theory to their own work.

I was interested in taking the primary responsibility for planning and editing this new volume and writing the Introduction. Our understanding was that I would turn to Mary, Blythe, and Jill often for advice, support, and help in editorial tasks. My name is listed first to reflect my special role; the other editors' names are listed in reverse order from the original alphabetical list.

While working on this book, the four of us marveled at how easily we fell into our old routines and collaborative spirit, even though each of us has "separated" from the group and gone on to work on special interests. This new book, then, is offered in the spirit of "we" as well as "I."

Nancy Goldberger
West Stockbridge, Massachusetts

INTRODUCTION

Looking Backward, Looking Forward*

NANCY RULE GOLDBERGER

THEORIES ARE STORIES and authors of theories are storytellers. In our 1986 book *Women's Ways of Knowing* (WWK), Mary Belenky, Blythe Clinchy, Jill Tarule, and I began a story of women's development of self, voice, and mind. Over the past decade our theory has grown, moved into the world, met skeptics as well as adherents along the way. Our theory,

*To say that my thinking as I planned and put together this collection of essays has been influenced by others would be an understatement. The encouragement of my friend and former BasicBooks editor Jo Ann Miller launched this book; Juliana Nocker, Jo Ann's successor, ably assisted me through the middle and final stages of production. From the earliest phases of envisioning contributions and contributors to the book to the later phases of editorial readings, I have also been supported and nurtured by my coeditors and favorite collaborators, Jill, Blythe, and Mary. I would especially like to thank Kathleen Strnad, who was so helpful in sorting through the citation indices, and Sally Ruddick, whose careful reading, thoughtful analysis, and caring advice are always welcome to me. I have benefited greatly from my interactions with other contributors to this book as we have discussed their chapters and my own; their questions and insights have spurred my thinking. And I am more aware than ever of how much I rely on my family—my husband, Leo; my daughter, Jessica; and my sister of the past and future, Jill Jakes—for honest reaction and loving attention to all I do. I am especially proud of Jessica, who is blossoming into an impressive scholar and a formidable editor.

1

as we and others have put it to use, has, like any story, shifted and changed over time in the telling and retelling. In this volume, my WWK coauthors and I, together with fourteen contributors, look backward over the decade since the book came out to see how our theory was taken up and used, evaluated and criticized, extended and elaborated, to accommodate new data and new thinking.

When *Women's Ways of Knowing* was first published, we authors, of course, had no idea of how it would be received nor what niche it would find in the psychological and women's studies literature. Our speculations and fears, however, were abundant. The author's nightmare is that a book will disappear into some void, never to be noticed, much less reviewed. Or it may find its way onto the bookshelves of good friends and colleagues whose interests in women's lives converge with ours. Our serious (and professionally ambitious) sides hoped that the book would enter the larger arena of academic discourse as a contribution to what was just becoming a new "hot" topic in the social sciences—that is, the social construction of knowledge and truth. And our human and feminist sides hoped that our words and observations would reach and resonate with the "ordinary women" who had shared their stories with us. The book has succeeded well beyond our expectations. It has reached and affected the lives of ordinary women, according to a multitude of testimonials we have received. And, according to citation index searches in the social sciences and humanities literature, it has been widely influential, and also criticized, over the past decade. It has generated interest in a wide variety of fields—psychology, philosophy, education, women's studies, diversity and culture studies, humanities, law and feminist jurisprudence, nursing, theology, and communications.

In this volume, we revisit WWK and pick up the narrative of how people know and come to think of themselves as knowers. Mary, Blythe, Jill, and I describe in our respective chapters the shifts and development of our thinking and research on personal epistemology, psychological development, and the complex interrelationships of ways of knowing, gender, race, class, and culture; we also address our critics and speak to what we believe are misreadings of the constructs and claims presented in WWK. In addition, the contributors describe in some detail how they have translated ways of knowing theory in their own work and in their own disciplines. Some contributors provide a general context for or overview of the public and academic reception of the ways of knowing theory; others address the utility and successful applications of the theory as well as criticisms and limitations they consider important. As a collection of coordinated essays, this book provides an expanded discussion of the nature of individual, institutional, and cultural differences in knowing and learning. It touches on such topics as power differentials in the construction and evaluation of knowledge, silence and power, loss of and attainment of voice, collaborative learning, connected knowing and teaching, cultural diversity and local knowledge, and what Sandra Harding (this volume) calls the "epistemological crisis of the West."

Because public and academic attention recently has turned (or returned) to debates about human differences and which differences make a difference, this book is particularly timely. According to academic and political voices from the right and alarmist reports in the popular media, feminism and multiculturalism (because of their focus on human diversity and the cultural construction of values) threaten "core" American canon and values. This book, by examining the history, politics, and heuristics of one particular theory of human diversity—that is, ways of knowing theory—should contribute to a more enlightened discussion of how "difference" research can raise important, unavoidable questions concerning how knowledge has been defined, validated, and claimed in twentieth-century America—and how only certain segments of the population have been empowered as valid and respected knowers.

A BRIEF REVIEW OF OUR
WAYS OF KNOWING THEORY

The original research behind WWK was undertaken to bring attention to the missing voices of women in our theories of how people know and learn. Following feminist theorist Carol Gilligan's pioneering work on the missing perspectives of women in psychology's theories of human development (Gilligan, 1982), the WWK authors reasoned that—since the only template for understanding shifts over time in an individual's assumptions about the nature of truth, knowledge, and the learning process was provided by the psychologist William Perry (1970) in his study of young men at Harvard—we should study women. Although Perry's scheme of personal epistemology and development in the college years was a persuasive and generative theory, and had been very influential in educational circles since its publication, it failed, we argued, to examine closely women's lives and women's experience.[1] Thus, the WWK project was begun as an extension and critique of the Perry scheme.

Our initial interview sample on which WWK was based was a diverse group of 135 women, of different ages, ethnic and class backgrounds; from urban to rural communities; with varying degrees of education (from high school dropouts to women with graduate or professional degrees). Compared to most developmental psychological research of the time, the sample was unusual in that it was demographically hetero-geneous—intentionally so, since we were quite aware of the limitations of prior research, which had worked with samples of convenience, that is, white, middle-class, and most often male. We argued that the diversity of the sample of women whom we interviewed would allow us "to see the common ground that women share, regardless of background" (Belenky, Clinchy, Goldberger, & Tarule, 1986, p. 13). Looking back now on what motivated our work in the mid-1980s, it is clear that we believed (and still do) that gender is a major social, historical, and political category that affects the life choices of all women in all communities and cultures. We (implicitly) asked, How were Western social constructions of gender and authority affecting women's sense of self, voice, and mind? In WWK, we zeroed in on two socializing institutions—the institutions of family and school—that communicate to growing girls how womanhood is to be defined, how and what they are to know, and how they are to make choices in their lives. Thus, in our analysis of women's life stories, we allowed the larger cultural, social, and political context of individual lives (now called "positionality") to recede as we focused instead on, and made central in the text, five knowledge perspectives that we believed captured some of the major ways women (regardless of class, race, or eth-nic background) think about themselves, authorities, truth, and life options. We did not discuss our findings in terms of class, racial, or eth-nic differences among the women, a decision that seemed reasonable at the time, given our relatively small and nonrepresentative sample and qualitative research methodology that does not lend itself to comparative statements and conclusions. Let us listen to the voices of diverse women, we thought, to hear what they say about the varieties of female experi-ence before we move to generalizations about differences among them that are related to class, race, ethnicity, or other social distinctions.

The five perspectives that we described in detail in WWK were:

1: *Silence*—a position of not knowing in which the person feels voice-less, powerless, and mindless.

2: *Received knowing*—a position at which knowledge and authority are construed as outside the self and invested in powerful and knowing oth-ers from whom one is expected to learn.

3: *Subjective knowing*—in which knowing is personal, private, and based on intuition and/or feeling states rather than on thought and articulated ideas that are defended with evidence.

4: *Procedural knowing*—the position at which techniques and procedures for acquiring, validating, and evaluating knowledge claims are developed and honored. We also described two modes of knowing that we first noticed as we described different procedures for knowing that women adopt: *separate knowing*, which is characterized by a distanced, skeptical, and impartial stance toward that which one is trying to know (a reasoning against), and *connected knowing*, which is characterized by a stance of belief and an entering into the place of the other person or the idea that one is trying to know (a reasoning with) (see Blythe Clinchy's chapter, this volume, for an extended discussion of connected and separate knowing).

5: *Constructed knowing*—the position at which truth is understood to be contextual; knowledge is recognized as tentative, not absolute; and it is understood that the knower is part of (constructs) the known. In our sample of women, constructed knowers valued multiple approaches to knowing (subjective and objective, connected and separate) and insisted on bringing the self and personal commitment into the center of the knowing process.

RECEPTION AND CONTROVERSY

As many of the contributors to this book demonstrate, the WWK scheme and categories have been put into action across many disciplines, both in support of and as fodder for feminist, postmodern, and people of color critics of theory, method, and practice in the social sciences. During the vital years between the mid-1980s and the mid-1990s, feminist theory itself proliferated, splintered, sometimes turned against itself, and struggled toward resolutions (for instance, see Alcoff, 1988; Nicholson, 1990; Hirsch & Keller, 1990; Herrman & Stewart, 1994). Among academic feminists, the WWK star has risen, fallen, and reappeared, as Frances Maher and Mary Kay Tetreault point out in their chapter. Feminist controversy has centered on essentialism versus constructionism, the misrepresentation of "women's" experience by white feminists, and the "flight from reason" that some people feel our work encourages. Among psychologists, educators, and others who have been putting the theory to use (as they teach, treat patients, or design educational and intervention programs), debate also centers on the validity of developmental stage theory (some classify WWK as such) and the meaning and "superiority" of constructed knowing as a developmental ideal.

To orient the reader to the chapters ahead, I will briefly describe the nature of some of the controversies, themes, and debates that revolve around ways of knowing theory. However, a word of caution to the reader: be aware that our ways of knowing theory is, as I have said earlier, a story—and a story that shifts in meaning and focus with whoever is doing the telling. In this volume, the original coauthors will address the challenges to our original theory even as we rethink and transform it and admittedly disagree among ourselves about meanings and implications. Over the past decade, we have been attentive to audience reactions as we have spoken across the country and abroad, attentive also to reviews and responses to our work and, as much as possible, to the ways others have interpreted and applied our theory. But authors of stories (and theories) lose control of their stories once they reach the world. Every reading is, in a sense, a revision. Other people's perspectives on ways of knowing and other people's analyses of the forces of oppression and the comforts of white privilege affecting women have caught us up short and challenged our thinking. We have evolved in the way we think about and present our story, as will be evident in our chapters ahead.

How we see ourselves and our theory may not gibe with the way other contributors talk about and interpret it; many of them, after all, are reacting primarily to the 1986 book and the constructs and categories as we described them then. Although the Rashomon effect is unavoidable, I will cross-reference the chapters in this Introduction so that the reader can more easily see how different authors present and discuss the same topic. However, each of the chapters deals with many of the following topics, so that the reader ultimately will have to find her or his own way through the discussions. The chapters are organized in three parts: Part I contains essays that describe how the ideas presented in WWK have been applied (and criticized) in different disciplinary areas over the past decade; Part II contains essays that expand on our theory and extend our thinking about connected and collaborative knowing (other chapters also deal with applications of connected knowing in various settings); Part III contains essays that are particularly focused on the role that power, positionality, and culture play in knowledge construction and strategies for knowing.

ESSENTIALISM VERSUS CONSTRUCTIONISM

The charge of "essentialism" (the postulation of enduring, distinctive, and possibly "natural" or biologically based sex differences) against our work and theory has certainly affected its reception among feminist theorists and its placement in array of "feminisms" and feminist strategies (Hare-Mustin & Marecek, 1990; Bordo, 1990; Morawski, 1994). Classified with Carol Gilligan, Sara Ruddick, Nel Noddings, Evelyn Fox Keller, among others who have been variously called "different voice," "alpha-bias," or "relational" theorists, the WWK group has been tagged as in the essentialist camp and out of the constructivist mainstream, which recognizes the centrality of the social construction of gender. As much of the following material will demonstrate (see especially chapters by Goldberger, Harding, Maher, and Ruddick), this reading of our work is an oversimplification.

Although many people have interpreted our work as arguing for essential gender differences, we did not claim that the five perspectives or ways of knowing that we described were distinctively female. We believed that those categories might be expanded or modified with the inclusion of a more culturally and socioeconomically diverse sample of women and men. However, it is so that we studied women only so that their perspectives, which had been masked or distorted by masculinist psychology, could come into view. In the mid-1980s, women-only studies were seen (by us and others) as correctives to psychology's historical neglect of women's experience; such studies represented an important phase in feminist theorizing, as Maher points out in her chapter. Readers may have been misled into thinking we were making an essentialist argument by the title of the book, which did emphasize *women's* ways of knowing. And perhaps they concluded that we must have meant to imply that there were distinctively different and unique *men's* ways of knowing. In fact, the constructs and categories we introduced have much in common with those of Perry (1970), who did study men. However, our interviews with women uncovered salient themes (missing or deemphasized in Perry's theory) related to the experience of silencing and disempowerment, lack of voice, the importance of personal experience in knowing, connected strategies in knowing, and resistance to disimpassioned knowing. Such themes suggested to us that there are hidden agendas of power in the way societies define and validate and ultimately genderize knowledge; the stories women told depicted a variety of different ways women understand, accommodate, and resist societal definitions of authority and truth. Our story of women's development and education was intended to describe not just different *ways* women know, but how women (in the United States) are socialized to know and how they respond to socializing forces. Essential gender difference was not part of our story as some have assumed; a detailed description of some women's experience of knowing *was* central to the story.

"WHITE" FEMINISM: WOMEN OF COLOR SPEAK OUT

The controversy and conflicting objectives that surround feminist theory, including ours, have been further complicated by critiques of "white" feminist theory by women of color who argue that the experience and perspectives of members of society who are marginalized by race or class are not well represented in the conceptual framework of much of feminist theory. In their chapter, Vanessa M. Bing and Pamela Trotman Reid give a historical overview of how psychology has (mis)understood and studied race and class, and how feminist theorists have tended to perpetuate this tradition in gender studies. Although Bing and Reid do not directly critique WWK in their analysis, I have included this chapter because this kind of analysis by women of color represents an important milestone in the study of difference.

Aída Hurtado, in her chapter, more directly addresses epistemology, race, class, and gender. She argues that the ways of knowing cultivated by the multiply stigmatized poor black female, for example, cannot be adequately explored or described if women are collapsed into one group without attention to race and class. WWK is vulnerable to this particular criticism. Even though in our original research we interviewed a demographically diverse sample, we stopped short of analyzing our data to highlight the role of social positionality and oppression in the construction of knowledge.

Over the past ten years, as we have listened to and learned from women of color and other culture theorists, we have become much more alert to the situational and cultural determinants of knowing and to the relationship between power and knowledge, left largely implicit in WWK. My new research, as well as that of my colleague Mary Belenky, is extending our thinking of how knowledge and knowing, class, race, gender, and culture intersect and shape one another.

As I have asserted elsewhere (Goldberger, 1996), in any society there are privileged epistemologies—the socially valued ways of knowing for establishing and evaluating truth claims—that assume normative standing. When a person's ways of knowing are at odds with the dominant or adoptive culture, he or she may experience a sense of coercion over "the right way to know" or may feel called on to silence or give up ways of knowing that are devalued. On the other hand, persons may develop strategies for knowing that are unique to their social positionality and history of oppression. In WWK, we argued that ways of knowing identified historically as feminine (in the United States, this includes both the intuitive or feeling-based knowing that WWK associates with subjective knowing and the empathylike procedural knowing we call *connected knowing*) have been devalued and discouraged in institutions of higher learning in favor of propositional knowledge and abstract, meta modes of knowing, particularly what we call separate knowing, which stresses impartiality and detachment. There is an implicit message that reaches us all, men and women, as we move through the American educational system and the workplace: If you want to succeed in this world, you cannot let emotions and personal considerations cloud your thought. You must toughen up and learn to think like (white) men. This message has affected the way (white) women in our society evaluate their intellectual potential, as we point out often in WWK. Note that this prevailing stereotype of masculine and feminine thought effectively ignores (renders invisible) the self-evaluations and ways of knowing of people of color, many of whom have assertive voices and positive self-regard and do not accommodate white norms and white sex role stereotypes (Fordham, 1993).

Several chapters in this volume (especially see Bing & Reid; Hurtado; Debold, Tolman, and Brown; Harding; Maher; and Goldberger) address further the relationship between knowledge and social power, a central consideration in what have come to be called *standpoint* epistemologies (Jaggar, 1983; Hartsock, 1983; Harding, 1986, 1991) and social *positionality* and *situated knowledge* (hooks, 1983; De Laurentis, 1986; Collins, 1990; Haraway, 1991).

THE "FLIGHT FROM REASON"?

Some people who have (presumably) read and written about our work believe that we endorse (even preach) the superiority of antirationalist, subjectivist epistemologies, an attitude we do not hold and in fact warn against (WWK, pp. 83–84). The essays by Blythe Clinchy and Sara Ruddick in this volume counter this assumption and explore what can be called alternative ideals of reason. Misunderstanding of our position seems to arise in part from a confusion of the naive relativism of subjective knowing (any opinion is as valid as any other), a position that many of our interviewees held, with the contextual relativism of constructed knowing (truth claims must be evaluated within the context in which they arise), a version of relativism that draws on reflection and reason and that we imply might be a developmental ideal. However, among certain critics from the political right, it is the spectre of "relativism" itself (and relativistic epistemologies) that is perceived as problematic, even threatening. Public experience of a growing cultural diversity in the United States, coincident with the feminist and culture critiques of tradition and normative policies, has led to an upsurge of sentiment against feminism and multiculturalism by those who are protective of American "truths" and foundational values (for example, D'Souza, 1991; Bloom, 1994; Sommers, 1994). Rather than embrace the fundamental value of human diversity in a democratic society—"affirmative diversity" (Jones, 1995)— and acknowledge the potential contributions and relevance of multiple perspectives to both theory and social problem solving and interventions, these conservative alarmist voices are encouraging a fearfulness that pervades even the most rational circles. As an example, an op-ed piece in the *Wall Street Journal* (July 15, 1995, byline: Christina Hoff Sommers) reported on a recent scientific conference organized to address the danger of a national "flight from reason." Irrationalism, Sommers and some of the conference participants claim, is being promoted by multiculturalists, feminists (including the WWK group), and environmentalists, who argue for the benefits of multiple approaches to knowing and who have questioned the integrity of standard science, which has dominated Western society's search for answers and evaluation of truth claims.

That this fear of irrationalism and subjectivist epistemologies is echoed even in feminist circles is perhaps best represented by the recent attack on women's studies ideology by Daphne Patai and Noretta Koertge (1994). Arguing that many practices of academics who "profess feminism" are contributing to dubious scholarship, these authors single out WWK as an influential text that has steered educators and students into an overvaluation of connected knowing, a way of knowing that Patai and Koertge claim disdains proof, disproof, and criticism. "Critical thinking," they assert, "is specifically ruled out by the (WWK) model of connected knowing" (p. 176). They add that "the *last* thing (students) should be taught is the dangerous proposition that all subjective opinions are equal" (p. 174). To be fair, it is true that Patai and Koertge recognize that it is not WWK's argument that connected knowing is the penultimate approach to knowing; it is, as they point out, the misapprehension of other people who use the scheme.

We have always taken the position that many women also value reason, although not necessarily the version of rationality espoused by separate procedural knowers. In WWK, we were struggling toward an alternative definition of reason in our description of connected knowing (a project that Blythe Clinchy pursues in this volume). We believe that connected knowing is not opposed to, but is an instance of, rationality. However, admittedly, in WWK we contributed to the erroneous assumption that we disclaim separate knowing as a viable strategy because we so heavily emphasized how Western history and a politics of knowledge delegitimize connected knowing and privilege separate knowing. Thus, although we do assert that connected knowing is a mode of knowing historically undervalued in American schools, professions, and workplaces, we do not argue that it is superior to or should replace separate knowing, a mode identified with the scientific method and some people's definitions of critical thinking. As Blythe Clinchy argues in this volume, Patai and Koertge seriously misunderstand connected knowing, which, she points out, is as thoughtful, effortful, and objective as separate knowing. Patai and Koertge (as well as Lorraine Code, 1991) also confound the naive relativism of subjectivism with the more reasoned relativism of constructed knowing—an epistemology that can be argued against, but not on the grounds that Patai and Koertge propose.

In a provocative essay in this volume, the philosopher Sara Ruddick discusses her interest in connected knowing and alternative conceptions of reason—reason's "femininity." She also reports on her several years spent teaching WWK and her experiences with students who feel reason is under attack by certain values expressed in WWK.

Several other contributors to this book extend our thinking about the utility of connected knowing by examining how it has been or could be applied in various knowledge arenas and in pedagogical settings. Carrie Menkel-Meadow examines how the concept and value of connected knowing, argued for in WWK, have played a role in feminist legal theory and feminist jurisprudence and have contributed to feminist challenges to the value of adversarial contestation; Mary Belenky shows how central connected knowing is to the nurturance and development of public leadership in communities; Michael Mahoney looks at connected knowing as one of the conceptual links between constructivist psychotherapy and feminist theory; Patrocinio Schweickart argues that connected knowing has important precedents in literary and composition studies and provides a conceptual gateway for challenging the philosopher Jürgen Habermas's postulation that dialogue is synonymous with argument; and Ann Stanton takes us into the arena where connected knowing as a guiding construct has been most frequently used and abused, that is, in education.

WAYS OF KNOWING AND DEVELOPMENTAL CHANGE

Whether or not our five knowledge perspectives represent a stagelike developmental sequence has been a matter of some confusion and debate. Numbers of people who have applied our epistemological framework, particularly in educational settings, have worked from the assumption that our five ways of knowing are arranged sequentially from less to more adequate (or less to more flexible), thus placing received knowing, for example, low on a developmental scale (presumably because, as we define it in WWK, it is a kind of passive and rigid way of knowing that assigns authority to sources external to the self). Entire educational curricula have been redesigned to promote movement from received knowing through the subsequent positions to what is assumed to be the endpoint of development: constructed knowing. Ann Stanton, in her extensive review of the educational literature citing WWK, takes a close look at some of the educational ventures that have used the WWK categories as a developmental map.

Other contributors to this volume ask whether movement from one way of knowing to another should be considered "development" and whether some ways of knowing can be deemed more adequate, more mature, more complex without examining the value assumptions and the ethnocentricism that probably underlie such a developmental schematic (see chapters by Ruddick and Goldberger).

Elizabeth Debold, Deborah Tolman, and Lyn Mikel Brown, in their chapter, question the model of development and trajectory of development that are suggested in WWK. In their own research with adolescent girls, they have been sensitized to how cultural practices and cultural authority shape how and what people know as well as how people develop.

In spite of the conflicting attitudes among our contributors as to whether "development" is a viable construct (the disagreement seems most marked between the psychologists and the philosophers), the notion of the WWK scheme as developmental sequence will not readily go away. Ultimately, anyone using the scheme has to face the question of what are the determinants that govern a person's shift in epistemological perspective over time and what are the determinants of, and how adequate is, reliance on one way of knowing to the exclusion of others. Are the determinants developmental? situational? strategic? political? cultural? These issues are likely to be debated for some time.

CONSTRUCTED KNOWING

Allied with the question of whether our scheme is developmental across stages is the question of whether we believe constructed knowing to be a superior or ideal epistemology. Arguing for ideals or normative developmental endpoints is particularly troublesome in this postmodern era in which universals and absolutes are decried. However, as I have said elsewhere (Goldberger, 1996) and also argue in this volume, constructed knowing can be considered "superior" in its flexibility and in the sense that it represents a meta perspective on knowing, a perspective at which one acknowledges "that different routes to knowing have their place, their logic, and usefulness" (p. 182). However, as Sara Ruddick in this volume and others (Code, 1991) point out, to the extent that constructed knowing is equated solely with epistemological relativism, it can lend itself to "a tepid epistemological laissez faire." Sandra Harding extends this point in her chapter by pointing out that the constructivism described in WWK can result in "either relativist or (anti-absolutist and anti-relativist) standpoint epistemologies." Needless to say, the debate continues on the definition and superiority of constructed knowing. Its value and ideality depend on who is doing the valuing and setting the definitional standards—and to what end.

NEW QUESTIONS AS THE THEORY GROWS

The story of the ways of knowing theory over the past decade is not just one of hard times and controversy. I believe, and several contributors will show, the theory is expanding, being rethought to accommodate new observations and new questions, and broadening its scope. Much of the new thinking brings ways of knowing into dialogue with other evolving theories in the social sciences, particularly in the areas of embodiment and embodied knowing: intersubjectivity, a construct used by the Russian psychologist Lev Vygotsky (1978) among others and now frequently discussed among psychotherapists and interpersonal clinical theorists; cooperative inquiry and the coconstruction of knowledge; and cultural psychology and postcolonial studies.

EMBODIMENT AND EMBODIED KNOWING

Mind–body dualism, tracked across time and the evolution of Western thought, has resulted in the pitting of reason against emotion and male against female. Such a split has contributed to the persistent dichotomizing and stereotyping of modes of thought and ways of knowing and being—and to the genderization of knowledge as we know it in the United States. Several chapters in this book address this topic. Elizabeth Debold, Deborah Tolman, and Lyn Mikel Brown show how at early adolescence the mind/body split perniciously affects the development of girls. Michael Mahoney discusses how the legacy of mind–body dualism in psychology has led to an artificial separation of cognition, emotion, and behavior and to a compartmentalized approach to the understanding of human experience. Embodiment—bringing the body back into the mind—as Mahoney shows, has the potential for influencing the practice of psychotherapy. In my chapter, led by the stories of persons from cultures in which bodily experiences are central in the knowing process, I explore the relationship of body knowledge and body knowing to the ways of knowing categories described in WWK.

SELF-IN-COMMUNITY: COMMUNITIES OF KNOWERS

When WWK was published in 1986, we believed that we had joined forces with other critical theorists who were examining the sexist and racist biases in social science method and theory. Although the vocabulary of constructivism and deconstructionism was just beginning to reach psychology, we identified with what we interpreted as the objectives of this kind of critical analysis—that is, the examination of how Western patriarchal intellectual tradition had shaped questions and answers in the social sciences. By focusing on the genderization of knowledge and knowing and on the vicissitudes of women's development in a patriarchal society, we contributed to the growing understanding of how gender is constructed in the lives of diverse women. What we have become more aware of over the past decade is that our emphasis on *individual* lives and the development of individual voice and mind directed our attention away from *individuals-in-communities* as a meaningful and useful unit of analysis. Knowing is not insular. How one knows is multiply determined within the array of relationships that define the self. Meaning making is not a solitary pursuit, but is interactional and negotiable; that is, knowledge is coconstructed. Persons are "situated" in communities of knowers in which the dynamics of power and status are often controlling factors in how one knows and what one knows.

Several chapters focus on knowledge as coconstruction. Jill Tarule examines how WWK metaphors of "voice" and "sense of voice" directed attention to an individual's sense of authority and mind as if the person were an isolated knower. She argues that metaphors better suited to the understanding of communities of knowers are those of "dialogue" and "conversation." With illustrations from her research with educator Bill Whipple on collaborative learning classrooms, she brings alive the notion of "dialogue communities."

Mary Belenky also has been drawn to the newer notion of the communal construction of knowledge in her studies of "public home-places"—women-based community organizations that can transform their members and the way they define truth and authority. Dialogue-rich communities like the public homeplaces she describes not only change the nature of knowledge but provide the breeding ground for political commitments and activism among their members.

Patrocinio Schweickart takes up the discussion of dialogue, rather than reflective monologue, as the basis for the production of conceptions of truth and morality. She contrasts Habermas's assertion that dialogue (though collaborative) is synonomous with argument with what Schweickart believes is an alternative conception of dialogue oriented toward caring and understanding. Schweickart explicitly links the Habermas view of argumentative discourse with what WWK calls separate knowing; a more "womanly" discourse, she feels, is similar to connected knowing. A unique contribution of Schweickart's analysis on discourse communities is her assertion that communicative action involves a receptive (listening) as well as an assertive (speaking) form of agency. Active listening to another, she says, is more than sitting quietly waiting for one's turn to speak; the ethic of care underlies active listening and the open receptivity to another. Mary Belenky in her chapter echoes Schweickart's appreciation of careful active listening.

Clinical interpersonal theorists, such as Robert Stolorow and George Atwood (1992), Stephen Mitchell (1988), and Daniel Stern (1985), have argued that a person's psychological makeup is constituted in interaction with other people. Meaning is not subjective and private, but resides in the intersubjective space between people; knowledge and meaning are coconstructions. Thus, the construct "connected knowing" as defined by WWK and Blythe Clinchy in this volume has much in common with the clinical construct "intersubjectivity." This point is touched on by

Clinchy in her chapter and more fully developed by Michael Mahoney in his, in which he explores the overlap and distinctions between constructivist and feminist theories of psychotherapy.

As I have indicated in the Preface, the collaborative construction of knowledge has preoccupied us in the years since WWK came out. We have been pushed to think about how we know as a collective by people interested in multiple authorship (Ede & Lundsford, 1990). Unfortunately, we have not yet written about or even articulated our process. To the extent that we have something to contribute about how people know in groups (Mary and Jill's new research is especially relevant here), we are linked conceptually with others who are exploring how knowledge is constructed in communities.[2]

CULTURE AND KNOWING

One of the most important changes in my thinking and research, and in my colleagues' as well, has been our increased concern with the way in which social context and culture shape knowing. I have been greatly influenced by the writing of people identified with the relatively new interdisciplinary "movement" called cultural psychology, which includes such culture theorists as Richard Shweder (1991; Shweder & LeVine, 1984), Roy D'Andrade (1984), Jerome Bruner (1990), and Arthur Kleinman (1988), who focus on how psyche and culture construct each other. In my new interviews with members of immigrant groups and diverse subcultures within the United States, I am exploring how indigenous ways of knowing can come into conflict with dominant culture epistemology. How this affects knowing at an individual level as a person accommodates or resists acculturation forces has been a central question in my studies on diversity in ways of knowing.

Aída Hurtado, in her essay, looks at how social identity (as opposed to personal identity), which is susceptible to structural forces of race, class, and gender, determines what access individuals have to knowledge and how one comes to perceive oneself as a knower. She describes five mechanisms—anger, silence/outspokenness, withdrawal, shifting consciousness, and multiple tongues—articulated by feminists of color that affect knowledge construction.

Mary Belenky has been involved in the study of woman-centered community action projects (some exclusively African American, others mixed-race and class organizations), in which she is studying models of "maternal leadership." Moving away from our earlier model of individual development, she is looking at how people and communities develop together and know together.

In her chapter, the philosopher Sandra Harding internationalizes the focus on culture and context by looking at "local knowledge systems" and the genderization of knowledge cross-culturally. She is interested in different standards for scientific knowledge and ways different knowledge emerges through the politics of historical and cultural knowledge-seeking projects. She identifies how Western criteria for knowledge acquisition and validation tend to obscure women's contributions to knowledge.

MORAL COMMITMENT AND MORAL ACTION

Several chapters in this book alert us to what seems to be a current preoccupation among both academics and the general public, that is, the rationale behind and justification for moral commitment and moral action. This is a particularly urgent issue, given the political climate in this country and elsewhere. As Sara Ruddick indicates, it is not just a question of how one knows, but what one knows and the morality that guides the uses to which knowledge is put. For instance, Ruddick asks, can we know (deem true) and assert that child beating is wrong when cultures around the world construe adult actions toward children in very different and conflicting ways? Does an acceptance of the relativity of truth preclude commitment to personal or community-defined truths? Does commitment entail entrenchment and parochialism?

As the world shrinks, differences among us are becoming magnified and too often perceived as threats. The inevitable globalization of economies, limits on natural resources, and migrating human populations are most probably among the primary causes of increasing nationalism and tribalism and fear of the "other." How are we to learn to live with each other when there are such apparent differences among us — in life-style, language, religion, worldviews and ways of knowing, values and strategies for living? In a pluralistic world, can individuals and communities justly set criteria for what is right, what is true, and what is good without demonizing strangers? A better understanding of how different people and cultures know and make truth claims is vital as we seek local solutions to a host of global problems.

This book will, I hope, set the reader thinking about some of these important questions and topics. I expect that it will raise more questions than it answers as our story about the ways people know continues to unfold.

NOTES

1. Perry, in fact, interviewed a few Harvard women, but excluded their stories in the text of his book. In the 1970s and early 1980s, both Blythe Clinchy (Clinchy & Zimmerman, 1982) and Nancy Goldberger (1978) used the Perry scheme to study undergraduate women and had begun to see limitations in its ability to capture women's educational experience.
2. Peter Reason and John Heron (1995), two well-known advocates of participatory action research, argue that "we are in the middle of a paradigm shift towards a participatory world view, one of the emergent expressions of which is cooperative inquiry."

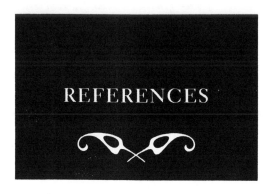

REFERENCES

Alcoff, L. (1988). Cultural feminism versus post-structuralism: The identity crisis in feminist theory. *Signs: J Women in Culture and Society,* 13(3), 405–436.

Belenky, M. F., Clinchy, B. M., Goldberger, N. R., & Tarule, J. M. (1986). *Women's ways of knowing: The development of self, voice, and mind.* New York: Basic Books.

Bloom, H. (1994). *The western canon: The book and school of the ages.* New York: Harcourt Brace.

Bordo, S. (1990). Feminism, postmodernism, and gender-skepticism. In L. Nicholson (Ed.), *Feminism/postmodernism.* New York: Routledge.

Bruner, J. (1990). *Acts of meaning.* Cambridge, MA: Harvard University Press.

Clinchy, B., & Zimmerman, C. (1982). Epistemology and agency in the development of undergraduate women. In P. Perun (Ed.), *The undergraduate woman: Issues in educational equity.* Lexington, MA: D. C. Heath.

Code, L. (1991). *What can she know? Feminist theory and the construction of knowledge.* Ithaca, NY: Cornell University Press.

Collins, P. H. (1990). *Black feminist thought: Knowledge, consciousness, and the politics of empowerment.* Cambridge, MA: Unwin Hyman.

D'Andrade, R. G. (1984). Cultural meaning systems. In R. A. Shweder and R. A. Levine (Eds.), *Culture theory: Essays on mind, self, and emotion.* New York: Cambridge University Press.

De Laurentis, T. (1986). Feminist studies/critical studies: Issues, terms and context. In T. de Laurentis (Ed.), *Feminist studies/Critical studies,* Bloomington, IN: Indiana University Press (1–19).

D'Souza, D. (1991). *Illiberal education.* New York: Free Press.

Ede, L., & Lunsford, A. (1990). *Singular texts/plural authors: Perspectives on collaborative writing.* Carbondale, IL: Southern Illinois University Press.

Fordham, S. (1993). Those loud black girls: Black women, silence, and gender "passing" in the academy. *Anthropology and Education Quarterly,* 24(1), 3–32.

Gilligan, C. (1982). *In a different voice: Psychological theory and women's development.* Cambridge, MA: Harvard University Press.

19

Goldberger, N. R. (1978). The relation between intellectual stage and the behavior of college freshmen in the classroom. Presentation at the Annual Meeting of the Eastern Psychological Association.

Goldberger, N. R. (1996). Women's constructions of truth, self, authority, and power. In H. Rosen & K. Kuehlwein (Ed.), *Constructing realities: Meaning making perspectives for psychotherapists.* San Francisco: Jossey-Bass.

Haraway, D. (1991). Situated knowledges: The science question in feminism and the privilege of partial perspectives. In D. Haraway (Ed.), *Simians, cyborgs, and women.* New York: Routledge.

Harding, S. (1986). *The science question in feminism.* Ithaca, NY: Cornell University Press.

Harding, S. (1991). *Whose science? Whose knowledge?* Ithaca, NY: Cornell University Press.

Hare-Mustin, R. T., & Maracek, J. (Eds.). (1990). *Making a difference: Psychology and the construction of gender.* New Haven, CT: Yale University Press.

Hartsock, N. (1983). The feminist standpoint. In S. Harding and M. Hintikka (Eds.), *Discovering reality.* Dordrecht: Reidel/Kluwer.

Herrman, A. C., & Stewart, A. (Eds.) (1994). *Theorizing feminism: Parallel trends in the humanities and social sciences.* Boulder, CO: Westview Press.

Hirsch, M., & Keller, E. F. (Eds.) (1990). *Conflicts in feminism.* New York: Routledge.

hooks, b. (1983). *Feminist theory: From margin to center.* Boston: South End Press.

Jagger, A. (1983). *Feminist politics and human nature.* Totowa, NJ: Rowman & Allenheld.

Jones, J. M. (1995). Our similarities are different: Toward a psychology of affirmative diversity. In E. J. Trickett, R. J. Watts, & D. Birman (Eds.), *Human diversity: Perspectives on people in context.* San Francisco: Jossey-Bass.

Kleiman, A. (1988). *Rethinking psychiatry: From cultural category to personal experience.* New York: Free Press.

Mitchell, S. (1988). *Relational concepts in psychoanalysis.* Cambridge, MA: Harvard University Press.

Morawski, J. (1994). *Practising feminisms, reconstructing psychology: Notes on a liminal science.* Ann Arbor, MI: University of Michigan Press.

Nicholson, L. J. (Ed.). (1990). Feminism/postmodernism. New York: Routledge.

Patai, D., & Koertge, N. (1994). *Professing feminism.* New York: Basic Books.

Perry, W. G. (1970). *Forms of intellectual and ethical development in the college years.* New York: Holt, Rinehart & Winston.

Reason, P., & Heron, J. (1995). Co-operative inquiry. In J. A. Smith, R. Harre, & L. Van Langenhove (Eds.), *Rethinking methods in psychology*. Thousand Oaks, CA: Sage.

Shweder, R. A. (1991). *Thinking through cultures: Expeditions in cultural psychology*. Cambridge, MA: Harvard University Press.

Shweder, R. A., & LeVine, R. A. (1984). *Culture theory: Essays on mind, self, and emotion*. New York: Cambridge University Press.

Sommers, C. H. (1994). *Who stole feminism? How women have betrayed women*. New York: Simon & Schuster.

Stern, D. (1985). *The interpersonal world of the infant*. New York: Basic Books.

Stolorow, R., & Atwood, G. (1992). *Contexts of being: The intersubjective foundations of psychological life*. Hillsdale, NJ: Analytic Press.

Vygotsky, L. S. (1978). *Mind in society*. Cambridge, MA: Harvard University Press.

PART I

The Past Decade:
Women's Ways of Knowing Applied

Reconfiguring Teaching and Knowing in the College Classroom

ANN STANTON

"WHAT WAS YOUR REACTION to *Women's Ways of Knowing* [WWK]?" I ask the eight students in the adult development seminar. Not unexpectedly, the response is positive, typified by that of Betsy, a single parent returning to college:

> The book was wonderful. It was my life and the stages I have gone through and continue to go through. I thought I was the only person that felt the way the women in those interviews did.

Other students call it "eye-opening" and are inspired by possibilities of growth. Comments Dorothy, a woman in her fifties:

> Those four women are powerful. They did everything—read the literature, they were creative, they were great listeners. I'd love to be a powerful thinker like that.

Ten years after its publication, WWK remains on my syllabus because it affirms and energizes students and encourages reflection about themselves as learners. They use the epistemological perspectives as a possible map of their own thinking, redrawing it where necessary.[1] In addition, the book promotes conversation, equipping us with a shared vocabulary.

What kind of impact has WWK had on other educators? How has it influenced the questions posed, the practices generated, the programs developed? These are the questions that shaped this chapter over months of reading, guided primarily by a citation index of more than five hundred listings.[2]

From the beginning, the opportunity to write this chapter has felt like a not entirely welcome invitation to cater a banquet. Although I'm a good (occasionally inspired) cook, the wealth of ingredients and the diverse tastes of prospective diners were daunting. I began in an exploratory mode, curious to explore possibilities.[3] There ensued a sorting process, based on how central WWK was to the educators' thinking and what aspects of the book were utilized.[4] Finally came the effort to blend and create coherence—to see what larger themes emerged, what conclusions could be drawn.

Education—what should be taught, and how, and whether we are getting our money's worth—always has been heavily contested terrain (Smith, 1990). That it matters so much may be a mark of our personal experiences in schools as well as the heavy freight of hope education bears, as we ask it to carry our dreams and solve our problems. *Women's Ways of Knowing* joined a long-lived, ongoing conversation—asserting its claims, disputing others, and offering its own version of hope.

When WWK entered that conversation in the mid-1980s, curricular debates took the form of arguments about the inclusiveness of the canon and the limits of objectivity (later trivialized into accusations of "political correctness"), and colleges and universities were instituting new programs such as African American Studies and Women's Studies. Demographic and structural changes were evident as well. After unprecedented post–World War II expansion in colleges and universities (including the successful advent of community colleges serving new populations), prosperity began to dwindle, as did the number of potential students. In the 1980s higher education was left with more slots to fill than traditional-aged students to fill them; thus, the gender and age compositions of undergraduate students shifted. By the late 1980s and early 1990s, more than half of undergraduate students were women and the majority of undergraduates were no longer "traditional-aged," that is, between eighteen and twenty-one. Thus, the student audience for WWK was older, was more diverse, had more life experience, and also was more female than any previous generation of college students. And faculty were aware, as never before, of the need to attract and retain students.

A developmental psychologist, I first encountered *WWK* while teaching at a small liberal arts college for women. Offered a position at the last minute to teach seven courses a year, I decided to consider myself a fellow learner with the students and to undergird all of my courses with a fundamental question: What does psychology have to say to and about women?

In these days when literature reviews routinely identify six and more varieties of feminism, it is interesting to remember what it felt like fifteen years ago to face a class of young women and generate questions such as why personality psychologists routinely excluded women as research subjects or why only mothers were studied in relation to child development. Harvard psychologist Carol Gilligan's seminal article in the *Harvard Educational Review* (1977) helped to explain why theories of human development had always left me feeling slightly fraudulent (if not aberrant)[5] and promised new sources and hypotheses. *Women's Ways of Knowing* was another welcome ally. Well versed in psychologist William Perry's (1970) theory of college student development, I was nonetheless mystified by students who were hardworking and bright but had significant difficulty participating in debates and critiquing one another's papers. The book offered a basis for approaching those dilemmas of practice. It simplified and concretized Perry's approach,[6] provided countless moments of recognition and insight about my students' struggles, and illuminated my own experience.

As I read the material gathered for this chapter, it seems to me that the broad appeal of *WWK* lies in its careful attention to dimensions of education that others take for granted or skim over. Principally, it takes women seriously as thinkers and knowers.[7] Rather than impose theories about cognition, the authors begin with their women respondents, listening carefully to how they define powerful learning experiences and go about gathering knowledge and making meaning. The women's own words are at the center of the book; and although the authors did not engage in actual dialogue with them, the reader senses an implicit exchange wherein the authors strain to hear and understand in order to arrive at their insights.

WWK also takes growth and development seriously. In the early and mid-1980s, adult development was still a somewhat new idea, not surprising, given that Sigmund Freud and Jean Piaget, the giants of developmental psychology, regarded developmental processes as basically complete by adolescence. Compounding this for educators was the long reign of behaviorist models of learning, which essentially define growth as the acquisition of content. *WWK*'s model of epistemological development was a welcome eye-opener, describing different underlying world-views or perspectives by which the women made sense of truth, knowledge, and themselves as knowers. There continues to be controversy about whether these perspectives are arranged in a stagelike hierarchy (some perspectives being more adequate than others). Nevertheless, it is supremely useful for educators to see those perspectives laid out so clearly—providing potential diagnostics of student functioning, professorial expectations, and an alternative to the behaviorist model.

Finally, WWK takes teaching seriously. Most college and university teachers have been carefully prepared as researchers, including a long stint of intensive labor on a highly specialized dissertation topic. They have little or no training and only limited experience as teachers (for example, leading discussion sections and grading tests). And despite Excellence in Teaching awards and the various institutes and conferences promoting undergraduate teaching, the culture of higher education rewards research more than teaching. Thus, WWK's attention to the importance of teaching and practices vital to good teaching was, and continues to be, both useful and heartening.

This is not to say that there are no critiques of the book. Some (e.g., Hare-Mustin & Maracek, 1989; Lewis, 1989) dismiss the authors as cultural feminists and "essentialists" who fail to recognize distinctions among women such as race, class, sexual preference, and ablebodiedness; they accuse the book of contributing to stereotyped views that restrict women's lives and possibilities. Others (e.g., Sweeney, 1994) are uncomfortable with categorizing ways of knowing, especially ordering categories hierarchically. However, others simply misread the book and attack it on the basis of their misunderstandings.[8]

How do I react to the criticisms? I find useful Rachel Hare-Mustin's and others' reminder to be attentive to the many ways in which women's experiences and perspectives differ. This points to a larger dilemma in social science: to what extent and for whom and for what purpose are generalizations possible?[9] Rather than dismiss the whole book as those critics do, a process of careful titration is required, filtering the findings against current understandings. In this case, arguing for WWK is its diverse sample, which included Hispanic and African American women from an inner-city community college, adult students who worked full-time, and students in a prestigious women's college. Fully one-third of respondents were poor rural women (who lacked access to higher education but found sources of knowledge in community institutions), whose voices are seldom heard by anyone. The authors chose to highlight larger patterns of commonality, providing many of the women's own comments but only occasionally identifying them by social background (and never by racial group membership) as a means to foreground the epistemological perspectives and make a plausible claim for their existence. This book, in its effort to reassess and extend the insights of WWK, is the most useful response to critics.

The problem with categories of ways of knowing, it seems to me, is not their use per se to organize information but rather their reification, which easily leads to a reductionism in which the person becomes no more than the category.[10] As one who codes interviews for epistemological perspectives, I am well acquainted with individuals' unique combinations of ways of knowing and how those may be configured differently across domains, with students responding differently (for example) to questions about knowledge in their major field versus new fields, informal learning versus classroom learning, disagreements with authorities versus disagreements with friends. Teaching in a tutorial mode, I have the luxury of sensing and adapting to subtle shifts in individual students' understanding.[11]

Yet even in large classrooms, the epistemological categories are potentially useful tools for assessing students' responses and deciding how to proceed. Consider, for example, how understanding the distinction between subjective knowing and connected knowing helps teachers facilitate student discussions differently. A "subjective" discussion would encourage students to air their opinions or relate their experiences in an atmosphere of nonjudgmentalness. While maintaining an aura of careful listening and acceptance, a "connected" discussion would go beyond that, pointing out where opinions are different, helping participants discover the sources of and reasons for the differences, exploring the implications of each position, and asking the class to reconcile different opinions.

Apart from such concrete applications, it is well to recognize that human minds gravitate to categories. It is better to base those judgments on ways of knowing categories derived from carefully considered interviews, than to use idiosyncratic (and ofttimes grumpy) categorizations of students as passive, intellectually lazy, and illogical.

The criticisms that label the authors of WWK as "cultural feminists" and "essentialists" are troubling primarily because they act to cut off dialogue and exclude the work from thoughtful consideration. Ironically, male theorists such as Foucault, Lacan, and Derrida are given considerable leeway so that feminists might mine their theories for useful nuggets, even as worthwhile feminist theories are dismissed with labels (Martin, 1994).

To a large extent, however, WWK has not been dismissed; dialogue around it has been rich and sustained. As the remainder of this chapter will document, educators across a variety of disciplines have engaged with its concepts and put it to use in inventing their own ideas and practices. I have organized what follows into three general themes. First is *epistemology*, signaling that teaching rests on assumptions about the nature of knowledge and that one's epistemological stance necessarily has implications for how the process of education is framed and practiced. Teaching is also a *mode of inquiry*. Most basically, this entails taking a particular perspective on material; for example, not only reading and assessing the scholarship in one's discipline but also thinking about how that can be re/presented to students. This, in turn, means understanding who the students are—their capabilities, motivations, and needs—and thinking about who, ideally, they might become: lifelong learners, producers of knowledge. Teaching is also a *practice*, one that brings together and embodies the other two themes.

TEACHING AND EPISTEMOLOGY

When learning about something you want to know, do you rely on experts? How do you know someone is an expert? Do you agree that . . . where there are no right answers anybody's opinion is as good as another's? How do you know what is right/true?

These are some of the questions the authors of WWK asked in their interviews of 135 women. The responses—focused on the nature of knowledge and truth and themselves as thinkers and knowers—formed the basis of five different epistemological perspectives: silence, received knowing, subjective knowing, procedural knowing, and constructed knowing (see table on page 31). The authors also detected the extensive use of the metaphor "voice," which links thinking and knowing with the capacity to articulate one's thoughts and feel heard.

The book encourages educators to understand that students bring epistemological assumptions into the classroom. They are not purely imbibing the contents of history or biology or psychology lectures and textbooks but are (for example) variously uncritically accepting/rejecting their teachers' expertise, comparing classroom material to their personal experiences and opinions, and seeking to understand and question how answers are arrived at, how knowledge is composed.

College teachers too engage in epistemological endeavors. At present

Women's Ways of Knowing

Silence (knowing-in-action)

Knowledge: Gets knowledge through concrete experience, not words

Mind: Sees self as "deaf and dumb" with little ability to think

Mode: Survives by obedience to powerful, punitive Authority

Voice: Little awareness of power of language for sharing thoughts, insights, and so on

Received knowing

Knowledge: Knowledge received from Authorities

Mind: Sees self as capable/efficient learner; soaks up information

Mode: Good listener; remembers and reproduces knowledge; seeks/invents strategies for remembering

Voice: Intent on listening; seldom speaks up or gives opinion

Subjective knowing

Knowledge: Springs from inner sources; legitimate ideas need to feel right; analysis may destroy knowledge

Mind: Own opinions are unique, valued; fascinated with exploring different points of view; not concerned about correspondence between own truth and external reality

Mode: Listens to inner voice for the truth that's right for her

Voice: Speaks from her feelings/experience, with heart; journals; listens and needs others to listen, without judging

Procedural knowing

Knowledge: Recognizes different frameworks, realms of knowledge; realizes positive role of analysis, other procedures for evaluating, creating knowledge

Mind: Aims to see world as it "really is"—suspicious of unexamined subjective knowledge

Mode: (Separate): logic, analysis, debate

(Connected): empathy, collaboration, careful listening

Voice: (Separate): aims for accuracy, precision; modulates voice to fit standards of logic or discipline

(Connected): aims for dialogue where self and other are clearly and accurately understood, even where different

Constructed knowing

Knowledge: Integrates strengths of previous positions; systems of thought can be examined, shaped, and shared

Mind: Full two-way dialogue with both heart and mind; seeks truth through questioning and dialogue

Mode: Integration of separate and connected modes

Voice: Adept at marshalling/critiquing arguments as well as empathic listening and understanding; speaks/listens with confidence, balance, and care

we are witnessing (and participating in) a crisis of knowledge and authority in academe wherein the traditional description of what we do—"the
discovery, extension and dissemination of knowledge" (Searle, 1995)—is
questioned from many sides. The very notion of knowledge and truth has
shifted, as critics call into question such concepts as universal and ahistorical laws of human behavior and the existence of an objective reality
that can be represented reliably by language. The idea that theory-
neutral facts are produced by objective scientists is no longer everywhere
tenable. Rather than an objective means of arriving at truth, science is
depicted as a process unavoidably biased in what and how it chooses to
investigate. Knowledge often is characterized as socially constructed,
inevitably influenced by such factors as historical time and place and
social position (Burbules & Rice, 1991; Greene, 1994; Lather, 1991;
Weiner, 1994; Riger, 1992).[12] With the foundations shaking, so to speak,
in every field, scholars must be aware as never before of the particularities of their own stance—the basis of their beliefs, knowledge, and practices (Minnich, 1990). This is especially true of those in education,
where epistemology and practice are thoroughly intertwined (Harrington, 1994; Lyons, 1990). If the knowledge and methods of the field are
being questioned, what does one pass on to one's students?

WWK was an early contributor to the chorus of questioning, and many
articles cite it as evidence of male bias in academic fields, commend its
methodology of interviewing and taking women's voices seriously, and/or
list and describe its epistemological perspectives.

More substantial use of the book's concepts and insights around issues
of epistemology was made by educators in diverse fields, among them
nursing (Bevis & Watson, 1989; Donley, 1988), occupational therapy
(Schwartz, 1991), composition (Hollis, 1992), economics (Bartlett &
Feiner, 1992), business law (Ingulli, 1992), and social work (Dore, 1994).
A common pattern across these articles finds authors discussing "the new
scholarship" (among which they include WWK) and questioning the
knowledge base of their fields. Then they move to consider curriculum
and pedagogy in their respective disciplines. Here WWK figures even
more prominently as the various authors outline strategies for transformed pedagogies. Nursing educators, for example, explicitly reject the
behaviorist/positivist orientation toward knowledge, with its curriculum
of measurable objectives, which has been entrenched in nursing pedagogy since the 1950s. They call instead for a human science that incorporates the ethic of caring into both theory and training of practitioners.
In the resulting pedagogy students and teachers would be regarded as
partners, with surfeit of content jettisoned in favor of hands-on active

learning and a curriculum honoring different ways of knowing (Bevis & Watson, 1989).[13]

WWK's concept of two modes of procedural knowing (separate and connected) has encouraged fruitful theorizing about what it means to teach students to think. Previously, most work concerning students' critical thinking focused on teaching concrete skills in areas such as logic and problem solving.[14] Nancy Sweeney (1994) marries philosopher Michael Polyani's concept of personal knowledge to WWK's constructed knowing to emphasize the knower as actively, passionately pursuing understanding. The two articles summarized next build on WWK in making eloquent arguments for new views of what constitutes good thinking.[15]

Anne Phelan and James Garrison (1994) propose a "feminist poetic" of critical thinking as a new way of conceptualizing what it means to be a rational person. They lead the reader in loving detail through the "irreconcilable yet complementary contraries" of separate and connected knowing, as well as other contraries posed by the theorists Sara Ruddick, Carol Gilligan, and Evelyn Fox Keller. Unwilling to appeal to a truth-seeking dialectic that would resolve the paradoxes, all these theorists embrace the contraries. Phelan and Garrison point out that alternating between (for example) separate and connected knowing works to enhance understanding and is reminiscent of how poets work, concerned as they are with meaning, interpretation, and insight. Poets use paradox to forge new connections. Harnessing this sort of thinking in pedagogy will lead to a new, less alienating definition of critical thinking.

Similarly, Kerry Walters (1990) makes amusing use of Mr. Spock and "Star Trek" to argue against viewing logic, proof, and analytic reductionism as the sum of rational thinking—which she refers to as the vulcanization of knowledge. She would redefine rational thinking to include creative "what if" thinking, imagination, and intuition and encourage students to seek "patterns of discovery," citing WWK as support for the need to go beyond the "calculus of justification."

Here, then, is a view of thinking itself that is less bounded, less restrictive, less rigid. There is room for passion, for caring, for imagination. Some critics might regard this as dangerous—a flight from rationality. I regard it as hopeful—a move toward embracing complexity, moving beyond simplistic polarization to consider where our thinking about thinking is incomplete and how we might transform our views and our practices.[16]

Other interesting uses made of WWK are those of scholars who place epistemology at the core of their work and who explicitly use WWK either as a source of inspiration in investigating the intertwining of epistemology and practice or as a springboard from which to make a case for different ways of knowing or construct new concepts. Two examples are Nona Lyons (1990) and Frances Maher and Mary Kay Tetreault (1994), who focus on teachers' epistemologies and the production of knowledge in a classroom, using extensive interviews with practicing teachers.[17] The WWK framework, especially concepts of voice and epistemological perspectives, are central to Lyons's study, which yields the theoretical concept of "nested epistemologies"—the interweaving of teacher and student epistemologies in knowledge production. Maher and Tetreault's *The Feminist Classroom* discusses emergent themes of mastery, voice, authority, and positionality in college classrooms in absorbing detail. Here, the influence of WWK is more indirect. The authors engage in conversation with the book, applying concepts of voice to their own educational autobiographies. In its methods, its determination to honor and take seriously the "female field" of pedagogy, and its careful attention to the actual practitioners, this book is reminiscent of WWK.[18]

In summary, WWK introduces college teachers to epistemology as relevant to what we do. Consider, for example, the two modes of separate and connected knowing. Although philosophers and even psychologists have grappled with similar concepts, relatively few college teachers prior to WWK had access to clear descriptions, redolent of their experience and concerns, of these different modes of making meaning. Being caught up as we most often are in our specialized training, it is illuminating to step out of that frame—to consider more generally what it means to know, what kind of thinking and means to knowledge we privilege and allow to prosper in our classrooms. As new visions of knowing arise, so do new possibilities for practice.

TEACHING AS INQUIRY

Listen as Kareen Sturgeon (1991), an evolutionary biologist, describes teaching environmental science to nonscientists:

> As I became more and more concerned with the urgency of teaching students to care about their world and the need for them to do something about it, the students seemed to become increasingly immobilized. . . . These students looked to me, a scientist—the expert—for answers and, because I had none, I began to think of ways I could get out of teaching this dismal course. Clearly, something was wrong (p. 166).

Sturgeon relates her ensuing search—questioning the meaning and purpose of scientific research vis-à-vis global problems, wondering about the aim of education (to inform? to motivate to action?), and experimenting with different teaching devices.[19]

> As an educator, I, too, was becoming transformed. I no longer carried the burden of feeling obliged to be an expert. . . . Rather, I was satisfied that I had encouraged the students to think and question and that I was learning and growing along with them. . . . The class, as a whole, seemed to take on a new personality (pp. 170–171).

Her quest, which transformed her perspectives on her discipline, her students, pedagogy, and, indeed, the universe, exemplifies teaching as inquiry. Such teaching involves contemplative questioning before, during, and after its practice. Although it may be truncated or even subliminal, it is ongoing. Teachers ask themselves not only what they know, but what the enterprise of education is all about, who they can be as a teacher, who the students are, and how to connect students with knowledge. They also engage in ongoing assessment of what happened, how it happened, how it can/should happen again.

I choose the term *inquiry* to recognize that at the core of WWK's message are the simple but powerful questions Who is the learner? What does s/he bring to the learning process? This provides an important counterbalance to the tendency of higher education to give center stage to disciplinary content, with the unspoken assumption that anyone with command of the material can teach and anyone who tries hard enough can learn. We professors know very little about who our students are, how they learn, and what they know and remember beyond the written products that we require them to deliver.[20]

WWK challenges us to attend to the learners, listening to their voices and observing their process in addition to grading their products. Moreover, WWK provides a device around which to organize what we've gathered—offering, literally, another way to frame. Perhaps that quiet student isn't passive but is working hard to receive knowledge. Maybe that opinionated student has just discovered that she has her own views; she needs encouragement to value and use evidence rather than being squelched.

Dedicated teachers who regard their efforts as energizing and creative partake in the spirit of inquiry. A majority of the articles that I have reviewed could fit into this section of the chapter.[21] To avoid such a glut, I have chosen to emphasize programmatic approaches that center not just on curriculum but on attention to who students are, the various ways they learn, and what their educational needs might be.

Making Connections was a program of three minicourses I devised for students at the women's college where I taught (Stanton, 1990, 1993). The immediate impetus for a programmatic response was the college's new president's calling for innovative approaches to improve retention and recruitment. I was more concerned with students' needs, having witnessed their struggling for coherence and meaning, wrestling with practical matters such as "How can I get through all this work?" and broader issues such as "Who am I and how is college changing me?" and "What do I want to do with my life?"

Deeply influenced by the concepts and insights of WWK,[22] the minicourses were designed as opportunities for students to engage in self-reflection and dialogue as well as learn relevant skills. Connecting with College aimed to ease first-year students' transition to college life by creating a small community of learners who would share their stories. It included interactive workshops on study skills and learning styles and reflective sessions on powerful learning experiences and self-as-knower. Connecting with Your Self invited first-semester sophomores "backstage" to learn about identity formation and epistemological development. The interactive workshop format encouraged them to share their own stories and imaginatively (through art and poetry) apply the concepts to their own lives, in an effort to create possible pictures of their own future development. In the spring semester, Connecting with a Major addressed sophomores' need to declare a major by providing a social context for the task. It included exercises and dialogue around values, skills and interests, workshops on life planning, alumnae mentors, and self-reflective essays.[23]

All minicourses lasted five to six weeks and were cofacilitated by a faculty member and a student service professional. To assess minicourse effectiveness, students interested in taking each course were randomly assigned to treatment or control groups when the courses were piloted, and their performances were compared. Evaluation results indicated that participants in the minicourses made greater gains in the first year on course grades, retention, ego development, and career development than did control subjects. Two years later they were utilizing more complex ways of knowing. As Marguerite tells us, in response to the question "How is the way you see yourself now different from the way you saw yourself before?":

> I see myself as much more confident now, much more capable. I feel that I know more; I can articulate more. I feel like I'm balancing my two ways of

thinking—both creatively and analytically—I haven't mastered it, but I'm close to mastering it. I clearly see . . . growth.

Notice how she has claimed concepts about voice and development for her own, using them as evaluative guides.

Concepts of voice, connected knowing, and collaboration permeated the minicourses' content and format. Faculty development accompanying the introduction of the courses included a week-long course, a regional conference addressed by the coauthors Mary Belenky and Blythe Clinchy, and ongoing in-service training for academic advisers. Thus, it is sobering to report the subtle resistance encountered. Only the first-year minicourse was approved by the faculty for academic credit (0.25 credit). When a faculty committee reworked the minicourse materials to incorporate them into year-long core courses, they erased components that emphasized students' shared dialogues, reflection on themselves as knowers, and gaining a voice. Instead, sole focus on content (albeit interdisciplinary) was reinstituted,[24] a reminder of how difficult it is to grasp and implement ideas from a new paradigm in a setting where traditional views about teaching and learning receive unquestioning support.

Ursuline College has been more successful with innovations designed around concepts from WWK (Carfagna, 1995). Asking themselves how to take the learning needs of women seriously (and responding to increasing enrollments of adult women students), the faculty studied educational philosophy, learning theory, and human development. They decided to use WWK's epistemological perspectives to guide the design of a core curriculum, reorganizing a somewhat loose collection of requirements into a meaningful framework. Students are now required to take fourteen different courses. At the first level is a seminar accompanied by satellite courses whose purpose is to move students from received into subjective knowing, encouraging them to gain a voice. Next, students take a common course and choose electives that expose them to a variety of perspectives and promote critical analysis, with the aim of moving subjective knowers into procedural knowing. The culminating seminar asks students to integrate their learning across disciplines, reflecting on the meaning of their education, creating new knowledge, and considering how to carry their knowledge responsibly into the world beyond college (moving toward constructed knowing). Ongoing long-term evaluation of students is under way to assess how successfully the new curriculum encourages personal development and social leadership.

This programmatic change was the result of in-depth study and thus "owned" by the faculty. The change was incremental in the sense that it did not depart from existing course structures; indeed, many existing courses could be folded into it. The key innovation was the faculty's adoption of gaining a voice—"enabl(ing) women to make their inner voices public voices with increasing grace and confidence"—as a goal. This was put into practice by such means as small classes, collaborative learning groups, and faculty team modeling (one faculty member facilitating content learning and the other attending to development goals, such as gaining a voice).

Perhaps the greatest programmatic effort to introduce changes in pedagogy in recent times has been the institution of women's studies programs across the nation. Beginning with the first at San Diego State University, San Diego, California, in 1970, there were 621 such programs by 1990 (Musil, 1992a). As a group, they questioned the dominant meaning system (Minnich, 1990), establishing new curricula and employing different pedagogical methods. None of this came easily. Whole programs were staffed with part-timers and people teaching overloads, for example; and through it all reverberated accusations that Women's Studies classes spread propaganda and promoted subjectivity.

The book *Courage to Question: Women's Studies and Student Learning* (Musil, 1992a)—the assessment of their women's studies program undertaken by faculty at seven different institutions—presents an interesting example of inquiry. In carrying out the collaborative evaluation, first the various faculties discussed the primary aims and purposes of women's studies in general and their programs in particular. Faculty from each site then framed their own questions and designed measures guided by a jointly conceived common core of questions that concerned disciplinary issues, pedagogical issues, and developmental issues.[25]

Noteworthy across all sites is how students' experiences and outcomes are placed at the center of the evaluations—their engagement (both intellectual and personal) with class material and in their own education, whether and how they think critically, and the pedagogical avenues followed to foster student voices and welcome their experiences into the classroom. Around such themes, this work shares with WWK a vision of transforming education, including taking women seriously and validating them, fostering dialogue, and teaching students how to produce as well as reproduce knowledge (Butler, Coyner, Homans, Longenechker, & Musil, 1991, p. 14).

Given the criticism of women's studies (and, by association, methods advocated in WWK) over the years, I found it particularly instructive to focus on site evaluations that compared women's studies courses and classes in other departments. Results were encouraging. At the University of Colorado, Boulder, students in women's studies courses were more likely to relate course material to their personal lives and social context[26] and consider how to take their knowledge into the world. Lewis and Clark College's comparative study revealed that students in gender-focused courses[27] acquire increased understanding of the social construction of gender and produce, rather than merely repeat, knowledge. Wellesley College found that women's studies students perceived themselves as more active and critical learners, with a self rooted in an intellectual agenda.

Daphne Patai and Noretta Koertge (1994) leveled a scathing attack on women's studies, including WWK in their scope. On the one hand, they provide a valuable service in alerting us to excesses that may occur if pedagogy promotes subjective knowing without recognizing its limitations. Their cautionary tales of hostile classrooms where politicized students intimidate fellow students (and teachers) call us to renewed vigilance and inquiry as teachers—Do such conditions exist on my campus? Where? What can be done?—and point out the need to be aware of the power of student subcultures, an aspect of students' learning that mostly escapes our notice (Fassinger, 1995). On the other hand, they seriously misunderstood the distinction between subjective and connected knowing and so contribute to the already overdetermined perspective that the only "real" thinking is logical and distanced. At the same time, their lack of a systematic research strategy—depending on unspecified interviews and on-line discussion groups and highly selective (if not distorted) readings of other sources for data—calls into question the basis of their conclusions. Findings from *The Courage to Question* and, more recently, *The Feminist Classroom* (Maher & Tetrault, 1994)—both of which carefully document the sources and kinds of data used, with thoughtful discussion of results and implications—do not indicate a problem of the scope implied by these critics.

The programmatic approaches cited here are explicitly concerned with student development, unlike in much of the work I reviewed. I find that somewhat dismaying[28] since, as a college teacher, I consider WWK's developmental possibilities to be a strong point (even as I recognize that developmental sequences may be culture- and situation-limited). Development goes beyond acquiring new information or new behaviors in specific situations; it involves acquiring more powerful ways of thinking. Any college professor who contemplates the various perspectives in WWK cannot doubt that procedural knowing—whereby students can evaluate evidence, judge conflicting claims, and understand material from a variety of perspectives—is more desirable than received knowing, where students uncritically accept an expert's claim as true, or subjective knowing, where students confine themselves to exploring their own perspective.

Most teaching effort at the college level is directed at matters of procedural knowing—presenting and utilizing the theories, methods, controversies, and findings of our fields. Most college teachers, however, overlook the pivotal perspective of subjective knowing. (If anything, we attempt to stamp it out—to make sure that students don't get away with unsupported personal opinions.) Viewed in the context of a developmental sequence, it becomes clear what gets lost if subjective knowing is dismissed—the student's sense of not only having but owning her own opinion—and how that capacity must be built upon to acquire more powerful thinking strategies.

In these days when the culture itself appears to promote subjectivity (Bellah, Madsen, Sullivan, Swidler, & Tipton, 1985), we ignore subjective knowing at our peril. How can we entice students to drop "I have a right to (it's only) my opinion" for a more nuanced procedural perspective? Paul Hettich (1990) offers the strategy of having students analyze their own journal entries according to Benjamin Bloom's educational taxonomy and Perry's developmental scheme. This has the advantage of using but building on subjective knowing.

In faculty development workshops on epistemological perspectives, professors often remark, "Well, I'm a received knower too when I'm learning something new like astronomy." Such remarks miss the point on two counts. First, a sophisticated knower recognizes that any field is more than a collection of facts and knows that there are undoubtedly theories, methods, and disputes about the knowledge that engage expert practitioners. (Received knowers make no such assumptions.) Second, those professors focus on the static categories rather than the dynamic quality of the developmental sequence.

The whole point of a developmental theory is not to pin the individual rigidly into a category but to locate her/him with reference to a sequence, providing a way to conceptualize where the student is and in what directions s/he might be ready to move. The power of a developmental theory resides in the expectation that the student is in the process of becoming a more capable and effective thinker, enabling the teacher to take a "believing" stance (Elbow, 1986) toward the student. There is an implied plan of action in a developmental sequence, beginning with where the student is but providing the encouragement and challenge for the student to develop further.[29]

What impels development? Jean Piaget (1964) identifies disequilibrium as a major underpinning of cognitive development. Encountering discrepancy and contradiction motivates students, who actively construct their own development, to revise their understanding in light of new material. WWK posits no such direct mechanism. But its critique of academic practices—for example, failure to affirm students as thinkers/knowers and exclusive use of adversarial techniques—and the recommendation ot "midwife teaching" imply that students will prosper in an environment of attentive support. The developmental sequence provides a basis for challenging students to use that support as a growth medium.

TEACHING AS PRACTICE

This moves us into the next theme—translating contemplation of epistemology and student characteristics and needs into action on the classroom level. My metaphor for teaching (Lakoff & Johnson, 1980) is that of a construc " .ite where the teacher, surrounded by apprentices, is simultaneously architect, general contractor, and supervisor and where a variety of tools are required, numerous action sequences must be coordinated vis-à-vis the design, and the emerging structure is continually tested for soundness. What are those tools and action sequences? What are design features? How does the structure hold up?

The most widely adopted design features from WWK are the concepts of voice and connection (connected knowing and connected teaching). Voice is related to students' capacity to formulate and air their thoughts, believing they have something worthwhile to say and feeling heard. In connected knowing, students enter into another's perspective and reason with the other to achieve understanding; in contrast, the more familiar separate knowing enta' c llenging the other's reasoning with particular attention to rules oi ιogic and sources of bias. Both are alternate modes of procedural knowing.

Unfortunately, the procedural basis of connected knowing is often missed. Perhaps the familiarity of the word *connected* permits readers to drift toward interpretations that focus on knowing that is tied primarily to experience, intuition, empathy, and feelings (e.g., Bartlett & Feiner, 1992; Enns, 1993; Harvey, 1994; Schwartz, 1991) and deemphasizes the goal—clear and undistorted understanding. Similarly, some critics (e.g., Freire & Macedo, 1995) fail to note the vigorous question posing and careful attention to understanding, comparing and reconciling different perspectives, implying that connected teaching is "touchy–feely."

Kate Begnal (1991) provides a clear and inspiring example of how literature can be conceived as an instrument of connected knowing, capable of evoking change by moving readers to think others' thoughts and participate in perspectives of/on narrators, characters, plot, and other readers. The critical thinking inherent in connected knowing is demonstrated as she shows how literature decodes and unmasks ideologies. Full of useful detail, this article describes how Begnal organized her syllabus around WWK perspectives (thus providing students with a way to think about their own knowing). She describes connected teaching techniques such as crediting students with the ability to think and know, sharing intellectual authority and responsibility with them, question posing, and facilitating collaborative work.

Blythe Clinchy (1995) is similarly attentive to rationale and detail in discussing a connected approach to teaching developmental psychology. She lays bare the fear of all college teachers: student reports that they adopt classroom knowledge only for the duration of a class, discarding it once grades are posted. In response, among other techniques, she elicits students' commonsense views of psychology and child development so that they can be openly discussed and assessed. Room is made for personal narrative in the classroom. Not only do students write in journals (a fairly common device these days), but dialogue is encouraged through excerpting and distributing (with permission) passages from those journals, which then serve as fodder for further reflection. Students interview each other, design experiments, and gather data. Underlying all these efforts are Clinchy's desire for students to understand that psychology is a creation of the human mind and her effort to convince them that they too can participate in that creation.

Topics such as women and literature and child development may be suited to connected knowing and teaching, but what about the sciences? On the face of it, the methodology and kind of knowledge required in courses such as mathematics, physics, and chemistry seem better suited to the separate mode of procedural knowledge. Thus, it is particularly interesting to hear how WWK has influenced the thinking and practices of science and math educators.

That there is a problem with college teaching of science is amply documented by Deborah Trumbull and Patricia Kerr's (1993) interview study of novice and experienced scientist teachers. All were motivated to teach well but had little pedagogical training and depended primarily on their own experiences as students for guidance in teaching and learning. Unfortunately, they expected things to "fall into place" for their students without recognizing that this had not happened for them until they conducted research in graduate school. Consequently, they often failed to help students understand, for example, the existence of scientific conflicts and how to solve conflicts through gathering and critically examining evidence. Although they clearly wanted students to gain more than rote knowledge, they had few ideas about how to help them generate deeper understanding, falling back on such strategies as repetition of material or the belief that some students had ability and others did not.[30] Trumbull and Kerr identified WWK's epistemological assumptions and teaching methods as an educational framework that could help scientist–teachers deal with the identified problems.

Inspired also by WWK, Jean Barr and Lynda Birke (1994) interviewed women students to ascertain their perceptions of and experiences with science.[31] Respondents saw scientists as both quite unlike ordinary people and endlessly engaged in solitary work (neither vision an appealing one). They saw themselves as passive consumers of scientific knowledge, possessing instead a more valuable "common sense." They not only felt excluded from science but actively resisted it in the form it was presented to them. Barr and Birke, too, call for transforming science education to be more open to different ways of knowing, sensitive to lived experience, and accessible to all citizens as necessary knowledge.

In light of such indictments, it is encouraging to read of programs that successfully incorporate new perspectives and teaching techniques. For example, the SummerMath program at Mount Holyoke College was designed to address the barriers still preventing women's equal participation in mathematical studies and careers. Deeming their program "reform in a feminist framework," the codirectors use WWK to identify overarching issues that then frame and define their curriculum. Their aim is enabling young women to experience mathematics as interesting, creative, and relevant, and to see themselves as confident and competent knowers and creators of knowledge (Morrow & Morrow, 1993, 1995).[32] The program challenges students with difficult problems, while providing an atmosphere of support that allows them to become independent (as opposed to isolated) and authoritative knowers. Although aimed at grades eight through twelve, this program is an excellent model of careful design that marries learners' needs and predilections with disciplinary knowledge and connected pedagogy.

Dorothy Buerk's (1985) teaching of mathematics hinges on the insight that while mathematicians' public presentations emphasize the separate mode of logic and analysis, they do their private work in the connected mode, searching for patterns and using intuitive, reflective, contextual strategies. Aiming to reach students who feel insecure, passive, or forced into rote learning, Buerk's "connected classroom" invites them to explore their own experience and ideas about mathematics through metaphors, journals, and math problems in nature. This leads them not only to solve difficult problems but to see the utility and beauty of mathematics and to see themselves as creative participants in the field (Buerk & Szablewski, 1993; Buerk & Kalinowsky, 1994). The work is deeply influenced by WWK, and a recent paper, "Enhancing Women's Mathematical Competence" (Kalinowsky & Buerk, 1995), is a potent teaching device for other teachers, showing how to use the epistemological perspectives as a lens for understanding individual students' approach to learning and for devising teaching strategies.

Underlying the methods and techniques of all these accounts is the issue of inclusiveness: Who belongs in science and mathematics classrooms? Critics of science teaching (Fensham, 1986; Tobias, 1990) point out that existing science education—by focusing on the future science and engineering majors—reaches only a minority of students, leaving others to believe that they can't learn or understand that realm and resulting in a high level of scientific illiteracy. These alternative models of science education provide a basis for broad-based literacy in the sciences. Where the goals are encouraging students' willing engagement with the material and fostering a long-term intelligent layperson's interest in mathematics or science, connected knowing classrooms are more defensible than traditional ones.

Another issue of inclusiveness is raised by the metaphor of voice. Whose voice gets heard? Some interesting responses come from teachers of composition, who ponder the exclusion of all but expository/argumentative discourse (Zawacki, 1992; Meyer, 1993) and seek to help students develop a voice that is both authentic and authoritative (Lamb, 1991).[33] As a group, teachers of composition seem unusually attuned to the link between voice and critical thinking and provide inspiring examples of how to forge and strengthen that link.

But voice goes beyond students' writing and speaking up in class. Just as it serves as a metaphor for women about thinking, voice is emblemmatic of larger issues in pedagogy. For example, narrative has been rescued from oblivion and introduced as a way to teach, to write, and to think (Witherell & Noddings, 1991). "The sounds of storytelling are everywhere," educational philosopher Maxine Greene (1991) tells us, reminding us too that

> the passion evoked by the discovery of "voice" and the moral and cognitive significance of the discovery have much to do with the belated recognition of "women's ways of knowing" (p. x).

Conversation and dialogue are advanced as pedagogical practices that encourage engagement and quest and open new avenues to seeking truth through mutuality, reciprocity, and care rather than detachment and distance (Helle, 1991; Vasquez-Levy, 1993).

WWK has contributed importantly to liberating women's voices: finding language to describe what had been suppressed or repressed about women's ways of knowing, providing a means to integrate the inner voice and the voice of reason, and encouraging a new kind of dialogue in the classroom (Greene, 1991).

STIRRING CONCLUSION

I write this heading only half in jest. It mocks and yet expresses my wish to stir readers' thoughts and visions. At the end of the long process of reading/thinking that went into this chapter, it is also an image of incompleteness: sauce not ready yet, still stirring. (One problem of writing this chapter has been the strain and the impossibility of communicating the richness of the material I have reviewed.)

As I rummaged through journals and texts, I kept encountering Maxine Greene—her scholarly acquaintance with educational thinkers and epistemologies, her commitment to bringing multiple voices into the conversation about teaching and knowing, and her insistence that education is a moral enterprise that requires our passionate commitment. She frequently cites and obviously admires *Women's Ways of Knowing* as an ally in her work, noting how it supported her in her efforts "to break through 'the frames and systems' provided by old authorities, and . . . create my own" (1990, p. 68).

To Greene's testimony, I add the following as my personal assessment of the place that WWK holds in my educational practice and research as a college teacher.

The enterprise of teaching is, for me, both engrossing and fulfilling, providing a life full of both thought and passion. That it is also a political activity in all senses is also important, although I have chosen not to discuss that here.[14] What WWK provides and helps me sustain is a moral vision of this enterprise, one that helps me see beyond the technological rationalism that undergirds most of modern life. While epistemology is featured, there is a strong subtext of an ethic of care.[15] As the midwife/teacher image dramatically conveys, education is relational—a relationship that involves knowledge, attentiveness, and care; care directed not only at disciplinary material but to who students are and what they can become. It involves responsiveness and a stance of hopefulness.

I now teach in a nearly ideal setting, working closely each semester with fifteen adult students who formulate their own study plans and engage in vigorous dialogue with me—a setting with multiple opportunities for mining narrative, relating theories to experience, and weaving them into a meaningful whole. Thus, it is easy for me to hope. But I remember all too well the travails of seven courses a year, too many students, and many of those distracted, glutted, resistant, confused. Given that and the current national disarray, most of us are in the position of Camus's Dr. Rieux in *The Plague*—doomed to persevere in doing what we know amid uncertainty and chaos. But we are not alone. With allies the like of WWK and colleagues such as those cited in this chapter, we may be part of a continuing conversation against despair.

NOTES

1. Many educators use the book in this way, including Begnal (1991); Eyres, Loustau, and Ersek, (1992), Hettich (1990), Ortman, (1993); Taylor and Marienau (1995). The latter monograph is an outstanding practical tool for educators working with adult women students.
2. Many thanks go to Kathleen Strnad, who provided very able assistance in the location and sorting through of these many references.
3. A developmental psychologist, I do not do my primary reading routinely in the area of education.
4. Interestingly, I found the uses of WWK corresponded roughly to the epistemological perspectives described in the book. Some writers cited it briefly as an expert source to back up claims about inadequacies of education for women or lack of women subjects in research or merely listed the epistemological perspectives as "the ways that women know." Another group of writers seized on concepts such as connected knowing and midwife/teachers but seemed to interpret them without careful reading of the original conceptual framework—a seemingly subjective use. Others used such concepts more procedurally, understanding the authors' original framework, finding ways to translate the concepts meaningfully into their specific fields, and creating new ways of teaching and thinking, inspired by WWK.
5. I had struggled to fit myself into categories (posited by theorists such as Lawrence Kohlberg) that were devised on the basis of research using male subjects. I could tell where I was "supposed" to fit but had to fudge and slightly distort my original reactions and inclinations in order to fit there.
6. The emphasis in Perry's book is on developmental positions and their variations; it speaks very briefly to concerns of teachers. In addition, the quotes by Perry's students were much longer and less focused (including repetitions and pauses). Students were only identified by year of college, with no additional social context provided. WWK's use of a more narrative text, with respondents' pseudonyms and life circumstances, makes connecting their examples with actual students and learning situations easier.

7. The implicit corollary is to take students seriously as knowers, although this may be more immediately obvious to those of us teaching primarily women students. The literature from nursing educators, for example, makes clear that WWK is important and relevant because of the gender composition of their students.

8. Britzman (1993), for example, implies that WWK posits inherent biological differences as the source of women's distinctive styles. Patai and Koertge (1994) confuse subjective knowing with connected knowing—ignoring the procedural basis of connected knowing—and belittle it as domestic and enfeebled.

9. This issue is not new—previous generations of psychologists discussed it under the rubric of nomethic versus idiographic research—but it is newly urgent in a society where diversity is being recognized and (sometimes) celebrated and the nature and sources of knowledge are being questioned.

10. Classroom teachers are all too prone to this kind of shorthand, understandably, since they rarely have the luxury of working individually with students. Thus, for example, in elementary school all third-graders may be forced to focus on math manipulatives, ignoring more abstract concepts, because (according to Piaget's theory) the children at this age "are" concrete operational.

11. An example would be Tom, a deeply devout Christian who wanted to learn about adolescent development so he could fix troubled lives. I never questioned his religious beliefs, which were couched in fundamentalist terms, but focused on his black-and-white judgments about what's wrong with families, with working mothers, and so on. I asked for more details of his thinking, posed questions, provided concrete counterexamples, and asked him to help me think through the implications of his statements. By the end of the semester, Tom framed issues differently, no longer searching for the right fix but believing that God had given him a mind for a purpose—to use in problem posing and thinking through complex issues. By working *with* his propensities instead of against them, he was enabled to do his own intellectual work and reconcile his deep faith with his newfound interest in questioning and formulating his own opinions.

12. The depth of the crisis in academe can be gauged by noting the extent to which academic disciplines have gained status and credibility for themselves by adhering to the traditional scientific research model—not only the mainstream social sciences but areas as far-flung as nursing (Bevis & Watson, 1989), business law (Ingulli, 1992), and composition (Peterson, 1991).

13. Those who use WWK as inspiration and foundational material also may over- or misinterpret its concepts. In this case, Bevis and Watson depict

the epistemological positions as "the way women think" and characterize procedural knowledge as masculine (pp. 179, 180), instead of recognizing that connected knowing is also procedural knowing.

14. Joanne Kurfiss's (1988) monograph provides a thoughtful summary of this literature that includes concrete suggestions for teachers. She also makes extensive use of WWK, clarifying how important it is to understand students' beliefs about knowledge before undertaking a skills approach to critical thinking.

15. For another illuminating view, see Nel Noddings (1991).

16. Carolyn Enns (1993) provides a good example of how to integrate and balance separate and connected knowing in the classroom through using Kolb's experiential learning model.

17. Maher and Tetreault also made extensive classroom observations and interviewed students.

18. It goes beyond WWK in engaging in actual dialogue with the participant informants and reflects a postmodern approach by focusing on the particularities of situations rather than seeking generalizations about ways of teaching across situations.

19. She credits WWK with affirming her experiences and contributing greatly to her ability to articulate her feelings and thoughts.

20. For interesting corrective material, see the anthropologists Moffat (1989) and Holland and Eisenhart (1990), as well as Baxter Magolda (1992a), the Harvard Assessment Seminars (Light, 1990), and Pillemer, Rhinehart, & White's (1986, 1988) research on what students remember as influential college experiences.

21. This is especially true for educators who are training others to be teachers. Notable examples include Cochran-Smith and Lytle (1992), Hollingsworth (1992), Holt-Reynolds (1992), and Peterson (1991).

22. I wrote the grant proposal that funded the program (FIPSE, Grant No. P116B91692-90) while on sabbatical leave, working with Mary Belenky and her coworkers on data from the Listening Partners project. In a very real sense, this program could be considered a Listening Partners for college students.

23. For further details, contact Stanton, Adult Degree Program, Vermont College of Norwich University, Montpelier, VT 05602.

24. In a small institution, personnel shifts can dramatically alter conditions, also. Within three years after the minicourses were introduced, the president, dean of students, and I, the principal architect of the Making Connections program, had left the college.

25. A companion volume, Students at the Center: Feminist Assessment (Musil, 1992b), discusses measurement issues and designs in detail.

26. In my experience, this means that the knowledge gained won't be jettisoned after the final exam.

27. This college has a gender studies rather than a women's studies program and has made efforts to mainstream gender-studies concepts across the curriculum.
28. To be fair, the authors of WWK laid out a developmental sequence but never fully claimed it as such, declining to call their perspectives hierarchical.
29. Other useful developmental theories for educators include Baxter Magolda (1992b), King and Kitchener (1994), and Kegan (1994). Slattery (1990) provides a good example of how to use both support and challenge in commenting on student papers.
30. Most troubling was how little the experienced scientist/teachers differed from the novices.
31. For additional material on science students' epistemologies, see Edmondson and Novak (1993), Novak and Musonda (1991), Roth (1994).
32. See C. Morrow (1995) for a useful chart of the issues, why they are important for connected teaching, and specifics of classroom structures and techniques.
33. Some cautionary words come from Seabury (1991) about how boring unmediated student discussions can be, and from Frey (1990) and Harvey (1994) on limitations of personal writing.
34. See Lewis (1990) for an engrossing example of bringing a political consciousness to bear in the classroom.
35. Articles by Elbaz (1992) and Rogers and Webb (1991) also stimulated me to think in these terms.

REFERENCES

Barr, J., & Birke, L. (1994). Women, science, and adult education: Toward a feminist curriculum? *Women's Studies International Forum, 17*(5), 473–483.

Bartlett, R. L., & Finer, S. F. (1992). Balancing the economics curriculum: Content, method, and pedagogy. *AEA Papers and Proceedings, 82*(2), 559–563.

Baxter Magolda, M. (1992a). Cocurricular influences on college students' intellectual development. *Journal of College Student Development, 33*, 203–213.

Baxter Magolda, M. (1992b). *Knowing and reasoning in college: Gender-related patterns in students' intellectual development.* San Francisco: Jossey-Bass.

Begnal, K. (1991). Knowing difference: Internationalizing a women-and-literature course. *Women's Studies International Forum, 14*(4), 285–294.

Bellah, R. N., Madsen, R., Sullivan, W. M., Swidler, A., & Tipton, S. M. (1985). *Habits of the heart: Individualism and commitment in American life.* New York: Harper & Row.

Bevis, E. O., & Watson, J. (1989). *Toward a caring curriculum: A new pedagogy for nursing.* Pub. #15-2278. New York: National League for Nursing.

Britzman, D. P. (1993). Beyond rolling models: Gender and multicultural education. In Biklen, S. K., & Pollard, D. (Eds.), *Gender and education.* 92nd Yearbook for the National Society for the Study of Education. Chicago: National Society for the Study of Education.

Buerk, D. (1985). The voices of women making meaning in mathematics. *Journal of Education, 167*(3), 59–70.

Buerk, D., & Kalinowski, J. (1994, October). *Tuning in women's voices: Strategies to enhance learning in mathematics.* Paper presented at the Conference on Reconciling Gender Issues in Higher Education, University of Vermont, Burlington, VT.

Buerk, D., & Szablewski, J. (1993). Getting beneath the mask, moving out of silence. In White, A. (Ed.), *Essays in humanistic mathematics* (pp. 151–164). Washington, DC: Mathematical Association of America.

Burbules, N. C., & Rice, S. (1991). Dialogue across differences: Continuing the conversation. *Harvard Educational Review, 61*(4), 393–415.

Butler, J. E., Coyner, S., Homans, M., Longenechker, M., & Musil, C. M. (1991). *Liberal learning and the Women's Studies major.* Report in conjunction with the Association of American Colleges National Review of Arts and Sciences Majors.

Camus, A. (1948). *The plague.* New York: Knopf.

Carfagna, R. (1995). A developmental core curriculum for adult women learners. In Taylor, K., & Marienau, C. (Eds.), *Learning environments for women's adult development: Bridges toward change.* (pp. 53–62). New Directions for Adult and Continuing Education, *65(Spring).* San Francisco: Jossey-Bass.

Clinchy, Blythe M. (1995). A connected approach to the teaching of developmental psychology. *Teaching of psychology 22*(2), 100–104.

Cochran-Smith, M., & Lytle, S. L. (1992). Communities for teacher research: Fringe or forefront? *American Journal of Education, 100*(3), 298–324.

Donley, R. (1988). Curricular revolution: Heeding the voices of change. In *Curriculum revolution: Reconceptualizing nursing education.* Pub. No. 15-2280. New York: National League for Nursing.

Dore, M. M. (1994). Feminist pedagogy and the teaching of social work practice. *Journal of Social Work Education, 30*(1), 97–105.

Edmondson, K. M., & Novak, J. D. (1993). The interplay of scientific epistemological views, learning strategies, and attitudes of college students. *Journal of Research in Science Teaching, 30*(6), 547–559.

Elbaz, F. (1992). Hope, attentiveness, and caring for difference: The moral voice in teaching. *Teaching and Teacher Education, 8*(5/6), 421–432.

Elbow, P. (1986). *Embracing contraries: Explorations in learning and teaching.* New York: Oxford University Press.

Enns, C. Z. (1993). Integrating separate and connected knowing: The experiential learning model. *Teaching of Psychology, 20*(1), 7–13.

Eyres, S. J., Loustau, A., & Ersek, M. (1992). Ways of knowing among beginning students in nursing. *Journal of Nursing Education, 31*(4), 175–180.

Fassinger, P. A. (1995). Understanding classroom interaction: Students and professors contributions to students' silence. *Journal of Higher Education, 66*(1), 82–96.

Fensham, P. (1986). *Science for all.* Invitational address at the annual meeting of the American Educational Research Association, San Francisco.

Freire, P., & Machedo, D. P. (1995). A dialogue: Culture, language and race. *Harvard Educational Review, 65*(3), 414–450.

Frey, O. (1990). Beyond literary Darwinism: Women's voices and critical discourse. *College English, 52*(5), 507–526.

Gilligan, C. (1977). In a different voice: Women's conceptions of self and morality. *Harvard Educational Review, 47*, 481–517.

Greene, M. (1990). The passion of the possible: Choice, multiplicity, and commitment. *Journal of Moral Education, 19*(2), 67–76.

Greene, M. (1991). Forward. In C. Witherell & N. Noddings (Eds.) *Stories lives tell: Narrative and dialogue in education.* New York: Teacher's College Press.

Greene, M. (1994). Epistemology and educational research: The influence of recent approaches to knowledge. *Review of Research in Education, 20,* 423–464.

Hare-Mustin, R. T., & Marecek, J. (1988). The meaning of difference: Gender theory, postmodernism, and psychology. *American Psychologist, 43*(6), 455–464.

Harrington, H. (1994). Teaching and knowing. *Journal of Teacher Education, 45*(3), 190–198.

Harvey, G. (1994). Presence in the essay. *College English, 56*(6), 642–651.

Heinrich, L. T., & Witt, B. (1993). The passionate connection and feminism invigorates the teaching of nursing. *Nursing Outlook, 41*(3), 117–124.

Helle, A. P. (1991). Reading women's autobiographies: A map of reconstructed knowing. In Witherell, C., & Noddings, N. (Eds.), *Stories lives tell: Narrative and dialogue in education.* New York: Teacher's College Press.

Hettich, P. (1990). Journal writing: Old fare or nouvelle cuisine? *Teaching of Psychology, 17*(1), 36–39.

Holland, D. C., & Eisenhart, M. A. (1990). *Educated in romance: Women, achievement, and college culture.* Chicago: University of Chicago Press.

Hollingsworth, S. (1992). Learning to teach through collaborative conversation: A feminist approach. *American Educational Research Journal, 29*(2), 373–404.

Hollis, K. L. (1992). Feminism in writing workshops: A new pedagogy. *College Composition and Communication, 43*(3), 340–349.

Holt-Reynolds, D. (1992). Personal history–based beliefs as relevant prior knowledge in course work. *American Educational Research Journal, 29*(2), 325–349.

Ingulli, E. D. (1991). Transforming the curriculum: What does the pedagogy of inclusion mean for business law? *American Business Law Journal, 28,* 605–647.

Kalinowski, J., & Buerk, D. (1995). Enhancing women's mathematical competence: A student-centered analysis. *National Women's Study Association Journal, 7*(5), 1–17.

Kegan, R. (1994). *In over our heads: The mental demands of modern life.* Cambridge, MA: Harvard University Press.

King, P. M., & Kitchener, K. S. (1994). *Developing reflective judgment: Understanding and promoting intellectual growth and critical thinking in adolescents and adults.* San Francisco: Jossey-Bass.

Kurfiss, J. G. (1988). *Critical thinking: Theory, research, practice and possi-*

bilities. ASHE-ERIC Higher Education Report No. 2. Washington, DC: Association for the Study of Higher Education.

Lakoff, G., & Johnson, M. (1980). *Metaphors we live by*. Chicago: University of Chicago Press.

Lamb, C. E. (1991). Beyond argument in feminist composition. *College Composition and Communication, 42*(1), 11–23.

Lather, P. (1991). *Getting smart: Feminist research and pedagogy with/in postmodernism*. New York: Routledge.

Lewis, M. (1989). The challenge of feminist pedagogy. *Queen's Quarterly, 96*(1), 117–130.

Lewis, M. (1990). Interrupting patriarchy: Politics, resistance, and transformation in the feminist classroom. *Harvard Educational Review, 60*(4), 467–488.

Light, R. J. (1990). *The Harvard assessment seminars: Explorations with students and faculty about teaching, learning and student life*. Cambridge, MA: Harvard University Graduate School of Education and Kennedy School of Government.

Lyons, N. (1990). Dilemmas of knowing: Ethical and epistemological dimensions of teachers' work and development. *Harvard Educational Review, 60*(2), 159–180.

Maher, F. A., & Tetreault, M. K. (1994). *The feminist classroom*. New York: Basic Books.

Martin, J. R. (1994) Methodological essentialism, false difference, and other dangerous traps. *Signs: Journal of Women in Culture and Society, 19*(3), 630–657.

Meyer, S. L. (1993). Refusing to play the confidence game: The illusion of mastery in the reading/writing of texts. *College English, 55*(1), 46–63.

Minnich, E. (1990). *Transforming knowledge*. Philadelphia: Temple University Press.

Moffatt, M. (1989). *Coming of age in New Jersey: College and American culture*. New Brunswick, NJ: Rutgers University Press.

Morrow, C. (1995). Women and mathematics: Avenues of connection. *Focus on Learning Problems in Mathematics*. Special Issue: Gender and Mathematics: Multiple Voices, *18*(1, 2, & 3), 4–18.

Morrow, C., & Morrow, J. (1993). Whose math is it, anyway? Giving girls a chance to take charge of their math learning. *Initiatives, 55*, 49–59.

Morrow, C., & Morrow, J. (1995). Connecting women with mathematics. In Rogers, P., & Kaiser, G. (Eds.), *Equity in mathematics education: Influences of feminism and culture*. London: Palmer Press.

Musil, C. M. (Ed.) (1992a). *The courage to question: Women's studies and student learning*. Washington, DC: Association of American Colleges.

Musil, C. M. (Ed.) (1992b). *Students at the center: Feminist assessment*. Washington, DC: Association of American Colleges.

Noddings, N. (1991). Stories in dialogue: Caring and interpersonal reasoning. In Witherell, C., & Noddings, N. (Eds.), *Stories lives tell: Narrative and dialogue in education.* New York: Teacher's College Press.

Novak, J. D., & Musonda, D. (1991). A twelve-year longitudinal study of science concept learning. *American Educational Research Journal, 28*(1), 117–153.

Ortman, P. E. (1993). A feminist approach to teaching learning theory with educational applications. *Teaching of Psychology, 20*(1), 38–40.

Patai, D., & Koertge, N. (1994). *Professing feminism: Cautionary tales from the strange world of women's studies.* New York: Basic Books.

Perry, W. G., Jr. (1970). *Forms of intellectual and ethical development in the college years.* New York: Holt, Rinehart & Winston.

Peterson, J. E. (1991). Valuing teaching: Assumptions, problems and possibilities. *College Composition and Communication, 42*(1), 25–35.

Phelan, A. M., & Garrison, J. W. (1994). Toward a gender-sensitive ideal of critical thinking: A feminist poetic. *Curriculum Inquiry, 24*(3), 255–268.

Piaget, J. (1964). Development and learning. In Ripple, R. E., & Rockcastle, V. N. (Eds.), *Piaget rediscovered.* Ithaca, NY: Cornell University Press.

Pillemer, D. B., Goldsmith, L. R., Panter, A. T., & White, S. H. (1988). Very long-term memories of the first year in college. *Journal of Experimental Psychology, 14*(4), 709–715.

Pillemer, D. B., Rhinehart, E. D., & White, S. H. (1986). Memories of life transitions: The first year in college. *Human Learning, 5,* 109–123.

Riger, S. (1992). Epistemological debates, feminist voices: Science, social values, and the study of women. *American Psychologist, 47*(6), 730–740.

Rogers, D., & Webb, J. (1991). The ethic of caring in teacher education. *Journal of Teacher Education, 42*(3), 173–181.

Roth, W. M. (1994). Physics students' epistemologies and views about knowing and learning. *Journal of Research in Science Teaching, 31*(1), 5–30.

Schwartz, K. B. (1991). Clinical reasoning and new ideas on intelligence: Implications for teaching and learning. *American Journal of Occupational Therapy, 45*(11), 1033–1037.

Seabury, M. B. (1991). Pedagogy of the distressed—comment. *College English, 53*(6), 714–717.

Searle, J. R. (1995). Postmodernism and the Western rationalist tradition. In Arthur, J., & Shapiro, A. (Eds.), *Campus wars: Multiculturalism and the politics of difference,* 28–48. Boulder, CO: Westview.

Slattery, P. (1990). Encouraging critical thinking: A strategy for commenting on college papers. *College Composition and Communication, 41,* 332–335.

Smith, P. (1990). *Killing the spirit.* New York: Viking.

Stanton, A. V. (1990, June 5). *Institutionalizing connected knowing: The Making Connections curriculum.* Paper presented at the International Interdisciplinary Congress of Women, New York City.

Stanton, A. V. (1993). Integrating student services: The Talent Development curriculum. Final Report on Grant P116B91692-90, Dept. of Education (FIPSE). Washington, DC.

Sturgeon, K. B. (1991). The classroom as a model of the world: Is there a place for ethics in an environmental science class? *Environmental Ethics, 13,* 165–173.

Sweeney, N. M. (1994). A concept analysis of personal knowledge: Application to nursing education. *Journal of Advanced Nursing, 20,* 917–924.

Taylor, K., & Marienau, C. (Eds.) (1995). *Learning environments for women's adult development: Bridges toward change.* New Directions for Adults and Continuing Education, 65 *(Spring).* San Francisco: Jossey-Bass.

Tobias, S. (1990). *They're not dumb: They're different.* Tucson, AZ: Research Corp.

Trumbull, D. J., & Kerr, P. (1993). University researchers' inchoate critiques of science teaching: Implications for the content of preservice science teacher education. *Science Education, 77*(3), 301–317.

Vasquez-Levy, D. (1993). The use of practical arguments in clarifying and changing practical reasoning and classroom practices: Two cases. *Journal of Curriculum Studies, 25*(2), 125–143.

Walters, K. S. (1990). Critical thinking, rationality, and the vulcanization of students. *Journal of Higher Education, 61*(4), 448–467.

Weiner, G. (1994). *Feminisms in education: An introduction.* Buckingham, England: Open University Press.

Witherell, C., & Noddings, N. (Eds.) (1991). *Stories lives tell: Narrative and dialogue in education.* New York: Teacher's College Press.

Zawacki, T. M. (1992). Recomposing as a woman—an essay in different voices. *College Composition and Communication, 43*(1), 32–39.

Women's Ways of "Knowing" Law

Feminist Legal Epistemology,
Pedagogy, and Jurisprudence

CARRIE MENKEL-MEADOW

INTRODUCTION

WOMEN'S RELATION TO STUDYING and practicing law has long been characterized by tension between optimistic faith in the ability of legal rights to provide gender (and human) equality and the fear and experience of law as a male-constructed, excluding domain. Unlike proponents of inclusion of women in the medical profession (Morantz-Sanchez, 1985), who based their arguments on intrinsic female ability to care and nurture, early women lawyers claimed that they were the same as men and could study, argue, and practice law just as men could (*Bradwell* v. *Illinois*, 1873). Where there were several separate female medical schools in the nineteenth century, the two female-only law schools were both integrated within a few short years (Menkel-Meadow, 1989a; Morello, 1986).

The early years of women's participation in the legal profession were characterized by the claim, in legal language, of equality and sameness—in learning, practice, competence, contribution, rights, and abilities. For instance, in the 1960s and 1970s when Supreme Court Justice Ruth Bader Ginsburg was a practicing lawyer, she was instrumental in making arguments to the Court that women were equal to men and could administer wills, serve liquor in bars, and receive government benefits for their families on the same basis as men (Ginsburg, 1988).

Beginning in the late 1970s, however, a "second" wave of feminism in the larger society affected legal culture as well. More radical law students, practitioners, and legal theorists recognized that many legal concepts were defined by men, based on "male" conceptions of reality, and excluded the experience of women (MacKinnon, 1979; West, 1985). Thus, for example, contracts involving promises pertaining to family life were unenforceable, where economic contracts were (Frug, 1985); rape was defined by concepts of "penetration" and "consent" interpreted by male jurists and lawmakers (MacKinnon, 1987); and employment and parenthood were treated by law in terms of the male experience (Littleton, 1987). The trickiest legal issue was presented by pregnancy—a physical condition argued by some legal feminists to be "equal" to men's disabilities (Williams, 1982), and by others to require "special treatment" based on its difference from male conceptions of body, health, and workplace availability (Wolgast, 1980; Kay, 1985).

As feminist practitioners debated how to deal with the pregnancy issue in legal doctrines of constitutional equality and workplace equity, legal scholars and theorists became aware of a deeper jurisprudential issue— legal categories and the very grounds of proper argumentation were based on a legal system that had been created exclusively by men (legal patriarchy, Rifkin, 1980) and continued to be perpetuated by a legal academy almost exclusively populated by men (Angel, 1988; Menkel-Meadow, 1987).

As feminist legal theory characterized itself was going through three simultaneous phases, equality–sameness, difference or cultural feminism, and postmodernism (Menkel-Meadow & Diamond, 1991; Menkel-Meadow, 1992a), law professors (Wildman, 1988; Finley, 1989; Ansley, 1991; Pickard, 1983) and law students alike (Worden, 1985; Weiss & Melling, 1988; Stanford Project, 1988) began to comment on the "silencing" of women and women's issues in the law school curriculum and classroom. Women students organized (in 1969) a national conference, Women in the Law, to focus on the legal issues affecting women that were omitted from legal education and legal rule making (Schneider, 1994). In the 1970s law schools began to offer Women in the Law courses, which merged, with increasing sophistication in both substantive and foundational matters, into courses on feminist jurisprudence and specific subject areas of interest to women—criminal law, family law, and employment law. Legal issues pertaining to women began to be "mainstreamed" as part of the legal curriculum (Menkel-Meadow, 1992a).

Thus, in law, the recognition that the very substantive structures of legal reasoning, lawmaking, and legal interpretation were connected to the way law was learned and taught was an important stage in what became known as feminist jurisprudence and pedagogy.

The publication, in 1982, of Carol Gilligan's *In A Different Voice* and, in 1986, of Mary Belenky, Blythe Clinchy, Nancy Goldberger, and Jill Tarule's *Women's Ways of Knowing* (WWK) had an important and evocative resonance for feminist legal scholars on both substantive and processual grounds (DuBois et al., 1985). Substantiating claims that there were multiple ways of reasoning (the logic of the ladder and justice and the morality of the web and relationship taken from Gilligan's work; see, e.g., Spiegelman, 1988) and learning (received, subjective, procedural, and constructed knowledge), these books provided legal scholars, practitioners, and educators with conceptual frameworks with which to explain possible alternative ways of learning law and constructing legal rules (Karst, 1984) and procedural systems.

In an outpouring of scholarship applying these ideas of moral philosophy, epistemology, and educational psychology to legal doctrine and legal knowledge, feminist theorists explored the correspondences of multiple ways of knowing with critiques of the adversary system, Socratic dialogue in the law school classroom, the use of abstract knowledge to teach law opposed to the "experiential" learning of clinical legal education, and the application of women's experience to legal knowledge, epistemology, narrative, and ethics (*Journal of Legal Education*, 1988; Goldfarb, 1991; West, 1993; Menkel-Meadow, 1994a; Rhode, 1993). In law, claims about the "social construction" of legal knowledge production (who "creates," "interprets," "teaches," and "practices" law and gives it its "meaning") have been controversial (Bartlett, 1990; Minow, 1987), raising foundational questions about the substantive formation of rules, standards, interpretation, and authority, inevitably leading to questions about the inclusiveness and legitimacy of our laws and legal system.

In this chapter I will describe some of the applications of "women's ways of knowing" to legal knowledge and pedagogy and their contributions to what we now call feminist jurisprudence and legal theory. Some of these applications elucidate the negative legal feminist critique of "silences" and suppressions (in the classroom) and "absences" (in the law) of women's voices and concerns. Others, related to the value of "connected" and relational knowledge, have been used to describe and expand a feminist pedagogy in law schools and a feminist consciousness in rule making and legal interpretation.

CRITIQUES OF LEGAL EPISTEMOLOGY AND PEDAGOGY

LEGAL KNOWLEDGE (LAW) AND ITS EPISTEMOLOGY

The field of law consists of multiple levels and layers of "knowledge" or "truth." This is consistent with what we learn from WWK—there are many ways of acquiring knowledge. Law and legal knowledge are expressed in cases (factual stories of what happened, analyzed and sorted by legal principles or rules); statutes (normative legislative generalizations about how we should live); administrative regulation (concrete codified applications of more generic principles, administered by agents of the state); legal treatises, books, and law review articles (codifications or contestations of legal rules and policy by academics)—the formal discourses of law. At less formal levels, there are the words of courtroom events (sometimes, though not always, recorded in transcripts), lawyer–client and lawyer–lawyer interactions (interviewing, counseling, negotiating sessions seldom preserved), classroom discourse, and the "law of the street" (where people interact with the force of the law and its human enforcers[1]).

Structurally, language has been constitutive of law (Finley, 1989), and thus conflicts about words and interpretation have long marked debates about what is right or wrong in law (particularly, but not exclusively, in constitutional law; West, 1993). Legal knowledge is produced by institutions (comprised, of course, by groups of individuals) such as courts, legislatures, and government agencies and structured in historically particular ways (for instance, the exclusion of whole classes of people, including women and people of color until quite recently). Among these institutions, law schools have been credited and criticized (some might argue disproportionately) for the creation of law (through scholarship) and socialization and perpetuation of legal concepts and understandings (through teaching).

Thus, law becomes "known" in many different ways by many different people, in part depending on whether the "knower" is the "recipient" of law (an object of the law or a student), an interpreter or maker of law (a judge or law professor), or an enforcer of law (a practicing lawyer or law enforcement official). Most modern critiques of legal knowledge and education, therefore, have sought to expand the expression of voices about the law, in the hope that it can more fully include all who are affected by it. Critiques of legal epistemology and the practice of legal knowledge that is the peculiar form of legal pedagogy are thus often battlegrounds over who will control what is "known" in law. Because law itself is often structured in bipolar forms, in which one side (plaintiff or defendant) wins and the other loses after adversarial and oppositional argument, and because legal institutions are also deeply hierarchical (in the multiple levels of courts, the employment structures of law firms, and the hierarchy of the classroom), these issues of contestation are often seen as either–or battles between traditionalists and radicals, doctrinalists and experientialists, men and women, whites and people of color, or the privileged and the excluded. These dichotomous approaches to the deep structures of legal knowledge produced by oppositional thinking and institutional hierarchies fail to recognize that knowledge (as WWK tells us) can be more inclusive, both of different kinds of learners and thus of more varied methods and ways of knowing.

What becomes more problematic when we evaluate how we know, in any field, is the valence of value attached to particular forms or structures of learning. Thus, in structuralist terms (as Frances Olsen [1990] has argued), in law reason is privileged over emotion, rationality over affective knowledge, the law in its doctrinal form over the more human arts of lawyering (Lopez, 1988–89; Goodpaster, 1975; Himmelstein, 1978), Socratic and hierarchical processes (and more conventional forms) of teaching over experiential, simulation, or clinical methods (Menkel-Meadow, 1988, 1994b). In a discipline that prides itself on its logical, inductive method in deriving rules from close contextual reading of the facts of cases that constitute common law, abstraction and general rules are still regarded as the coin of the realm. Conventional law students clamor to know "what the rules are," while professors attempt to teach the art of "thinking like a lawyer" by demonstrating the elusiveness of absolute "truth" through "arguments on both sides."

To "gender" legal knowledge and legal education is a risky business, though there has been no shortage of ink spilled on the project. Although in most disciplines, including law, feminists have argued for increasing emphasis on the context of knowledge, with a critique of universal, abstract knowledge, legal scholars have pointed to the common law method (Kronman, 1994) of focus on the "prudential" application of discrete facts to general legal principles as the process through which legal problems are solved. In a sense, the traditional method of legal reasoning (by specific, concrete case) appears responsive, not only to feminist critiques of knowledge, but to postmodernism as well (Rosenau, 1992).

Nevertheless, feminists and race theorists continue to critique the way in which law is structured, learned, and taught. Despite law's alleged focus on context, for example, women and people of color have argued that certain narratives are either excluded from, repressed, or denied in the telling of legal stories in the cases (P. Williams, 1991; Lawrence, 1992; West, 1993). Patricia Williams eloquently argues that as the descendant of slaves she is "acted upon" in law, rather than acting, and this perspective affects how she views lawmaking and interpretation. Thus, as in other fields, law has been urged to take a "narrative turn" to include the stories of those who have been oppressed or ignored by conventional legal doctrine and reasoning (Abrams, 1991; Massaro, 1989; Henderson, 1987). The claim for narrative method to supplement, if not supplant, legal logic rests on an important epistemological point, reflected in WWK's empiricism: some people (ideally, lawmakers) will learn to seek principles like justice more inclusively if they learn, through emphatic responses and "connected knowing," of other's experiences (Menkel-Meadow, 1992a, 1992b) and begin to understand the effects of law differently than their own experience of assumed "neutrality" or "objectivity" allows (Minow, 1987).

Though these claims for narrative, storytelling, and a focus on the experience of those acted on in law are now associated with the critiques of feminists and critical race theorists, they also have their roots in traditional legal philosophy and method. The argument for the "many ways of knowing law" can trace its origins to Oliver Wendell Holmes (who said that "the logic of the law is experience") and legal pragmatists and realists (Brint & Weaver, 1991; Radin, 1990). Men then claim, as do women, that traditional legal epistemology—the application of rules to facts (deduction) or facts to rules (induction)—has had philosophical as well as political limitations, as the preferred method for "knowing" law.

Other critiques of the epistemology of law focus on its need for partisan and polarized argument (with only two sides to most questions vested in a plaintiff or defendant), often resulting in a win–lose result in court (Menkel-Meadow, 1984, 1995a). This on–off, yes–no, "I'm right; you're wrong" structure of legal argument and remedies is counterpoised to claims of the "indeterminacy" and "manipulability" of most legal doctrines and principles (D. Kennedy, 1990). Any argument is "right" if it convinces a judge, a teacher, or an opponent. Thus, students of law often feel adrift in competing seas of total uncertainty, the need for an "answer," and the tight structure of hierarchy (encountered in the law school student–teacher relationship, law firm associate–partner relationship, and courtroom lawyer–judge relationship). The field is, then, characterized by both the fluidity of language, argument, narrative, and persuasion and the draconian certainty of grades, employment evaluations, partnership decisions, and court judgments and verdicts. Law and legal education have produced their share of intellectual and emotional vertigo.

LEGAL EDUCATION AND PEDAGOGY

A series of empirical studies of the legal education process in the 1980s and 1990s have documented the gendered nature of legal education, elaborating on how the "standard" legal curriculum and law school structures may disadvantage women students (and teachers) (Guinier, Fine, Balin, Bartow & Stachel, 1994; Homer & Schwartz, 1989–90; Stanford Project, 1988; Weiss & Melling, 1988). Many of the findings of these studies are consistent with earlier results documenting the "chilly climate" in classrooms in higher education generally (Hall & Sandler, 1982) and the work that initially inspired WWK.

More recently, legal scholars of color, particularly women, have explicated similar structural and cultural patterns in how "white" legal education may serve to disempower students of color or the economically disadvantaged law student as well (Crenshaw, 1989; Jin-Myung Oh, 1992; Banks, 1990–91; Berkeley W. L. J. Symposium, 1990–91; Scales-Trent, 1992). This important work explores the importance of "deessentializing" the critique of legal education as reflecting only the experience of particular women and has joined with older, class-based, and humanistically based critiques to demonstrate how dysfunctional conventional legal pedagogy may be.

The common themes reported in these empirical studies demonstrate a pattern of less engagement with the educational process in law schools when it is structured exclusively around the study of abstract rules derived from appellate cases in a large, Socratically led classroom (the most common form of standard first-year legal instruction). The issues lie in both form (classes of hierarchy, teacher domination, abstraction, individual competitiveness, adversary argument) and content (the almost relentless use of the same material—the appellate case, deconstructed as a text for factual variations in the applications of a standard set of abstract rules).

Though the Socratic method was originally intended by its founder, Christopher Columbus Langdell, to impart the substantive "science" of law by developing a systematic scheme of knowable "rules" derived from the "data" of cases, the legacy of the Socratic method has been purely process—the propounding of questions and hypotheticals to large groups of students in the hopes of teaching a particular form of reasoning: "thinking like a lawyer," as if there were a "right way to know" (Goldberger, 1996). The studies demonstrate repeatedly that those who feel "outside" the system—women, students of color, those less economically advantaged—feel alienated and "silenced" by this form of classroom discourse (Banks, 1988) as it appears to exclude any form of "reasoning" that falls outside the purview of what is denominated "legal and analytic" (Harris & Schultz, 1993; Finley, 1989). Women students and students of color are much more likely to report that they feel they must leave behind, when they enter law school, whatever else they "know"—their life experiences.[2]

Though legal education does not generally involve the use of lecture and the "banking" or "received" knowledge of didactic presentations of information (Belenky, Clinchy, Goldberger, & Tarule, 1986) and is thus intended, through Socratic questioning, to be more "active," the actual effects on students are not much different from the passivity and acceptance of "authority" reported in other studies of education. Students who feel themselves to be "different"—whether more emotional, angry, older, poorer—from the assumed norm of law student and lawyer report a "loss of voice" or fear of taking on either teachers or fellow students.

Perhaps more insidious in legal education than in other forms of education, the informal curriculum or "peer" learning, emphasizing the currency of legal practice—competition, individual achievement, elitism and hierarchy, produced by harsh competition for jobs, and the mandatory curves imposed in grading—produces a narrow spectrum of acceptable behaviors and "answers" that often inhibit exploration of social, political, and other issues that interact with legal principles. Many law students begin to demonstrate the dangers of "received" learning—a desire to conform to the expectations of "authority"—both of teachers and of the narrow peer culture of corporate law practice.

Most disturbing in the reports of the experience of legal education is that women students with equal (or even better) admissions credentials do not fare as well in the grading competition or other measures of law school success (law review, moot court, faculty-recommended honors). Guinier, Fine, and Balin's (1994) recent study of the University of Pennsylvania experience (demonstrating, among other things, lower performance in the first year, greater hostility to the process of legal education, loss of a greater commitment to public service among female students) is currently being replicated at a number of other institutions to test whether the presence of more female faculty, more innovative teaching methods (reviewed later), and different school and legal cultures might have different effects on the educational climate at different legal institutions.[3]

Some have argued that the very structure of the legal curriculum manifests the same "male bias" as the allegedly "neutral" categories of law. To the extent that the "business" curriculum (corporations, tax, securities regulation, bankruptcy) is seen as "core" and subjects of greater interest to women (family law, welfare and poverty law, civil rights, employment discrimination, and legal ethics) are perceived to be marginalized (Bartlett, 1994), women may suffer a "push–pull" effect in their legal studies and legal work as their own "interests" are channeled and segmented by subject stratification (Menkel-Meadow, 1989b). Others have noted the parallel stratification of women as law teachers by the value of the subjects they teach (Angel, 1988; Chused, 1988).

In any event, the feminist (and critical race) critique of legal education (consistent with earlier critical theory and humanist critiques) can be summarized as pointing to the deleterious effects of an emphasis on competitive individualism, rote rule learning, hierarchy in classroom structure and control, adversary argumentation, zero-sum conceptions of grading and achievement, moral relativism (one must be prepared to argue the merits of any position), and dominance of cognitive, objective, instrumental, and analytic forms of knowledge over affective, subjective, moral, and synthetic methods of problem solving.

The experience of legal education is often thought to be alienating and degrading as a process of "professional hazing" to everyone (Turow, 1977), but women students (and students of color) do report a disproportionate loss of self-esteem, confidence, and feeling of inclusion in the educational process. The Guinier, Fine, and Balin (Penn) (1994), Berkeley (1989–90), Stanford (1988), and Yale (Weiss & Melling, 1988) studies (all of elite schools) reveal similar patterns of closer camaraderie between dominant white male faculty and students, mentorship relationships, peer group formation (first-year study groups and writing groups), and classroom interactions — thus illustrating the effects of social interaction of like groups as yet another level of critique of legal education superimposed on the earlier structural and content critiques.

As in the analysis of different ways of learning and knowing demonstrated by feminist epistemologists (Harding, 1991; Belenky, Clinchy, Goldberger, & Tarule, 1986), feminist critiques of legal education have exposed the role of the interpersonal, interactionist, and human aspects of learning and knowing that have not been emphasized by other critics more focused on the content and structure of legal education.

Thus, as I controversially claimed fifteen years ago (Menkel-Meadow, 1981, 1987), just allowing new, previously excluded entrants into legal education (as students and teachers) is likely to lead to critique, reform, and change of the legal education process. My argument then depended (as it still does) on some version of nonessentialist difference feminism (now much criticized in law, as elsewhere; J. Williams, 1989). This claim for particular contributions to the legal education process focuses on how the social exclusion of women and the sociocultural segmentation of work and other social roles structures knowledge (by experience). The recent empirical studies of legal education confirm this differentiated experience of legal education, though not without their critics, and we await the results of further research at other institutions. Whether "difference," "equality," "dominance," or "postmodern" feminism will prove most robust in continuing critiques of legal education and doctrine, we know that the critique of legal education from a gendered perspective has led to a flowering of pedagogical reforms, in conjunction with other movements in legal education, that are only now beginning to be assessed, and to which I now turn.

WOMEN'S WAYS OF KNOWING LAW: OF FEMINIST PEDAGOGY AND ITS EFFECTS ON LEGAL KNOWLEDGE AND PRACTICE

The categories of learning originally developed in WWK—"received," "subjective," "procedural," and "constructed" knowing—in many ways reflect both the critiques and the contributions of feminist pedagogues to the diversification of legal education methods in the last fifteen or so years. The different processes of "meaning making" for women as learners also describe the different ways of making meaning in learning and creating legal knowledge. Some of these methods can be associated with gender, others simply with the postmodern acknowledgment that our knowledge (of many things) now has a greater diversity of sources and comes with a greater humility about its claims for universal truth across time and cultures.

The experience of "silence" is still described by students (female and people of color) who feel excluded from the norms of a legal education constructed through abstraction and cases of particular kinds. I encountered one of the most poignant examples of this for me some years ago, when I was interviewing male Latino and African American students at a state university law school who had recently gained access to legal education but were troubled by how they were learning. Fearing race and class stereotypes, they were afraid to speak out when their criminal law professor assumed that members of their class identified more fully with the interests of prosecuting attorneys than with the defendants in the criminal cases. Some of these men told me the "stories" they read in the cases reminded them of their brothers, their cousins, themselves, and they felt silenced and excluded by the assumptions made by teachers and fellow classmates about who was good and who was evil in the stories. Women students relate similar experiences of being "silenced" during legal discussions of rape and its legal defenses and, increasingly, in discussions of abuse and domestic violence. Thus, with the assumed homogeneity of a group of "gentlemen" in law schools, legal educators have had to realize that their assumptions often silence students who do not conform to traditional pictures of white male lawyers (Epstein, 1970). The slight increase in diversity of the professoriate has come to recognize and build on this growing human resource in the classroom (Hing, 1993; Freedman, 1990), by drawing in, rather than excluding, those who might otherwise be silenced. Law teachers now try to arrange for actual litigants to talk to their classes (Menkel-Meadow, 1988) or, as in clinical programs, to include clients in the teaching and learning process (Shalleck, 1993). One African American law professor writes of her own changes in hairstyles as a reflection of her own changing needs, first to assimilate (with straightened hair) and then to claim her identity as a law professor who challenges "conventional" demographic expectations (Caldwell, 1991).

To the extent that law students are "receivers" of knowledge, passive recipients dependent on the approval of authority, women may be no different in their desire to please and "imitate" the language of law than male students (Schwartz, 1980). Yet there is some evidence in the studies reported that women are slightly more likely to enter law school with the motivation of working in the public interest (Stover, 1989; LaRussa, 1977), which they abandon as they slowly become assimilated to the dominant pattern of commercial and corporate law at many (certainly the elite) law schools (Guinier, Fine, & Balin, 1994).

For many students of the law, the emotional and intellectual vertigo described earlier dislodges their sense of what they already know—the self is thus subjected to a particular form of "legal earthquake" in which the ground is always shifting and there seem to be "no right answers." In the words of the research of WWK, however, the "truth" discovered from self-knowledge has become one of the most powerful resistances to and "eruptions" in conventional legal knowledge. It has been largely through methods such as journal writing (Cain, 1988) and consciousness-raising methodologies in some legal seminars that women have learned to speak of their own experiences in the law school classroom and by doing so have helped to create new legal theories, causes of action (bases for legal claims), and ways of analyzing old problems. Thus, by claiming that sexual harassment, rape, and domestic violence were experiences of women that the law did not recognize, women learned to frame new legal theories, some based on older principles (employment discrimination, redefinitions of "consent"), others based on whole new definitions of legal "wrongs" (MacKinnon, 1987; West, 1985; Bender, 1994). Taking the experiences of self seriously in law has caused women, people of color, and gay, lesbian, and physically challenged students to resist conventional categories of teaching and of lawmaking. Although conventional legal education has often sought to suppress the subjective as an inappropriate measure of truth and justice, modern assertions of the student self in law have caused law to expand its categories of coverage and its methods for evaluating truth claims.

In what has become one of the few canonical texts of modern feminist legal epistemology, the short story "A Jury of Her Peers" by Susan Glaspell (originally a play called *Trifles*) (Glaspell, 1993) is often taught to demonstrate how the "silent, intuitive and subjective" knowledge of women may be more effective at solving some legal problems (Camilleri, 1990; Menkel-Meadow, 1988). In the story, a group of men, including the town sheriff, are sent to investigate the murder of a man who lived in a remote and isolated area with his wife. Accompanying the men are some women who are acquaintances of the one suspect—the man's wife, who is imprisoned. As the men seek conventional legal clues in the form of physical evidence of murder weapons or evidence of the crime, the women sit silently among the artifacts of domestic life in the kitchen, which the men have abandoned as not relevant to "motive"—"Nothing here but kitchen things," one of them says. As they wait, the women discover some "crazy" stitching in the wife's quilt; they discover a broken birdcage and finally, a little bird with a broken neck wrapped up in a piece of silk. Silently, the women communicate their dawning comprehension of the loneliness, isolation, and violence that Mrs. Wright, the dead man's wife, must have suffered at the hands of her husband. As they realize that he killed not only the bird's but his wife's own "song," they realize they have pieced together the "clues" of motive that the skeptical men could not imagine they would ever understand. "But would the women know a clue if they come upon it?" asks the doubting man. Silently the women acquit the victim of likely physical, as well as emotional, abuse and remove the one piece of evidence that only they, as women, understand might prove motive. As they acquit the lonely woman they also come to appreciate their own guilt, in contributing to her isolation by not visiting more often and creating more human connections for their solitary sister. They come to appreciate a different form of "guilt" and "innocence" that is both more and less than the law would allow and encompasses individual and collective responsibility.

This story, now used to teach law students, lawyers, and judges about justice, standards of legal responsibility, legal knowledge, and "evidence," demonstrates the power of feminist epistemology by illustrating how women's knowledge can illuminate the most traditional of legal subjects—evidence and proof of criminal intent and motive. But it also illustrates the complexity of one of law's most difficult contemporary problems: the standards for criminal excuse and justification as a defense in the murder of a battering partner (Schneider, 1986). Women's knowledge is thus relevant to the law—in understanding fact, motive, evidence, and moral justification. In this story, the failure of men to take "women's ways of knowing" seriously likely impairs their investigation.

Legal "truth," then, can be learned from many sources, not just law books and rules, but different human experiences. To be unable to envision or imagine the experience of others not like oneself (as the men in the story are unable to do) is to limit what we can know of what may be legally relevant or important. The failure of the men in this story to "know" and understand "kitchen" clues to murder has also been reflected in recent feminist studies of the exclusions and sexist treatment of issues in law school texts (Frug, 1985; Coombs, 1988; Erickson, 1988). In response, feminist law teachers are increasingly represented in the writing and editing of texts in the core first-year curriculum of civil procedure, contracts, property, torts, and criminal law.

The description of Women's Ways of Knowing's "procedural" knowledge (Belenky, Clinchy, Goldberger, & Tarule, 1986, pp. 87–130) has been especially evocative for legal knowledge, since much of legal education and the development of legal knowledge is based on procedures for evaluating and knowing things. To the extent that traditional knowledge of rules and doctrine appears to be "separate" knowledge (pp. 103–112) most often understood through vigorous adversarial debate or Socratic method with the use of hypotheticals, where the knower stands apart from the known, more recent forms of experiential learning and engagement with the interaction of law and its subjects, through clinical and other forms of legal education, reflect more "connected" knowing (pp. 112–123).

The authors of *WWK*, like many feminist legal scholars, have attempted to detach these seemingly polarized forms of knowing from gender (Goldfarb, 1991; Tronto, 1993, Menkel-Meadow, 1995b) by suggesting that both are necessary (separate knowledge to develop critical evaluative faculties and connected knowledge to understand ideas and people through empathic and emotional responses). Nevertheless, considerable controversy concerning feminist pedagogy centers on whether "caring" knowledge is female or feminist or whether it should be a part of all good lawyering (Ellmann, 1993).

Proponents of Harvard psychologist Carol Gilligan's "ethic of care," one of the most evocative and contested debates in legal education and theory, have argued that women are more likely to reason in law, as in morality, from a relational, needs-based, contextual, and people-oriented perspective, as contrasted to the more male focus, described by psychologist Lawrence Kohlberg, on universal principle, rights-based abstract justice, and rules (Menkel-Meadow, 1985, 1994b; Spiegelman, 1988). Using analysis of Gilligan's Kohlbergian hypotheticals and fables, legal scholars continue to debate whether gender differences can be statistically verified, both in legal education attitudes and performance and in practice (Menkel-Meadow, 1994b; Granfield, 1994). One study of differences in lawyers' ethical reasoning demonstrated that when the rules of the profession were clear (as in ethics requirements for zealous advocacy in criminal law) men and women responded to ethical dilemmas quite similarly. When the rules were less clear and the facts more ambiguous or general approaches to morality were questioned, women were more likely to question the rules (Jack & Jack, 1989). Other studies have claimed no gender difference with respect to negotiation performance (Craver, 1990) of law students, and so the debate continues (somewhat inconclusively, I believe). What these studies may demonstrate is that context matters and so may socialization and training. Thus, where the "rules" are clear, they may "trump" gender-differentiated sensibilities, especially where the expectations of the "rules" and the practicing profession have been created by men and women seek to assimilate to the culture of professionalism. Attitudes toward law school are clearly influenced by race, class, and occupational goals in a world where women are no longer merely "tokens," but have themselves come to represent the growing diversification of the student body and the profession (Granfield, 1994). What is more interesting is the growing attention being paid to the issues and concepts raised by the "ethic of care" and similar concepts (such as "advocacy of protection"; Kotkin, 1996) by both male and female legal scholars and practitioners (Ellmann, 1994). Clinical teachers in particular have begun to consider the variety of ways that lawyers may practice their craft and interact with clients.

The engagement with real clients that has become the hallmark of clinical and experiential education in law draws on both separate and connected knowledge of law and the people it affects. This relatively new development in legal education is derived from several simultaneous social movements—the left politics of the 1960s, feminism, civil rights, access to legal services for the poor, and the "relevance" movement in education born of the student activism of the 1960s. This form of "engaged" and activist learning demonstrates a pedagogical commitment to focusing on more effective methods for teaching students to *be*, not just *think*, like lawyers (Bellow, 1973; Schon, 1983; *Hastings Law Journal*, 1992).

Feminist legal educators have drawn attention to the importance of the relationship between lawyer and client (see, for example, Shalleck, 1993; White, 1990), consistently with the intellectual development of relational feminism, but they have been joined by many men (Alfieri, 1991; Ellmann, 1992, 1993; Spiegel, 1979). Vigorous debates in legal scholarship and clinical legal education now focus on such matters as who should make decisions in attorney–client interactions; how groups as well as individuals can be empowered in the legal process; and whether lawyers of powerful corporate clients should retain some greater moral independence from their clients and reject the interdependence that leads to unquestioning loyalty. This is not the place to review all of these substantive debates, but it is important to understand that issues have been framed by a new focus on relationship inside legal education that was completely absent a generation ago.

As the focus on lawyer–client relations grew, in part, out of relational feminism, so has greater attention to the relationship between teachers and students grown out of more systematic attention to the people, not "things" of legal education (Lesnick, 1992; Himmelstein, 1978, Dvorkin, Himmelstein, & Lesnick, 1981). In some respects, legal education was a "Jeannie come lately" to the innovations of feminist education in other parts of the academy (Culley & Portuges, 1985; Maher & Tetreault, 1994; Griffin 1992). Although small classes and seminars have always characterized a segment of the advanced curriculum in law, it was not really until the 1980s that feminist teachers began to use more participatory modes of education. Borrowing from their colleagues in women's studies programs, they began to employ such methods as journal writing, use of narratives and personal experiences, creative writing about legal encounters, student-led seminars, consciousness-raising process in class (such as circular seating and round-robin talking and sharing), small group exercises within large classes, empirical studies of women's participation in the legal system (Jackson, 1994), and the role plays and experiential performances and feedback of clinical education in both "simulated" and "live-client" settings.

The variety of teaching methods championed by feminists, humanists, "crits," and clinical teachers have been instrumental in affecting the production of legal knowledge as well. Thus, although traditional legal education remains remarkably resistant to radical reform, it must also be said that the 1970s and 1980s have, at least, spawned a variety of diverse "add-ons" to types of classes and methods of teaching, which have also affected our scholarship and methods of knowing and evaluating legal claims. Given the outpouring of recent books on what's wrong with the legal profession (Kronman, 1994; Glendon, 1994; Linowitz, 1994), one senses an insecurity in the land—the center of traditionalism will no longer hold. The "new" forms of legal thinking—feminism, critical legal theory (see Kelman, 1977), clinical education, critical race theory, sociolegal studies, economic analysis of law, the "narrative" turn, law and literature (Heilbrun & Resnik, 1990), and even postmodernism's gossamer influence on legal studies—have broadened what we think is relevant to understanding "the law." Feminist approaches to traditionally "female" issues—such as family law, employment law, and criminal law—have now moved on to treat the "core" issues in legal education and theory: corporate law (Lahey & Salter, 1985), torts (Bender, 1994), labor law, and even taxation and bankruptcy (Menkel-Meadow, 1992a). Issues about whether there are "women's ways" of structuring a progressive taxation system now involve traditional legal scholars in issues of "essentialism" or "standpoint" theories in legal knowledge (R. Kennedy, 1989).

Thus, in law, we have moved from the "separate" knowledge of stylized adversarial debate about doctrine, to more "connected" ways of understanding how people interact with the "law on the streets," as well as the law on the books. We have begun to consider the role of marginalized individuals and groups in constructions of legal knowledge, through narrative, as well as conventional lawsuits and demands for legal rights. We have shifted to consider other ways of knowing than the "purely" rational, including empathy (Ward, 1994), with all of the difficulties that such oppositions entail, especially when associated with gender and race in what are considered "essentialist" claims (a controversy that continues to rage).

Most significantly, it is not only "knowledge" that has been affected by this flowering of intellectual and pedagogical production, but legal institutions as well. Thus, in the terms of *WWK*, we have used the new epistemologies of law to "construct" not only knowledge but new forms of educating about and "doing" law. Specialized women's law journals now exist at almost every major law school. Clinical education has become an institutionalized form of both experiential learning and service to underrepresented communities in many law schools in the country. For those who have focused on nonadversarial methods of resolving disputes and drawing clients and parties into participation in solving their own legal problems in a more democratic mode, new forms of "alternative dispute resolution" such as mediation (even with feminist critiques of power imbalances and inequalities ongoing; Grillo, 1991) have produced both new forms and more creative resolutions to at least some legal problems.

Women have gone from being "silenced" to arguing about whether they have a "different voice" or not, to measuring whether they are heard in the courtrooms of America. For the last ten years, over thirty-five states and several federal districts have formally studied whether there is gender or racial bias in the operation of the justice system (Resnik, 1993; Schafran, 1989). A multitude of concrete reforms have been proposed, ranging from judicial education to substantive changes in family, criminal, and procedural law. Interestingly, some of these studies have substantiated vast "perceptual gender gaps" in what men and women see as fair or discriminatory treatment in the courts (Ninth Circuit Gender Bias Task Force Report, 1993).

These efforts, though not all uniformly successful or even welcomed, have required legal education and legal knowledge to take account of the experiences of women and others who have been excluded from discourses about the law. Women have also had to take account of their own ambivalence about law as both rights-creating and equality-enhancing, at the same time that law often fails to protect or account for women's experience and ability to control or effect justice. Years ago, I said that women remain ambivalent about the state (and its law)—we need it to protect us (from violence and in times of economic need) but it can also oppress us (in the creation of its categories and recognized legal claims and the power it bestows on those with control over us) (Menkel-Meadow in Dubois, Dunlop, Gilligan, MacKinnon, & Menkel-Meadow, 1985).

The work of the last fifteen years has demonstrated that we have been somewhat successful in integrating the voices of clients, students, women, people of color, and gay men and lesbians in the traditional legal discourse of doctrine and policy spoken by judges, legislators, law professors, and lawyers. We have added "narrative" and the stories of people behind the rules; we have created new claims for legal redress (sexual harassment, antipornography campaigns) and redefined others (rape, divorce, and family law reform) as we still struggle with others (domestic violence, reproductive rights, and welfare). We continue to press for legal recognition of women's hurts and harms before the law (West, 1985). We have helped create some new institutions and methods for resolving legal and social problems (mediation) while continuing to adapt older forms to new claims (legal class actions for women's health issues). We have argued about whether a particular feminist sensibility will increase or change the focus of our aspirations for justice and a moral world. We, like others, have focused on the contradictions and ambiguities of the relations among law, justice, and morality (West, 1993; Jack & Jack, 1989; Menkel-Meadow, 1995b). The fact that there are more women in both the legal academy and the profession has clearly made a difference, even if that difference includes a continuing debate about whether difference matters.

That legal knowledge is contingent, context-driven, and "constructed," not "given," is hardly a new insight about how law is made or interpreted. The field of legal epistemology or jurisprudence (the study of the philosophy and meaning of law and legal institutions) has been concerned with these questions for years. Yet, the importance of the political, social, and, yes, gendered "construction" of law and legal institutions has been exposed in the last fifteen years by an explicit focus on how law is studied, made, and interpreted by people in particular "positions" of knowing. This focused analysis has been driven by feminists who make specific claims about how law has been "known" by women from both the "inside out and the outside in" (Belenky, Clinchy, Goldberger, & Tarule, 1986, p. 135).

Feminist critiques of law, legal education, and legal institutions have joined with others and empowered others to examine critically the assumptions of legal certainty and determinacy; the value of adversarial contestation as a method for achieving justice, if not truth; the role of power in the creation of legal knowledge and the distribution of its services; and the historical and political contingencies that define legal categories. The growing diversity of law students, faculty, lawyers, judges, and other lawmakers has expanded the participation of different kinds of people in the processes of learning and making law. This has produced greater uncertainties and lack of clarity about what law means and when it is just. Many fear this postmodern opening out of a field that many wish would provide clear answers or at least a commitment to the shared values of "lawyer–states*men*" (Kronman, 1994).

Those of us who see law as a humanistic tradition—made by people, interpreted by people, used by and for people—acknowledge the greater complexity that increased participation in the law produces, and we welcome it, so that law, which governs as well as educates, can be as fully "human" as a discipline founded on justice should be.

NOTES

1. Traditional legal knowledge taught in law schools has not concerned itself much with this "actual" experience of law. A separate interdisciplinary field, "law and society" or "sociolegal studies," has developed to study empirically the interaction of law with human beings (see Menkel-Meadow & Seidman, 1991). Some legal jurisprudes have also been concerned with the coercive or violent aspects of law (Cover, 1985; Minow, Ryan & Sarat, 1992).

2. At least one legal educator has attempted to reverse this relationship to knowledge, urging students to use their "lay knowledge" in their legal work (Lopez, 1983). Gerald Lopez's focus on legal education is similar to and draws on similar themes from the more experiential "connected" knowledge of WWK, as well as the work of bell hooks (1994) and Paulo Freire (1970).

3. A number of law schools have been quick to claim that they do not experience the same demoralization of women students, with similar educational practices but with different teacher–student ratios, diversity of faculty and students, and other "institutional cultural" factors.

REFERENCES

Abrams, K. (1991). Hearing the call of stories. *California Law Review, 79,* 971.

Alfieri, A. V. (1991). Reconstructive poverty law practice: Learning lessons of client narrative. *Yale Law Journal, 100,* 2107.

Angel, M. (1988). Women in legal education: What it's like to be part of a perpetual first wave or the case of the disappearing women. *Temple Law Review, 61,* 799–846.

Ansley, F. L. (1991). Race and the core curriculum in legal education. *California Law Review, 79,* 1512.

Banks, T. (1988). Gender bias in the classroom. *Journal of Legal Education, 38,* 137.

Banks, T. (1990–91). Two life stories: Reflections of one black woman law professor. *Berkeley W. L. J., 6,* 46–56.

Bartlett, K. (1990). Feminist legal methods. *Harvard Law Review, 103,* 829.

Bartlett, K. (1994). Feminist perspectives on the ideological impact of legal education upon the profession. *North Carolina Law Review, 72,* 1259–1270.

Belenky, M., Clinchy, B., Goldberger, N., & Tarule, J. (1986). *Women's ways of knowing: The development of self, voice, and mind.* New York: Basic Books.

Bellow, G. (1973). On teaching the teachers: Some preliminary reflections in clinical education as methodology. In *Clinical education for the law student.* New York: Council for Legal Education and Professional Responsibility, Ford Foundation.

Bender, L. (1994). Teaching torts as if gender matters: Intentional torts. *Virginia Journal of Social Policy and the Law, 2*(1), 115–163.

Berkeley Women's Law Journal (1990–91). *Black women law professors: Building a community at the intersection of race and gender, a symposium. Berkeley Women's Law Journal, 6,* 1–201.

Bradwell v. Illinois (1873) 16 Wall. 130; In *Re Bradwell,* 55 Ill. 535 (1870).

Brint, M., & Weaver, W. (Eds.). (1991). *Pragmatism in law and society.* Boulder, CO: Westview Press.

Cain, P. (1988). Teaching feminist legal theory at Texas: Listening to difference and exploring connections. *Journal of Legal Education, 38,* 165–182.

Caldwell, P. (1991). A hair piece: Perspectives on the intersection of race and gender. *Duke Law Journal, 2,* 365.

Camilleri, M. (1990). Lessons in law from literature: A look at the movement and a peer at her jury. *Catholic University Law Review, 39,* 557.

Chused, R. (1988). The hiring and retention of minorities and women on American law school faculties. *University of Pennsylvania Law Review, 137,* 537.

Coombs, M. (1988). Crime in the stacks, or a tale of a text: A feminist response to criminal law. *Journal of Legal Education, 38,* 117–136.

Cramton, R. (1978). The ordinary religion of the law school classroom. *Journal of Legal Education, 29,* 247.

Cover, R. (1985). Violence and the word. *Yale Law Journal, 95,* 1601–1629.

Craver, C. (1990). The impact of gender on clinical negotiating acheivement. *Ohio State Journal of Dispute Resolution, 6,* 1.

Crenshaw, K. (1989). Foreward: Toward a race-conscious pedagogy in legal education. *National Black Law Journal, 11,* 1–6.

Culley, M., & Portuges, C. (Eds.) (1985). *Gendered subjects: The dynamics of feminist teaching.* Boston: Routledge & Kegan Paul.

Davis, P. C. (1991). Contextual legal criticism: A demonstration exploring hierarchy and "feminine style." *New York University Law Review, 66,* 1635.

DuBois, E., Dunlap, M., Gilligan, C., MacKinnon, C., & Menkel-Meadow, C. (1985). Feminist discourse, moral values and the law—a conversation. *Buffalo Law Review, 34,* 11–87.

Dvorkin, E., Himmelstein, J., & Lesnick, H. (Eds.) (1981). *Becoming a lawyer: A humanistic perspective on legal education and professionalism.* St. Paul, MN: West.

Ellmann, S. (1992). Empathy and approval. *Hastings Law Journal, 43,* 991–1016.

Ellmann, S. (1993). The ethic of care as an ethic for lawyers. *Georgetown Journal of Legal Ethics, 81,* 2665.

Epstein, C. F. (1970). *Women's place: Options and limits in professional careers.* Berkeley: University of California Press.

Erickson, N. (1988). Sex bias in law school courses: Some common issues. *Journal of Legal Education, 38,* 101–116.

Erickson, N. (1990). Final report: Sex bias in the teaching of criminal law. *Rutgers Law Review, 42,* 309.

Estrich, S. (1992). Teaching rape law. *Yale Law Journal, 102,* 509.

Finley, L. (1989). Women's experience in legal education: Silencing and alienation. *Legal Education Review, 1;* 101–106.

Finley, L. (1989). Breaking women's silence in law: The dilemma of the gendered nature of legal reasoning. *Notre Dame Law Review, 64;* 886.

Freedman, A. (1990). Feminist legal method in action: Challenging racism, sexism and homophobia in law school. *Georgia Law Review, 24;* 849.

Freire, P. (1970). *Pedagogy of the oppressed.* New York: Seabury Press.

Frug, M. J. (1985). Re-reading contracts: A feminist analysis of a contracts casebook. *American University Law Review, 34;* 1065.

Gilligan, C. (1982). *In a different voice: Psychological theory and women's development.* Cambridge, MA: Harvard University Press.

Ginsburg, R. B. (1988). Remarks on women becoming part of the constitution. *Law and Inequality, 2;* 19–25.

Glaspell, S. (1993). In Rabkin, E. S. (Ed.), *Lifted masks and other works.* Ann Arbor, MI: University of Michigan Press/Ann Arbor Paperbacks.

Glendon, Mary Ann (1994). *A nation under lawyers: How the crisis in the legal profession is transforming American society.* New York: Farrar, Straus & Giroux.

Goldberger, Nancy. (1996). Women's constructions of truth, self, authority and power. In Rosen, H., & Kuehlwein, K. (Eds.), *Constructing realities: Meaning making perspectives for psychotherapists.* San Francisco: Jossey-Bass.

Goldfarb, P. (1991). A theory-practice spiral: The ethics of clinical teaching. *Minnesota Law Review, 75;* 1599.

Goodpaster, G. (1975). The human arts of lawyering. *Journal of Legal Education, 27;* 5.

Granfield, R. (1994). Contextualizing the different voice: Women, occupation goals, and legal education. *Law & Policy Quarterly, 16*(1); 1–26.

Griffin, G. B. (1992). *Calling: Essays on teaching in the mother tongue.* Pasadena, CA: Trilogy Books.

Grillo, T. (1991). The mediation alternative: Process dangers for women. *Yale Law Journal, 100;* 1545.

Grillo, T., & Wildman, S. (1991). Obscuring the importance of race: The implication of making comparisons between racism and sexism (or other -isms). *Duke Law Journal, 1991;* 397–412.

Guinier, L., Fine, M., Balin, J., with Bartow, A., & Stachel, D. L. (1994). Becoming gentlemen: Women's experiences at one Ivy League law school. *University of Pennsylvania Law Review, 143;* 1–110.

Hall, R., & Sandler, B. (1982). *The classroom climate: A chilly one for women?* Washington, DC: Project on the Status and Education of Women, Association of American Colleges.

Hantzis, C. (1988). Kingsfield and Kennedy: Reappraising the male models of law school teaching. *Journal of Legal Education, 38;* 155–164.

Harding, S. (1991). *Whose knowledge? Whose science? Thinking from women's lives.* Ithaca, NY: Cornell University Press.

Harris, A., & Schultz, M. (1993). A(nother) critique of pure reason: Toward civic virtue in legal education. *Stanford Law Review, 45;* 1773–1806.

Hastings Law Journal (1992). Theoretics of practice: The integration of progressive thought and action. *Hastings Law Journal, 43;* 717–1257.

Heilbrun, C., & Resnik, J. (1990). Convergences: Law, literature and feminism. *Yale Law Journal, 99;* 1913.

Henderson, L. (1987). Legality and empathy. *Michigan Law Review, 85;* 1574.

Himmelstein, J. (1978). Reassessing law schooling: An inquiry into the application of humanistic educational psychology to the teaching of law. *New York University Law Review, 53;* 511.

Hing, B. O. (1993). Raising personal identification issues of class, race, ethnicity, gender, sexual orientation, physical disability, and age in lawyering courses. *Stanford Law Review, 45;* 1807–1834.

Homer, S., & Schwartz, L. (1989). Admitted but not accepted: Outsiders take an inside look at law school. *Berkeley's Women's Law Journal.* 5:1–47.

hooks, b. (1994). *Teaching to transgress: Education as the practice of freedom.* New York: Routledge.

Jack, R., & Jack, D. (1989). *Moral vision and professional decisions: The changing values of women and men lawyers.* Cambridge, England; New York: Cambridge University Press.

Jackson, V. C. (1994). Empiricism, gender and legal pedagogy: An experiment in a federal courts seminar at Georgetown University Law Center. *Georgetown Law Journal, 83,* 461–524.

Jin-Myung Oh, C. (1992). Questioning the cultural and gender-based assumptions of the adversary system: Voices of Asian-American law students. *Berkeley Women's Law Journal, 7,* 125.

Karst, K. (1984). Woman's constitution. *Duke Law Journal, 1984,* 447–508.

Kay, H. H. (1985). Equality and difference: The case of pregnancy. *Berkeley's Women's Law Journal, 1(1):* 1–38.

Kelman, M. (1977). *A guide to critical legal studies.* Cambridge, MA: Harvard University Press.

Kennedy, D. (1990). Legal education as training for hierarchy. In Kairys (Ed.), *The politics of law.* New York: Pantheon.

Kennedy, R. (1989). Racial critiques of legal academia. *Harvard Law Review, 102,* 1745.

Kotkin, M. (1996). Professionalism, gender and the public interest: The advocacy of protection. *St. Thomas Law Review,* Vol. 8, 157–173.

Kronman, A. T. (1994). *The lost lawyer: Failing ideals of the legal profession.* Cambridge, MA: Harvard-Belknap Press.

Lahey, K., & Salter, S. (1985). Corporate law in legal theory and legal scholarship: From classicism to feminism. *Osgoode Hall Law Journal, 23,* 543.

LaRussa, G. W. (1977). Portia's decision: Women's motives for studying law and their later career satisfaction as attorneys. *Psychology of Women Quarterly, 1,* 350.

Lawrence, C. R. III (1992). The word and the river: Pedagogy as scholarship as struggle. *Southern California Law Review, 65,* 2231.

Lesnick, H. (1992). Being a teacher, of lawyers: Discerning the theory of my practice. *Hastings Law Journal, 42,* 1095–1106.

Linowitz, S., with Mayer, M. (1994). *The betrayed profession: Lawyering at the end of the twentieth century.* New York: Charles Scribner's Sons.

Littleton, C. (1987). Reconstructing sexual equality. *California Law Review, 75,* 1267.

Lopez, G. P. (1983). Lay lawyering. *UCLA Law Review, 32,* 1–60.

Lopez, G. P. (1988–89). Training future lawyers to work with the politically and socially subordinated: Anti-generic legal education. *West Virginia Law Review, 91,* 305.

MacKinnon, C. (1979). *Sexual harassment of working women.* New Haven, CT: Yale University Press.

MacKinnon, C. (1987). *Feminism unmodified: Discourses on life and law.* Cambridge, MA: Harvard University Press.

Maher, F. A., & Tetreault, M. K. T. (1994). *The feminist classroom.* New York: Basic Books.

Massaro, T. (1989). Empathy, legal storytelling and the rule of law. *Michigan Law Review, 87,* 2099.

Menkel-Meadow, C. (1981). Women as law teachers: Toward the feminization of legal education. In *Humanistic education in law: essays on the application of humanistic education in law.* New York: Columbia University Press.

Menkel-Meadow, C. (1984). Toward another view of legal negotiation: The structure of problem solving. *UCLA Law Review, 31,* 754–842.

Menkel-Meadow, C. (1985). Portia in a different voice: Reflections on a women's lawyering process. *Berkeley Women's Law Journal, 1*(1), 39–63.

Menkel-Meadow, C. (1987). Excluded voices: New voices in the legal profession making new voices in the law. *Miami Law Review, 42,* 29–53.

Menkel-Meadow, C. (1988). Feminist legal theory, critical legal studies and legal education or the "fem-crits" go to law school. *Journal of Legal Education, 38,* 61–85.

Menkel-Meadow, C. (1989a). Exploring a research agenda of the feminization of the legal profession: Theories of gender and social change. *Law and Social Inquiry, 14*(2), 289–319.

Menkel-Meadow, C. (1989b). The feminization of the legal profession: The comparative sociology of women lawyers. In Abel, R., & Lewis, P. (Eds.), *Lawyers in society: Comparative theories.* Berkeley and Los Angeles: University of California Press.

Menkel-Meadow, C. (1992a). Mainstreaming feminist legal theory, *Pacific Law Journal, 23*(4), 1493–1542.

Menkel-Meadow, C. (1992b). The power of narrative in empathetic learning: Post-modernism and the stories of law. *UCLA Women's Law Journal, 2,* 287–307.

Menkel-Meadow, C. (1994a). Narrowing the gap by narrowing the field:

What's missing from the MacCrate Report—of skills, legal science and being a human being. *Washington Law Review, 69,* 593–624.

Menkel-Meadow, C. (1994b). Portia redux: Another look at gender, feminism, and legal ethics. *Virginia Journal of Social Policy and the Law, 2*(1), 75–114.

Menkel-Meadow, C. (1995a). *The trouble with the adversary system in a postmodern, multi-cultural world.* New York: Hofstra University.

Menkel-Meadow, C. (1995b). What's gender got to do with it? The politics and morality of an ethic of care. *New York University Journal of Law and Social Change, 22,* 100–131.

Menkel-Meadow, C., Minow, M., & David Vernon, D. (Eds.) (1988). *Symposium: Women in legal education—pedagogy, law, theory and practice. Journal of Legal Education, 38,* 1–193.

Menkel-Meadow, C., & Diamond, S. S. (1991). The content, method and epistemology of gender in sociolegal studies. *Law & Society Review,* 25(2), 221–238.

Minow, M. (1987). The Supreme Court, 1986 term—foreword: Justice engendered. *Harvard Law Review, 101,* 10.

Minow, M., Ryan, M., & Sarat, A. (1992). *Narrative, violence and the law.* Ann Arbor, MI: University of Michigan Press.

Morantz-Sanchez, R. (1985). *Sympathy & science: Women physicians in American medicine.* New York: Oxford University Press.

Morello, K. B. (1986). *The invisible bar: The woman lawyer in America: 1638 to the present.* Boston: Beacon Press.

Ninth Circuit Gender Bias Task Force Report (1993). Special section. *Stanford Law Review, 45,* 2143–2209.

Olsen, F. (1990). The sex of law. In Kairys, D. (Ed.), *The politics of law: A progressive critique.* New York: Pantheon Books.

Pickard, T. (1983). Experience as teacher: Discovering the politics of law teaching. *University of Toronto Law Journal, 33,* 279.

Radin, M. (1990). The pragmatist and the feminist. In M. Brint, & W. Weaver, (Eds.), *Pragmatism in law and society.* Boulder, CO: Westview Press.

Resnik, J. (1993). Ambivalence: The resiliency of legal culture in the United States. *Stanford Law Review, 45,* 1525–1546.

Resnik, J. (1988). On the bias: Feminist reconsiderations of the aspirations for our judges. *Southern California Law Review, 61,* 1877–1944.

Rhode, D. (1988). Perspectives on professional women. *Stanford Law Review, 40,* 1163–1207.

Rhode, D. (1993). Missing questions: Feminist perspectives on legal education. *Stanford Law Review, 45,* 1547–1566.

Rifkin, J. (1980). Toward a theory of law and patriarchy. *Harvard Women's Law Journal, 3,* 83.

Rosenau, P. M. (1992). *Post-modernism and the social sciences: Insights, inroads and intrusions.* Princeton, NJ: Princeton University Press.

Scales-Trent, J. (1992). Sameness and difference in a law school classroom: Working at the cross-roads. *Yale Journal of Law and Feminism, 4,* 415.

Schafran, L. (1989). Ge·· ¹ ·· bias in the courts: An emerging focus for judicial reform. *Arizona . ·· .aw Review,* 237.

Schneider, E. (1986) Describing and changing: Women's self defense work and the problem of expert testimony on battering. *Women's Rights Reporter, 9,* 195–222.

Schneider, E. (1994). Feminist lawmaking and historical consciousness: Bringing the past into the future. *Virginia Journal of Social Policy and the Law, 2*(1), 1–12.

Schon, D. (1983). *The reflective practitioner: How professionals think in action.* New York: Basic Books.

Schwartz, A. (1980). Law, lawyers and law school: Perspectives from the first year class. *Journal of Legal Education, 30,* 437.

Shalleck, A. (1993). Constructions of the client within legal education. *Stanford Law Review, 45,* 1731–1753.

Spiegel, M. (1979). Lawyering and client decisionmaking: Informed consent and the legal profession. *University of Pennsylvania Law Review, 128,* 41.

Spiegelman, P. (1988). Integrating doctrine, theory and practice in the law school curriculum: The logic of Jake's ladder in the context of Amy's web. *Journal of Legal Education, 38:* 243–270.

Stanford Law Review Project (1988). Gender, legal education, and the legal professions: An empirical study of Stanford law students and graduates. *Stanford Law Review, 40,* 1209.

Stover, R. (1989). *Making it and breaking it: The fate of public interest commitment during law school.* (Howard Erlanger, ed.). Urbana, IL: University of Illinois Press.

Tronto, J. (1993). *Moral boundaries: A political argument for an ethic of care.* New York and London: Routledge.

Turow, S. (1977). *One l.* New York: G. P. Putnam's Sons.

Ward, C. (1994). A kinder, gentler liberalism: Visions of empathy in feminist and communitarian literature. *University of Chicago Law Review, 61,* 929.

Weiss, C., & Melling, L. (1988). The legal education of twenty women. *Stanford Law Review, 40*(5), 1299–1369.

West, R. (1985). The difference in women's hedonic lives: A phenomenological critique of feminist legal theory. *Wisconsin Women's Law Journal, 3,* 81–145.

West, R. (1993). *Narrative, authority and law.* Ann Arbor, MI: University of Michigan Press.

White, L. (1990). Subordination, rhetorical survival skills and Sunday shoes: Notes on the hearing of Mrs. G. *Buffalo Law Review, 38,* 1.

Wildman, S. (1988). The question of silence: Techniques to ensure full class participation. *Journal of Legal Education, 38*(1–2), 147–154.

Williams, J. (1989). Deconstructing gender. *Michigan Law Review, 87,* 797–845.

Williams, P. (1991). *The alchemy of race and rights: Diary of a law professor.* Cambridge, MA: Harvard University Press.

Williams, S. (1993). Legal education, feminist epistemology, and the Socratic method. *Stanford Law Review, 45,* 1571–1576.

Williams, W. (1982). The equality crisis: Some reflections on culture, courts and feminism. *Women's Rights Law Reporter, 7,* 145.

Wolgast, E. (1980). *Equality and the rights of women.* Ithaca, NY: Cornell University Press.

Worden, K. C. (1985). Overshooting the target: A feminist deconstruction of legal education. *American University Law Review, 34,* 1141–1156.

Embodying Knowledge, Knowing Desire[*]

Authority and Split Subjectivities in Girls' Epistemological Development

ELIZABETH DEBOLD,
DEBORAH TOLMAN,
AND LYN MIKEL BROWN

COMING TO KNOW

"I DON'T REALLY KNOW anything that's true, outside myself," explains Alisar, during an interview in the spring of her senior year. This is Alisar's last annual interview as part of a longitudinal study of girls' development at the Laurel School for Girls in Cleveland (see Brown, 1989; Brown & Gilligan, 1992). Asked to describe "how you ever know what is the truth," Alisar says,

[*]We would like to thank Mark Tappan for his generosity and insight into some of the finer points of structural developmental theories and the work of Bakhtin; Dalma Heyn for her suggestion and insights into the eighteenth-century development of a psychology of women; Heather Willihnganz for pulling together the references; and Nancy Goldberger for her helpful suggestions.

85

Just as a personal thing, not worldwide or anything. . . . I think it's very hard to know. How do I know it? I guess if it feels right, then I feel I know it, and if it feels bad — if this conscience is acting up, then you really don't know. . . . You just know when something is true about yourself and you feel like satisfied with yourself and there is a sense of relief in your head or something, that you have come to this fact and you have absorbed it and it feels right and you know it, it is an inner thing — for me, I think, anyway.

Alisar's statement is evidence for the "subjectivist" position in the *Women's Ways of Knowing* (WWK) scheme (Belenky, Clinchy, Goldberger, & Tarule, 1986) — a position that the authors and, more recently, Nancy Goldberger (this volume) have noted often describes knowing as grounded in bodily sensation, typically of what "feels right." For the women in the ways of knowing study, the "subjectivist" position represents a turning away from external, often male, authorities to a newfound, "inner source of strength" (p. 54). From the subjectivist perspective, truth is "personal, private, and subjectively known or intuited" (p. 54), just as Alisar has defined it.

The move into subjectivism is, the authors believe, "a particularly significant shift" and often a "personally liberating event" (p. 54). They note that nearly half of the 135 women interviewed for WWK were "predominantly subjectivist in their thinking" (p. 55). As the authors note, the subjective way of knowing still contains "remnants of dichotomous and absolutist thinking." Subjectivist thinking, thus, is positioned as a less evolved way of knowing and hearkens to "myths and stereotypes about women's thought." However, they also note that realizing one's subjective truth is "an important adaptive move in the service of self-protection, self-assertion, and self-definition," and, thus, "has repercussions in her relationships, self-concept and self-esteem, morality and behavior" (p. 54).

Yet, in Alisar's case, and in the stories of many girls we have talked with and interviewed, the transition into subjectivism, while perhaps a refuge, tells a more complicated and troubling story. Within a Western culture that authorizes as knowledge the products of a mind abstracted from material reality — of the body, of human relationship, of the particulars of people's lives — we have found that girls coming of age and coming to know the dominant culture typically find themselves torn and, ultimately, split from their own power to authorize their experience as real and as knowledge (see, e.g., Brown & Gilligan, 1992; Debold, 1994; Gilligan, 1990; Taylor, Gilligan & Sullivan, 1995; Tolman & Debold, 1994). While not contradicting the basic findings of our ways of knowing colleagues, we offer another approach to epistemological development, one rooted in girlhood and in an explicitly poststructuralist frame, that we believe explains some of the tensions now apparent within WWK.

In the last decade, a chorus of voices erupting out of near silence within the human sciences has provided new ways of listening and new themes to hear. The ways of knowing project furthered our collective ability to hear women's voices and the ways they know, to hold open possibilities of alternative forms of rationality, and to engage with the complex relationship between intellectual development and cultural authority. And yet—and not to diminish their accomplishment—WWK was written during a particular historical moment. At that moment, "a different voice" (Gilligan, 1982) in psychology—let alone multiple voices—was a radical notion. Carol Gilligan's "different voice" was joined by those articulating experiences of being raced, classed, disabled, and dissed within a culture and a psychology (as a culturally sanctioned discourse) that privileged the values, thinking, and experience of educationally advantaged, middle-class white males (see, e.g., Fine & Asch, 1988; Fordham, 1988; Reid, 1993; Robinson & Ward, 1991; Tatum, 1992; Ward, 1990; Weis & Fine, 1992). Furthermore, postmodern and poststructuralist critiques of the unitary, epistemic subject—that son of the Enlightenment—have been explored within feminism in ways that the authors of WWK could hardly have predicted (see, e.g., Bartky, 1990; Bordo, 1987, 1993; Brennan, 1993; Butler, 1990, 1993; Cixous, 1981; Diamond & Quinby, 1988; Grosz, 1990, 1994; Irigaray, 1985; Jaggar & Bordo, 1989; Keller, 1986; Sawicki, 1991).

In this chapter, we offer a way of listening to voices of culturally diverse girls using a Foucauldian framework that explores how authorized, that is, culturally sanctioned, forms of knowledge effect girls' bodily and psychological experience of subjectivity. As philosopher Susan Bordo (1993) explains, "Cultural practices, far from exerting power *against* spontaneous need, 'basic' pleasures or instincts, or 'fundamental' structures of body experience, are already and always inscribed 'on our bodies and their materiality.' . . . Our bodies, no less than anything else that is human, are constituted by culture" (p. 142). French philosopher Michel Foucault (1983) observes that "there are two meanings of the word *subject*: subject of someone else by control and dependence, and tied to his [sic] own identity by a conscience or self-knowledge. Both meanings suggest a form of power which subjugates and makes subject to" (p. 212). Self, or subject, becomes divided against its self through an incorporation of knowledge that functions as a form of power. Developing knowledge of what is right, true, or moral creates "normalizing" discourses that are then incorporated as human subjectivity through the power of these discourses to create desire to be normal, that is, right, true and moral. Yet, while the existence and, thus, incorporation of power relations is constant, the particular manifestation is not. Foucault (1983) points to historical times of resistance and outbreak of conflict "to bring to light power relations, locate their position, find out their point of application and the methods used" (p. 211). Power relations, though ubiquitous, are made evident through human struggle and conflict.

By taking up a Foucauldian framework offered by one of us, Elizabeth Debold (1994, 1996), we trace culturally diverse girls' struggles both between self-authorization—their capacity to know, value, and articulate their experience—and cultural authority, and between integration and splits in their subjectivity (Brown, 1989, 1991; Brown & Gilligan, 1992; Debold, 1990a, 1990b; Tolman & Debold, 1994). Debold (1994, 1996) argues that human subjectivity becomes engendered as children struggle against and incorporate what is "normal" for males and females within the larger culture and their particular social environment. Over the course of development, children develop increasing cognitive capacities to understand the potential impact of social expectations on their selves and relationships. Exploring the intersection of body, psyche, and culture, Debold (1994, 1996) traces differences in what is known as "masculine" and "feminine" personality, and gender differences in psychopathology, to power/knowledge about "normal" gender roles and expectations that become systematically, cognitively available to boys and girls in early childhood and early adolescence (see Gilligan, 1991a, 1991b, 1996). For boys in early childhood, the understanding that gender is a binary category requires them to divide themselves internally and socially from what they have understood to be maternal and female (see also Chodorow, 1978). Debold theorizes that girls feel required to make a similar, but substantially different, internal and social division as they reach adolescence and the capacity for abstract thinking. With the power of abstraction, girls divide from aspects of themselves and from other women and girls as they come to know the patriarchal, heterosexual dynamic of social power relations. While desiring to be "normalized," boys and girls simultaneously engage in active struggle and resistance— evident in psychological distress—to normalizing expectations of gender because such expectations require loss and dis-integration of self (see also, Brown & Gilligan, 1992; Gilligan, 1991a, 1991b, 1996).

Our chapter has four primary sections; the first two provide critique and the latter two our alternative reading of epistemological development. In the first section, we bring questions to the WWK framework relating to issues central to the enterprise of understanding and articulating "the development of self, voice, and mind" in women. We use Foucault's insight into the relationship between power/knowledge and subjectivity as the basis of our critique. In the second section, we ask whether the authors' emphasis on "mind" enforces a "bifurcation of being" that subtly reinscribes dominance relations that engender women's subordination (Grosz, 1994, p. 3). The historical positing of gender difference and a "different voice" in literature and human psychology has left women, identified with body, positioned outside the realm of authorized knowledge. We argue, admittedly from the advantage of hindsight, that any attempt to understand women's epistemology needs to engage directly with how authorized knowledge has been engendered. The third section explores younger girls' epistemology and girls' resistance to cultural authority as presenting another ground for epistemological development. Finally, we provide a brief case study of a seventeen-year-old girl.

POST HOC POSTSTRUCTURALISM

Alisar resorts to a subjective, personal truth as a way of holding on to what she knows in the face of disagreement and potential loss or exclusion. Born in Lebanon and coming of age in America during crises in the Middle East, Alisar reports that she's changed as a learner and thinker: "I am more skeptical and I have more cynicism when I learn about things, especially when I watch the news or study history or something. . . ." Watching news about Middle East conflicts, she wonders about what is presented to her as objective truth: "I don't know if it is paranoia or what, but I think a lot of it is American propaganda. Then when I go to Europe or something, and I read their articles or hear European people talk about the same subjects, . . . you get a totally different perspective that wasn't shown on television here." The authorized American view differs from what Alisar and her family understand "about the back history of what has led up to these events." As she explains, "I was born in Beirut, and I didn't know any Jewish people there. . . . There were Palestinians, a lot of them. And I grew up with a lot of them. . . . In the beginning my thoughts were totally against what people thought here." Fearing that she would offend others and be labeled "a prejudiced person," Alisar "kept [her] mouth shut" because, she feels, "I mean I want to speak my mind, but if that is how people are going to feel about it, then it is not really worth my talking to them about it. I don't care." When faced with a culture and context that are hostile to her perspective, Alisar protectively disengages from discussion of complex ideas that she cares about deeply.

Against the words of authorities in school who hold the key to her future, Alisar's understanding of the context-dependence of historical and political truth leads her to split the ways she knows into public belief and private doubt. While she believes that she needs a "good education" to realize the American dream of "get[ting] a good job and mak[ing] lots of money," she doubts the substance of what she is learning at school— putting the two at cross-purposes:

> I don't think that you have to trust anything to get a good education. I don't think you have to trust any facts. You can know about them but you don't have to believe in them to get a good education, as long as you know about all the facts—or nonfacts. As long as you know, but you don't have to believe in it.

As an accommodation to a hostile surround, Alisar has found a way to divide knowing into "know[ing] about all the facts—or nonfacts" that she is asked to learn and believing or trusting in truth that is "a personal thing."

Alisar does not become one of the privileged "hidden multiplists" described in WWK who are "the polite listeners, the spectators who watch and listen but do not act" (p. 66). Over three years of interviews, between the ages of fifteen and seventeen, Alisar finds herself deeply at odds with her surroundings. Like the adage that the cynic is a failed idealist, Alisar splits subjective from "objective" truth because the world and educational system in which she finds herself have failed to give her a way to maintain her integrity and, so, truly to "feel right" about what she knows. While Alisar says she finds herself "really irritated by it and I don't know what to do," she knows that being able to mouth American truths in American classrooms is critical for her to achieve academically in this country, and that, in turn, is key to her future economic success.

Incorporating a public–private split between doubting espoused American truths and believing in her personal experience, can Alisar simply be called a subjectivist thinker and knower? Certainly, she is very clear that truth is a personal, felt understanding. Alisar's curiosity about different perspectives and understanding that "for some questions there are no right or wrong answers" show more than nascent awareness that knowledge is constructed, contextual, and changing. Such "constructed knowledge" is the most integrative position within the WWK framework: the result of a search "for a unique and authentic voice." At the same time, however, Alisar can be heard within the WWK framework as a "received knower," because even though, on one level, she resists accepting American truths, on another, she takes in this knowledge and gives back the "right" answers. Oddly enough, by rejecting the substance of what she is taught, she seems to leave that information unprocessed, raw, without knowing how she might critique it without risking dismissal.

We have two primary questions about the premises of the ways of knowing work raised by this short excerpt from Alisar's interview. First, what does it mean that, within this framework, a woman is categorized primarily in one of five epistemological positions?[1] As we have noted, Alisar appears to acknowledge several ways of knowing that vary with her relation to authority across contexts. Second, and related to the first question, what does development mean within the WWK framework? Alisar's transition into a public–private split cannot simply be understood either as a regression or as developmental progress.

While the authors acknowledge that their categories "cannot adequately capture the complexities and uniqueness of an individual woman's thought and life," we are concerned with a seeming contradiction: on the one hand, that categorizing women in one epistemic perspective (give or take a half stage above or below this perspective) supports the notion of a unitary self, and, on the other, that underscoring that these epistemic positions themselves relate deeply to women's relationships with predominantly male authority suggests that across the contexts of women's lives, individual women will exhibit the characteristics of more than one position. In other words, if women's engagement with authorized knowledge relates to their relationships with male authorities, then assuming a unitary epistemological perspective obscures power struggles that women may necessarily incorporate as splits in subjectivity and different ways of knowing.

Structural theories of human development, on which the ways of knowing framework has been based, skip over theoretical questions of self and subjectivity to describe holistic, stagelike transformations in knowing and understanding (Broughton, 1978; Erikson, 1968; Fowler, 1981; Kegan, 1982; Kohlberg, 1981; Loevinger, 1976; Perry, 1968; Piaget, 1983). Similarly, most empirical measures of personality assume a unitary self that, within a single test-taking context, reveals its unitary truth and, issues of developmental change aside, is relatively stable (see, e.g., Bem, 1981; Spence, Helmreich, & Stapp, 1974; Loevinger & Wessler, 1970; Rosenberg, 1965; Offer, Ostrov, & Howard, 1981). In WWK, "self" is frequently used to convey a global sense of personness. Designating each woman to a unique epistemological perspective, and placing these perspectives in an order parallel to William Perry's (1968) stages of intellectual development, further underscore an assumption that there is a unique, unitary self that normatively and ideally makes progress along a certain path of development.

However, the authors simultaneously suggest that, both within the women's responses and in their use of "self," there are more complexity, conflict, and tension than are implied by such singular epistemological perspectives. The women struggle to describe experiences that point to the *process* of being a knowing "I" who changes over time and with context. For example, a subjectivist knower says, "I keep discovering things inside myself. I am seeing myself all the time in a different light" (p. 85), or, the authors describe constructed knowing, "as an effort to reclaim the self" through integrating knowledge (p. 134). This aspect of self, the "self-as-knower" (James, 1892, cited in Damon & Hart, 1982), describes an ongoing process in which "I" creates self from moment to moment within the context of internalized and situational power relations.

The authors of WWK note women's "tendency . . . to ground their epistemological premises in metaphors suggesting speaking and listening," which places self-as-knower within relationship but can obscure the power relations inherent in social interaction (p. 18). The changing social nature of selfing process is accurately expressed, conceptually and literally, in "voice": self process is known, to others and to our selves, through speaking as an "I" (see Gilligan, 1982/1992; Wertsch, 1991). Moreover, it is developed within and by the complex social interaction and experience of language (see Bruner, 1986; Stern, 1985). George Herbert Mead (1934/1967) concluded that "there are all sorts of different selves answering to all sorts of different social reactions" (p. 142). Learning when to speak, to whom, and how to be heard is critical to the development of subjectivity and to subjection (see Taylor, Gilligan, & Sullivan, 1995). Power relations inhere in this learning.

For Mikhail Bakhtin (1981), as for Lev Vygotsky (1978, 1986), language mediates the functioning of the psyche; thus, the activity of authoring (which is his term for the selfing process) always takes place in the context of a relationship, in ongoing dialogue between self and others (see also Day & Tappan, 1996; Tappan, 1991). In Bakhtin's (1981) terms, the process of "ideological becoming" occurs as words, language, and forms of discourse enter and become part of the psyche—that is, become part of "inner speech." Words are internalized via different speaking voices that a person hears in the context of her various relationships and social interactions—voices engaged in the ongoing dialogue that constitutes the social world. Bakhtin (1981) hints at the power relations inherent within this discourse-based process; he notes that certain voices are more "internally persuasive" than others. Human mind is persuaded by discourses that promise sustenance, love, and security, and, conversely, limit anxiety, danger, and harm; all are forms of power/knowledge/desire that normalize subjectivity.

Within this context, Carol Gilligan's (1982/1992) work not only outlined different gendered selves-as-knowers, as the authors of WWK note, but also argued that selves are multiply voiced within relations of power. In the method developed for reading interviews of individuals' lived moral conflicts (Brown et al., 1988; Brown, Debold, Tappan & Gilligan, 1991; Brown & Gilligan, 1990), two moral voices, "care" and "justice," are typically evident within each subject's interview narratives. However, a subject tends to align with—that is, be internally persuaded by—one voice over another in ways that then typically align her selves with normalizing discourses about gender, power, and morality. Gilligan and her colleagues' work suggests that the psychic interplay of these voices relates to men's and women's, and boys' and girls', differing relationship with cultural authority (see Gilligan, Ward, & Taylor, 1988).

The finding that so many women in the ways of knowing study predominantly embraced subjective knowing undermines the concept of a simple developmental path of simply unitary subjects. Of the 135 women involved in the study, "almost half were predominantly subjectivist in their thinking" (p. 55). As the authors observe, subjective knowers "appeared in every educational and agency setting included in the study. They cut across class, ethnic, age, and educational boundaries" (p. 55). The presence of so many diverse women within one category suggests that the category itself might be more of a "catch-all" than a unique epistemological perspective. The authors note both that "it was not easy to absorb and generalize about . . . this large group of women" and that "at first it was difficult to see what linked the women in so diverse a group" (p. 55). Within the WWK framework, the authors explore a developmental logic that moves from subjectivity and attention to relationship to "connected procedural knowing," wherein the knower uses empathy and subjectivity to learn from and with others, and culminates in "constructed knowing," in which feeling and thinking, the personal and the authorized method, are integrated in a process of knowing that emphasizes the relationship of the self and other in the context of knowing. The fact that so few women move across this trajectory and come to know knowledge as constructed could be due to the justifiable difficulty women have in explicating reason outside authorized rational discourse—needing an *écriture féminine* (see Dallery, 1989; Irigaray,

1985)—or to the possibility that the WWK framework itself still privileges authorized ways of knowing that divide mind from body or, finally, to developmental problems with the trajectory itself.

Similarly, women were clustered at Stage 3 in Lawrence Kohlberg's (1981) structural theory of moral development, a middle stage that captured reasoning related to "interpersonal accord and conformity." Deconstructing this overburdened stage led Sharry Langdale (1983) to argue that it was poorly conceptualized and Carol Gilligan (1982/1992) to hear within it a "different voice" with its own logic. Concern for relationship, in Kohlberg's theory, and body-based subjectivity, in the WWK framework, are engendered feminine within Western cultural representations and practices, thereby placing them outside authorized discourses of knowledge. As the work of Luce Irigaray (1985) and Hélène Cixous (1981) tantalizingly suggests, the historical fact that author-ity and reason have been gendered masculine may leave other forms of reason, particularly a body of knowledge, outside authorized discourse and without a rational language with which to speak audibly. Women's struggles with hegemonic representations of development can be seen as both their resistance to authorized cultural power relations and their embeddedness within a system of power that historically has excluded the female from reason (see Bordo, 1987; Lloyd, 1984/1993).

Unitary theories of self also imply—or even state—that only one mode of knowing and being is "normal," "healthy," or "mature" through tracing a single developmental path. In two separate analyses with our colleagues, we have observed that what is, in conventional terms, defined as regression in adolescent girls' development of self and knowing may actually indicate their struggles with and resistance to external authorities—that is, with notions of how they *should* feel and think and act. Using the WWK perspectives to analyze questions about knowing in interviews with a cross-section of the Laurel seventh- and tenth-grade girls, Judith Dorney and Elizabeth Debold observed that more tenth-graders expressed themselves predominantly as either received, that is, accepting authority as the source of truth (29 percent versus 16 percent) or subjectivist, defining truth as personal (45 percent versus 31 percent) knowers, than seventh-graders. Surprisingly, more seventh-grade girls (53 percent) than tenth-graders (26 percent) articulated procedural knowing, which takes truth and knowledge out of the dichotomy of public/external/other and private/internal/self to embrace systems and methods for knowing. While seventh grade, a transitional year for these girls, marks a time when they struggle actively with who defines their reality—they or the authorities in their lives—the tenth-grade girls, notes Lyn Brown

(1989), "give external authorities the power to define goodness and value" (p. 197). Girls' conflicts between their own experience and their increasing knowledge of cultural expectations at early adolescence may lead them to give up on developing methods for knowing (that is, procedural knowing), and in so doing, either to accept what authorities say as true (received knowing) or to attempt to hold on to a personal truth (subjectivist knowing).

Annie Rogers, Lyn Brown, and Mark Tappan (1994) support this preliminary analysis in a three-year longitudinal study of ego development with these seventh- and tenth-grade girls. While ego development is not the same as epistemological development, they are deeply interrelated. Ego, or self-system, notes Jane Loevinger (1987), referring to Harry Stack Sullivan, is the "gatekeeper" of knowledge, "the template or frame of reference within which each of us perceives and conceives the interpersonal world" (p. 91). Rogers, Brown, and Tappan write, "In the seventh grade group, 50% of the girls regressed at least one level in ego development by the ninth grade. Many of these girls regressed from the conscientious-conformist stage to the conformist stage, moving from beginning to question conventions into a simpler and easier acceptance of conventions" (p. 12). We see this regression as parallel to the epistemological shift from knowing through procedures to relying on authorities—that is, convention—for knowledge. Moreover, the authors found that this pattern of regression continued through high school:

> In the 10th-grade group, 45% of the girls regressed at least one level [by twelfth grade] from a range of different levels. . . . Among the girls who regressed there were two distinct patterns: girls who regressed two or three levels from the highest stages, and girls who regressed on average one level, from the conscientious stage to the conscientious-conformist stage. Regardless of the level from which the 10th graders regressed, all of these girls moved into a less complex and differentiated understanding of themselves and of their relationships according to Loevinger's theory. (p. 12)

As girls approach the end of their high school experience and begin to move into college (the destination of virtually all of these educationally privileged girls), they continue to reconsider their relationship with themselves and with authorities, embracing more simple and more conventional ways of being and knowing.

While both of these preliminary analyses used methods that rely on simple ratings of position or perspective, they challenge the structural hierarchy, linearity, and unidimensionality of such developmental frameworks.

If girls are capable of more complex ways of knowing and being when they are younger than when they are older, then the implicit link between age and developmental progress that undergirds developmental theory—the assumption that "every day in every way things are getting better and better," to paraphrase Voltaire—is called into question (Kaplan, 1967).[2] We argue, and will explain in more detail, that the transformations in girls' selves and relationships in early adolescence, and arguably again at the end of their high school experience, place these girls under pressure to conform—to subject themselves—to cultural standards that do not embrace either the reality or the complexity of their experience.

By presenting women at a single epistemological perspective and by placing those perspectives in a normalized developmental sequence, the authors caught themselves in a double bind: within the system that they present, women do not appear to be developing "normally" or to "advanced" stages of knowledge, but were the authors to stay with the women's experience, it would undermine their implied notions of self and development. However, the tensions within WWK about self and development can be read post hoc within a more poststructuralist framework. The varying uses of "self" and "voice" can be heard as evidence for a subjectivity that is not unitary, but created by dialogue within varying power relations. The presentation of a fixed developmental progression, expressed with ambivalence by the authors, is undermined by women's and girls' experience. Developmental theories, taken up as practices within education, are normalizing discourses of power/knowledge: they articulate what forms of subjectivity, ways of knowing, and systems of value are granted cultural authority and function as mechanisms of control and discipline. Women and girls, as historical subjects on the margins of cultural power and authority and, thus, in a subordinate power relation to that authority, both resist and are subjected within such developmental discourses. Trying to hear women's voices without an explicit critique of developmental discourse as an expression of power relations, and the kind of self/subjectivity inherent in it, leads to an ambiguity that can subject the women themselves to negative interpretations of their capacities and knowledge. In other words, it can unwittingly reinscribe cultural power relations that subject and subordinate women.

SPLITTING MIND FROM BODY

As Alisar moves between believing and doubting, she knows how her world splits along divisions integral to Western culture. Asked whether she has ever experienced work that she loved, she responds with some surprise, "No." Her interviewer then asks whether that is something that she is looking for, and Alisar answers:

> See, that is what I want. I want to do some work that I love doing, but I don't know if it is in my nature to love work. You know what I mean. I would love to have a career where I would love doing it, be happy doing it. I think there is a difference, be happy doing it, and loving to do it. But I just don't find myself loving to do work. I think that's where the self-discipline kind of thing comes in.

Is there something that you love to do?

> I love to learn about new things and experience new things and I think that goes with traveling, that is what traveling is, just seeing new things and experiencing them. I love doing that. I love just talking with my friends, or just with people, I guess. I love cooking. I love eating. I hate dieting. So those are the type of things. I love being infatuated, you know, things like that.

Dividing her world along Sigmund Freud's split between work and love, Alisar finds her self similarly divided between self-discipline and embodied, passionate experience. Later, asked what kind of teacher would help her to learn the most, Alisar continues to divide herself and her world:

> So far I haven't experienced that. I feel I will be more interested and I would give more of myself to it than anything else. . . . How can [history] possibly affect you? That's how you get out the real emotion, you know, feelings to understand or want to learn more about something, where your curiosity starts working.

What would it take to have people teaching like that?

> Someone who loves his work. And I don't know how many people feel like doing that, are willing to do that. I mean, and I don't know what the benefits are.

Although Alisar no longer knows what the benefits are of loving work, she desires this deep feeling, this connection between what "you think and care," between the historical and the present, between embodied passions and intellectual love. Alisar speaks of a "self-discipline" that is in conflict with giving "more of [her]self . . . than anything else." The "self" that is disciplined cannot be infatuated, satiated, or wholly involved: such a self is sapped of passion and desire.

Evidencing a classic mind–body antagonism that splits her self, Alisar struggles with the "self-discipline" to control the hungers and passions that threaten her American dreams. Work and love inhabit two separate spheres aligned with the public and private worlds of industrialized cultures. Alisar cannot find a way that work and love are integrated in her life because the self-discipline of work—dieting, competition, academics—is critical to the personal aim of "achieving my goals." She has taken in, incorporated, a notion of self and body that bifurcates the "lower" bodily material experience from the "higher" disembodied intellectual inherited from René Descartes and Plato. Thus, to achieve her goals, she must overcome the unruly passions and desires of the body. At the end of her last year of high school, Alisar has set her sights on an American dream of individual wealth "to be financially independent, to do whatever I want and not have anybody step in my way," yet her path to success depends on her triumph over her desires, passions, and needs, and, thus, splits her from relationship with herself and with others.

Alisar incorporates the splits in the culture by splitting off that part of herself that believes passionately, that hungers for food and knowledge. As she states, "I don't think you have to trust anything to get a good education. I don't think you have to trust any facts. You can know about them but you don't have to believe in them." By embracing the recipe for middle-class success, Alisar also splits into an achievement-oriented, individual public self that appears to believe in the American dream of meritocracy, in American educational and cultural authorities, and a private self that disagrees strongly with those authorities and feels passionately about experiences shared with her family and culture. While choosing her own felt sense of truth may be a brave and defiant stance, the choice in itself embodies her loss of integrity within a culture built on dualisms of mind–body, passion–reason, love–work, as well as of rich–poor, black–white, and male–female. Alisar's move to a privately held subjectivism is an act of resistance to cultural authority. Her resistance may cost her both the passion that so often undergirds sustained intellectual endeavor and the procedures through which she may voice and question her own feelings. Her splitting, particularly if parts of her self and her passion become increasingly silenced, may also leave her vulnerable to psychological or even somatic distress (Brown & Gilligan, 1992; Debold, 1991, 1994, 1996; Freud, 1895; Gilligan, 1991b).

That Alisar holds on to a private subjective truth as a function of a mind–body split is particularly intriguing given the fact that subjective knowers often rely on bodily feelings that communicate truth to them. Moreover, in WWK reliance on subjective truth often is related to anti-intellectualism and disdain for rationality, particularly scientific rationality. While the authors rightly note the solipsistic dangers of subjectivism and the stereotyping of women's thinking as irrational and intuitive, their ahistorical emphasis on mind as separate from body threatens to rein-scribe women's historical, cultural subordination to men's authority and authoring of knowledge. The concept of "mind" within Western culture comes out of a discourse within which women, and the body, are subordinated within a subjectivity constructed as irrational.

WWK explores the problematic relationships women have with cultural authorities and authorized ways of knowing as related to gender but does not go far enough to negate the cultural equation of mind, authority, and masculinity. Even though the authors make important distinctions relating to gendered authority between their work and the work of William Perry (1968), the fact that they have made these distinctions does not fully problematize disembodied, masculine reason. Perry describes the struggles of (white male) Harvard students in the 1960s to move beyond simplistic dualistic epistemology as a response to the question "What do They want from me?" Whether, as father's favored son, the men try to give "Them"—cultural Authorities—what they want, or in Oedipal defiance, they try to stake their own ground and stand alone in their truth, there appears to be little question that the process will at least lead these white Harvard students toward greater personal authority, and most likely, to acknowledged cultural Authority. Moreover, Perry argues that Oedipal rebellion is the better choice because it enables an emotional separation that facilitates what Susan Bordo (1987) has called "the flight to objectivity," that is, to becoming the Cartesian epistemic subject (see Keller, 1986). For Perry's young men, the development of an authoritative epistemology is related both to their position as "sons" to cultural authority and to their ability to separate from feeling.

For women, the question "What do They want from me?" in relation to authority or Authority is more problematic because it is asked within a gendered power relation—both on the level of discourse and in actual relationships. Not only are the authorities in women's lives often men, but women and the "feminine" as we know them are historically connected to the body and separate from, but controlled by, (masculine) public authority. A large number of women in the WWK study had at one time been sexually exploited by social authorities, such as fathers, uncles, doctors, professors, ministers, employers (pp. 58–59). For too many women, the response to "What do They want?" holds an implication of male sexual desire and aggression. The authors note that many of these women were subjectivist, bodily knowers who eschew the abstract rationality authorized as knowledge. These women's refuge in a private knowledge based in their personal subjectivity seems, then, protective, and echoes the historical creation of women's knowledge within a distinct domestic sphere.

Research in the various disciplines of history (Foucault, 1980, 1983, 1986; Laqueur, 1990), literary criticism (Armstrong, 1987), and philosophy (Bordo, 1987; Rorty, 1979) points to the early modern period as engendering institutional systems of knowledge and desire that persist in middle-class life today. Descartes's private pursuit of reason through pure mental reflection helped to legitimate and create the private, psychological self understood since then as the basis of human subjectivity (Armstrong, 1987; Bordo, 1987). As the rise of the middle classes upset the historic social and moral order based on heredity, a new social and moral order was defined on the basis on sex difference, thus engendering Western culture (Armstrong, 1987) and creating a "psychology" for each gender.[3] The historical relationship between women and the material body (due both to childbirth and to men's projections) became a basis for aligning women's psyches and essential subjectivity with passivity and emotion (see Lloyd, 1984/1993). A woman's social worth—and, thus, what a woman desired—changed from being based on social class to being based on the degree to which she embodied domestic virtues that balanced nascent capitalism's sordid political economy.

The essentially feminine subject, outside authorized knowledge and political authority and aligned with the body, was created by inciting women's desires for power and security. Armstrong (1987) observes that middle-class women (and those who aspired to middle-class life) actively embraced and created the proffered domestic sphere of influence and the power it offered separate from male authority in the workplace, academy, and government. From the anxiety raised by the dissolution of the hereditary order, the question of how women could obtain class security and prevent victimization was increasingly answered through the achievement of a "natural" feminine subjectivity (Armstrong, 1987; Debold, in press). Giving up identity as a member of a sociopolitical class, women came to know themselves *as women* by their ignorance of the political economy and the desire to embody a domesticated goodness.[4] For security and the power to influence, then—as now—the feminine subject we recognize as woman is essentially depoliticized and subjected through authority over feeling and the care of bodies.

Intrinsic to the maintenance of the balance of separate, gendered spheres, and middle-class hegemony, then, was a reconfiguring of women's desires. Historian Thomas Laqueur (1990) observes that women's sexual desires, previously assumed to be similar to, if not greater than, men's, were transformed into passivity and ignorance of sexual desire to legitimate women's exclusion from public life. "Woman," the psychologically feminine subject, became increasingly privatized and idealized. In an extraordinary tension, women's domestic sphere of knowledge became the body—its feelings, appearance, comportment, acculturation, and nurturance—even as the desirable woman became disembodied through ideals of bodiless purity and domesticated good-ness. By the Victorian era, women's psychological connection with the body, within a culture that deeply embraced splitting passive body from active reasoning mind, led science (and medicine) to question whether women should engage at all in intellectual activity (Russett, 1989) or were even capable of the activity of orgasm (Laqueur, 1990). "Woman," then, as a body of knowledge, became sanctioned—and desired by middle-class men and women alike—as the passive subjective body, out-side the realm of the active, objective masculine mind.[5]

Susan Bordo (1993) observes pointedly that the dualism of mind and body intrinsic to Enlightenment rationality is not a sterile philosophical concept from centuries ago but a cultural practice through which we understand what is normal and become subjects/subjected. "Rational-ity," philosopher Genevieve Lloyd (1984/1993) notes, "has been con-ceived as transcendence of [the body, and by association, of] the femi-nine. . . . Women cannot easily be accommodated into a cultural ideal which has defined itself in opposition to the feminine" (p. 104). When the feminine has been constructed as oppositional to mind and autho-rized knowledge in the public domain, women are bound to have con-flict assimilating standards of rationality that oppose their cultural basis for being. Dominant cultural knowledge of the feminine subject is essen-tial to middle-class life, which provides the framework of desire and sub-jectivity within American culture.

Too often the attempt to articulate a different experience of mind is defeated by an analysis using traditional dualistic categories that grant "objective mind-separate-from-body" dominance or repetitively recon-struct the mind–body split through a designation of body as inchoate feeling (see Grosz, 1994). WWK began to articulate a possibility for knowing that defies traditional categorization, but, by starting with Perry's (1968) work as a starting point, reasserted a bias for mind-over-body rationality that aligns with cultural authority. This difficulty in articulating alternate forms of and ground for reason is mirrored by the struggles of the women within the study. Many of the women resisted masculine authority and authorized methods of knowing, embedded within cultural discourse that equates masculinity–mind and femininity––body, by embracing bodily subjectivity or experiencing alienation from authorized masculinity. Thus, these women reinscribed the mind–body split even as they may have been struggling to articulate something different (see also Goldberger, this volume). As we discuss further in the next section, the difficulty in deconstructing this split arises from the fact that language, authorized discourse, and our gendered subjectivity are all constructed to re-cognize and know mind—and often self—as distinct and separate from body. Rationality that does not reinscribe mind separate from body would reconceptualize knowing through corporeality, through the sentient body, and authorize diverse, complex subjects (see Clinchy, this volume; Grosz, 1994; Ruddick, this volume).

NEW DEVELOPMENTS

Alisar cultivates a "self-disciplined" public self that strives for the normalizing ideal of the American dream because she has developed the cognitive capacity to recognize cultural ideals and systemic power relations, which, in turn, has divided her against her embodied desires for pleasure and relationship (see also Bartky, 1990). Her love of eating is radically split from her self-disciplined, dieting self because, as she says in her tenth-grade interview, "Society doesn't like fat people and I want to be liked. That's the whole thing, right?" Similarly, the love of making art that she describes in eleventh grade—"I really enjoy doing it. . . . I like the reward of looking at it after I'm finished"—is transformed by normalizing standards made available to her through her increasing ability for self-reflection, by which she views her work. As she explains in her twelfth-grade interview, "I thought I really loved my art and everything and then I found out . . . I am not as good as I thought I was," and so, "I don't enjoy it as much."

Alisar is also divided from her own ignorance and isolation and from others as she embodies a normalizing discourse about class relations. Her visceral, bodily responses are shaped by her knowledge of what is good and right as an upper-class subject. Repeatedly, she articulates what is a normalized moralistic discourse about poor people: "The worst is being a bum on the street" or "I don't want to end up like them, you know, I don't want to end up with no education, pregnant, you know, just ignorant about the whole world and everything. I mean they know nothing about nothing." As Alisar develops as an abstract thinker, she viscerally incorporates a discourse that reviles the poor: simply seeing "the rat freaks . . . [who] live out on the farms, with the teenage kids and . . . greasy hair and blond and they wear these tight jeans . . . made [her] want to throw up." Her own anxiety about money and success, perhaps intensified by her knowledge of racial power relations as a young woman of color, echoes a long-standing social Darwinist cultural discourse that incites desire by creating moral as well as material anxiety. Alisar's capacity for abstract thought subjects her self as a divided subject. She may not be able to know her own ignorance, which might make her like the poor people she hates, nor be able to integrate her pleasure with her desire for achievement without feeling that she would risk her chances for success.

Our work and that of our colleagues have led us to hear a developmental counterpoint to Enlightenment progress toward increasing cognitive abstraction and bodiless objectivity that both suggests another potential ground for reason and makes visible the dark side of incorporating cultural knowledge about oneself and the world (e.g., Brown, 1989; Debold, 1990b; Debold & Brown, 1991; Gilligan, 1991a). Through our studies with diverse preadolescent and adolescent girls, we have come to realize that Alisar's dichotomous dilemmas are an incorporation of her struggle for self-authorization and knowledge in the face of cultural authority that privileges certain forms of subjectivity and experience while devaluing others. Normalized, divided subjects are not simply gendered but also, at least, raced and classed. A subject's particular material body—its race, ethnicity, disabilities, color, weight, height—are all subject to cultural knowledge that creates desire and divides subjectivity. Alisar's incorporation of and resistance to cultural ideals that deny the power and vulnerability of her self and experience trace a process that parallels that of many girls who come of age in a patriarchial, racist, and classist culture (Brown, in prep.; Brown, 1989; Brown & Gilligan, 1992; Debold, 1990a, 1990b; Taylor, Gilligan & Sullivan, 1995; Rogers & Gilligan, 1988; Tolman, 1992; Tolman & Debold, 1994). Girls' accommodation, not simply in the narrow Piagetian sense, to cultural expectations, ideals, and categories by dividing their selves is both a tribute to human resilience and evidence of the incorporation of power relations.

Elizabeth Debold and Lyn Brown (1991) observed that preadolescent girls from the Laurel School were less subject to splitting along cultural divides than their older peers, such as Alisar. Although younger girls are not precultural, their limited capacities for abstract reasoning constrain the degree to which they can know and, therefore, desire as enculturated subjects.[6] As developmentalists John Broughton (1978) and William Damon and Daniel Hart (1982, 1988) also have noted, preadolescent children speak less in terms of Enlightenment categories of rationality and the private, psychological self. While Damon and Hart note that younger children have ways of knowing psychological, or inner, experience, as children move into adolescence they increasingly use psychological concepts, articulate agency and volition, and create an intellectual construct of self through the process of self-reflection. Such explanations, as power/knowledge discourses themselves, legitimate an understanding of younger children's concrete thinking as less worthwhile, less developed, less complex than that of older children and adults. Ignored in this explanatory discourse is an appreciation of girls' capacity to subvert categories of experience and knowledge that divide middle-class life through their mind–body integrity.

The young middle-class girls in the Laurel study—that is, girls between the ages of seven and eleven—know from a mind–body integrity and value ways of interacting that are not normative aspects of either Cartesian knowing or its constructed opposite, middle-class femininity (Debold, 1990a, 1990b, 1994, 1996; Debold & Brown, 1991; see also, Brown & Gilligan, 1992). These younger girls live in a world that is vivid and clearly defined by their senses and feelings. The visible differences between people are neither liberally glossed over nor reacted to as categorical. "Different people have different opinions," explains nine-year-old Margaret, "because you have a different mother and a different family, and a different skin, different color, different color eyes, color hair, and intelligence." Experience, and differences in experience, are the ground of knowledge and knowing. Nine-year-old Toni argues that it's "good to be different" because "it's like if everybody had the same feelings, it'd be kind of like the same. . . . If you're all alike and you do everything alike, they'll like know everything you'll know . . . and that's not good." While not innocent of the categories by which society makes judgments—"Some people like [others] because they're popular . . . skinny . . . [or] pretty"—nine-year-old Amy and many of her classmates reject such categorical distinctions as the basis of relationship: "And I think that it doesn't matter because I have a friend, she's not really attractive, but she's a nice friend to be with and she makes me laugh a lot, . . . and she's a nice friend to be with." As Amy says later, "I've known her long enough to judge her, and I like her a lot." Jill, another nine-year-old, also knows how image-conscious people are, that is, how physical differences are used to judge, but places value elsewhere: "How [someone] feel[s] is what really counts because it doesn't matter what you look like because that's not really your feelings." Unlike the subjectivists in WWK whose personal knowledge becomes truth that often prohibits engagement and leads to a search for sameness, these girls take differences as a given ground of knowledge, not a system of judgments, that is the basis of real engagement.

Differences, as these girls know, can lead to disagreement and difficult feelings. While nearly all of them echo the mantra of middle-class femininity—Be nice, be quiet, be good, get along with everyone—they haven't fully incorporated that discourse such that they are able to live it and judge themselves by it because they do not yet have the cognitive capacity to do so. Alison, at nine, not only takes fighting for granted but feels it is part of what's exciting about relationship: being an only child is "always boring because there's no one to fight with, no one to do anything with." Girls' knowledge of difference also gives them insight into the relativity of truth as a source of disagreement. Clara, at ten, struggles to find the right words to describe how her great aunt's interpretation of events differs from her and her brother's interpretation: "Sometimes in her head it's different than it really happened. I mean, it happened the way she's telling it, but not in her thinking; it processes different than in our thinking." Clara demonstrates a very sophisticated ability to distinguish between her great aunt's narrative of events and the interpretive spin that they each put on those events (see also Brown & Gilligan, 1992).

From different bodies and different contexts, girls realize that people develop different opinions, feelings, and thinking—words that they often use interchangeably. For these girls, knowing comes out of a felt experience that is both mind and body, feeling and thinking, rather than out of a privately held subjectivism created in varying ways in opposition to authorized forms of rationality. Seeing someone walk away from her best friend, Judy, at nine, notices that her friend is left "just talking into space" and goes to her "so she wouldn't feel bad." Asked in her interview, "How can you tell when you think someone's going to feel bad?" Judy erases the distinction between thinking and feeling. "I don't know," she says, "I just feel it in my mind." While she finds such knowledge "hard to explain," Judy says further, "You can just kind of see them walking away or getting sad or something, but you can't tell right then and there she's going to get hurt or anything, but you just feel it." Through a keen distinction between being able to "tell right then" and being able to "feel it," Judy articulates a felt difference between an intellectual re-cognition and a mind–body awareness that leads her directly to action. Her use of the word *mind*, then, encompasses far more than intellective cognition. Rogers (1993) calls on a medieval, pre-Enlightenment definition of "courage," the "capacity to speak one's mind with all one's heart," that connects feeling and thinking, mind and body, to describe the integrity with which girls live.

Listening to poor and working-class girls in early adolescence, some of whom have experienced sexual, physical, and emotional abuse, Lyn Brown (in prep.) demonstrates that, living literally and figuratively on the margins of middle-class culture, these girls have concepts of mind and norms of femininity that embody a vibrant resistance and self-authorization. The girls articulate and value their experience, as they struggle against incorporating cultural notions of themselves as bad and stupid (Brown, 1989, 1991). These girls, similar to poor girls in an urban setting studied by Betty Bardige (1988), experience and articulate knowing that is a unity of thought, feeling, and action. The seventh- and eighth-grade girls in Brown's study feel and express their self-righteous anger at what they perceive to be unpredictable, inconsistent, and unfair treatment by those in positions of power and authority—particularly, in their case, their middle-class women teachers. To a fault, the fracture of which runs along class lines, these girls declare their personal truths openly and aggressively, their loud and indignant voices covering an emerging anxiety and insecurity around their abilities to know and contribute in the classroom. As their teachers react to their hostility rather than to the vulnerability that underlies it, the girls become more distrustful and further removed from their teachers and their education. For these girls, their determined and certain experiential knowledge places them in constant tension with authority figures, in part because who they are and how they express themselves undermine "appropriate," that is, white middle-class, feminine behavior.

Whether a move to silence, noted as an outcome of poverty and abuse in the WWK study, is imminent for these poor and working-class girls or not, we cannot say at the moment.[7] However, to project that such trouble and tension would undermine working-class girls' sense of self and their confidence in their ability to know and learn, particularly in those contexts where white middle-class values and norms prevail, seems reasonable. Perhaps, for some, the reliance on boyfriends and husbands to negotiate public spaces will become the soil in which further insecurities take root and in which the potential for oppression and abuse grows. Perhaps not. In any case, these girls point to struggles with authority that persist throughout the lifespan that have a profound effect on what develops and how selves can know—and on their capacities to negotiate and resist oppression.

As our collective work demonstrates (Brown, 1989, 1991; Brown & Gilligan, 1992; Debold, 1990a, 1994, 1996; Debold & Brown, 1991; Debold & Tolman, 1991; Gilligan, 1990, 1991a, 1991b; Gilligan, Brown & Rogers, 1990; Rogers, 1993; Steiner-Adair, 1990; Taylor, Gilligan & Sullivan, 1995; Tolman, 1992; Tolman & Debold, 1994), the changes of mind and body in adolescence, and the social and cultural interpretation of those changes, lead girls to know themselves and their worlds differently, and place them in complicated—often contentious—relationship with cultural authority. Both girls' knowledge and this conflict create severe pressure on girls to split, divide from aspects of their selves, lose mind–body integrity and create themselves as normalized subjects within the dominant middle-class culture as well as in particular cultural communities.

In our developmental analyses of girls at the Laurel School, we observed that they undergo a crisis with cultural authority during adolescence (Brown, 1989, 1991). Brown (1989) tracked the relationship between self-authorization and external authorities in girls between the ages of seven and sixteen. Second-grade girls, she found, tended to trust their own voices and believe in the wisdom and beneficence of authorities in their lives (undoubtedly related to their educational privilege), while seventh- and tenth-grade girls increasingly struggled with inner and outer authority. Moving into adolescence, girls articulate increasing self-doubt evidenced by the persistent echo of "I don't know" in their speech (Brown & Gilligan, 1992; Debold, 1990a; Gilligan, 1990). Girls' faltering ability to voice their experience with authority is expressed as an epistemic confusion, often signified through the repetitive qualifier "I mean"; they no longer know themselves or what they once knew (Debold, 1990a).

As girls develop the cognitive ability to understand their worlds more abstractly, to comprehend cultural values and expectations, they begin to doubt the authority of their own experience—and divide their selves—as they experience their selves as increasingly vulnerable to loss or danger within a patriarchal culture (Brown, 1989, Debold, 1990, 1994, 1996). Brown (1989, 1991; Brown & Gilligan, 1992) identifies an idealized "Perfect Girl" within predominantly white middle-class girls' interview narratives as a damaging source of comparison between self and ideal that is evidence of their incorporation of knowledge of femininity. These middle-class girls' cognitive ability to hold a cultural ideal and compare self to that ideal as a way of guaranteeing security, love, and connection divides them against themselves. Perhaps similarly, working-class and poor girls often identify as ideal both models and celebrities in early adolescence, and, in later adolescence, the successful young, middle-class career woman (Brown, in prep.; Taylor, Gilligan, & Sullivan, 1995). For these girls, the desire created by knowing middle-class hegemony leaves them split between that knowledge—their dreams—and experienced relational closeness within their social class—their reality. Steiner-Adair (1990) noted that young women who took in and adopted as their own the cultural ideal of the "Superwoman" were at risk for eating disorders, evidencing a dangerous split between an embodied desire for relationship, known through experience and culturally defined as feminine, and an incorporated ideal of competitive achievement, defined culturally as masculine.

Debold (1994, 1996) hypothesizes that girls' growing capacity to comprehend normalized, systemic power relations, otherwise known and desired as "reality," as their bodies develop sexually leads them to disintegrate mind from body as they re-cognize themselves in danger and split for safety. As Tolman's work (1992) on girls' experience of sexual desire clearly shows, girls know that fully embodying their sexual(ized) bodies places them at risk to lose close relationships, particularly with family members; lose their sense of their own goodness, having incorporated cultural knowledge about morality and sexuality; and lose their physical integrity, realizing that rape and sexual assault are all too real. These risks are frightening and mildly traumatizing. Girls' resistance to these losses, evidenced by internal conflict, acute distress, and/or "acting out," marks this point in development as a struggle for hegemony between a more experiential mind–body integrity and cultural power relations. Ironically, girls' struggles to maintain relationship, knowledge, voice, and vibrant embodiment as they develop the cognitive capacity to incorporate as knowledge/desire cultural divisions (between masculine and feminine, sexual subject and sexual object, mind and body, public and private, rich and poor, black and white) often lead them to reproduce within their selves the same divisions because these divisions have become known to them as "reality." Girls, at adolescence, become subjects subjected to cultural power relations.

LILY: SUBJECTED SEXUALITY

For many girls, the most acute pressure to split themselves comes from what they learn and know about sexuality. Here we would like to listen to Lily, a high school senior at an urban school, talk about her knowledge and experience of her self within the context of an interview about girls' sexual desire.[8] Lily, at seventeen, lives with her Colombian father, who is divorced from her white mother. The psychological complexity of the splits within her subjectivity that Lily makes to be safe, loved, and thought well of—by herself and others—provides some idea of the effect of power as a literal incorporation of culture.

Lily is asked what makes her feel sexy. She responds by explaining how her boyfriend evaluates her appearance each morning; when he "says that I look sexy, that's one of my sexy days." While asked a question about her subjective experience, about her knowledge of how she feels, she replies from a position as the object of another's judgment; that is, she knows herself in the realm of "sexy" as the object of male desire. When her interviewer persists in trying to learn what she can tell about feeling sexy, Lily answers again from a perspective that privileges her boyfriend's knowledge about her: "I feel good . . . it's just nice to think that he thinks of me as a way he would think of somebody walking down the street that, you know, that he would say, oooh, she's so hot, or whatever." Incorporating the normative power relation that girls and women are objects of male sexuality, objects that are at constant risk for violation or abandonment by being supplanted by other, more attractive objects, Lily cannot know her own sexiness as something within the scope of her own authority or embodied feeling. In this socially condoned construction of sexuality, agency is all male and female sexuality seems limited to looking good; her embodied feelings just do not figure. Throughout her interview, we track Lily's process of "selfing," of creating herself as a powerful subject and knower, while trying to avoid being subjected to abuse or abandonment, which, unwittingly, creates subjectivity-as-object—safe, perhaps, but deeply divided against herself.

Lily appears to be subjected as the object. We hear her as accepting the culture's authority that displaces her sexual subjectivity with the need and desire to be a "good object." As an adolescent, Lily knows herself as an object within dangerous power relations; she now enacts a sexual objectification of herself whereby, as feminist theorist Sandra Bartky (1990) says, "her sexual parts or sexual functions are separated out from the rest of her personality and reduced to the status of mere instruments or else regarded as if they were capable of representing her" (p. 26). Not only is this a dis-integration of mind–body, but, as Bartky notes, Lily is "alienated" from full personhood because "part of [her] being [has been] stolen by another" (p. 32). And yet, at this point, the incorporation of the Other's view of herself is so thorough that Lily herself acts as the thief. Listening to her, we hear a cultural discourse uncritically emerging from and creating her with the full force of its authority.

Lily is not a passive robot programmed to voice and represent the "culture." As her story within her interview tells us, she has embraced and incorporated what appears to be a path to safety, respect, and relationship. Her division from her self probably feels right, that is, "normal," as well as good, in a moral sense if not in terms of embodied pleasure. Her first experience of intercourse at twelve was unexpected and not at all about her pleasure or agency: "I just did it because I didn't even know what I was doing at the time, we were just kissing and all of a sudden it just happened and I didn't, I didn't even know that it was happening when it was happening. . . . I never thought about not wanting to or wanting to. I never really thought about doing it at all." Like many adolescent girls, sexual intercourse is something that "just happened" to Lily. Her desire or pleasure was not only absent, it did not even figure for Lily as a relevant aspect of this experience. Yet, that difficult experience led to catastrophic relational consequences for her, as she explains:

> The guy that I lost my virginity to was about four years older than I was, and I was twelve. And, it was a really big thing, cause I got a really bad reputation for that, but I went out with him for three years after that, and I really thought we loved each other, and we always planned on getting married and everything. . . . My mother didn't know how old he was. . . . I think the only reason why I stayed with him was because he was my first, so that kind of had, that had a big influence on my life, I guess, because if I wasn't with him, my mother wouldn't of found out, my mother wouldn't have sent me to Boston.

Her sexual behavior garnered Lily not only a bad reputation but rejection by and loss of her mother. Recasting a frightening story within a culturally available romance narrative, she describes this boy as "the first"—although she leaves ambiguous whether "the first" modifies "love" or "time"—and immediately begins discussing marriage. Lily "normalizes" her relationship by placing it within the context of marriage. Within her peer group and the culture at large, girls who have sex outside a long-term relationship are open targets for verbal, if not physical, abuse and ostracism. Thus, her desire to stay with this boy is simply intelligent. As she explains further, Lily "knows" and understands her experience, shaped within cultural power relations, through the story told in her family's culture and in dominant American culture that a woman's happiness is dependent upon marriage, motherhood, and sex after marriage. The lessons Lily learns map perfectly with cultural practices, rooted in constructed norms of femininity, that deny young women sexual subjectivity.

Since then, Lily has located herself safely in relationships that enact normative power relations between the active masculine and passive feminine. Her own body is more a site of potential vulnerability than a source of empowerment or connection to herself or others through pleasure. Her abrupt and disorienting induction into intercourse, a later date rape, her bad reputation, and her mother's rejection have taught her the price of living outside the bounds of normalized femininity as she understands it within her own environment. She says sexual pleasure is not in her own body because

> I don't, I don't think that it's there, because for me, if I said it was someplace on my body, then that means anybody can go there and touch it and I would feel sexual pleasure, but that doesn't happen. So for me, I guess sexual pleasure would be in somebody that I love, that we kind of share, you know, maybe, maybe it's half in me and half in him, and then when we share it, then, then that's where it is, I guess it just comes from nowhere, from inside, you know.

Knowing from experience that boys can touch her and that it is not pleasurable, Lily refuses to accept a construct of her self wherein her body is a locus of sexual pleasure, regardless of context, as a way of protecting herself from participating in her own violation. Instead, she locates pleasure in relationship.

Despite the interviewer's pressing for an acknowledgment that she feels sexual desire within her body, Lily resists such a construction of her self. Trying to maintain her experience of pleasure as relational, she begins to locate her self in the gendered split of sexuality into male physicality and female emotionality. Lily has a visceral response to the idea of sex without love: "I couldn't, even, even if I felt good physically with somebody, if I didn't love them, I would just be totally disgusted being with them." Yet, within relationship, sex without desire is fine. As she explains about her relationship with her boyfriend,

> I would, I would, I mean if I didn't enjoy having sex, I would do it for him, just because he likes it, but he makes me enjoy it, so I do. And, I mean, it's not like he forces me to, but he does things, so I, so I do. . . . But if I didn't, I would still do it for him, because I don't really care how it feels physically, because it, it doesn't really [sigh] I don't know, like I said before, it's the emotional thing.

Lily demonstrates how complex the splits are that she has incorporated: while she would be physically repulsed by pleasurable sex with someone she didn't love, it is fine to have unpleasurable sex within a "love" relationship. In both cases, however, it is clear that the person physically enjoying sex is the male. The traumatizing events of her early sexual experience may have propelled her to incorporate a gendered cultural split so fully that her body responds with revulsion to the idea of sex outside the safety of relationship and, yet, doesn't tremble at intercourse within relationship when she's not aroused.

Lily cannot fully ignore or split off her desires for pleasure, for direct action and agency. "The best time, the nicest time, the funnest time, the most incredible time" in her relationship with her boyfriend in terms of the power of her embodied passionate feelings occurs when she can rationalize why she wasn't agentic. During this experience, Lily recounts that she was both drunk and just waking from a sound sleep:

> We were drinking and I went to sleep in the bedroom, . . . he just woke me up, and, and that was like, it was like a dream, you know, cause I was, I was still half asleep, and it was, it was so incredible, I don't know, it was like, it was like, um, my skin was so sensitive or something, maybe cause I was drinking and then I sleeping too, and just ever, everytime he touched him I was just so, it was really sensitive, everywhere. And, it was like a dream.

Released from the constant vigilance of complying with norms of femininity which require that she focus on providing him with pleasure and satisfying his desire rather than pay attention to her own passion, Lily remembers the power of her bodily feelings and her sense of emotional connection with him—an integrity of body and mind that is virtually impossible to describe under the tenets of a social construction of womanhood that leaves out or demonizes women's embodied passion—only within a context in which she can rationalize that she wasn't fully responsible as a result of the effects of alcohol and sleep.

The ways that cultural norms guard the split between girls' bodies and minds are exquisitely illustrated in Lily's exegesis of her occasional transgression of these norms, earning her the label (by her boyfriend) of "wild girl": "When I want to do something sexually it's amazing because then I'll, then I do it, and, and then my boyfriend's happy. And he thinks that I'm just this wild girl who does anything, but it just happens once in a while, and, and that's when I, I do it." When she is asked what is going on when that happens, she reflects, "I don't know. I, sometimes I just feel, I don't know, I don't know the words for it, brave I guess [laugh]." This question takes Lily to a territory within her self where there are no words for the feeling or impulse or desire that engages her sexually, evidence of how split her sexual body and feelings are from her mind and knowledge. Suggesting that being "wild" is dangerous, risky, or frightening, and, so, requires bravery, Lily does not elaborate on what she sees her transgression to be. Instead, she describes her occasional defiance of the straitjacket of femininity within the normative context of the never-ending cultural imperative for women to look good and to be "put together":

> Sometimes I'm just like, I'm not in the mood to do anything. Like sometimes I'm not in the mood to have sex because I just have all my clothes on, everything is fine, I just, maybe I just did my hair or something, and I don't want to just have to take off all my clothes, especially when I'm wearing panty hose, and then have to put them back on, and and, that's probably the time when he wants it most, and I don't, . . . And so when I do things like that, he gets surprised and even though it's inconvenient for me, sometimes I just have this feeling, well I just don't care, if I have to put my panty hose on or not. You know. So.

Divided between having to look good and to respond to her boyfriend's sexual demands, sometimes Lily responds to this conflict by not caring about her appearance and surprising her boyfriend by being "wild." Interestingly, Lily does not call her feeling "desire" and resists associating it with the "sexual," perhaps because it may be as much an expression of anger and aggression at the normative boundaries and demands she feels she must meet.

Within the normative bounds of femininity, voicing sexuality is a male practice. Lily describes her own participation in such a discourse as another way that she transgresses and here she explicitly marks her behavior as male. Describing when she and her friends talk about sex, she says:

> And guys, guys have, they have no shame talking about it. We talk about it and we laugh, and then it's over, and we feel embarrassed, and, and that's it, . . . But they say it to embarrass people. To embarrass other people. But we say it just to . . . just to act like them, I mean if they can say it, then we can say it. But we won't say it around them, because we don't want them to know that we're just like them, cause you have to kind of play the game of, if they talk about stuff like that, then you have to say, oh that's gross, don't talk about that in front of me, you know.

For Lily, to continue to be seen as a normal, presumably good, girl means that she cannot take action, even verbally, about sex.

For Lily, being a girl who will not be rejected, ostracized, or abused means living a split that divides herself against her self and incorporates as "normal" or "okay" a system of relationships in which she exists as a fairly passive sexual object. Lily knows her self, is subjected, within a power/knowledge matrix wherein the public expression of sexuality, the desire for sexual pleasure, aggressive pursuit of sexual objects, and control over other's reputations are all masculine. She has heard that she might be able to be an agent of her own pleasure, a pleasure to which she is entitled and through which she could be empowered: "I've heard people calling up Dr. Ruth and Dr. Ruth saying, well, you should show them where, where you like it and where, you know, what you like and whatever, and they're just like, no that's not for me." Dr. Ruth's authority is not authoritative enough to counteract the collective weight of her own harsh experiences, her desire for love and safety, and her understanding of what it is that girls who don't get exploited do. Repeatedly in this interview, Lily asserts that she does not feel sexual desire. Reflecting on her experience of having been essentially raped while on a date, she connects this past experience with how her sexuality is organized now, where love displaces desire: "I was so scared. . . . So I guess that's where all my feelings, my emotional things, come from." If being safe means being dissociated from her body, virtually treating her own body as an object which serves somebody else's pleasure, then that might be better and, in fact, give her a greater sense of control than acting openly as a sexual agent.

Even though Lily can be adamant that, for her, sexuality is about her emotional feelings, she does describe complex experiences with her own sexual pleasure that suggest a powerful and wonderful physical aspect. Her experiences do not fit well into the mold of "good" womanhood that she knows well; in addition, Lily has conveyed her painful personal knowledge of how defying these conventions can mean the loss of important relationships. Lily negotiates a minefield of conventions, expectations, punishments, and pleasures that push her to split her mind from her body, her heart from her knowledge. Lily's seeming embrace of conventions and norms of feminine behavior—updated somewhat to a 1990s urban setting—belies a complex struggle that has left her divided against herself and subjected within cultural discourse and her intimate relationships. For Lily, as for many girls, the struggle for safety and relationship within systems of power relations embedded in cultural discourses and practices makes it dangerous for them to know themselves sexually and divides them from a body/mind integrity so evident in the narratives of younger girls.

CONCLUSION

We would argue, along with Nancy Goldberger (this volume), that the epistemological perspectives in WWK are varying strategies that subject women from different material and social contexts. For different women, the different faces and voices of patriarchy—known through husbands, fathers, media, or textbooks—offer different possibilities for creating self and knowledge. We, thus, take the authors' central insight that women's epistemological development has to do with women's relationships with male authority further to argue that the WWK perspectives track women's different possibilities as subjects/subjected within patriarchal (and other hegemonic) discourses and in relation to patriarchal authority. Yet, in the search for integration between public and private authority, between mind and body, that so many women within WWK articulate, we suggest further that listening to younger girls holds promise for understanding the conflicts that women experience and for a ground to epistemology that is not rooted in the dis-integration of sentient body or a division between masculine rationality and feminine emotionality (see Debold & Brown, 1991).

By using William Perry's scheme (1968) for epistemological development in the college years as a foundation for their work on women, the authors inherited not only a framework that relies on a unitary, monovocal self but also one that rests on a relatively unproblematic relationship with culturally authorized knowledge that divides mind and body. Perry's young men's relationship with authority, even when oppositional, is relatively straightforward because they do stand to inherit the kingdom. For women and girls, however, such inheritance is far less likely given the historical persistence of cultural subordination perpetuated by the creation of women as subjects outside public discourse and power.

Listening to young girls, and to girls' struggles with self-authorization and dis-integration at adolescence, radically transforms thinking about epistemological development. As Gilligan (1990) noted when revising the hypothesis she had presented in In a Different Voice (1982/1992), "The sequence that I had traced by following adolescent girls and adult women through time and through crisis did not seem rooted in childhood. Instead, it seemed to be a response to a crisis, and the crisis seemed to be adolescence" (p. 9). Adolescence is a crisis for girls because the knowledge that girls develop—through their increased capacity for abstract reason as they become sexually mature and know their selves and the culture differently—subjects them to splits within both themselves and their relationships. What girls know leads them to losses and dis-integration that leave them vulnerable psychologically, physically, and economically.

Yet, what girls know in childhood—and few maintain in adolescence—before the Enlightenment categories of subjectivity and knowledge subject them offers us hope that we might be able to claim the sentient body as the ground for rationality and create new ways of knowing and being a subject (see Clinchy, this volume; Grosz, 1994). We are neither suggesting a return to some idealized Golden Age in childhood, nor are we locating it in medieval times, but we suggest that we might, oddly enough, learn from the constraints placed on young girls' knowing to question those cultural divisions created in the seventeenth and eighteenth centuries. While the idea of creating culture without forms of subjectivity that subject us to power relations is an impossibility, we can privilege and authorize ways of knowing and being that do not divide us in the way we are now. The beginning of the enterprise is the point where Descartes started: bringing the body into knowledge. Creating a corporeality or corpo-rationality will simultaneously begin to deconstruct the categories of gender that have engendered our social worlds. Perhaps then we can revision a world in which Alisar can have work that she loves without experiencing that as a fundamental contradiction in life.

NOTES

1. We recognize that there is considerable disagreement among the authors of *Women's Ways of Knowing* on this point. However, from what is evident in the book, it appears that a woman can be coded in half steps, that is, one half position above or below a particular epistemological position, or can be given a major and a minor score, such as 3(2). Nevertheless, like other structurally based coding schemes (for example, those of Kohlberg, Kegan, Loevinger), a unitary, stage-specific-"structural whole" is assumed to underlie a person's way of knowing.

2. Piaget observed that concrete forms of experience in early development are recapitulated in later, more abstract experience. Thus, as an individual begins to exhibit more abstract thinking, he or she appears to repeat an analogous developmental sequence. While we accept Piaget's basic observation, the point that we make is that there are ways of knowing and knowledge that appear to be split off in this process (see also Stern, 1985).

3. Before the seventeenth century, writes Thomas Laqueur (1990), "To be a man or a woman was to hold a social rank, a place in society, to assume a cultural role, not to *be* one or the other of two incommensurable sexes" (p. 8). To be a man or woman, then, was not to consider one's self to be "masculine" or "feminine" or even a private psychological being, but to be a member of a sociopolitical class. The proliferation of conduct books and novels for and about women through the eighteenth and nineteenth centuries established a new code of desire and new spheres of knowledge that embodied women as the epitome of moral virtue safe within a distinct domestic sphere (Armstrong, 1987).

4. Through increased literacy, conduct books and the novel authorized a subjectivity that granted safety and security through a sexual and economic exchange of a woman's virtue for a man's economic security (Armstrong, 1987). Throughout the early modern period, women were instructed to prove their true moral goodness by denying any motivation to marry for economic gain and thus ignoring, that is, not knowing, their economic vulnerability within a changing socioeconomic order

(Grieco, 1993; Armstrong, 1987). Through multiple discourses in fiction, nonfiction, education, science, and medicine, women's economic anxieties were assuaged by inciting their desire through the promise of security paradoxically dependent on a feminine subjectivity dissociated from economic and political reality.

5. This does not mean that this discourse does not effect masculine bodies. The authorized relationship of a man to his body is one that parallels the dominance relation of mind–body and masculine–feminine.

6. Note that the value placed on abstract reasoning and formal operations within psychology is in itself a cultural discourse that divides self. For persons who value education or desire to become middle- or upper-middle-class subjects, such a privileging of a certain form of rationality creates and encourages an incorporation of the Cartesian split.

7. Silent knowers find themselves nearly speechless and depend "on the continual presence of authorities to guide their actions" (WWK, p. 28). The authors point to the fact that these women share similar backgrounds of family violence with lack of positive interaction and dialogue through which they could develop a trust in their selves.

8. This case is part of a larger study of adolescent girls' experiences of their own sexual desire conducted by Deborah Tolman (see, e.g., Tolman, 1994a, 1994b, 1996; Tolman & Higgins, 1996). She interviewed thirty girls who were juniors in an urban and a suburban high school. Lily was one of the few girls in this study who said that she did not feel sexual desire. The majority of these young women said that they experienced sexual desire and that desire posed a profound dilemma for them about how to be good girls who had intense feelings in their bodies in a culture that denies and denigrates their sexual feelings. They described an understanding of this dilemma as an individual problem that they struggled to solve in private, because speaking about desire is such a taboo for girls and women. This study was supported by the Henry A. Murray Dissertation Fellowship, administered by the Murray Center at Radcliffe College.

REFERENCES

Achenbach, T. M. (1982). *Developmental psychopathology.* New York: Wiley.

Armstrong, N. (1987). *Desire and domestic fiction: A political history of the novel.* New York: Oxford University Press.

Bakhtin, M. (1981). *The dialogic imagination.* (C. Emerson and M. Holquist, Trans.). Austin: University of Texas Press.

Bardige, Betty. (1988). Things so finely human: Moral sensibilities at risk in adolescence. In C. Gilligan, J. Ward, & J. Taylor (Eds.), *Mapping the moral domain.* Cambridge, MA: Harvard University Press.

Bartky, S. L. (1990). *Femininity and domination: Studies in the phenomenology of oppression.* New York: Routledge.

Belenky, M., Clinchy, B., Goldberger, N., & Tarule, J. (1986). *Women's ways of knowing.* New York: Basic Books.

Bem, S. L. (1981). *Bem sex role inventory professional manual.* Palo Alto, CA: Consulting Psychologists Press.

Bordo, S. (1987). *The flight to objectivity.* Albany: State University of New York Press.

Bordo, S. (1993). *Unbearable weight: Feminism, body, and western culture.* Berkeley: University of California Press.

Brennan, T. (1993). *History after Lacan.* New York: Routledge.

Broughton, J. (1978). Development of concepts of self, mind, reality, and knowledge. *New Directions for Child Development, 1,* 75–100.

Brown, L. (1989). *Narratives of relationship: The development of a care voice in girls ages 7 to 16.* Unpublished doctoral dissertation, Harvard University, Cambridge, MA.

Brown, L. (1991). Telling a girl's life: Self-authorization as a form of resistance. In Gilligan, C., Rogers, A., & Tolman, D. *Women, Girls, and Psychotherapy.* Binghamton, NY: Haworth Press.

Brown, L. (in prep.) *Stones in the road: Anger, class, and adolescent girls.* Cambridge, MA: Harvard University Press.

Brown, L., Argyris, D., Attanucci, J., Bardige, B., Gilligan, C., Johnston, K., Miller, B., Osborne, R., Ward, J., Wiggins, G., & Wilcox, D. (1988). A *guide to reading narratives of conflict and choice for self and relational voices* (Monograph No. 1). Cambridge, MA: Harvard Graduate School of Education, Project on Women's Psychology and Girls' Development.

Brown, L., Debold, E., Tappan, M., & Gilligan, C. (1991). Reading narratives of conflict and choice for self and moral voice: A relational method. In W. Kurtines & J. Gerwitz (Eds.), *Handbook of moral behavior and development: Theory, research, and application*. Hillsdale, NJ: Erlbaum.

Brown, L., & Gilligan, C. (1990, August). *Listening for self and relational vices: A responsive/resisting reader's guide*. Paper presented at the annual meeting of the American Psychological Association, Boston, MA.

Brown, L., & Gilligan, C. (1992). *Meeting at the crossroads: Women's psychology and girls' development*. Cambridge, MA: Harvard University Press.

Bruner, J. (1986). *Actual minds, possible worlds*. Cambridge, MA: Harvard University Press.

Butler, J. (1990). *Gender trouble: Feminism and the subversion of identity*. New York: Routledge.

Butler, J. (1993). *Bodies that matter: On the discursive limits of "sex."* New York: Routledge.

Chodorow, N. (1978). *The reproduction of mothering: Psychoanalysis and the sociology of gender*. Berkeley: University of California Press.

Cixous, H. (1981). The laugh of the Medusa. In E. Marks & I. de Courtrivon (Eds.), *New French Feminisms*. (K. Cohen & P. Cohen, Trans.). New York: Schocken.

Dallery, A. (1989). The politics of writing (the) body. In A. M. Jaggar & S. Bordo (Eds.), *Gender/body/knowledge*. New Brunswick, NJ: Rutgers University Press.

Damon, W., & Hart, D. (1982). *The development of self-understanding in childhood and adolescence*. New York: Cambridge University Press.

Damon, W., & Hart, D. (1988). *Self-understanding in childhood and adolescence*. New York: Cambridge University Press.

Day, J., & Tappan, M. (1996). The narrative approach to moral development: From the epistemic subject to dialogical selves. *Human development, Vol. 39*, pp. 67–82.

Debold, E. (1990a). Learning in the first person: A passion to know. Paper presented at the Laurel-Harvard Conference on the Psychology of Women and the Development of Girls, Cleveland, Ohio.

Debold, E. (1990b) *The flesh becomes word*. Paper presented at the Association for Women in Psychology, Western Massachusetts and Vermont Region.

Debold, E. (1991). The body at play. In C. Gilligan, A. Rogers, & D. Tolman (Eds.), *Women, girls, and psychotherapy*. Binghamton, NY: Haworth Press.

Debold, E. (1994). Toward an understanding of gender differences in psychological distress: A Foucauldian integration of Freud, Gilligan and cognitive development theory. Unpublished qualifying paper. Harvard University, Graduate School of Education.

Debold, E. (1996). Knowing bodies: Gender identity, cognitive development and embodiment in early childhood and early adolescence. Unpublished doctoral dissertation. Harvard University, Graduate School of Education.

Debold, E. (in press). Paradise divided: Engendered knowledge and Stoppard's "Arcadia." In J. Fisher & E. Silber (Eds.), *Analyzing the different voice: Feminist psychological theory and literary texts.* Totowa, NJ: Rowman & Littlefield.

Debold, E., & Brown, L. (1991). Losing the body of knowledge: Conflicts between passion and reason in the intellectual development of adolescent girls. Paper presented to the 16th National Conference of the Association for Women in Psychology, Hartford, CT, March 1991. In C. Gilligan, L. Brown, A. Rogers, & E. Debold, *A Selection of Working Papers through 1991.* Cambridge, MA: Harvard Graduate School of Education.

Debold, E., & Tolman, D. (1991, January). Made in whose image? Paper presented at the Ms. Foundation for Women's Fourth Annual Women Managing Wealth Conference, New York, NY.

Diamond, I., & Quinby, L. (Eds.). (1988). *Feminism and Foucault: Reflections on resistance.* Boston, MA: Northeastern University Press.

Elbow, P. (1973). *Writing without teachers.* New York: Oxford University Press.

Erikson, E. (1968). *Identity: youth in crisis.* New York: WW Norton.

Fine, M., & Asch, A. (Eds.) (1988). *Women with disabilities: Essays in psychology, culture and politics.* Philadelphia: Temple University Press.

Fordham, S. (1988). Racelessness as a factor in black students' success: Pragmatic strategy or pyrrhic victory? *Harvard Educational Review,* 58(1) 54–84.

Foucault, M. (1980). In C. Gordon (Ed.). *Power/knowledge: Selected interviews and other writings, 1972–1977.* New York: Pantheon.

Foucault, M. (1983). Afterword: The subject and power. In H. Dreyfus & P. Rabinow (Eds.). *Michel Foucault: Beyond structuralism and hermeneutics* (pp. 208–226)(2nd ed.). Chicago: University of Chicago Press.

Foucault, M. (1986). *The history of sexuality.* Vol. 3. *The care of the self* (R. Hurley, Trans.). New York: Vintage Books.

Fowler, J. W. (1981). *Stages in Faith.* New York: Harper & Row.

Freud, S. (1895). Fraulein Elisabeth von R. In J. Strachey (ed.), *The standard edition: Studies on hysteria,* Vol. II, 135–181. London: The Hogarth Press.

Gilligan, C. (1982/1992). *In a different voice: Psychological theory and women's development.* Cambridge, MA: Harvard University Press.

Gilligan, C. (1990). Teaching Shakespeare's sister. In C. Gilligan, N. Lyons, and T. Hamner (Eds.), *Making connections: The relational worlds of ado-*

lescent girls at Emma Willard School, 6–27. Cambridge, MA: Harvard University Press.

Gilligan, C. (1991a). Joining the resistance: Psychology, politics, girls and women. In L. Goldstein (Ed.), *The female body*. Ann Arbor, MI: The University of Michigan Press.

Gilligan, C. (1991b). Women's psychological development: Implications for psychotherapy. In C. Gilligan, A. Rogers, & D. Tolman (Eds.), *Women, girls, and psychotherapy*. Binghamton, NY: Haworth Press.

Gilligan, C. (1996). The centrality of relationship in human development: A puzzle, some evidence, and a theory. In G. Noam, & K. Fischer (Eds.), *Development and vulnerability in close relationships*. Mahwah, NJ: Lawrence Erlbaum.

Gilligan, C., Brown, L., & Rogers, A. (1990). Psyche embedded: A place for body, relationships, and culture in personality theory. In A. Rabin et al. (Eds). *Studying persons and lives*. New York: Springer-Verlag.

Gilligan, C., Ward, J., & Taylor, J. (Eds.). (1988). *Mapping the moral domain*. Cambridge, MA: Harvard University Press.

Grieco, S. F. M. (1993). The body, appearance, and sexuality. In G. Duby & M. Perrot (Gen. Eds.), N. Zemon & A. Farge (Eds.), *A History of Women in the West*. Vol. 3. *Renaissance and Enlightenment Paradoxes*. Cambridge, MA: Harvard University Press/Belknap.

Grosz, E. (1990). *Jacques Lacan: A feminist introduction*. New York: Routledge.

Grosz, E. (1994). *Volatile bodies: Towards a corporeal feminism*. Bloomington, IN: Indiana University Press.

Guidano, V. (1987). *Complexity of the self: A developmental approach to psychopathology and psychotherapy*. New York: The Guilford Press.

Irigaray, L. (1985). *This sex which is not one*. (C. Porter, Trans.). Ithaca, NY: Cornell University Press.

Jack, D. (1991). *Silencing the self: Women and depression*. Cambridge, MA: Harvard University Press.

Jaggar, A. M., & Bordo, S. (1989). *Gender/Body/Knowledge*. New Brunswick, NJ: Rutgers University Press.

Johnston, D. K. (1988). Adolescents' solutions to two dilemmas in fables: Two moral orientations—two problem solving strategies. In C. Gilligan, J. Ward, & J. Taylor (Eds.), *Mapping the moral domain*. Cambridge, MA: Harvard University Press.

Kaplan, B. (1967). Meditations on genesis. *Human Development, 10*, 65–87.

Kegan, R. (1982). *The evolving self*. Cambridge, MA: Harvard University Press.

Keller, C. (1986.) *From a broken web*. Boston: Beacon Press.

Kohlberg, L. (1981). *Essays in moral development*. Vol. 1. *The philosophy of moral development*. New York: Harper & Row.

Langdale, S. (1983). Moral orientations and moral development: The analysis of care and justice reasoning across different dilemmas in females and males from childhood through adulthood. Unpublished doctoral dissertation, Harvard Graduate School of Education, Cambridge, MA.

Laqueur, T. (1990). *Making sex: Body and gender from the Greeks to Freud.* Cambridge, MA: Harvard University Press.

Lloyd, G. (1984/1993). *Man of reason: Male and female in Western philosophy.* Minneapolis: University of Minnesota Press.

Loevinger, J. (1976). *Ego development: Conceptions and theories.* San Francisco: Jossey-Bass.

Loevinger, J. (1987). The concept of self or ego. In P. Young-Eisendrath, & J. Hall (Eds.), *The book of the self: Person, pretext, and process.* New York: New York University.

Loevinger, J., & Wessler, R. (1970). *Measuring ego development I: Construction and use of a sentence completion test.* San Francisco: Jossey-Bass.

Lyons, N. (1983.) Two perspectives on self, relationships, and morality. *Harvard Educational Review, 53,* 125–145.

Mead, G. H. (1934/1967). *Mind, self, and society.* Chicago: University of Chicago Press.

Offer, D., Ostov, E., & Howard, K. (1981). *The adolescent: A psychological self portrait.* New York: Basic Books.

Perry, W. G. (1968). *Forms of intellectual and ethical development in the college years.* New York: Holt, Rinehart & Winston.

Piaget, J. (1983). Piaget's theory. In P. Mussen (Ed.), *Handbook of child psychology* (4th Ed.) Vol. 1. *History, theory, and methods,* 103–128, W. Kessen (Ed.). New York: Wiley.

Reid, P. (1993). Poor women in psychological research: Shut up and shut out. *Psychology of Women Quarterly, 17,* 133–150.

Robinson, T. & Ward, J. V. (1991). "A belief in self greater than anybody's disbelief:" Cultivating resistance among African American female adolescents. In C. Gilligan, A. Rogers, & D. Tolman (Eds.), *Women, girls, and psychotherapy.* Binghamton, NY: Haworth Press.

Rogers, A. (1993). Voice, play and a practice of ordinary courage in girls' and women's lives. *Harvard Education Review, vol. 63,* pp. 265–295.

Rogers, A., Brown, L., & Tappan, M. (1994). Interpreting loss in ego development in girls: Regression or resistance? In A. Lieblich & R. Josselson (Eds.), *Exploring identity and gender: The narrative study of lives,* Vol. 2 (pp. 1–36). Thousand Oaks, CA: Sage Publications.

Rogers, A., & Gilligan, C. (1988). Translating the language of adolescent girls: Themes of moral voice and stages of ego development (Monograph no. 6). Cambridge, MA: Harvard Project on Women's Psychology and Girls' Development, Harvard University, Graduate School of Education.

Rorty, R. (1979). *Philosophy and the mirror of nature.* Princeton, NJ: Princeton University Press.

Rosenberg, M. (1965). *Society and the adolescent self image.* Princeton, NJ: Princeton University Press.

Russet, C. E. (1989). *Sexual science.* Cambridge, MA: Harvard University Press.

Rutter, M., & Garmezy, N. (1983). Developmental psychopathology. In E. M. Hetherington, (Vol. Ed.), P. Mussen (Ed.), *Handbook of child psychology. Vol. 4. Socialization, personality and social development,* 775–911. New York: Wiley.

Sawicki, J. (1991). *Disciplining Foucault: Feminism, power and the body.* New York: Routledge.

Schonert-Reichl, K., & Offer, D. (1992). Gender differences in adolescent symptoms. In B. Lahey, & A. Kazdin, (Eds.), *Advances in clinical child psychology,* Volume 14. (pp. 27–60).

Spence, J. T., Helmreich, R., & Stapp, J. (1974). The personal attributes questionnaire: A measure of sex-role stereotypes and masculinity-femininity. *JSAS Catalog of Selected Documents in Psychology, 4,* 43–44, MS617.

Steiner-Adair, C. (1990). Normal female adolescent development and the development of eating disorders. In C. Gilligan, N. Lyons, & T. Hanmer, *Making connections: The relational worlds of adolescent girls at Emma Willard School* (pp. 162–182). Cambridge, MA: Harvard University Press.

Stern, D. (1985). *The interpersonal world of the infant: A view from psychoanalysis and developmental psychology.* New York: Basic Books.

Tappan, M. (1991). Narrative, language, and moral experience. *Journal of Moral Education, 20*(3), 243–256.

Tappan, M. (1991). Narrative and storytelling: Implications for understanding moral development. In M. Tappan & M. Packer (Eds.), *Narrative approaches to moral development* (pp. 5–25). San Francisco: Jossey-Bass.

Tatum, B. (1992). Talking about race, learning about racism: The application of racial identity development theory in the classroom. *Harvard Educational Review, 62*(1), 1–24.

Taylor, J., Gilligan, C., & Sullivan, A. (1995). *Between voice and silence.* Cambridge, MA: Harvard University Press.

Tolman, D. (1992). Voicing the body: A psychological study of adolescent girls' sexual desire. Unpublished doctoral dissertation. Harvard University, Graduate School of Education.

Tolman, D. (1994a). Daring to desire: Culture in the bodies of adolescent girls. In J. Irvine (Ed.), *Sexual cultures and the construction of adolescent identities* (pp. 250–284). Philadelphia: Temple University Press.

Tolman, D. (1994b). Doing desire: Adolescent girls' struggles for/with sexuality. *Gender and Society, 8*(3), 324–342.

Tolman, D. (1996). Adolescent girls' sexuality: Debunking the myth of the urban girl. In B. Leadbetter and N. Way (Eds.), *Urban girls: Resisting stereotypes, creating identities.* New York: New York University Press.

Tolman, D., & Debold, E. (1994). Conflicts of body and image: Female adolescents, desire, and the nobody body. In P. Fallon, M. Katzman, & S.

Wooley (Eds.), *Feminist perspectives on eating disorders*. New York: Guilford.

Tolman, D., & Higgins, T. (1996). How being a good girl can be bad for girls. In N. Bauer Maglin and D. Perry (Eds.), *Good girls/bad girls: Women, sex, violence and power in the 1990s*. New Brunswick, NJ: Rutgers University Press.

Vygotsky, L. S. (1978). M. Cole, V. John-Steiner, S. Scribner, & E. Souberman (Eds.), *Mind in society: The development of higher psychological processes*. Cambridge, MA: Harvard University Press.

Vygotsky, L. S. (1986). *Thought and language*. A. Kozulin (trans. & ed.). Cambridge, MA: The MIT Press.

Ward, J. V. (1990). Racial identity formation and transformation. In C. Gilligan, J. Ward, & J. Taylor (Eds.), *Mapping the moral domain*. Cambridge, MA: Harvard University Press.

Weis, L., & Fine, M. (Eds.). (1992). *Beyond silenced voices: Class, race and gender in American schools*. Albany: State University of New York Press.

Wertsch, J. V. (1991). *Voices of the mind*. Cambridge, MA: Harvard University Press.

Young-Eisendrath, P., & Hall, J. (1987). *The book of the self: Person, pretext, and process*. New York: New York University Press.

Connected Knowing in
Constructive Psychotherapy*

MICHAEL J. MAHONEY

What stands out most strongly in narratives of constructivist women, and particularly in the part of their story that pertains to the future they foresee for themselves, is their desire to have "a room of their own," as Virginia Woolf calls it, in a family and community and world that they helped make livable. They reveal in the way they speak and live their lives their moral conviction that ideas and values, like children, must be nurtured, cared for, placed in environments that help them grow. (Belenky, Clinchy, Goldberger, & Tarule, 1986, p. 152)

IN 1986 I WAS HALFWAY through a ten-year writing project that was starting to feel overwhelming in its scope and demands. My editor, Jo Ann Miller, phoned to check on my progress and to tell me about something hot off the presses that was ground breaking. It was the book *Women's Ways of Knowing* (WWK). She sent me a copy and I was enthralled by what Mary Belenky, Blythe Clinchy, Nancy Goldberger, and Jill Tarule had rendered. Their interviews were captivating illustra-

---

*This chapter is dedicated to my mother, Zita Ellen Fitzgibbons Mahoney, who died tragically while it was being written. I am also deeply indebted to Nancy Goldberger for her patience and her generous help in connecting my knowing with that of the other contributors to this volume. It is an honor to participate in the continuing dialogue begun by *Women's Ways of Knowing*.

tions of personal epistemologies. Moreover, their organization of this material into five epistemological categories was intriguingly creative, and I was particularly taken with their elaborations on constructed knowledge and the differences between separate and connected knowing. Their collaborative and dialogical writing style was also inspiring. I remember being moved by their words in the Preface: "During our work together, the four of us developed among ourselves an intimacy and collaboration which we have come to prize. We believe that the collaborative, egalitarian spirit so often shared by women should be more carefully nurtured in the work lives of all men and women. We hope to find it in all of our future work" (p. iv).

I am sure that I am only very partially aware of their influence on my own writing project, *Human Change Processes*, which appeared in 1991. I do know that reading their book deepened my interest in feminist studies and awakened me to the fact that some of the most creative and caring work in constructivism was taking place in that area. I do not pretend to be an expert on feminism or women's studies—the gaps and "positionality" (Maher & Tetreault, this volume) in my knowing are becoming more and more apparent to me—but I am an avid student, and the editors and contributors of this volume have been both gentle and generous in guiding my explorations. The process of writing this chapter—not just the generation of words, but the readings, reflections, and dialogues entailed—has stimulated an expansion in my understanding that feels both welcome and transformational. Like Jill Tarule's student (this volume), I often don't know what I think until I hear myself saying it or read myself writing it. And, like Ann Stanton (this volume), I have often felt the strain and impossibility of communicating the richness of the material reviewed in the process of my writing. In their own contributions to this volume, the editors reflect on how their ideas have evolved and elaborated over the course of the ten years since the publication of *WWK*. That evolution and elaboration were not simply the result of incubation over time, but were forged through an active exploration and reflective self-questioning that resound with their lively engagement with people (students, research participants, communities, and so on). It reminds me of Alice Walker's (1996) courageous reflections on her own development during and after the filming of *The Color Purple*. With colleagues and teachers so willing to share their personal experiences of development, I have felt more encouraged and connected in sharing my own.

My goal in this chapter is to voice some reflections on how the metaphors of connection and construction suggested in *WWK* relate to conceptualizations and practices in psychotherapy. In the process I shall propose that WWK is a contemporary classic in the literatures of constructivism. To flesh out that proposal, I will briefly discuss constructivism in the context of historical traditions in epistemology. Terminology becomes important here in that there appear to be significant differences in the intended meanings of constructive words. Moving to a more experiential level, the centrality of personal realities and personal epistemologies will be explored. Finally, I will comment on the complexities and rewards of conducting psychotherapy in a way that is consistent with the caring and collaborative spirit evident in WWK.

CONSTRUCTIVISM AND FEMINIST THEORY

I believe that one of the most significant contributions of feminist theory and women's studies has been their recognition that our attempts to understand ourselves and our worlds are necessarily constrained by our embeddedness in cultures and traditions (Goldberger, this volume; Hurtado, this volume). What we (think we) know is always a reflection of our methods of inquiry, and our methods necessarily reflect the legacy of traditions (Hoshmand & Martin, 1995; Polkinghorne, 1983; Toukmanian & Rennie, 1992). As readers are probably well aware, today's most visible and recognized traditions of knowing also reflect a legacy that is largely Western, white, and male (Alic, 1986; Keller, 1985; 1992; Kelly, 1984; Lennon & Whitford, 1994; Nye, 1990; Tuana, 1989).[1] The major themes in Western traditions have centered around issues of authority and power, a point that has been recognized and successfully challenged by feminist theory. Noteworthy here is the fact that the two primary and presumably different sources of knowing authorized by classical rationalism and logical empiricism were the mind and the senses. The workings of the mind were to be aided by the laws of logic; the renderings of the senses were to be helped by instrumentation and public inspection. In either case, the object of inquiry was external to the person and the methods of knowing required a disconnection or detachment from that which is known. This has perhaps been the most basic illusion of Western white male epistemology: that reality is a rational order revealed by reason and public sensibility. This is the assumption that lies at the heart of objectivism, a tradition that still dominates contemporary worldviews. In that tradition, truth and reality are singular, stable, and external to the person. Such a view essentially denies plurality, perspective, diversity, change, and the private realm—rendering meaningless any discussion of multiple, personal, or dynamic realities. The roots of objectivism lie in the misguided attempt to separate the personal knower from the process of knowing (Bernstein, 1983; Kegan, 1982; Mahoney, 1991). *Objectivity* comes from the Latin root *ject*, which means "to throw." With the prefix *ob*, meaning "off" or "away," objectivity implies an intentional distancing. Literally translated, *subjectivity* involves an "under-throwing" that results in an allegedly insufficient separation of the knower and the known.

Objectivism has had its vocal detractors, of course, and its dominance has come under increasing challenge in the last half of this century. The arguments against "detached" knowing and in favor of a more holistic and "connected" knowing are far-ranging and beyond the scope of my intentions in the present chapter. A brief sketch of a scaffolding for those arguments may be useful, however.

Amid the eighteenth-century growth of science there was also another development in epistemology. It has come to be called "constructivism" because of its emphasis on the active participation of the knower in the structuring processes that characterize knowing. Giambattista Vico (1668–1744) is generally recognized as the originator of this position, and Immanuel Kant (1724–1804) later elaborated a view of the human mind as an active complex of construction processes. Later constructivists were to include Hans Vaihinger, Wilhelm Wundt, Jean Piaget, Frederic Bartlett, Friedrich Hayek, and Jerome Bruner.[2] Constructivism is today an active and evolving theme in philosophy, psychology, and psychotherapy (Griffin, Cobb, Ford, Gunter, & Ochs, 1993; Mahoney, 1991, 1995; Neimeyer & Mahoney, 1995). As will be elaborated, it is also an approach to epistemology that resonates deeply with the central tenets of feminist theory.

Attempts to capture the essence of constructivist philosophy are challenged by the fact that it is a dynamic and diverse perspective that defies fixation in static symbols. At its core, I believe, are five interdependent themes: (1) activity, (2) order, (3) social-symbolic processes, (4) identity, and (5) development. The activity of the organism is a central theme. Rather than being a passive and reactive object of manipulations by external forces, the living system is viewed as a proactive agent that participates in its own life. Psychologically, this means that the person is both "the changer and the changed" (to borrow from feminist singer and songwriter Cris Williamson). She cocreates the personal realities to which she responds and thereby participates in a reciprocity—not only between her environment and her body, but also within different levels of her own activities.

According to constructivism, all living systems work to establish, maintain, and elaborate a patterned order in their experience. We organize
our worlds by organizing ourselves. This process of self-organization continues throughout the lifespan. Although the order of experience
becomes very complex and unique to each individual, it is always fundamentally carved out of organizing contrasts (same–different, female–male,
young–old, good–bad, right–wrong, self–other, and so on). Common
themes in such self-organization seem to be reality (for example, perceptual constancy and predictability), power (including issues of control
and possibility), identity (phenomenological continuity and the human
relationships that define self), and value (moral and emotional domains).
Adding further complexity to the mysteries of human self-organization,
the vast majority of these order-serving processes operate at levels well
beyond our awareness. It is noteworthy that quests for order and personal
meaning are common concerns of persons in psychotherapy, and it is not
coincidental that studies of psychopathology are focused on the causes
and correlates of "disorder."

In humans, self-organizing activities are embedded in social and symbolic contexts. The social and "intersubjective" dimensions of human
experience have been a central theme of feminist writers (Chodorow,
1978, 1989; Watkins, 1990). Symbol systems, including languages, are
formalized expressions of the social fabric of experiencing. Among other
important implications, this theme in constructivism emphasizes the
importance of human relationships and their role in both personal and
collective experiences. Relatedly, the experience of personal identity —
the lifespan project of self — is viewed as inseparable from the interpersonal realm. Identity development and, indeed, all human experiencing
take place within contexts of human relationships — hence the growing
interest in "connections" and intersubjectivity (Clinchy, 1993, this volume; Stolorow & Atwood, 1992). Even though individuals are always
unique and diverse, their individuality emerges within (and not apart
from) their human bonds. From this perspective, the self is not the isolated entity revered in Western male images of individualism. More consonant with feminist and Eastern viewpoints, the constructive self is a
dynamic, diversified, and thoroughly "connected" complex of processes.
Not only is the self embedded in social systems, but social systems pervade the self. Developments in one necessarily influence the other.

The fifth theme of constructivism is development. Here the emphasis
is on the ongoing complexity of processes that contribute to the unfolding of living systems. Personality development, for example, is viewed as
an individually expressed lifespan process of ongoing self-construction.

Although that development may be constrained and channeled by a variety of circumstances, it is essentially an expression of the person navigating those circumstances. Such development is viewed as fundamentally dialectical—meaning that new order emerges out of interactions among contrasts. Among other things, this implies that dialogue and diversity play central roles in the elaboration of lives. Moreover, from a constructive viewpoint, resistance to change is not necessarily an unhealthy or self-defeating phenomenon. Rather, it is a natural and common self-protective expression of attempts to maintain the integrity of a system that experiences itself as being pushed too quickly or too far beyond the boundaries of its familiar functioning.

All in all, then, constructivism portrays the individual as an active agent seeking order and meaning in social contexts where her uniquely personal experiences are challenged to continue developing. This portrayal is, I believe, deeply resonant with that offered by a number of feminist theorists (Chodorow, 1978, 1989; Enns, 1992; Harding, this volume; Lennon & Whitford, 1994; Maher & Tetreault, this volume). Above, beneath, and beyond their endorsement of equal rights for women and of human rights in general, expressions of feminism have challenged the central dogmas of Western epistemology. In so doing, they have encouraged truly revolutionary trends in diverse areas of science and scholarship:

> Considered as a whole, the feminist perspective and impulse has brought forth perhaps the most vigorous, subtle, and radically critical analysis of conventional intellectual and cultural assumptions in all of contemporary scholarship. No academic discipline or area of human experience has been left untouched by the feminist reexamination of how meanings are created and preserved, how evidence is selectively interpreted and theory molded with mutually reinforcing circularity, how particular rhetorical strategies and behavioral styles have sustained male hegemony, how women's voices remained unheard in centuries of social and intellectual male dominance, how deeply problematic consequences have ensued from masculine assumptions about reality, knowledge, nature, society, the divine. Such analyses in turn have helped illuminate parallel patterns and structures of domination that have marked the experience of other oppressed peoples and forms of life. (Tarnas, 1991, p. 408)

Among the most striking examples of this illumination are the works of Barbara McClintock (Keller, 1983), the Nobel Prize–winning geneticist. McClintock's felt connection with the chromosomes she was studying was remarkable:

I found that the more I worked with them, the bigger and bigger [the chromosomes] got, and when I was really working with them I wasn't outside, I was down there. I was part of the system. I was right down there with them, and everything got big. I even was able to see the internal parts of the chromosomes—actually everything was there. It surprised me because I actually felt as if I was right down there and these were my friends. . . . As you look at these things, they become part of you. And you forget yourself. (Keller, 1985, pp. 164–165)

Her "feeling for the organism" led not only to major breakthroughs in genetics, but also to a challenge of the dogma that separate (objectivist) knowing is the only path to true understanding.

Feminist scholars have often employed the metaphors of constructivism in their descriptions of feminism, women's experience, and women's development (Clinchy, 1993; this volume; Crawford & Marecek, 1989; Enns, 1992; Goldberger, this volume; Kimmel, 1989; Margolis, 1989; Wartenberg, 1992). Across diverse expressions of feminist philosophy there are clear resonances with the constructivist themes of activity, organization, social-symbolic processes, diversity of individuality, and ongoing development. Before illustrating some of this relevance in the realms of personal epistemology and clinical practice, however, it is important to note the diversity of meanings associated with derivations of the verb *to construct*. Some contrasts now being explored, for example, have to do with differences among "radical constructivists," critical or "developmental constructivists," and "social constructionists." Radical constructivists believe that individuals totally create (rather than cocreate) their personal realities. "Whoever is conscious of being the architect of his or her own reality would be equally aware of the ever-present possibility of constructing it differently" (Watzlawick, 1984, pp. 326–327). Such a person is said to have "total freedom" in the creation and change of his or her personal experiencing. This is an extremely agentic and individualist epistemology. At the other extreme are the social constructionists, who maintain that there can be no truly personal knowledge because all knowing is embedded in social, cultural, and historical contexts (Gergen, 1985). For the social constructionists, personal agency and the experience of a private self are illusions. Between these extremes (at least in my own construction of this domain) are the developmental constructivists, who walk a path that attempts to respect both individual (self-generative) agency and dynamic social embeddedness (Guidano, 1987, 1991; Mahoney, 1991; Markus & Nurius, 1986). Dialogues about these differences are important to the elaboration of a range of issues, not the least of which is the contrast between separate and connected knowing that was a central theme of WWK.

CONNECTED KNOWING
AND PERSONAL REALITIES

The essential resonance of contructivist philosophy and feminist theory is readily apparent in the realm of clinical practice. I shall not here attempt a review or synthesis of the extensive and rapidly growing literatures on feminist therapy (for example, Brown & Brodsky, 1992; Enns, 1992; Goldberger, 1996; McNamara & Rickard, 1989; Nevels & Coché, 1993). Nor will I use these pages to present a formal description of "constructive psychotherapy" as I now understand it. Rather, my purpose in this section is to share some emerging thoughts and feelings about how the perspective developed in WWK and elaborated in the present volume can be applied to some of the most difficult and important aspects of understanding another person and facilitating his or her development.

Let me first say something about personal realities. This is a concept that both tacitly and explicitly pervades this and the previous volume. It is so familiar to those of us who are "friendly users" that we forget how difficult it may be for some people to understand. How can reality be personal, let alone plural? This flies in the face of objectivist dogma, and it can be a frightening idea for individuals who experience it as challenging the ground of their being. This realization came around again for me just a few days ago when my friend Bob Neimeyer was visiting. We were sharing our respective experiences in teaching and supervising constructive psychotherapy. I was excited about my "connected reading" of the other chapters in this volume, and I was trying to relate some of the ideas that were dancing around inside me. Bob was telling me stories about some students' reactions to his and my work (Neimeyer & Mahoney, 1995) and the fear that they reported about considering reality to be a constructed or coconstructed phenomenon. We reflected on the inertia of objectivism, not only in science but in popular culture, and on the likelihood that it will be a long time before participatory epistemologies are widely embraced.

In my opinion, the emphasis on personal epistemologies and personal realities in WWK was an important punctuation in the evolution of our understanding of ourselves and others.[3] Our styles of knowing and our constructions of reality are not things we "have" in the sense of possessions, but processes we live. We do not just "think" them; we eat and breathe them. Metaphors of containment fail to convey this absorption (Lakoff & Johnson, 1980). We live "out of" or "through" our personal epistemologies and realities, but it is misleading to say that they are totally "inside" us. Other than WWK and the work reported in this volume, there have been relatively few attempts to understand differences in personal epistemologies and their associated experience patterns (Ebersole & Flores, 1989; Hersh, 1980; Jackson & Jeffers, 1989; Janoff-Bulman, 1989; Johnson, Germer, Efran, & Overton, 1988; Mahoney, 1991; Unger, Draper, & Pendergrass, 1986). Moreover, much of this sparse research has been conducted (or at least reported) in a separate knowing style such that individual differences and the dynamic complexities within (let alone between) individuals are not explored.

In reading Blythe Clinchy's recent work (1993, this volume) on connected knowing, I was impressed not only by the evolution of her thinking over the past decade but also by the parallels between her elaborations and major developments in epistemology. In 1962 philosopher Bill Bartley published an unprecedented analysis of Western rationality in which he noted that a central assumption for twenty-five hundred years has been that knowledge claims can be "justified" by invoking "authority" (in diverse forms, such as revelation, logic, evidence, expert opinion). He concluded that all such attempts at justification ultimately "retreat to a commitment," a nonrational leap of faith (for example, regarding the invoked authorities). Nonjustificational epistemologies, which have been endorsed by a few psychologists (Burrell, 1987; Mahoney, 1976; Weimer, 1979), do not make absolute knowledge claims, which means that they seek to encourage ongoing dialogue rather than seeking to end such dialogue and "win the argument" with some final authoritarian chess move.

What Blythe Clinchy (this volume) describes is, in my opinion, a form of respectful, compassionate, and authentically interested inquiry into another's experiences in a way that also acknowledges the complex relations between self-knowing and knowing of others. The relevance of this approach to psychotherapy is readily apparent (see later discussion). Instead of looking for flaws, arguing, and doubting, the connected knower and the connected therapist are predominantly empathic, exploratory, and affirming. Her reference to theologian Martin Buber's "bold swinging . . . into the life of the other" emphasizes the important difference between theoretical intersubjectivity and experiential presence to the selves, voices, and minds of other beings. Moreover, such presence with others both requires and deepens a presence with self—a capacity to see, hear, smell, taste, feel, and intuit the multiplex "selfing process" from which all presence to others springs. As Clinchy aptly notes, this connected self-knowing does not come easily, partly because of the critics who inhabit our beings—critics who are born out of social intercourse. These invisible guests need not be exclusively hostile, however, and psychologist Mary Watkins (1990) has done an invaluable service in demonstrating how "imaginal dialogues" can create and reflect healthy and enriching self-relationships.

Here we are moving toward the domain of human services, but let me dwell a bit on some of the questions that reverberate through my own imaginal dialogues. How does connected knowing relate to the concept of intersubjectivity? There is a "lie" in absolutizing the contrast between separate and connected knowing, of course, but how do these modes of being coordinate to afford us the capacity to navigate through changing daily seas? And how are we to teach about boundaries to our children, our clients, and our selves? For me, these and related questions lie at the heart of our constructions of the worlds we live in (and that live in us). And it is here that the dialogical emphasis of WWK resounds as an evolving melody—not as a repetitive sequence of sounds, but as a meaningfully caring exchange that encourages something like dialectical harmonics.

Pursuing such questions in dialogue and other forms of research and practice continues to be a burning challenge for me. I am captivated, for example, by the potential synergy of constructivist metatheories, women's studies, and the sciences of complexity. Recent writings in the latter suggest some very deep resonances (Kauffman, 1995; Mahoney & Moes, in press). Moreover, my research on self and self-relationships has changed substantially. In the 1970s I was fascinated with issues of "self-control," a relationship to self that was probably closer to one of dominating power rather than caring agency. Over the years my research has moved progressively deeper into the subtleties of self-knowledge and lifespan developmental processes. Almost invariably, I have taken questions from personal, clinical, and teaching/learning experiences into the laboratory for exploration and elaboration. Journal work, life review, sensory deprivation, attention, imagery, meditation, stream of consciousness, movement, massage, creative writing, artististic expression, music, exercise, sports, and self-care have been woven into this unfinished fabric of questions. One current theme of research is the relationships among self-complexity, psychological development, and emotional diversity and resilience. In a series of studies still being elaborated by my students[4] and me, we are using such tasks as "mirror time" (Mahoney, 1991), in which participants spend time in front of a mirror. In the laboratory we can measure dynamic variations in their physiological response while tracking their visual focus. More interesting in a connected way are their reports of their phenomenology while engaged in variations of the mirror task. During early studies of mirror time, I was struck by the variable power of the procedure, the range of individual experiences, and the gap between what I was seeing in the laboratory and what was happening with clients. (Such gaps have created a continuing ferment in me that is expressed in explorations of more connected ways of conducting research.) Common patterns of mirror experience include a preliminary preoccupation with "superficial" issues of appearance—hair, complexion, weight, facial features, and so on. Some participants and clients remain predominantly in a mode of self-scrutiny, which is often critical and self-rejecting.[5] Intermittently, however, there will be brief excursions "inside"—glimpses and whispers, if you will, of deeper layers and private diversities. Individuals exhibit uniquely personal patterns of "leveling" of their momentary focus that are like the approach–avoidance oscillations of a startled toddler. We are now trying to elaborate ways of gently encouraging explorations of new patternings while respecting individual pacing and interest.

SELECTED IMPLICATIONS FOR PSYCHOTHERAPY

Connected or constructive knowers are perennial students of life, and their studies are all the more ardent when they are also psychotherapy practitioners. They may, in fact, go through stages of understanding and practice that parallel those outlined in WWK (Skovholt & Rønnestad, 1992). Throughout their development as persons and professionals, however, there are general themes that pervade practice from a constructive perspective. The first is an emphasis on the human relationship as a safe and caring "secure base" in and from which the client can experience, explore, and experiment with her ways of knowing (herself, her world, her current concerns). Each person knows a somewhat different world, of course, and knows in his or her own style. Essential to the safety and caring dimensions of the therapeutic relationship is an authentic and compassionate regard for the individual. This theme of individuality or uniqueness reflects a respect for the diversity of human experience and the very personal nature of individual lives. The phenomenology of the client is respected as his or her personal reality, his or her currently active construction of how things are and what that might mean. Thus, therapy begins and remains fundamentally tied to the personal phenomenology of the client. Among other things, this means that the therapist must be sensitive and flexible enough to adapt herself to the client's current capacities and concerns. Rather than assuming that every client can be adequately treated with the same techniques, each client is viewed as a unique expression of life-seeking processes. Each has a "personal reality"—a dynamic and interactive web of personal meanings—that has emerged from a unique history of human relationships and personal experiences. The individual's ways of knowing—knowing who she is, what she can or should do, and so on—are also idiosyncratic, even when they reflect general stages of epistemic development. A helpful therapist must be sensitive to these individual and developmental differences.

Getting to know a client involves the same processes as getting to know any other person, but with some important additional challenges and responsibilities that are entailed because the knowing is embedded in a special, professional helping relationship. Among the most important of these additional challenges and responsibilities, I believe, are issues of reciprocity and boundaries. Unlike traditional friendships and other intimate relationships, the exchanges between a professional helper and her client are explicitly focused on serving the well-being of only one of the participants, the client. Even though the therapist often benefits from the exchange (psychologically, financially, or otherwise), this is secondary to the purpose of therapy. The primacy of the client's well-being is also at the heart of professional codes of ethics that place boundaries on the relationship. Current versions of such codes emphasize prohibitions against various forms of exploitation (for example, sexual, financial, emotional). The recognition and active reform of abuses of power in human relationships have been among the central contributions of feminism. Ironically, objectivist wordings of such reforms have sometimes pushed professional codes even further toward the disconnected prototype.[6]

A therapist operating from a constructive perspective recognizes that her capacity to know another person is inseparable from her ever developing abilities to know herself. Indeed, the process of serving clients is likely to bring her into frequent contact with her own psychological life and may result in accelerated personal development (Mahoney & Fernandez-Alvarez, 1995; Nevels & Coché, 1993; Skovholt & Rønnestad, 1992). This does not mean, however, that such a therapist is constantly self-conscious in her interactions with clients. It does mean that the therapist's self-knowledge is an instrument in the service of the work being collaborated on with the client. Common concerns of therapists—ranging from beginning beginners to veteran beginners—are the fre-

quency and extent to which they see themselves in their clients. Many of
these concerns are born of the assumption that there should be dramatic
differences between therapists and their clients. My experience has been
that the most helpful therapists are those who can resonate deeply with
their clients' experiences and, importantly, who can dance the dialectic
between their own and the other's experiencing. Differences then
become important not because they create or maintain a separating distance but because they afford opportunities for both participants to learn
about and explore new ways of being themselves.

The overall strategy of constructive psychotherapy is—with the client's
consent and active collaboration—to create a safe human context in and
from which the client can explore and experiment with new ways of
knowing and experiencing herself, her world, and their possible relationships. The therapeutic relationship is thus viewed as central to the
entire enterprise—even in single-session or time-limited therapy. That
relationship cannot replace (and should not diminish) the network of
human connections that the client has outside therapy. Likewise, the
therapeutic relationship is created by its participants, the most important
of whom is the client. But the therapist must also be emotionally accessible and empathically engaged in the creation of that relationship
(Kahn, 1991).

The therapeutic relationship is a context for facilitating the changes
that clients are seeking in their lives. For some clients the processes of
establishing and elaborating that relationship will be integral to important personal changes. Being heard and understood, being respected and
trusted, having their experiences validated and their efforts affirmed,
being cared about—these may make invaluable contributions to clients'
development. From the context of the secure bases they have developed—with their therapist and with others—clients may begin to experiment with different ways of living their lives. Some of those experiments
will be focused on specific concrete problems. Others may deal with
longstanding patterns. The specifics of the experiments are as diverse as
the persons and circumstances involved, and their results are often a mixture of trial-and-error persistence, creativity, and chance.

It is in the face of these experiments and their results that a therapist's
skills and abilities are most frequently challenged. Most problems are not
simple, and their solutions may be frustratingly elusive. Even when clear
and significant improvements are made, clients may become confused or
paradoxically discouraged. Their faith—in themselves, in therapy, in
life—may wax and wane, as may their engagement in all three. This is
where philosophical foundations, interpersonal sensitivity, and an appre-

ciation for the complexities of human development become critically important. The constructive therapist recognizes that personal development is a dynamic, nonlinear process with many unanticipated turns and an infinite variety of unknowns. She respects the oscillations that characterize many developmental trajectories. Resistance to change is also respected as an expression of self-protection that is better worked "with" rather than "against." And she realizes that hope lies at the heart of life engagement.

How are these beliefs enacted in the conduct of constructive psychotherapy? The diversity of expressions is infinite. My own clinical work reflects the aforementioned general themes and working assumptions about human development, and it is mostly experience-led in the sense of being woven from the actual moments of my interaction with a particular client. I try to encourage an atmosphere of trust and safety, and I allow the individual to move in and out of different levels of focus from moment to moment or session to session. At times the individual's focus will be on concrete personal problems; other times she may reflect on her emerging awareness of some pattern or patterns in her past history and current circumstances. From time to time she may catch herself or me in a "here and now" moment of living, a glimpse of the ongoing processes by which she or we are creating or construing present possibilities. I usually try to "lead from behind" on such shifts in attentional focus, encouraging the client to use my presence as a reliable tether and source of relatedness in her self-paced explorations.

Over years of practice I have found myself increasingly attuned to matters of "voice," both literally and figuratively, and this is probably one of the reasons I was so enthralled with WWK. Being heard and hearing their own voice expressing strong feelings are often important to individuals. I encourage clients to dialogue with themselves and with the voices within themselves (Watkins, 1990). I invite them to explore exercises of whispering, listening, singing, yelling, and screaming. How and when they pursue those explorations are highly individualized, and they often lead to discoveries and developments that neither of us could have anticipated. I remember one woman, whom I shall here call Ellen, who was afraid to disclose her inner life to me because she expected rejection and my termination of her therapy. Slowly she began to share more and more—giving me glimpses and samples of her private life in the form of diary entries, excerpts of her favorite music, and copies of meaningful statements from books she was reading. One of her diary entries referred to a part of her she called "the Voice." When I asked about the Voice, Ellen became frightened and did not want to discuss it. Much later she came to elaborate her relationship with that part of her, and the Voice emerged as a strong and protective "intralocutor" that had helped her endure and survive many childhood tragedies.

Just as there are undeniable connections between the knower and the known, the same is true of realms usually separated into "mind" and "body." Mind–body dualism has dominated psychology and psychotherapy for the last century, and the legacy of such dualism is a compartmentalized approach to human experiencing. Cognition is not something that goes on in the head while behavior and emotion take place in the body. These three processes—all of which serve to order experience—cannot be meaningfully separated. But the therapist does not need to introduce the topic of the body to psychotherapy. It is always already there, in at least the two bodies of client and therapist. A more important practical question, I believe, is how does an active and appreciative awareness of embodiment influence the practice of professional helping?

I have tried to elaborate such influences elsewhere (Mahoney, in press, a; in press, c). The essence of embodying emphases in my own practice does not conform to a particular school of thought and rituals in the somatic therapies. I rarely prescribe anything in the authoritarian sense of that practice. I do, however, encourage dialogue and explorations of people's bodily histories and present consciousness and evaluation of their patterns of sensation, emotion, and activity. This may sound abstract, but it becomes particular and concrete in a unique way with each client. With as little judgmentality and expectation as possible, I inquire about bodily patterns (sleep, work, play, food, drugs, sex, and so on). At times I may reflect on or recommend possible patterns of experimental movement. Examples include experiential exercises that explore basic bodily awareness and that deepen an appreciation for a basic life-seeking and self-protective wisdom in bodily activities.

I encourage some clients to experiment privately and responsibly with dimensions of their bodily experience—range of movement and balance, for example, often beginning in slow motion. Some find these explorations more helpful than others. Some begin taking classes in movement, meditation, or dance. For clients who wish to explore the dimension of nonsexual touch, I collaborate with skilled and connected massage therapists in the community. I encourage people to write, to draw, to sculpt, to create— and we dialogue more about the process than the products. In working with each client as an individual who knows more about herself than I do and than she realizes, we collaborate on developing novel exercises for her continuing exploration of who she is, how and what she does, and so on.

But these are simply illustrations of how an epistemological appreciation of embodiment can be translated into practice. The practical particulars are less important here than is the core insight on which they are based. Embodiment is where constructivist epistemology invites connected knowing—a kind of knowing that is capable of relating subjects and objects as dialectical processes. The therapist does not come to know her client solely by means of the five senses and a functioning association cortex. These are helpful tools, to be sure, but they are neither the heart nor the whole of the knowing that evolves in psychotherapy (or any other form of human interaction). That heart and that whole are necessarily a dynamic dance of two beings in search of a changed life for one of them. Moreover, there are multiple dialectical dances going on within each of them at every moment, only very little of which they will ever observe, understand, or communicate. This connected knowing is thus an ongoing process of pilgrimages into relationships—connections—with others and with self.

Finally, I think it is important to acknowledge that there are emotional challenges to being connected and present as a psychotherapy practitioner. The more skilled one becomes in entering into the experiential worlds of one's clients, the more deeply one feels their struggles and suffering. People rarely enter psychotherapy while they are happy and functioning well. Hence, the therapist's day (and life, for that matter) is filled with heart-wrenching stories of abuse, injustice, and tragedy. Those stories do not go away when the client does. They remain with us, haunting our dreams and popping up from time to time in our waking consciousness. As psychotherapists we are socially sanctioned protectors of hope, trust, and compassion, and yet in our work we must daily confront very personal and painful violations of human rights and needs. At the same time, of course, we are also privileged to witness the strength, resilience, and tenderness of the human spirit, and we cannot help but be enlarged by our intimate participation in so many lives. As humanistic psychotherapist Jim Bugental put it:

> I am not the person who began to practice counseling or psychotherapy more than thirty years ago in an army hospital. And the changes in me are not solely those worked by time, education, and the life circumstances shared by most of my generation. A powerful force affecting me has been my participation in so many lives. A psychotherapist had best recognize that the profession will continually press on her or him to change and evolve. (1978, p. 149)

This is why I believe it is so important that psychotherapy practitioners place a high priority on self-care and the quality of the systems supporting their personal lives and lifespan development.

CONCLUSION

A central theme in this chapter has been the proposal that the connected knowing elaborated in and since WWK is essentially resonant with the philosophical tradition of constructivism, which has recently begun to be more actively explored and translated into practice by health service providers. I have briefly discussed the history of traditions in epistemology, and I have characterized constructive theory in terms of five themes. In the second part of the chapter I have discussed connected knowing and aspects of a constructive approach to psychotherapy.

It should come as no surprise that I consider the developmental trajectory of constructivism and constructive psychotherapy impossible to predict. This is simply an acknowledgment of the truly humbling limitations of our knowing and of the poverty of our power to understand objectively or control rationally many (if not most) of the particulars of our lives. I doubt that constructive psychotherapy will be successfully translated into operations manuals—such operationalization and attempted objectification are antithetical to its epistemological essence. I also doubt that evaluations and elaborations of constructivist theory will rely heavily on traditional objectivist methodology. It will not be numbers on a grid that most interest or influence constructive researchers and practitioners (Hoshmand & Martin, 1995; Polkinghorne, 1983; Toukmanian & Rennie, 1992). Nor are they likely to support societal health care policies that unduly constrain professional decisions or otherwise jeopardize the quality of care. I believe it is more likely, however, that constructivists will play an increasingly active role in protecting and promoting dialogue about just such issues. They are also likely to be protectors of diversity and human rights, emphasizing that compassionate—not just peacefully coexistent—human relationships form the heart of conscious community.

NOTES

1. Sandra Harding's (this volume) nonspatial categorization of Northern and Southern positionalities is a refreshing and creative alternative to the habitual contrast between Eastern and Western civilizations.
2. A scholarly history of women constructivists has yet to be written. When it is, I suspect that it will include such figures as Charlotte Bühler, Mary Whiton Calkins, and Barbel Inhelder.
3. As I come to understand and elaborate connected knowing more deeply, I feel that the adjective *revolutionary* is less apt than *evolutionary* for WWK in that the former suggests an adversarial rather than emergent and dialectical process.
4. I am indebted to more students/colleagues than I can name here. Current projects include the works of Luis Amunátegui, Carol Baldwin, Chris Buntrock, Nancy Diehl, Linda Galijan, and Amy Moes. Information about their work appears in *Constructive Change*, a publication of the Center for Constructive Change, 894 E. Boise Ave., Boise, ID 83706.
5. For an incisive critique of "the heresy of self-love" in the history of Western civilization, see Zweig (1980).
6. Prohibitions against any form of physical contact between therapist and client have left many students and practitioners worried about the legitimacy of a compassionate touch of the hand, the propriety of a hug, and the proper therapeutic distance and posture when a client is crying. Objectivist views have long established the body as a boundary of impropriety. Constructive and feminist alternatives have resisted rendering the body as an object and have incorporated responsible acknowledgements of embodiment into common practice (Chodorow, 1992; Mahoney, in press, a).

REFERENCES

Alic, M. (1986). *Hypatia's heritage: A history of women in science from antiquity through the nineteenth century.* Boston: Beacon Press.

Bartley, W. W. (1962). *The retreat to commitment.* LaSalle, IL: Open Court.

Belenky, M. F., Clinchy, B. M., Goldberger, N. R., & Tarule, J. M. (1986). *Women's ways of knowing: The development of self, voice, and mind.* New York: Basic Books.

Bernstein, R. J. (1983). *Beyond objectivism and relativism: Science, hermeneutics, and praxis.* Philadelphia: University of Pennsylvania Press.

Brown, L. S., & Brodsky, A. M. (1992). The future of feminist therapy. *Psychotherapy, 29,* 51–57.

Bugental, J. F. T. (1978). *Psychotherapy and process: The fundamentals of an existential-humanistic approach.* Reading, MA: Addison-Wesley.

Burrell, M. J. (1987). Cognitive psychology, epistemology, and psychotherapy: A motor-evolutionary perspective. *Psychotherapy, 24,* 225–232.

Chodorow, N. (1978). *The reproduction of mothering.* Berkeley: University of California Press.

Chodorow, N. (1989). *Feminism and psychoanalytic theory.* New Haven, CT: Yale University Press.

Chodorow, N. (1992). Sophia's dance. *American Journal of Dance Therapy, 14,* 111–123.

Clinchy, B. M. (1993). Ways of knowing and ways of being: Epistemological and moral development in undergraduate women. In A. Garrod (Ed.), *Approaches to moral development: New research and emerging themes* (pp. 180–200). New York: Teachers College Press.

Crawford, M., & Marecek, J. (1989). Psychology reconstructs the female: 1968–1988. *Psychology of Women Quarterly, 13,* 147–165.

Ebersole, P., & Flores, J. (1989). Positive impact of life crises. *Journal of Social Behavior and Personality, 4,* 463–469.

Enns, C. Z. (1992). Toward integrating feminist psychotherapy and feminist philosophy. *Professional Psychology: Research and Practice, 23,* 453–466.

Gergen, K. J. (1985). The social constructionist movement in modern psychology. *American Psychologist, 40,* 266–275.

Goldberger, N. (1996). Women's constructions of truth, self, authority, and power. In H. Rosen & K. Kuehlwein (Eds.), *Constructing realities: Meaning making perspectives for psychotherapists.* San Francisco: Jossey-Bass.

Griffin, D. R., Cobb, J. B., Ford, M. P., Gunter, P. A. Y., & Ochs, P. (1993). *Founders of constructive postmodern philosophy.* Albany: State University of New York Press.

Guidano, V. F. (1987). *Complexity of self.* New York: Guilford.

Guidano, V. F. (1991). *The self in process.* New York: Guilford.

Hersh, T. (1980). The phenomenology of belief systems. *Journal of Humanistic Psychology, 20,* 57–68.

Hoshmand, L. T., & Martin, J. (Eds.). (1995). *Research as praxis: Lessons from programmatic research in therapeutic psychology.* New York: Teachers College Press.

Jackson, L. A., & Jeffers, D. L. (1989). The attitudes about reality scale: A new measure of personal epistemology. *Journal of Personality Assessment, 53,* 353–365.

Janoff-Bulman, R. (1989). Assumptive worlds and the stress of traumatic events: Applications of the schema construct. *Social Cognition, 7,* 113–136.

Johnson, J. A., Germer, C. K., Efran, J. S., & Overton, W. F. (1988). Personality as the basis for theoretical predilections. *Journal of Personality and Social Psychology, 55,* 824–835.

Kahn, M. (1991). *Between therapist and client: The new relationship.* New York: Freeman.

Kauffman, S. (1995). *At home in the universe: The search for the laws of self-organization and complexity.* Oxford: Oxford University Press.

Kegan, R. (1982). *The evolving self: Problem and process in human development.* Cambridge, MA: Harvard University Press.

Keller, E. F. (1983). *A feeling for the organism: The life and work of Barbara McClintock.* New York: Freeman.

Keller, E. F. (1985). *Reflections on gender and science.* New Haven: Yale University Press.

Keller, E. F. (1992). *Secrets of life, secrets of death: Essays on language, gender and science.* London: Routledge.

Kelly, J. (1984). *Women, history, and theory.* Chicago: University of Chicago Press.

Kimmel, E. B. (1989). The experience of feminism. *Psychology of Women Quarterly, 13,* 133–146.

Lakoff, G., & Johnson, M. (1980). *Metaphors we live by.* Chicago: University of Chicago Press.

Lennon, K., & Whitford, M. (Eds.) (1994). *Knowing the difference: Feminist perspectives in epistemology.* London: Routledge.

McNamara, K., & Rickard, K. M. (1989). Feminist identity development: Implications for feminist therapy with women. *Journal of Counseling and Development, 68,* 184–189.

Mahoney, M. J. (1976). *Scientist as subject: The psychological imperative.* Cambridge, MA: Ballinger.

Mahoney, M. J. (1991). *Human change processes: The scientific foundations of psychotherapy.* New York: Basic Books.

Mahoney, M. J. (Ed.) (1995). *Cognitive and constructive psychotherapies.* New York: Springer.

Mahoney, M. J. (in press, a). *The body in psychotherapy: A constructive integration.* New York: Guilford.

Mahoney, M. J. (in press, b). *Constructive psychotherapy: Principles and practice.* New York: Guilford.

Mahoney, M. J. (in press, c). *Constructive techniques in psychotherapy.* New York: Guilford.

Mahoney, M. J., & Fernandez-Alvarez, H. (1995). *The personal life of the psychotherapist.* Unpublished manuscript, University of North Texas.

Mahoney, M. J., & Moes, A. J. (in press). Complexity and psychotherapy: Promising dialogues and practical issues. In F. Masterpasqua & P. A. Perna (Eds.), *The psychological meaning of chaos: Self-organization in human development and psychotherapy.* Washington, DC: American Psychological Association.

Margolis, D. R. (1989). Considering women's experience: A reformulation of power theory. *Theory and Society, 18,* 387–416.

Markus, H., & Nurius, P. (1986). Possible selves. *American Psychologist, 41,* 954–969.

Neimeyer, R. A., & Mahoney, M. J. (Eds.) (1995). *Constructivism in psychotherapy.* Washington, DC: American Psychological Association.

Nevels, L. A., & Coché, J. M. (1993). *Powerful wisdom: Voices of distinguished women psychotherapists.* San Francisco: Jossey-Bass.

Nye, A. (1990). *Words of power: A feminist reading of the history of logic.* New York: Routledge.

Polkinghorne, D. (1983). *Methodology for the human sciences: Systems of inquiry.* Albany: State University of New York Press.

Skovholt, T. M., & Rønnestad, M. H. (1992). *The evolving professional self: Stages and themes in therapist and counselor development.* New York: Wiley.

Stolorow, R. D., & Atwood, G. E. (1992). *Contexts of being: The intersubjective foundations of psychological life.* Hillsdale, NJ: Analytic Press.

Tarnas, R. (1991). *The passion of the western mind.* New York: Ballantine.

Toukmanian, S. G., & Rennie, D. L. (Eds.) (1992). *Psychotherapy process research: Paradigmatic and narrative approaches.* London: Sage.

Tuana, N. (Ed.) (1989). *Feminism and science.* Bloomington, IN: Indiana University Press.

Unger, R. K., Draper, R. D., & Pendergrass, M. L. (1986). Personal epistemology and personal experience. *Journal of Social Issues, 42,* 67–79.

Walker, A. (1996). *The same river twice: Honoring the difficult.* New York: Scribner.

Wartenberg, T. E. (Ed.) (1992). *Rethinking power.* Albany: State University of New York Press.

Watkins, M. (1990). *Invisible guests: The development of imaginal dialogues.* Boston: Sigo Press.

Watzlawick, P. (Ed.) (1984). *The invented reality: Contributions to constructivism.* New York: Norton.

Weimer, W. B. (1979). *Notes on the methodology of scientific research.* Hillsdale, NJ: Erlbaum.

Zweig, P. (1980). *The heresy of self-love: A study of subversive individualism.* Princeton NJ: Princeton University Press.

5

Women's Ways of Knowing in Women's Studies, Feminist Pedagogies, and Feminist Theory

FRANCES A. MAHER
WITH MARY KAY TETREAULT

INTRODUCTION

> In considering how to design an education appropriate for women, suppose we were to begin by asking, simply: What does a woman know? Traditional courses do not begin there. They begin not with the students' knowledge but with the teacher's knowledge. The courses are about the (dominant) culture's questions, questions fished out of the "mainstream" disciplines. If the student is female, her questions are unlikely to intersect with the culture's questions, since women, paddling in the bywaters of the culture, have had little to do with positing (its) questions or setting (its) agendas. (Belenky, Clinchy, Goldberger, and Tarule, 1986, p. 198)

This excerpt from *Women's Ways of Knowing* (WWK) is about the educational and epistemological implications of this pathbreaking work. In chapters 9 and 10, the authors elaborate a series of pedagogical approaches that they call "connected teaching," approaches that are specifically designed to encourage women students to develop their own questions and agency as learners and to claim an education that relates to their agendas. In this chapter we wish to explore the impact of *WWK* on the academic fields that are most specifically concerned with the question "What does a woman know?" namely, feminist theory and women's studies.

We want first to look at the important place of WWK both in terms of developments in feminist theory and as a guide for pedagogical innovations undertaken by feminist teachers. As one of the authors, Jill Tarule, stated, the book started a conversation, and they then found themselves in the middle of it. Second, we want to ask how this conversation has changed over time, and how the issues raised by WWK address the specific challenges for feminist theory, women's studies, and feminist pedagogies today.

Throughout this essay, we will refer to representative writings on these topics over the last ten years, as well as make use of ideas we learned through writing *The Feminist Classroom*, an ethnographic study of the classrooms of seventeen feminist college professors in six institutions nationwide during the late 1980s and early 1990s (Maher & Tetreault, 1994). WWK, and the conversations it started, became formative influences on our initial conception of our own project, along with the increasing amount of scholarly work on women's studies curriculum development and on feminist pedagogy to which both of us had contributed (Maher, 1985a, 1985b, 1987; Tetreault, 1985, 1985b, 1986). The faculty informants for *The Feminist Classroom* are teachers in both Women's Studies and specific academic disciplines who have been concerned with issues of pedagogy as well as course content. Very early they helped us to see that pedagogies and content are inextricably intertwined in the classroom construction of knowledge, and that women's studies and feminist pedagogies are related aspects of the same epistemological shifts in higher education.

Indeed, both because of this emphasis on the social construction of classroom knowledge and because of the continuing influence of major trends in feminist theory on our ongoing research and writing, we were led in a different direction in our work, away from WWK's central focus on individual development. In this chapter we wish to begin by placing WWK in the context of the feminist thought of the late 1980s, then show how the challenges of diversity and poststructuralism have transformed feminist theory and women's education. By enlarging the grounds of analysis to include a focus on the interpersonal setting, on the social construction of knowledge, *The Feminist Classroom* examined classrooms as examples of shifting and relational arenas in which interpretations of people's multiple positions in society can be developed, articulated, and shared. Extending WWK's individually based cognitive stages into a different context, we used an insight of Jill Tarule and others, that learning is constructed not only in individual minds, but through the interactions of communities of knowers (Maher & Tetreault, 1994, p. 22; see also Tarule's chapter, this volume). Specifically, we moved their last stage of "constructed knowing" away from its place as a marker of individual development, and began to see this epistemologial approach emerging within the multivocal contexts given by a range of classroom settings. We could thus explore some of the specific challenges created by the diversity that preoccupies feminist theory today.

However, today the conversation has also grown more bitter. Women's studies and feminism itself are buffeted by attacks from "feminists" who critique all women's studies classrooms as being destroyed by an unscholarly emphasis on "personal experience" and a self-referential "identity politics" that leaves no room for shared knowledge or traditional academic achievement (Patai & Koertge, 1994). Exploiting criticisms from some feminists of themselves and each other for replacing scholarly vigor with sentimentality and for valorizing and generalizing about "all women's experiences," these critics want to go back to traditional models of academic discourse. We will argue that, on the contrary, truly multicultural, gendered classrooms and curricula can be built through what we call "pedagogies of positionality," which use the idea of constructed knowing—both for the individual and in the classroom context—as a jumping-off place, not a final destination. We also want to suggest that these discourses are structured by—and must move into—difficult worlds beyond the classroom as well.

WOMEN'S WAYS OF KNOWING
IN FEMINIST THEORY

As many of the chapters in this volume attest, WWK had an electrifying effect on people in every discipline who work with women, because of its delineation of alternative ways of seeing the world outside traditional models of knowledge and of knowing, of epistemology. WWK is a prime examplar of an important earlier phase of feminist theory and women's studies characterized *by some* as bifocal scholarship. This scholarship has been transformative, because it represents a paradigmatic shift from a perspective that views men as the norm to one that opens up the possibility of seeing the world through women's eyes. One of the first and most influential works in this genre came in the field of moral development. Carol Gilligan's *In a Different Voice* articulated an "ethic of care," challenging Lawrence Kohlberg's "ethic of justice" in which women usually occupied lower stages than men (Gilligan, 1982).

By charting a new course through the cognitive-developmental stages first analyzed by developmentalists William Perry and Arthur Chickering, Mary Belenky, Blythe Clinchy, Nancy Goldberger, and Jill Tarule showed how women's thought patterns are more contextual and more embedded in relational concerns than those of men. Challenging the rationalism, separation, and false "objectivity" of masculinist models of knowledge, they insisted on women's knowing as a hallmark of sophisticated thought and judgment, as Gilligan had. In the process they revealed traditional stage theory as reflective of the experiences and growth of one group, namely, privileged males, rather than as a series of universal steps by which all could be judged and some, often women, be found wanting.

The revolutionary impact of the idea that women may inhabit different worlds than men spawned new complexities, however. As feminist theorists began to think about "truths" for women and men in WWK and other work in this genre, they began to see some of the limitations inherent *in basing theoretical distinctions exclusively on gender.* Despite statements by the authors of WWK that their insights were "gender-related rather than gender-specific," and in spite of their careful delineation of specific cultural contexts for their informants, their ideas began to be read by many as dualistic and dichotomized. Implicit in these approaches, critics stated, was the idea that a single element of identity, gender, determines one's development and ways of knowing. They charged that such a generalized view of women and men played into more simplified and essentialist views of gender that erased both differences among women and commonalities among women and men sharing similar histories. It did not allow for distinctions within groups as large and complex as women and men. Important factors such as historical period, geographic location, societal structural barriers, race, culture, religion, sexual orientation, and social class, to name a few, clearly made a difference (Tetreault, 1985b; Minnich, O'Barr, & Rosenfeld, 1988; Schuster & Van Dyne, 1985).

This ground-breaking scholarship thus spawned a proliferation of new topics and issues for women's studies, raised by women of color, lesbians, and members of other groups uncomfortable under the umbrella label of "all women." It also led, more unfortunately, to a later theoretical position known as "cultural feminism," a set of ideas that exploited an overly simplistic valorization of "women's experiences" and virtues in order to claim that women are essentially different from and superior to men.

These developments have helped to create the current complexities in women's studies and feminist theory today, as discussed later.

WOMEN'S WAYS OF KNOWING
IN FEMINIST PEDAGOGY

Within the emerging field of feminist pedagogy, WWK also occupied an important position, helping feminist teachers articulate some principles and practices that would particularly empower women students. The authors' metaphor of "the teacher as midwife," who would encourage students to talk about their own experiences and work through their uncertainties, was combined with general ideas of the teacher as a nurturer and a facilitator, rather than a distant and expert authority figure. They offered a model of "connected teaching," which would encourage students to answer their own questions and manage their own intellectual growth.

> The connected class provides a culture for growth. . . . The connected teacher creates groups in which the members can nurture their thoughts to maturity. . . . In a connected class no one apologizes for uncertainty. It is assumed that evolving thought will be tentative. (Belenky et al., 1986, p. 221)

Many writers on issues of feminist pedagogy picked up on these ideas to articulate specific approaches to teaching women students; several ideas were "in the air" anyway, as feminist professors adapted principles and techniques of the consciousness-raising groups of the women's liberation movement to the classroom (Bunch & Pollack, 1983; Culley & Portuges, 1985; Davis, 1985). For example, in a 1987 special issue of *Women's Studies Quarterly* devoted to feminist pedagogies, a third of the essays referred to WWK, and many others published around this time mentioned similar ideas for working with women (Schniedewind & Maher, 1987). In *The Feminist Classroom*, we noted the bifocal quality of this literature; it constructed "a somewhat simplistic and dichotomized view of the authoritarian, male-dominated, 'traditional classroom' versus the idealized 'feminist teacher.'

> Like the construct of "woman's nature" in some feminist theories, like Gilligan's, of the early 1980s, this teacher was democratic rather than authoritarian, cooperative rather than competitive, and concerned with "connected"

and relational rather than "separate" and rational approaches to learning. (Maher & Tetreault, 1994, p. 11)

Because of the enthusiastic reception given to WWK and these ideas about teaching women, such concepts became important features of the pedagogical version of feminist theory's "equality versus difference" struggle of the mid- to late 1980s. Out of the premises of bifocal scholarship emerged debates over whether or not, in fact, women and men were in essence the same or different; and if they were different, how could women be treated equally to men? The pedagogical version of this question became, How is feminist teaching any different from any other progressive, alternative teaching methods? Are passive women students any different from men who are also silenced by the traditional classroom discourses of power and dominance?

Along with these pedagogical concerns arose related ones, namely, how to deal with differences of power, authority, and voice *among* classroom participants, not only those of gender but of race, culture, age, and other important factors. One major difference for the classroom in particular concerned the superior power enjoyed by the feminist teacher, whose "sisterhood" with her students was complicated by her scholarly authority and motivations, as well as by her power and responsibility to give grades. Questions like these became the opening wedge for critiques over the past six or seven years, critiques that would ultimately transform feminist pedagogies (and Women's Studies) from the "women-centered" approaches of WWK and other feminist work of the time to a more complicated and nuanced view of feminist pedagogy, of Women's Studies, and perhaps of women's development as well.

RETHEORIZING FEMINIST PEDAGOGIES: FROM WOMEN'S WAYS OF KNOWING TO POSITIONALITIES

The first responses to the question, Why is feminist pedagogy different from liberatory models? were either to say that at bottom it is not, or to cite its particular concern for women students. For example, one representative article asserts:

It is clear to us that much of the agenda of radical education in the last thirty years has involved emphasis on the agency of both teacher and student, and a focus on collaboration rather than competition that are key features of what these feminists call "interactive teaching and learning." (Kenway & Modra, 1992, p. 158)

On the other hand, women's studies faculty members were more likely to say, like one of our informants, that their commitments to feminist pedagogies were based on feminism, not models from the field of education:

> The reason we call this feminist pedagogy is because those of us here who are doing it came at it through thinking about feminist theory. We have chosen to call it feminist because we arrived at it through that route. I call myself a feminist teacher because that is the particular mode of analysis that I use to arrive at what I am trying to do. (Maher & Tetrault, 1994, p. 13)

Attempts to "write across" this gap took the form of several articles comparing the approaches of feminist teachers to the philosophies of liberatory teaching espoused by Paulo Freire, the Brazilian educational philosopher, and his followers (Freire, 1970). Many writers criticize Freire for insufficient attention to gender, asserting that the inclusion of gender would enrich his approaches (Maher, 1987; Weiler, 1991; Kenway & Modra, 1992). Frances Maher used what she called "gender models of teaching" to challenge Freire's unidimensional model of the oppressed as all speaking with the same voice. She asked, What about people, such as many men, who occupy the position of both oppressed *and* oppressor? More broadly, what about differences of power, authority, and perspective *within* the feminist (or any other) classroom?

Elizabeth Ellsworth, a feminist educator, uses the conflicts in her course Media and Anti-Racist Pedagogies to critique theories of "critical pedagogies" (and by extension feminist pedagogies) for adopting an abstract and acontextual set of prescriptions for the teacher to promote a generalized view of student empowerment. Such theories, she asserts, obscure the nature of the teacher's power, overlook the implications of differences among students, and make it impossible to engage successfully with the competing viewpoints of agendas of all groups in a given situation, even those working against oppression.

> Critical pedagogues consistently answer the question of "empowerment for what?" in ahistorical and depoliticized abstractions [such as] "human betterment" [or] agency, democratic community, and transformative social action. Student empowerment has been defined [in ways] that fail to challenge any identifiable social or political position, institution, or group.
>
> "Emancipatory authority" is a contortion, for it implies the potential for an emancipated teacher. . . . No teacher is free of the learned and internalized oppressions [of racism, classism, or sexism]. Nor are accounts of one group's

suffering and struggle immune from reproducing narratives oppressive to another's—the racism of the women's movement in the United States is one example. (Ellsworth, 1992, p. 99)

As Ellsworth explained, new directions in critical pedagogy were needed to address these problems adequately.

Other writers in both women's studies and feminist theory were also beginning to raise the issue of "difference." Indeed, in the years since the publication of WWK, several important movements have enlarged the conversation among these writers and transformed these fields. First were the demands by women of color, lesbians, Third World women, and others silenced by the universalizing tendencies of earlier stages in feminist thought, to be included in the range of women's experiences being researched, theorized, and taught. Just as WWK had revealed the false universalism of traditionalist male theory, so, now, theories of different "identities" had begun to reveal the limitations of WWK and other work in its field in speaking for all women, without sufficient attention to variations among them. For example, although the authors of WWK included black and working-class women in their study, the two black women they discussed, whose stories concerned unreliable men or "superwomen" mothers, were used to illustrate how these women constructed their thinking in relation to the epistemologies in the book—which represented the thinking of women in general (Belenky et al., 1986, p. 58, 173).

Explorations of their own histories on their own terms by members of these and other marginalized groups gave rise to a number of so-called identity, or standpoint theories.[1] As feminist theorist Catherine Stimpson put it recently:

Women's Studies fissured into academic cohorts that fused the study of sex and gender with at least one other powerful element of biological, social, and/or cultural identity: class for Marxist feminist studies; sexual preference for Lesbian studies; colonization for post-colonial or Subaltern studies; religion for feminist spirituality; and race and ethnicity for Black feminist studies, Latina or Chicana studies, Native American or Asian-American women's studies. (Stimpson, 1995, p. 6)

For example, feminist theorist Patricia Hill Collins articulated a series of distinctive epistemologies for African American women in her *Black Feminist Thought.* In it, she drew heavily on both the "women's epistemologies" described in WWK, such as knowledge from personal experience and thought patterns from African and African American culture, such as action and community validation as hallmarks of knowing. Similarly, Sandra Harding outlined a specific lesbian epistemological stance, one that illuminates the operations of heterosexism in the society in a way that earlier, heterosexist theory could not (Collins, 1990; Harding, 1994; but see essays by Harding, Goldberger, and Hurtado in this volume that extend and transform these ideas in new ways similar to those suggested later).

The proliferation of such standpoint feminisms represented a new set of problems, namely, those generated by the implications of a series of parallel "knowledges" that existed alongside each other without intersecting, or being able to claim knowledge of each other except as regards those experiences held in common. The results have been (and still are) the stalemates of "identity politics," where members of different dominated and exploited groups, in trying to understand who they are, struggle against the barriers between them and other groups that these same identities create.

The second major transformation in feminist thought, however, has challenged the fixities of identity politics. Feminist postmodernism replaces the wholistic and unitary worldview of any group with an emphasis on the constructedness, through shifting language, discourse, and histories, of all "identities." Identities are multiple, not only within and between groups, but also between and within individuals. These concerns with the multiple (and ultimately indeterminable) realities of experience between and within each person have broken down the proliferation of the binary oppositions woman/man, black/white, black woman/white woman, and so on, that have plagued feminist theory and Women's Studies. Postmodernist feminists have instead asked us to look at these terminologies as markers of false dichotomies, and to uncover the relations of power and domination they mask. For example, some women of color theorists have gone beyond "black" and "white" to look at relationships of race and culture globally, asking about the roles of African Americans in relation to the global diaspora; others have pointed out that the term *multicultural* does not designate *nonwhite* studies but rather a description of the real world beyond white solipsism: as one put it, "Multiculturalism is not an ism; it just is" (Chinosole, 1994).[2]

These newer discourses in feminism allow Ellsworth to reflect on her own course on racism:

> Current writing by many feminists working from antiracism and feminist poststructuralist perspectives recognizes that any individual woman's politi-

cized voice will be partial, multiple and contradictory. The literature on crit-ical pedagogy does not confront the ways in which any individual student's voice is already a "teeth-gritting" and often contradictory intersection of voices constituted by gender, race, class, ability, ethnicity, sexual orientation, or ideology.

The particularities of historical context, personal biography, and subjec-tivities split between the conscious and the unconscious will render each expression of student voice partial and predicated on the absence and mar-ginalization of alternative voices. It is impossible to speak from all voices at once, or from any one, without the traces of the others being present and interruptive. Thus the very term "student voice" is highly problematic. Plu-ralizing the concept as voices implies correction through addition. This loses sight of the contradictory and partial nature of all voices. (Ellsworth, 1992, pp. 103–104)

Meanwhile, in the course of working on *The Feminist Classroom*, we were emboldened by these developments in feminist theory to change our own approaches as well. We had found our original categories of analysis, based on the putative approaches of a modal and individualized feminist teacher, inadequate. Not only were they idealized and dichotomized, but, like most of the work in pedagogical theory, they made the teacher's approaches the main focus of concern. Although postmodern approaches as interpreted by writers like Ellsworth are widely understood to offer a more complex account of "identity forma-tions" than was previously possible, another, equally important aspect of postmodern feminism has been undertheorized, especially in accounts of feminist pedagogy: the necessity for a methodological shift away from the *individual* as the only source and end point of our knowledge. We began to look not only at the individual student or teacher's development but at the evolution, processes, and relationships of students and teach-ers in the particular settings themselves—not only as arenas in which to examine individuals but as worthy of attention themselves.

WWK's model, as is common in the field of psychology as a whole, is both individual and universalized. That is, the authors used examples from a number of interviews with individuals to make generalizations about all members of a group, in this case women, which are illustrated with anecdotal material. Working with a wide range of women, they focused on commonalities in their personal development.

When the context is allowed to vary, as it did in our study, because we included women of widely different ages, life circumstances, and back-grounds, universal developmental pathways are far less obvious. We describe in this book epistemological perspectives from which women know and view the world. (Belenky et al., 1986, p. 15)

Culling statements from interviews that illustrated these epistemological perspectives,

> We moved back and forth between these excerpts and the unabridged interviews. This enabled us to maintain a dual perspective, hearing the statements as exemplars of a particular epistemological position but hearing them also in the context of a woman's whole story. (Belenky et al., 1986, p. 17)

Yet in the course of WWK, few of these individuals' "whole stories" are heard. The resulting focus on the universal misses the importance of the varied societal and structural contexts they use—those conferred by race, class, age, culture, and other relational dynamics—for shaping the ways individuals grow and become who they are. Thus, even though the last "stage" in WWK, "constructed knowing," is formulated as an individual epistemology, a different and fuller articulation of this stage may emerge through attention to the multiple situations within which people find themselves, and thereby construct their understandings of self and the world.

For *The Feminist Classroom*, as we looked at both identity and knowledge as socially constructed, shifting, and dependent on context, not only did we have to move beyond the individual as our sole object of study, we also had to change our methodological categories to emphasize relationships rather than entities, to study *not* the "objects" themselves—whether they be curricula versus pedagogies, teachers versus students, male versus female or black versus white students—but how these "identities" construct each other in different settings. We thus sought new methodological categories to capture networks and webs of meaning rather than separate trajectories, wanting to follow multiple narratives and their relations rather than a single argument. We analyzed our informants' classes through the use of four themes, each of which represented both an individual *and* a relational lens (Maher & Tetreault, 1994, pp. 15–24). These are described in the sections that follow.

Mastery.

Our first theme was mastery, or the question of what it is that the students are supposed to learn. Mastery has traditionally meant the goal of rational comprehension of the material on the teacher's and expert's terms. On a more fundamental level, mastery has always been concerned with telling students who they should be, and where they should fit, as well as what they should know. Becoming educated has been the process by which people are constructed in their relationship to the mainstream culture. Because all our teacher informants resisted, in some measure, the traditional curriculum's definition of who women are, they all have wrestled with the relationship between who their students are—both as individuals and as groups—and what they need to "master," or know. Looking at these relationships, we came to redefine mastery as more than an issue of individual achievement. We began to see it as interpretation and to look for interpretations based on particular contexts, both in the layers of interpretation arrived at in the class discussions we saw and in the multiple interpretations offered to us as researchers by our situations.

Voice.

The theme of voice is twofold: first, it is about the new forms of personal student expression available in these classrooms; second, it is about the construction of communities of discourse as teachers' and students' voices interact with, influence, and construct each other. In the first sense, voice concerns the relationship within an individual of what can be expressed and not expressed, and how that relates to who one "is" and who one can become. This "coming to voice" for previously silenced women is an important theme in WWK.

We were concerned also, however, with the fashioning of voice in terms of classroom settings and appropriate classroom languages. These classrooms created communities that were powerful supports, but they also engendered silences, conflicts, and the bumping together of different discourses. In other words, as with mastery, we saw voice as an interpretive device for looking at the construction of classroom discourses, rather than solely as a marker of individual expression.

Authority.

As we had the others, we examined the theme of authority partly because the issue of the teacher's authority had been rendered so problematic by the earlier literature on critical and feminist pedagogy. A central question for these professors was the source of their authority in relationship to their disciplines, their students, and the institutions in which they work. Traditionally professorial authority arises from superior knowledge of a field; it is lodged in the hierarchical relationship of expert to teacher to student and is enforced institutionally by the power and duty to assign grades. For us, authority, like mastery and voice, became an evolving factor within the framework of each classroom, reflecting professors' and students' varying relationships with each other as well as the material. In fact, we learned that students often become authorities to each other, and that authority, like voice, is situational and constructed.

Positionality.

Our last theme, positionality, is the concept, articulated by postmodern and other feminist thinkers, that knowledge of any topic is valid only as it acknowledges the knowers' varying positions in any specific context, positions always defined by the enactments of the dynamics of gender, race, class, and other significant dimensions of societal domination. Of the four themes, positionality is the only one that cannot be viewed solely through the lenses of individual development, as the term itself signals that context is a key to understanding. An individual's *position*, as opposed to his or her "identity" or even "standpoint," is relational and evolving, in the sense that the concept "maleness" implies and creates meanings for "femaleness," and vice versa; "blackness," and certainly the phrase "of color," rests on the simultaneous construction of the idea of "whiteness." Thus peoples' positions, unlike their "identities," are susceptible to critique and change as long as their own locations (and relations) within these networks are explored rather than passed over, individualized, or universalized.

It was in the articulation of this theme that we used the insights of postmodern feminism most consciously, particularly as offered in political theorist Linda Alcoff's theory of positionality (Alcoff, 1988; see also Harding, this volume). Critiquing the essentialism of cultural feminism and the groundlessness of much postmodern theory, she marks positionality as a construct by which women can articulate their oppression without being fixed in a restricted (and essentialized) identity "woman":

> The positional definition of "woman" makes her identity relative to a constantly shifting context, to a . . . network of elements involving other people, economic conditions, cultural and political institutions and ideologies, and so on. If it is possible to identify women by their position within this network of relations, then it becomes possible to ground a feminist argument for women . . . on the claim that their position within this network lacks power and mobility and requires radical change. (Alcoff, 1988, pp. 433–434)

The classroom became for us an instructive example of one of these "constantly shifting contexts," within which we could examine knowledge about how women are constructed. We saw how, in each classroom, students and professors carried with them the complex power relations representing their different positions in the wider society, but also were able to use the (relative) neutrality of classroom spaces to examine, challenge, and reconstruct those positions.

We used our four themes to examine these processes in the classes of the seventeen professors in our study. In so doing, we were able to look at individual development *in context* and make connections between the meanings made by individuals and those emerging in the wider discourse, the classroom community of knowers.

COMMUNITIES OF KNOWING

Our focus on the classroom construction of knowledge has illuminated for us some of the present issues of diversity and identity politics within feminist theory. Looking back on a few vignettes, we can see the usefulness of the theoretical framework of WWK for dealing with these issues.

For example, in a Feminist Criticism class, an all-female group of thirteen with one African American student, a student journal entry kicked off a discussion of Toni Morrison's *Sula*. The class had read an article by literary critic Barbara Smith, "Towards a Black Feminist Criticism," which interprets *Sula* as a lesbian novel. (Maher & Tetreault, 1994, 167–170). The entry, written by a white student, began:

> Barbara Smith says, "Writing about Black women writers from a feminist perspective and about Black lesbian writers from any perspective at all (is) something dangerous." This assures that the attempt of a non-Black reader to write about the Black woman writer will be far more dangerous, if not impossible—at least to write from a Black perspective.
>
> Perhaps it would be *less presumptuous and less offensive* for the White woman critic to try to comprehend the "feminist" or "lesbian" issues within Black women's literature. These ideas and issues may prove to be starting points for Black and White women to understand and interpret each other's literature more intelligently. While White women can never expect to express a total understanding of the Black woman's experience they can express concern and understanding in those areas of Black women's lives and literature that parallel their own.

WWK helped us to analyze this passage, and the possible lesbianism of the main characters, Sula and Nel, as an excellent example of the subjective knowing of these students. Indeed, WWK's stage of subjective knowing, and the authors' criticisms of its limitations, may also be seen as a warning against the devolution of bifocal scholarship into "cultural feminism." They point out that where "truth" is based on personal experience, each person's truth rests on an essentialized uniqueness and is unknowable to the other. Similarly, for cultural feminism, the "truth" of each gender is unknowable to the other. We began to see subjective knowing as the epistemological phase that characterizes not only the cultural feminist emphasis on "all women's experiences," but also the reliance on other essentialized identities that are part of other "feminist standpoint" theories described earlier. We said about this and other, similar discussions in our book:

> As we have been looking again at the previous chapters with barriers to positional epistemologies in mind, we were struck by a commonality between some of these ideologies of "cultural" feminism, the epistemological stage of subjective knowing noted by the authors of Women's Ways of Knowing and discussed in Chapter Four, and the individualism of the dominant culture. The idea that "woman's nature" is in essence different from that of men could be read . . . as a "subjective" phase of feminism, extending the notion of an individual's uniqueness into that of a group's uniqueness.
>
> The idea (expressed by this journal entry) becomes that only women can understand women's "experiences," only black people can understand black peoples' experiences, and that white women can understand women of color only through the "woman" piece of their identity—not the African American one. "True" understanding of another becomes possible only in the increasingly limited ways that they are seen as "the same." The underlying notion is that the ultimate unit of meaning must be *individual* experience. As Grey Osterud (one of the teacher informants) put it to us,
>
>> Late adolescents especially are concerned about negotiating their identity, and that makes some of them more individualized, and if identity politics is seen as the basis for knowledge, then no one's getting beyond that. But I do think that in the period of time when you observed these peoples' practice, that was a real phenomenon in the state of feminist politics. (Maher & Tetreault, 1994, pp. 224–225)

We went on to say, "In contrast to the isolation of 'fixed identities,' positional approaches bring different forms of identity into relation to each other, showing, for example, how gendered experiences, far from being 'natural,' are constructed by class and race, and vice versa, each factor contextualizing and specifying the circumstances under which the others are experienced."

In fact WWK's articulation of a cognitive stage called *subjective knowing* might be a clue to the reasons "identity politics" is such a plague for feminist theory in general. Subjective knowing is also the quintessential epistemological stage of individualism, one of the most pervasive and mystifying ideologies in our culture because it suggests that we stand or fall, progress or not, only as individuals and not as occupants of societal positions of power and domination. Theories of identity, including cultural feminism, do not really challenge this because in substituting the notion of a group's uniqueness for that of an individual's uniqueness, they posit an essential "unknowability" between groups. This unknowability is considered traversible through aspects of identity that are held in common across these groups, but the increasing proliferation of categories of knowable selves and "unknowable" others means that, ultimately, no one can fully understand anyone else.

Introducing the notion of "positionality" to pedagogical and epistemological formulations changes this situation. It suggests that rather than being composed of any fixed "essence" or individual identity, we all develop amid networks of relationships that themselves can be explored, analyzed, and changed, as long as people understand that they are *not* simply individuals, but differentially placed members of an unequal social order. It is in this context that we might return to WWK's stage of "constructed knowing" and see how it might emerge within positional approaches to knowledge. The authors say, for example, that this "way of knowing and viewing the world began (for several interviewees) as an effort to reclaim the self by attempting to reclaim knowledge that they felt intuitively was personally important with knowledge that they learned from others" (Belenky, Clinchy, Goldberger, & Tarule, 1986, p. 134).

In *The Feminist Classroom*, because of the "state of feminist politics" noted by Grey Osterud, one of our teacher participants, here and by us earlier, discussions that represented such positional approaches to the formation of knowledge and identity were quite rare. However, discussions interpreted this way offer some insights about the social construction of classroom knowledge that reflect the struggles with diversity and identity engaging feminist theory and offer clues to some contexts within which "constructed knowing" can be developed.

As one possible example, the following discussion focused on the need for people in oppressed groups to name themselves, and the simultaneous pitfalls of this need. It took place in a coeducational liberal arts college, in the course Feminism in Historical Perspective/Feminist Theory, which is the final course in the college's Gender Studies program. In this particular discussion, students of color (although only three in a class of thirty) dominated (Maher & Tetreault, 1994, pp. 108–113). In a classroom dialogue provoked by the absence of race in Sheila Rowbothams's *Women's Consciousness, Man's World,* an African American student named Roy used the language of margin and center to suggest the relationship between identity and positionality:

> In a way to get at the center you have rings of light to bring to light what is marginal and spread it. And the only way to do that being a woman or being a Black person whose experience is marginalized, you have to talk about that experience, you have to establish some kind of identity.

A white female student asked next how blacks could "gain strength as individuals trying to deal with white people," in a subtle acknowledgment of racism. Cheryl, a Filipina American, and Roy took up her question to explore the necessity for people of color to form an identity in opposition to the dominant culture. But such visibility is "threatened, dangerous," because it exposes some people as marginal without exposing the relations of marginality; it leaves the relations of domination, the center, in darkness:

CHERYL: But they all have to form an identity first . . . but in a lot of ways it doesn't exist, in that it is so threatened given—
ROY: I think it's dangerous to form, the question of whether we have the wherewithal to form groups without first knowing who you are.
NICK (A WHITE MALE): But if identity, if group consciousness is necessary for you to acquire an identity then you are caught in a vicious circle.
ROY: Caught in the loop again.
CHERYL: You know just part of it is the individual knowing his or her cultural experience, historical experience.

A few comments later Beth, a student who described herself as "mixed Hispano and Native American," said:

> And sometimes I think about marginal people just sort of floating around not really being able to name what is going on, not really knowing your identity. It's just knowing that for some reason they're not up there with the rest of society and that just finding names and creating an identity through naming together takes a big thing.

ROY: It's a good thing for a while, it's a good springboard but I don't think you can really carry it with you. If you carry it with you, you're just carrying with you those same notions of those distinctions between me or we, me and them, or me and you or us and them. The celebration of difference gets you into a a different bind.

BETH (LATER): I think one thing interesting about learning political language that the mainstream culture understands [is] so that you can as an oppressed group be validized. But once you learn how to communicate then I think it is necessary to go back to your own language, your own identity, your own culture and I guess they, we, the marginal people face sort of a problem on the one hand to be autonomous and form an identity and reevaluate it on the other hand, be able to communicate to—

ROY: So there will always be a double consciousness, sisters under the veil.

To Cheryl's point that most feminist theory is written by white women "with their ideologies and values," Roy replies,

> But that's the whole point, that's how language is used to oppress people. People close the doors and talk about all this stuff and I'm saying that theory provides a key to that door—it also presents a way of changing meaning, changing the way things are.

In the book, we commented that "this discussion dramatizes the tensions inherent in the interplay of personal voice, the languages of theory and experience, and the construction of personal identities. It shows what can happen when personal narratives of race and gender oppression and invisibility emerge into public discourse and intersect in the classroom." This dialogue also may be read as an example of the challenge, difficulty, and even pain of struggling out of identity politics into a more positional state of mind. Cheryl speaks both of individual experience and of the broader issues of "cultural experience, historical experience"; she, Beth, and Roy then explore the ramifications of needing to formulate group identities without being trapped by the societally inferior positions forced on those identities by the dominant culture. By "double consciousness" they mean the need to situate their formulations of themselves in different ways for different contexts, working through changing forms of representation and self-construction to a point where language and theory, rather than being used to oppress people, can be used to "change meaning, change the way things are." This is an example, then, of a push from identity politics to positionality.

However, this discussion could also fruitfully be read as an instance in which not individuals, but a *group*, struggles with the transitions from subjective knowing, through procedural knowing, to a kind of constructed knowing hinted at in the end. The students begin with identity, conceptualized as "group consciousness," but then seem to seek outside knowledge in the form of "cultural and historical experiences." Significantly, this turn to the procedures and knowledges of the disciplines doesn't help them very much; the "political language" of the mainstream culture offers a validation of oppression, but no means of communication for them within its terms. Therefore, as in the transition from procedural to constructed knowing, these students need to include their own perspectives.

Yet because the view from the mainstream disciplines, the dominant culture, is different from theirs, this move leads not to an integrated epistemology, but rather to a double consciousness. This is not an individual journey so much as a search for broader, theoretical explanatory frameworks to fit group experiences, frameworks that neither fix people in stereotypic molds *nor* assimilate them into the mainstream only as individuals. These students are therefore led to articulate the need for a new language and a new theory, one that does not oppress them in the ways practiced by the dominant discourse. Ultimately, they want to construct their own theory—to "change the way things are," by transforming the meaning-making apparatus itself. Indeed, the major challenge to the achievement of constructed knowing in diverse communities of knowers may be how it develops when different constructions are under dispute, and when those disputes themselves reflect the differential place of various constructions of "identity" in an unequal society.

THE CHALLENGES OF POWER RELATIONS
TO COMMUNITIES OF KNOWING:
THE EXAMPLE OF WHITENESS

In *The Feminist Classroom*, as in women's studies and feminist theory until recently, the focus was on the emergence of the stories and experiences of hitherto marginalized groups, and the effects of this emergence on the classroom. However, the use of the theme of positionality to analyze classroom discourse has also pushed us to formulate new research questions for ourselves, going along with more recent developments in feminist and postmodern theory. We have now decided to revisit our classroom vignettes and observe them not from the viewpoint of the marginalized, but rather from a perspective that looks at the *relationships* of margin and center. As Grey Osterud mentioned to us in 1993, "Your whole section (on positionality) treats positionality as it arises from marginality. It doesn't make the dominant position clear. So much feminist theory comes from understanding marginality. Feminists from the dominant group haven't even noticed."

We have thus completed an essay on "whiteness," in which we explore the ways in which assumptions of whiteness as the norm, and the pervasiveness of white privilege, create racialized relationships of oppression within which all identities are embedded (Frankenberg, 1993; McKintosh, 1988; Tatum, 1992). Going back again to the two classroom vignettes, we can now note that the failure to name whiteness, even as an identity, created impossible stumbling blocks to positional understandings in both discussions. That is, only people of color are forced into having an identity; if whiteness were revealed, then the other identities, far from being "essential" or fixed attributes of individuals, would be revealed as markers of unequal places in complex sets of power relations.

As in the postmodern insight that the notions "man" and "woman" rely for their basic conceptualizations on their opposition to each other, so, also, and perhaps even more so, there is no such essential identity as "blackness." Rather, the concept of blackness, or being "of color," maintains the set of polar opposites by which an assumed and "normal," unracialized, illusory, and pure white world is developed, defended, and constantly maintained without ever being spelled out. Not only are "white" and "black" or "of color" always constructed in relation to each other, they never existed except as they construct each other. Whiteness is a category, a "political color," that not only justifies racialized oppressions of nonwhite others, but represents a falsified and idealized self-identification that needs blackness in order to exist (Roediger, 1994).

Thus we can now see in the *Sula* excerpt the resistance in the student's journal entry to naming the power relations governing the difficulties for "black and white women to understand and interpret each other's literature intelligently." We can also see Cheryl's, Roy's, and Beth's struggle with identities in a new way. It was partly the silent assumption of whiteness as the norm that channeled the conversation, stilled its possibilities, and frustrated Roy's attempts to cast light on the center. What is that center, if not the whiteness (and other forms of privilege) of the dominant culture? As Beth put it, "Marginal people are just sort of floating around, not really being able to name what is going on, not really knowing your identity," because the others will not reveal theirs; the mainstream culture will not look at itself.

In our ongoing look at our own data through the shifting lenses of positionality, we can see a new role for constructed knowing, and that is as part of a much broader view of feminist theory and women's studies than was possible when WWK was first published. Constructed knowing, articulated not only as a perspective within individual development but as a means for looking at communities of knowledge as well, may show us how to get beyond the traps of identity politics, both within the classroom and beyond it (see also Harding, this volume). Indeed, feminist theorists and others have begun to look at race, gender, sexuality, culture, and other issues in a "constructed" (and constantly changing) way, as indicating complex dynamics of power relationships within which the operations of the dominant groupings have begun to be analyzed as well.

Meanwhile, however, opponents of feminism have been using the weaknesses of cultural feminism and identity politics to attack the whole field of women's studies and multicultural education (Patai & Koertge, 1994; Sommers, 1994). Partly these critiques represent the rightward shift in the academy and in the society as a whole, wherein assaults on women's studies are used to justify the current backlash against feminism, against the left, and against all social welfare programs. But to the extent that they pick up on weaknesses in feminism, it is the weaknesses of cultural feminism, of identity politics, and of the epistemology of subjective knowing that these theories rely on, that they are attacking. When they dichotomize "subjective experience" and "objective research," they are reflecting (and excoriating) the dichotomies first raised in bifocal scholarship, and in their desire to return to the traditional classroom they simply reinscribe those dichotomies to the detriment of women. In short, they want to return to "received knowing."[3] But the feminist movement has gone beyond this, and we may now be in a position to recreate constructed knowing as a desired epistemology, not only of individual students and learners, but of women's studies classrooms and feminist theory as well.

Catherine Stimpson recently spoke of the needs articulated by students in Women's Studies classes today:

> First, they want to hear their own stories, both personal narratives and histories of the groups in which they claim membership. But no matter how necessary these stories are, they are not sufficient. They also want large, cohering narratives, and unless women's studies can write them in accessible language, they will turn elsewhere.
>
> My students want to learn how the postmodern global economy works and

how to find a place in it from which they can support themselves and their families—however they define family. . . . The desire for a helpful economic narrative crosses class, gender and racial lines—a defining feature of a big, sprawling, multicultural center. [Finally], they are suspicious of a stress on individual rights that seems to ignore social relations. They like the feminist political theory that seems to connect the self with others; that reassures them that they are free, feminists, and active members of human communities. (Stimpson, 1995, pp. 12, 13)

These needs speak to our responsibilities as feminist academics, to understand, if not to focus on, the theoretical approaches we use in the classroom with the multiplication of topics that must be addressed. We must look at not only sexuality but acquired immunodeficiency syndrome (AIDS), not only the second shift but the global economy's differential effects on women and men, not only domestic violence (in both senses of the word *domestic*) but the global violence against women as refugees and victims of war. We must approach these topics not simply as separate problems or "experiences" for different groups of women, or as matters of "objective" study, but through a focus on the relationships among these issues and among those most affected by them. Then we may be helping our students to locate themselves in the multiple contexts necessary for them to find their way.

In a recent Feminist Theory class, my students were eager to talk about the complex connections they felt to women in the Third World; they were most engaged by readings that situated them as recipients of class, race, and political privilege in relation to other women. These positional understandings helped them, like many of the informants in our book, make sense of themselves not just as individuals but as occupants of a certain place in the world. In *The Feminist Classroom*, we used the following quote from a student as an example of the positional understanding that comes with constructed knowing, and vice versa.

One of the things that came out in class was that (a certain poem) was about a woman going through a lesbian experience. It had never occurred to me that the woman had chosen to have sexual experiences with women. It never entered my mind. I realized that there was a lot I didn't see. I was looking at things in my own views. I really liked finding that out. I mean I really *liked* finding out that I was limited. One of the things I found out about myself in that course was that I really tried; that I had a tolerant attitude towards others. I thought all people were alike, but what I really believed was that they were all like me. You know? Even black people. Black people can be like black people, you know, their own cultures, their own ethnic views. I always thought in terms of myself. (Maher & Tetreault, 1994, p. 96)

It is in the development of constructed knowing, as the epistemological stage whereby these perspectives are gained, that WWK continues to offer the most important insights. However, because we are always in the act of being "constructed" within communities of knowers, it is important to make those communities as diverse and broad as possible in the classroom, to counteract the increasing isolation of individuals and groups in contemporary society. It is important to see constructed knowing as a function of whole communities of learning, as well as of individuals. This is still the main contemporary challenge for feminist theory, women's studies, and feminist pedagogies both within and outside the classroom.

NOTES

1. There is some confusion over the terminologies used for these theories, and the relative emphasis given in each articulation to each group's "essence" (which is usually the basis of "identity" theories) *versus* their societal position and the contribution people occupying that position make to feminist knowledge construction (which is usually the basis of "standpoint" theories). In terms of these distinctions, *positionality*, described later in terms of feminist political theorist Linda Alcoff's work, may be seen partly as a further extension of standpoint theory.

   However, positionality suggests not only the importance of position but also, unlike standpoint theories, that positions are mutually constructed, rooted in issues of language and representation, and therefore always changing and changeable. Although the lines are thin, I mean to draw a distinction here between both "identity" politics and "standpoint" theories, on the one hand, and "positionality," on the other, on the basis that the former generalize about all members of a particular group as in some way fixed, and also reflect a notion of language as a transparent reflection of an unchanging "reality." See Sandra Harding's essay in this volume for another series of extensions on these ideas.

2. Spelman College recently instituted a course on the African diaspora. See also Rosaldo (1989, 1990), and Nancy Goldberger's essay in this volume.

3. For example, in a critical review of *The Feminist Classroom*, historian Elizabeth Fox Genovese remarks, "The authors tie good teaching to an emphasis on subjective experience. . . . Objective knowledge and the authority it pretends to convey emerge as the main dragons for our feminist pedagogues to slay" (Genovese, 1994).

REFERENCES

Alcoff, L. (1988). Cultural feminism versus post-structuralism: The identity crisis in feminist theory. *Signs, 13*(3): 405–436.

Belenky, M. Clinchy, B., Goldberger, N., Tarule, J. (1986). *Women's ways of knowing: The development of self, voice, and mind.* New York: Basic Books.

Bunch, C., & Pollack, S. (Eds.) (1983). *Learning our way: Essays in feminist education.* Trumansberg, NY: The Crossing Press.

Chinosole (1994). Dear Mary Kay and Frinde: Reflections on a five-year dialogue about feminist pedagogy. *Concerns: Women's Caucus for the Modern Languages, 24*(2), 25–29.

Collins, P. H. (1990). *Black feminist thought: Knowledge, consciousness and the politics of empowerment.* Boston: Unwin Hyman.

Culley, M., & Portuges, C. (Eds.) (1985). *Gendered subjects: The dynamics of feminist teaching.* London: Routledge & Kegan Paul.

Davis, B. H. (Ed.) (1985). *"Feminist education"*, Special Topic Edition of *The Journal of Thought: An Interdisciplinary Quarterly,* Vol. 20, 2, Fall.

Ellsworth, E. (1992). Why doesn't this feel empowering? Working through the repressive myths of critical pedagogy. In Luke, C. & Gore, J. (Eds.), *Feminisms and Critical Pedagogy,* 90-119. New York and London: Routledge.

Feminist Teacher. Norton, MA: Wheaton College.

Frankenberg, R. (1993). *White women, race matters: The social construction of whiteness.* Minneapolis: University of Minnesota Press.

Freire, P. (1970). *The pedagogy of the oppressed.* New York: Continuum.

Genovese, E. F. (1994, November 6). Teaching and the gender agenda: A review of *The feminist classroom. Education Review, Washington Post,* 1–3.

Gilligan, C. (1982). *In a different voice: Psychological theory and women's development.* Cambridge, MA: Harvard University Press.

Harding, S. (1992). *Whose science? Whose knowledge? Thinking from women's lives.* Ithaca, NY: Cornell University Press.

Harding, S. (1994). Thinking from the perspective of lesbian lives. In Herrman, A. C., & Stewart, A. (Eds.), *Theorizing feminism: Parallel trends in the humanities and social sciences*, 343–357. Boulder, CO: Westview Press.

Herrman, A. C., & Stewart, A. (Eds.) (1994). *Theorizing feminism: Parallel trends in the humaniti· ·nd social sciences*. Boulder, CO: Westview Press.

Kenway, J., & Modra,)92). Feminist pedagogies and emancipatory possibilities. In Luke, C., & Gore, J. (Eds.), *Feminisms and critical pedagogy*. (pp. 138–166). New York and London: Routledge.

Luke, C., & Gore, J. (Eds.) (1992). *Feminisms and critical pedagogy*. New York and London: Routledge.

McKintosh, P. (1988). *Understanding correspondences between white privilege and male privilege through women's studies work*. Unpublished paper.

Maher, F. A. (1985a). Classroom pedagogy and the new scholarship on women. In Culley, M., & Portuges, C. (Eds.), *Gendered subjects: The dynamics of feminist teaching*, 29–48. London: Routledge & Kegan Paul.

Maher, F. A. (1985b). Pedagogies for the gender balanced classroom. *Journal of Thought*, 20(3), 48–64.

Maher, F. A. (1987). Toward a Richer Theory of Feminist Pedagogy. *Journal of Education*, Vol. 169(3), 91–99.

Maher, F. A., & Tetreault, M. K. T. (1994). *The feminist classroom: An inside look at how professors and students are transforming higher education for a diverse society*. New York: Basic Books.

Minnich, E. K., O'Barr, J., & Rosenfeld, R. (Eds.) (1988). *Reconstructing the academy: Women's education and women's studies*. Chicago: University of Chicago Press.

Patai, D., & Koertge, N. (1994). *Professing feminism: Cautionary tales from the strange world of women's studies*. New York: Basic Books.

Roediger, D. (1994). *Towards the abolition of whiteness: Essays on race, politics and working class history*. London and New York: Verso.

Rosaldo, R. (1989). *Culture and truth: The remaking of social analysis*. Boston: Beacon Press.

Rosaldo, R. (1990, February). Others of invention: Ethnicity and its discontents. *Village Voice Literary Supplement*, 82, 27–29.

Schniedwind, N., & Maher, F. (Eds.) (1987). Feminist Pedagogy. Special Issue of *Women's Studies Quarterly*, XV, 3, 4.

Schuster, M., & Van Dyne, S. (Eds.) (1985). *Women's place in the academy: Transforming the liberal arts curriculum*. Totowa, NJ: Rowman & Allanheld.

Sommers, C. H. (1994). *Who stole feminism: How women have betrayed women*. NY: Simon & Schuster.

Stimpson, C. (1995). *Women's studies and its discontents*. Unpublished paper given as the Deborah L. Rhode Lecture at Stanford University, May 24.

Tatum, B. D. (1992). Talking about race, learning about racism: the application of racial identity development theory in the classroom. *Harvard Educational Review, 62*(1), Spring 1–24.

Tetreault, M. K. (1985a). Feminist phase theory: An experience-derived evaluation model. *Journal of Higher Education, 56*(4), 363–384.

Tetreault, M. K. (1985b). Phases of thinking about women in history: a report card on the textbooks. *Women's Studies Quarterly, 13*, 35–47.

Tetreault, M. K. (1986a). Integrating women's history: The case of United States history high school textbooks. *The History Teacher, 19*, 211–262.

Tetreault, M. K. (1986b). Its so opinioney. *Journal of Education, 168*(2), 78–95.

Weiler, K. (1991). Freire and a feminist pedagogy of difference. *Harvard Educational Review, 61*(4), 449–474.

6

Unknown Women
and Unknowing Research

Consequences of Color and Class
in Feminist Psychology

VANESSA M. BING
AND PAMELA TROTMAN REID

INTRODUCTION

THE PORTRAYAL OF WOMEN and people of color in both traditional psychology and feminist psychology literature is laden with problems and inaccuracies. This situation is due to several factors: (1) the adoption of a narrow lens through which women and people of color are viewed; (2) a general lack of attention to differences among women, particularly differences based on class and race/ethnicity; and (3) psychologists' frequent use of inappropriate assumptions and strategies when they do attempt the study of women's differences.

Rather than providing a place where the many voices of women could be dissected, understood, and "heard," for many years the discipline of psychology silenced women and undervalued people of color. Further, although considerable progress has been made over the years in breaking through the barriers of sexism, racism, and classism in scientific and psychological research, such barriers remain. Even feminist researchers are

175

implicated in the silencing of women of color and the economically disenfranchised. Thus, it is our contention that there remain large numbers of *unknown* women and *unknowing* research studies in feminist and psychology literature.

In order to extend our knowledge about women in general, we must acknowledge the differences and the tensions that exist between White women and other women. Before we can reconstruct theory and the bases of our research, we must examine past and present assumptions and reassess the intentions of research.

In this paper we plan to (1) provide an overview of the history of psychology's approach to research on women, people of color, and social class differences, noting the trends, issues, and objectives as they have evolved; (2) examine feminist psychology and its treatment of women who have come to be considered "nontraditional" (that is, women of color); and finally, (3) discuss how feminist psychology can begin to approach "knowing" those "other" women through an analysis of the barriers to knowing and suggestions for change.

It is our goal to encourage and stimulate the continued efforts of researchers seeking to develop social constructionist models that explicate women's experiences by providing a historical context and analytic framework for understanding the deficiencies of the past. Further, through such an analysis, we hope to provide continued support for the development and identification of models that are more inclusive and that more adequately describe the experiences of women representing all races and social classes. We believe such models will extend the work begun by Mary Belenky, Blythe Clinchy, Nancy Goldberger, and Jill Tarule, feminist authors and scholars whose seminal work *Women's Ways of Knowing* (WWK) provided an examination of experiential processes unique to women.

A HISTORY OF UNKNOWING RESEARCH: PSYCHOLOGY'S BEGINNINGS

During the late nineteenth century when psychology was emerging as a discipline, there were myriad factors influencing and shaping the direction and attitude psychology would take in the research of women and people of color. The sociopolitical climate was ripe for biased approaches used in such studies as the atmosphere was fraught with overt racism and discriminatory practices. These practices stemmed from a strict adherence to a number of nativistic positions that prevailed at the time. Psychology, which initially began as an extension of philosophy, began to make a paradigm shift in an effort to be legitimized as a true "science." To this end, scientific models grew, largely as a result of early experimentalists such as Gustav Fechner and Wilhelm Wundt. Fechner, a German scholar, physiologist, and psychophysicist, studied sensory perceptions and was considered a forerunner in the development of psychology as a science (as his theories described a relation between the mind and body/the mental and material worlds). Wundt, a physiologist, actually developed a conception of psychology as an independent and experimental science, and was responsible for establishing the opening of the first experimental laboratory at the University of Leipzig in 1879 (thus founding a new science). It was with the establishment of laboratory settings where "hardcore" research could take place.

A EUROCENTRIC AND ANDROCENTRIC PAST

The field of psychology in its beginnings grew out of the scientific models used in the laboratories of Wilhelm Wundt in Germany and William James in the United States. Psychology was inherently biased in that it focused without concern or reflection on male European populations. Further, researchers adopted the philosophy and methodology of empiricism, emphasizing "observable facts" and completely ignoring context. Measurable observation, as the empiricists defined it, relied on the experimental method as the means of developing a pure knowledge base.

Ethnocentric, androcentric, and sexist biases have been revealed in psychology since the late 1800s (Sherif, 1994), and the women's rights movement in the 1960s provided the context for a reexamination of the biased theoretical assumptions that plagued the field. Feminist challenges to psychology called for an examination of the experimental methodologies, the nature of the experimental questions under study, the method of subject selection, the choice of measures (qualitative versus quantitative), and the interpretation of results (Dutton-Douglas & Walker, 1988).

In addition to biased experimental methods, early psychology developed a number of nativistic views, such as social Darwinism, which sanctioned a hierarchical view of people based on racial dimensions. Human differences were seen as the results of internal, innate causes, rather than as responses to environmental influences exacted by society. Social Darwinistic views were used to explain the deficiencies and inadequacies of people of color. Blacks, for example, were typically singled out and regarded as lower forms of people.

Charles Darwin's *Origins of Species* (1859) described evolutionary changes that occurred in nature and introduced the doctrine of "survival of the fittest." Social Darwinism extended this idea by suggesting that only the strongest and most intelligent would survive in the struggle between individual and individual and individual and environment. Darwin's theory recognized the importance of individual differences and placed the onus of an individual's plight on that individual. This view gave credence to the idea and perpetuation of "deficit theories" that would be used to explain the deficiencies of people of African descent and other persons of color. Those of European descent were believed to be "winning" the struggle for survival and were superior to the darker races.

Social Darwinism was one of the bases of conceptual support for imperialistic moves made by the United States and Western Europe in the late nineteenth century, as well as of White supremacy movements including Nazism. These views, along with the promulgation of eugenics (a science of heredity) and theories of heritability (which describe variations caused by genetic differences) to explain intelligence, promoted through the works of British scientist Sir Francis Galton (*Hereditary Genius: Its Laws and Consequences* [1869]; *Natural inheritance* [1889]) and more recently by British educational psychologist Cyril Burt (1959, 1961), American hereditarian Arthur Jensen (1964), and American physicist William Shockley (1966), supported, among other things, the idea that racial improvement could be achieved through selective mating and sterilization of those deemed "unfit."

William McDougall, who has been referred to as the father of social psychology, similarly promulgated a theory of instinct in humans, suggesting that inborn and unlearned response tendencies determined social behavior. He and others provided an explanation for the stereotyping of non-Europeans, particularly Blacks (Guthrie, 1991). Such theories provided fertile ground for research efforts in psychology that would be grounded on racist, biased, and stereotyped views of people of color.

In a review that explored the dynamics of interracial therapy, clinical psychologist Beverly Greene (1986) provided an overview of the history of racism in psychology and noted that such figures as G. Stanley Hall (the first president of the American Psychological Association) referred to Blacks as "a primitive race in a state of immature development" and that psychoanalyst Erik Erikson, writing about Black babies, stated that their sensory experiences "helped to build a slave identity." Psychiatrist

Alexander Thomas and psychologist Samuel Sillen's (1972) seminal work, *Racism and Psychiatry*, similarly exposed psychology's racist assumptions. The following examples are cited by Thomas and Sillen:

• Carl Jung spoke of the "childishness of the Negro" and explained repression in whites as a defensive maneuver against "living together with lower races, especially with Negroes."

• William McDougall demonstrated that "black people have an instinctive need to be pushed around by white people."

• Dr. W. M. Bevis, a psychiatrist at St. Elizabeth's Hospital in Washington, D.C., wrote in the *American Journal of Psychiatry*, that the Black man tries to "compensate for psychic inferiority by imitating the white race." Bevis similarly suggested that the mental development of Negro children "starts freezing at puberty."

• The nineteenth-century statesman John C. Calhoun stated, "The African is incapable of self-care and sinks into lunacy under the burden of freedom. It is a mercy to give him the guardianship and protection from mental death." (This was clearly a rationalization for slavery).

These examples of views held by the pioneer thinkers in psychology demonstrate how in its early years the discipline dealt with people of African descent. Certainly, the average student of psychology is hardly made aware of the racist assumptions and tenets that grounded its beginnings. Other disenfranchised peoples were similarly mischaracterized, and women, of course, were almost totally ignored.

KNOWING AND UNKNOWING: PAST RESEARCH AND THEORY ON WOMEN

It has been recognized for some time that psychology has promulgated biased views about women (Allport, 1954). The sexist views were predicated on an androcentric approach, which relegated women to a status of inferiority. Indeed, psychoanalytic theories must hold some of the responsibility for keeping women in a lesser position in society. Sigmund Freud's early studies on hysteria (Breuer & Freud, 1893; Breuer & Freud, 1895) and his psychosexual theory of human development (Freud, 1905, 1924, 1925) laid the groundwork for erroneous assumptions about women. He not only confirmed some previously existing views (for example, of women as dependent, less competent), he also provided new biases (women as hysterical and masochistic).

Freud's theory of psychosexual development was largely built around the experiences of male children. He attempted to fit females into a masculine schema that culminated in his construction of the theory of the *Oedipus complex*. In this theory, females are seen as deficient and envious of that which they do not possess (the penis). Furthermore, Freud saw the resolution of the Oedipus complex in the formation of the superego, or the moral agency of the psychic structure. The resolution of the Oedipus complex would naturally be more difficult for the female since the formation of the superego was largely tied to "castration anxiety" (fear of losing the penis/fear of mutilation) and ability to identify with the aggressor.

Freud suggested that there would be differences in men and women, in that "for women, what is ethically normal is different from what it is in men." He concluded that women "show less sense of justice than men, that they are less ready to submit to the great exigencies of life, that they are more often influenced in their judgments by feelings of affection or hostility" (Freud, 1925, pp. 257–258).

Other theorists, including Erikson (1950), Swiss psychologist Jean Piaget (1965), and cognitive developmental theorist Lawrence Kohlberg (1969), similarly developed theories that were largely predicated on research conducted with male subjects and (almost as an afterthought) extended their findings to include females. Women have been portrayed as inferior to men along cognitive and social dimensions. Females' capacity for higher-order moral and cognitive development and the attainment of autonomy and competence has, therefore, been seen as limited.

Just as there were challenges to the experimental approaches in psychology, there were similar efforts to correct the ill-conceived theories about women. Beginning with the work of psychoanalyst Clara Thompson in the early half of the century (Thompson, 1941, 1950), feminist theory has attempted to develop a clear psychological explanation of women's development for use by researchers and practitioners of psychotherapy. Thompson's writings challenged existing theories while also addressing the lack of specific hypotheses about women. She asserted that explanations were needed to explicate the unique properties and experiences of the female gender. She did not consider it sufficient merely to offer a reflection or some variant of a theory on men's development.

UNEXPLORED INFLUENCES OF SOCIAL CLASS

In addition to these representations of women as deficient, it was assumed that those with White middle-class backgrounds were the standard to which all others were to be compared (Reid, 1993). The acceptance of this standard has been borne out in a variety of publications that purport to describe the development and behavior of women. Research that has attempted to explicate issues affecting all women has consistently been based on responses obtained from a traditionally limited sample of women. Indeed, authors "flag" those studies that deal exclusively with women of color or other disenfranchised women by advising the reader in the title that the study used a "minority sample." Thus, articles on or about women that *do not* make an ethnic, racial, or class distinction are assumed (and likely) to represent research that has been based on a White middle-class sample.

Feminist scholar and developmental psychologist Pamela Reid and her student Elizabeth Kelly (1994) noted that even in journals dedicated to the study of women, the bias of class and ethnicity was maintained. In the larger psychology literature, UCLA psychologist Sandra Graham (1992) similarly noted the paucity of research dealing explicitly with people of color, but was less clear about class status. A content analysis reported by Reid (1995) of over five hundred psychological abstracts confirmed that social class status is rarely reported and even more seldom analyzed.

UNKNOWN WOMEN: AFRICAN AMERICAN WOMEN

When examining issues of gender that have been obscured by psychological theory and practice, the need to reveal an essential nature of women often arises. This problem, however, is made difficult by a number of fundamental differences among women in their experiences, past and present.

The treatment of women in U.S. society, the expectations of and assumptions about women, all vary greatly, depending on whether one considers the experiences of White women or women of color. Particularly profound are the differences between White and African American women.

Historically, African American female slaves worked alongside their male counterparts, performing tasks (for example, in the cotton fields) that required near-equal levels of strength and endurance. The African American female could not be regarded as a delicate, genteel "fair maiden" to be spared harsh labor. African American women did not share access to the White power structure that was available (albeit marginally) to White women. Ultimately, they had to face a dual burden. No matter what stigma a White woman had to bear, the Black woman had the double burden of dealing with that stigma as it related specifically to her gender, while concomitantly having to cope with the sanctions of racism.

As early as 1851 at the Women's Rights Convention, Black abolitionist and women's rights activist Sojourner Truth highlighted the difference between women of color and White women in their relationship to men (the White power structure) and in the role they played in society. Her well-known eloquent words spoke to the inherent contradictions in the women's movement that created a separation between African Americans and Whites:

> That man over there say that women needs to be helped into carriages, and lifted over ditches, and to have the best place everywhere. Nobody ever helps me into carriages, or over mud-puddles, or gives me any best place! . . . And ain't I a woman? . . . I have ploughed, and planted, and gathered into barns, and no man could head me! And ain't I a woman? I could work as much and eat as much as a man—when I could get it—and bear the lash as well! And ain't I a woman? (Cited in Schneir, 1972, pp. 94–95)

Post–Civil War activities likewise revealed the schism between African American and White women. When African American men received the right to vote, many African American and White suffragists united to protest the continuing exclusion of women. However, some White women, particularly those from the southern states, sought to separate themselves from Blacks. For example, Elizabeth Cady Stanton, a leader in the woman's suffrage movement, used divisive language that pitted White women against African American men. "I protest against the enfranchisement of another man of any race or clime until the daughters of Jefferson, Hancock, and Adams are crowned with their rights" (cited in Hurtado, 1994, p. 139).

Equally disturbing was the language used by Stanton before the New York State Legislature in 1860, which appeared to trivialize the struggles of Blacks in America:

> The prejudice against color, of which we hear so much, is no stronger than that against sex. It is produced by the same cause, and manifested very much in the same way. The negro's skin and the woman's sex are both prima facie

evidence that they were intended to be in subjugation to the White Saxon man. The few social privileges which the man gives the woman, he makes up to the negro in civil rights. The woman may sit at the same table and eat with the white man; the free negro may hold property and vote. The woman may sit in the same pew as the white man in church; the free negro may enter the pulpit and preach. Now with the black man's right to suffrage, the right unquestioned, even by Paul, to minister to at the altar, it is evident that the prejudice against sex is more deeply rooted and more unreasonably maintained than that against color.

Such strategies served to push African American women away from the women's suffrage movement. African American suffragists had not wished to separate themselves from their men, fighting for fair and equal treatment for all. Still, they were perceived by some as disloyal to the "women's cause."

The racism that existed (and to some extent still exists) in the women's rights movement and was exemplified when African American men received the vote, although very startling, did not signify the emergence of the race struggle between African American and White women. The negative sentiments that were felt toward African American women at that time had much to do with the prevailing social order, which deemed Black women to be "morally impure" (hooks, 1981). What is more important to recognize is that White and Black women did not share a common agenda nor perspective on the political and social situation. Neither did they have a common experience. The differential treatment accorded African American and White women during the nineteenth century is discussed by Black feminist and political activist Angela Davis (1981) in her book *Women, Race, and Class*, who notes that Black women consistently struggled in subservient and second-class roles and could not take refuge in the role of the "weaker sex."

Over the years, the differences between White and Black women appeared to some to diminish. Yet, their experiences and access to the power structure continued to contribute to differences in outlook and perception. Thus, the political agenda set by White women seeking entrée and acceptance in the workplace was not viewed as a universal need for all women. Indeed, this was considered of little concern for African American women, who had always worked; Black women never had to make a choice between work and family. In 1960 a Black woman who did not *have* to work was extremely rare and she was typically the talk of the neighborhood and the envy of her peers.

THE PSYCHOLOGY OF GENDER AND ETHNICITY

When ethnicity and gender were considered together, psychology continued to demonstrate its bias and prejudice. The best example may be found in studies on African American women, since the limited research conducted on women of color is based on this group. Psychologists have generally approached the study of African American women by using a deviance model that described women of color as different from the norm. Few researchers explored the strengths or the normative practices of African American women. In fact, many found ways to turn those strengths into weaknesses. Stirred by a report by Daniel Patrick Moynihan in the mid-1960s (Moynihan, 1965), there was a growing interest in the study of the African American family with an eye to understanding its dysfunctional nature. A special focus was an examination of the myriad dysfunctions *caused* by the African American woman.

The "Black matriarchy theory" was developed and used to explain all that was wrong with Black America. It purported to demonstrate how African American women were instrumental in the oppression of African American men and responsible for their continued absence from the home. Scant attention was given to the impact of economic, political, and social injustices that permeated the day-to-day existence of African Americans, and how these factors, rather than the Black female, contributed to the development of problems evidenced in the African American community. Additionally, rather than look at the strengths of African American women who were able to rear families in the absence of male figures, research focused on the African American family's weaknesses and deviations from middle-class American life.

It is interesting to note that the designation of "Black matriarchy," aside from being prejudicial, was also a clear misnomer. The term *matriarch* implies the existence of a social order in which women exercise social and political power (hooks, 1981). This clearly did not reflect the condition of African American women in society. Yet, the label provided an opportunity to tear apart systematically the competency of the African American female. It is illuminating to consider that African American women's ability to demonstrate effective coping (bearing children, raising families, while also performing "manly" work) posed a threat to patriarchal myths about the nature of women and their weaknesses (presumably derived from inherent physiological differences). The fact that African American women were able to perform men's work and survive in the absence of men who held power in society contradicted the existing sexist order. Thus, African American women were derogated, mas-

culinized, and subhumanized because of their competencies (or perceived lack thereof).

Nevertheless, American society remained patriarchal. Furthermore, a
racially imperialistic base, as well as a framework of sexual dominance,
was maintained from the inception of this nation. As hooks (1981)
declares in her discussion of racial imperialism:

> No degree of patriarchal bonding between White male colonizers and Native
> American men overshadowed White racial imperialism. Racism took prece-
> dence over sexual alliances in both the White world's interaction with Native
> Americans and African Americans, just as racism overshadowed any bonding
> between African American women and White women on the basis of sex.
> (hooks, 1981, p. 122)

We do not deny that sexual imperialism is in fact more endemic to societies throughout the world than is racial imperialism. However, in America, racial imperialism, as it has been peculiarly instantiated, may be
found to supersede sexual imperialism in many instances. (This is known
to be a highly debatable point, however, and specific circumstances are
the key to which factor may dominate in any particular setting.)

THE TRIPLE WHAMMY:
GENDER, ETHNICITY, *AND* CLASS

There has been considerable difficulty addressing class in psychological literature, where a "generic norm of middle class status has prevailed,
falling in with the common notion of the United States as a 'classless
society'" (Brown, 1994, p. 69). The scholarly writings of psychologists,
including feminists, have regularly engaged in exclusionary practices by
omitting poor and working-class women. As indicated previously, participants of research studies typically represent White populations from
middle-class backgrounds. There is also a pervasive underlying assumption that addressing issues of racial diversity will subsume the issues of
class, thus perpetuating the dominant culture's stereotype, which equates
middle-class status with White people and poverty with people of color.
While it is true that women of color are disproportionately represented
among poor and working-class women, this does not negate the fact that
White women are the majority group among the poor.

As psychologists we know very little about the experiences, constructions, and worldviews of women living in poverty, since the study of poor

women has been largely ignored in psychological research. There has been some indication that class differences exert influences on a variety of factors including aspirations and social perception. However, we have little to no understanding of the differences that may exist among poor women or women of varying ethnic backgrounds.

We do know that poor people represent a cross section of America and that the majority are women. They are Asian, African American, Latina, and White women. They are teenage mothers, high school dropouts, immigrants, and homeless individuals. They are low wage earners (receptionists, clericals, domestic workers, and college students); they reside in major cities (such as Newark, New York, Chicago, Los Angeles), as well as more rural areas (the mountains of Appalachia and the flat lands of the Midwest); and they hail from varied family and cultural backgrounds, as exemplified in the diversity of their religions, languages, customs, and parenting practices.

The poverty of women, however, must be underscored. Indeed, women constitute over 70 percent of persons with incomes under four thousand dollars per year. This is due in large part to the fact that women generally earn less than their male counterparts, and that a growing number of families are headed by women who are the sole earners. Furthermore, over 46 percent of families with children living in poverty are maintained by women, as compared with less than 8 percent that are maintained by husband–wife teams. The disproportionality of women of color, however, must be noted as a significant feature. Over 50 percent of all families maintained by African American and Latina women are poor, as compared with about 25 percent of families maintained by White women (Rotella, 1990).

The absence of research on poor women and women of color that accurately depicts the issues, problems, and life experiences of this segment of the population is further exacerbated by other research assumptions and practices. There has been, for example, a demonstrated propensity to use women of color when researchers are seeking to uncover *atypical* phenomena, psychopathology, or other nonmainstream behavior. It can be expected, for example, that research on teenage pregnancy, homelessness, and criminal behavior will more often be based on women of color, while more "adaptive concerns" will be addressed through the study of White middle-class women.

The primary consequence of this approach is to pathologize women of color, while leaving their other concerns unaddressed. The continued exclusion of culturally and economically diverse women from research on ordinary problems and issues allows the entire discipline to remain ignorant of the experiences of these women. It also permits their continued relegation to a lowered status typified by criminality, deviance, and dysfunction.

While it is fairly simple to indict psychology on its abuses and failed research practices, it is more important to identify viable suggestions for developing new approaches. Before doing this, however, it is helpful to gain an understanding of the underlying "forces" that have allowed such abuses. Psychology merely represents a discipline within the social sciences that resides in a culture built on a model of oppression. The prevailing practices and zeitgeist of a culture typically dictate the ways in which research is conceived of and pursued. Certainly, the sociopolitical climate in America over the last century has provided the context for ignoring women of color and other disenfranchised groups. A review of the historical context is thus warranted to illuminate how the changing social climate that gave rise to feminist theory and a feminist psychology has shaped and continues to shape the research direction in the psychology of women, and constructionist approaches in feminist literature.

FEMINISM, FEMINIST THEORY, AND WOMEN OF COLOR

Feminist scholars (such as Matina Horner, 1968; Nancy Chodorow, 1978; and Carol Gilligan, 1982) have attempted to refute some of the existing theories and shed light on the inherent problems in conceptualizing women using constructs developed for men. They, along with many others, were instrumental in spearheading the feminist movement in psychology and in advancing feminist discourse and theory. Feminist ideas are based, by and large, on theories that hold that women suffer discrimination as a result of a social inequality and an imbalance of power between men and women. Women have needs that are unmet, and addressing those needs necessitates a radical shift in the social, economic, and political order. Feminism represents the collection of political philosophies that aim to overthrow patriarchy and end inequities and power imbalances based on gender through cultural transformations and radical social change (Brown, 1994). Feminism also assumes a shared experience of all women by virtue of their gender and regards gender-based inequalities in patriarchal society as problems to be eradicated.

Patriarchy is the structure and system where the value of women is obscured or diminished, and where women are devalued through gender-based inequalities in areas such as employment, education, and social activities. The inequities may be subtle (such as the higher cost of dry-cleaning or haircuts) or blatant (exclusion from certain jobs, salary differential in occupations shared by men, derogation of women in lesbian relationships), but they all represent socially sanctioned methods of keeping women in a lesser position than men.

The feminist movement has gradually assumed an essential identity among women, based on the guiding belief that women share the same experiences, including economic oppression, commercial exploitation, and legal discrimination, often leading to feelings of inadequacy and a limited vision of what they can accomplish or achieve. However, this notion of a "shared experience" has not always been useful; rather than being a unifying point, it has actually been at the root of a splintering in the feminist movement, and the subsequent creation of factions divided along racial lines. Feminist scholar Rosalind Delmar notes that "unity based on identity has turned out to be a very fragile thing. What has been most difficult for the women's movement to cope with has been the plethora of differences between women which have emerged in the context of feminism" (Delmar, 1994, p. 7).

FEMINIST THEORIES AND WOMEN OF COLOR

One of the major problems confronting feminist thinking and feminist theories has concerned its application to women of color. In the effort to be inclusive of all women, feminist writings have propagated the use of words that suggest unity, for example, emphasizing the "shared *gender* experience" while negating other experiences of women that are not gender based. This has helped create a paradox in contemporary feminist theory most often revealed through the jargon of "sisterhood," which was intended to reflect the collective voices of all women but in actuality has negated the voices of culturally diverse women (i.e., feminist literature has striven to reflect the voices of Black women, Asian women, Latinas, and Native American women—to name a few—but has in fact failed to represent the voices of these culturally distinct women; the jargon of sisterhood has not reflected the issues and concerns of these women as well as poor women).

There exists an imbalance of power between White women and women of color that is often overlooked in analyses of power imbalances in feminist literature (Greene, 1994). Because the underlying assumption of most feminist theories is that gender alone is the primary locus of oppression, there has been a failure to recognize other forms of oppression (race, sexual orientation). Or, if these factors are recognized, they are often trivialized, with the result that the interaction of these factors is not examined. Feminist scholar Aída Hurtado (1994) makes the point that gender alone does not determine whether a woman holds a superordinate or subordinate position in society. Rather, "socially constructed markers" determine placement and relative power. Race, ethnicity, class, and gender are such markers.

Most feminist theories have not explicitly recognized the relevance or the role of such markers. Thus, feminist discourse has primarily emanated from White educated women who accept the middle-class perspective. While there has been some lip service noting that it is important to include the experiences of diverse women, the writings fail to reflect a fundamental premise—that for women of color, race, class, and gender subordination are experienced *simultaneously* and that the oppressors of women of color are not only their male counterparts, but also White males *and White females.*

THE STATUS OF PRIVILEGE:
REFUTING WHITE FEMINIST PHILOSOPHY

Although White feminists may have made an intellectual commitment to addressing race and class, their experiences living in the dominant culture (with all the rights and privileges that accrue to being White) have undoubtedly affected their perspective. In fact, such privileges have so generally been unexamined that they may have fostered a skewed view and limited understanding of the oppression that women of color experience. Greene (1994) suggests that failure to acknowledge this "locus of privilege" is tantamount to avoidance behavior in the research process as it prevents feminist researchers from inquiring into how this position of privilege is used, why it is used, and whom its use may victimize. Furthermore, such a position allows a tendency to minimize the lack of access of women of color to institutional power and thus further perpetuates their lower status.

Psychologist and women's studies scholar Elizabeth Rave (1990) defines White privilege as all that is conferred to Whites by virtue of their skin color, specifically, the "automatic access" that is bestowed as a result of and living in a historically racist society. True feminists, who presumably believe in the equality of all people, should by definition be antiracist. However, while this may be a theoretically sound position, it does not necessarily reflect reality. Rave (1990) sees this condition as a function of White women's inability to understand the effects of White privilege, to see how White feminists contribute to White privilege, and how they can act against racism.

The "antidote" resides largely in White feminists' learning to become "culturally literate": that is, learning about the diversity within and between cultures and working toward developing respect and understanding for cultural differences. Additionally, it calls for recognizing how White privilege affects Whites as individuals, and how it affects their work, beliefs, values, and actions (Rave, 1990).

The delineation of White privilege and the process of understanding its impact may well be difficult, as they require individuals to regard themselves as both outsiders (oppressed White females fighting for equality) and as insiders (privileged White females who are members of the dominant culture). As clinical psychologist and researcher Maria Root (1990) notes, it is difficult for White feminists to understand how they are the "perpetrator, enforcer, the reinforcers of White privilege" (p. 320).

It has been suggested that White feminists typically focus on agendas that reflect the politicization of the personal (that is, they emphasize issues that arise from their examination of their everyday interactions with men). Feminists of color, on the other hand, have often taken on more "public" issues that affect all people of color (affirmative action, racism, school desegregation, voter registration, and prison reform) (Hurtado, 1994). This emphasis on public issues may be perceived by some feminist activists to reduce or altogether exclude specific gender-based issues.

The divergence of political and personal agendas is not a new phenomenon. Indeed, it has been a recurring point of contention between White feminists and women of color (Reid, 1984). The level of hostility and acrimony that has at times been generated by this fissure is not typically discussed in psychological literature. However, private reactions and daily observations bear witness to it. Such an event was recently experienced by the first author during a stroll through New York City's Greenwich Village.

On a Saturday afternoon two well-dressed White women with placards in hand were attempting to get people (women) to sign a petition against female pornography. In a span of about fifteen minutes, although many had passed, no women of color had stopped either to sign the petition or to inquire about the "cause." This occurrence alone could be loosely interpreted to support the idea of a schism between African American's and White women's agendas. However, a statement made by an African American female passer-by brought more clearly into focus the disparity in African American and White women's views of the other's stance on gender-based issues. The African American female commented to her friend: "These rich White bitches must have entirely too much time on their hands. If women want to make money showing off and selling their bodies, then that's their business!"

Certainly, this street corner remark cannot be taken to represent any one other than the speaker's views on pornography. Yet, we may view it as a sign that women of color are reluctant to align themselves with White women whose focus may be seen as trivial—trivial because the White women appeared to negate the *economic* circumstances of women who choose to appear in pornographic films—a class issue with which more women of color may be able to identify. In this scenario, pornography—a gender-based issue that affects *all* women—was seen as a "White middle-class issue" because the women who were attacking it appeared to be unaware of their own power and economic privilege. Indeed, as long as White middle-class women are believed to be operating on a different agenda that fails to incorporate the experience of women of color and poor women in America, there will be a divide.

In 1981 the African American writer bell hooks argued that most White women were unwilling to surrender allegiance to race, class, and sexual preference in order to bond on the basis of a shared ideology—a shared political belief of "sisterhood." She declared that White women's feminist ideology was both "elitist" and "racist." This assertion has been both confirmed and challenged over the past fifteen years, as researchers and theorists on both sides have begun to address the question of where women of color fit into the feminist agenda (Boyd, 1990; Brown, 1990; Collins, 1991; Greene, 1994; hooks, 1981, 1989; Hurtado, 1994; Reid, 1993; Reid & Kelly, 1994).

BLACK FEMINISM:
DIFFERING FOCI OR OPPOSING IDEOLOGIES

It is clear that within the women's movement, there has historically been a divide along racial lines. Thus, the rise of the Black feminist movement was inevitable. We must note that included in the Black feminist movement are women of African descent from countries outside the United States (for instance, Dutch social researcher Philomena Essed) and Latinas, although the earliest and most visible proponents were African American women.

In addressing Black feminist thinking, the Combahee River Collective, a Boston-based African American feminist collective begun in 1974, wrote, "We believe that sexual politics under patriarchy is as pervasive in Black women's lives as are the politics of class and race. We also find it difficult to separate race from class from sex oppression because in our lives they are most often experienced simultaneously."

The collective also addressed the difference between White and African American women with regard to their relationship to their male counterparts and spoke to African American women's unwillingness to separate from their men: "Although we are feminists and lesbians we feel solidarity with progressive African American men and do not advocate the fractionalization that White women who are separatists demand. Our situation as African American people necessitates that we have solidarity around the fact of race, which White women of course do not have with White men, unless it is their negative solidarity as racial oppressor" (Combahee River Collective, 1982, p. 16).

NEW APPROACHES TO KNOWING WOMEN OF COLOR

Belenky, Clinchy, Goldberger, and Tarule (1986) described "women's ways of knowing" by developing five different perspectives from which to understand how women view their reality and draw conclusions about truth, knowledge, and authority. They illustrated how dramatically different voices of women may be, by including in their sample ethnically and culturally diverse women. However, the voices of economically disadvantaged women and women of color were still, for the most part, unheard. This effort, nonetheless, marked an important step toward demystifying and depathologizing women of color and poor women. Still, further strategies are needed to begin to explain the needs and to hear the voices of the women who are still unknown in psychological research.

It remains important to deconstruct these ways of knowing by examining the differences that occur across racial and class lines and understanding how the different types of "knowing" may appear when placed in a culturally dissimilar context. If we consider the voices of women who have been systematically oppressed because of their race, for example, we can appreciate that these women have had to create different voices—ones that are contextually determined. Similarly, women silenced by their lack of access to education, financial resources, and other types of social power must "speak in tongues" not recognized by those who control what is heard.

It is essential that we examine the silencing of women of color and economically disadvantaged women by "institutional blockouts." Researchers who limit their study of women to geographically and ethnically homogeneous communities risk perpetuating discrimination and tacitly engaging in methods of oppression. Researchers who offer weak "disclaimers" and do not discuss the implications of not having a more representative sample of women similarly contribute to the maintenance of the status quo. The message they appear to send is that the voices of "minority" culture are not important. They imply that women from diverse backgrounds do not count in the formulation of psychological theories and policies.

Culturally derived power relations must also be examined in any attempt to understand women's ways of experiencing the world. Women of color have traditionally held powerful positions within their families. However, this power is stripped in the larger sociopolitical milieu where these women function daily. If we accept the idea that the way a woman "knows" or experiences her world changes as her position changes in an ever-shifting cultural context, we are forced to explore the meaning of context and examine its full implications. Otherwise, we accept the continued derogation of women of color, who already hold a tenuous position in the power structure, and prevent them from having a meaningful voice in society.

In a racially polarized society such as ours, the true voices of women of color may continue to go unheard until researchers find improved ways of communicating (this means listening and hearing them, as well as speaking to them). We must, therefore, call for truly radical paradigm shifts, as well as a thorough reexamination of traditional research strategies. Such radical shifts may represent more "action-oriented" approaches, which, as feminist scholar Patricia Bell Scott (1982) suggests, will inevitably involve the sensitizing of society to the roots and workings of overt, covert, and institutional racism and sexism. Until that time, women's constructions and ways of knowing will continue to be understood from the vantage point of White middle-class women — women who represent only a subsection of the population.

BARRIERS TO KNOWING: TRADITIONAL METHODS, ASSUMPTIONS, AND PRACTICES

Feminist scholars have attempted to debunk traditional experimental methodologies by criticizing not only the approaches used but the value-laden assumptions that undergird many of those questions and choices of measures (Douglas & Walker, 1988). Science, they contend, is not value-free and theories are riddled with biases, inasmuch as ideological biases influence the kinds of research questions raised and the results obtained. Black psychologist and scholar William Hayes (1991) agrees:

> The scientific posture assumed by psychology has led to a selectivity among white psychologists characterized by the unwillingness or inability to hear and process points of view contrary to their own intellectual and cultural biases, except those conclusions of psychological research that are consistent with their biases. (p. 68)

Indeed, psychology has adopted rules of science that allow its practitioners to "find expression for their cultural and racial biases while presenting themselves as scientific investigators of human behavior" (Hayes, 1991, p. 65).

Hayes further contends that there exists a myth of the "scientist" in psychology. This "myth," according to Hayes, would have us believe that the researcher is "objective" and "emotionally detached" and has as his or her only interest "the advancement of knowledge." Hayes refutes this notion and concludes that the psychological researcher is indeed biased given that *what* s/he chooses to investigate is largely a function of his/her interest, knowledge, training and therefore is naturally determined by his/her biases, prejudices, and racism. These practices have resulted in a "cultural elitism" of sorts.

In a critique of psychology's approach to research on women, Reid (1993) has also discussed the problem of elitism. She too notes that some research practices significantly contribute to the misunderstanding of women of diverse backgrounds, these factors are responsible for diminishing the potential for sound research on poor women and women of color. These barriers to knowing women of color Reid labels personal affiliation, effort maximization, and investigator training.

Reid defines *personal affiliation* as the researcher's personal connection and commitment to the area chosen for investigation: male psychologists' interest in studying men; female psychologists' interest in women; gay and lesbian psychologists' interest in gays and lesbians; and ethnic minorities' interest in studying other minorities reflect such personal commitments. Of course, self-interest need not be construed as having a deleterious influence. In fact, it can be credited with bringing investigators' assumptions into clear view. Previously, investigators were assumed to approach their subjects of study with the same subjectivity with which one might study inanimate objects; this is no longer assumed. Thus, it has become necessary for psychologists, whether they are examining populations with backgrounds different from or similar to their own, to make explicit their personal biases and experiences.

Effort maximization is a concern for getting the most benefit for the work involved in conducting research. Reid and Roseanne Flores (in press) note that research on working-class and poor populations typically requires greater effort than similar studies on middle-class populations. Poor "subjects" are likely to reside in different communities and speak a different language from the researcher conducting the investigation. Further, they may hold attitudes or suspicions (founded or unfounded) that are likely to make them less cooperative. Standard measures may be useless in this population. Thus, constructing more culturally appropriate measures, pilot testing, and attempting to establish "norms" for these new measures may require extensive effort. This raises the financial costs of the research and may diminish the cost–benefit ratio. These issues, coupled with the fact that many of the more traditional and prestigious journals in psychology appear to be less interested in publishing such topics (as is evidenced by the dearth of research concerning minority and poor populations), provide already reluctant researchers with enough "reasons" for backing away from studying such topics, judging them to be less than viable research.

Investigator training contributes negatively in two ways to the access to information about diverse women. First, most psychologists and researchers are trained to conduct research in a traditional manner (with assumptions based on White middle-class standards). Second, training to consider diverse populations is considered unnecessary for the scientific base of the discipline. Thus, psychologists are not trained to work with ethnically, culturally, and economically diverse populations. Such training, if it is offered at all, is very limited and typically considered outside any academic core. Even for researchers and practitioners who will consider diverse populations in their daily work, specific training for poor or female or ethnic populations is not mandated in the clinical or research curriculum.

Academic institutions largely comprise faculty members who represent the dominant culture and whose training reflects a Eurocentric and androcentric bias. Indeed, more traditionally trained academicians often use the ideology of "academic freedom" and the guise of "traditional standards" to protect the status quo. They typically assert that academic freedom means that they cannot be "forced" to infuse the content of their courses or investigations with issues of race or class. It is interesting to note how often such issues are deemed inappropriate or irrelevant to their investigations even though no evidence has been collected to substantiate such a claim.

The lack of explicit training in areas of cultural differences received by psychologists and other researchers severely limits the outcomes of psychological investigations. Limited exposure to low-income and/or ethnic populations diminishes a researcher's ability to interpret results appropriately. A poorly developed theoretical base renders it almost impossible for a researcher to prepare himself or herself to choose the appropriate methodology and tools to assess and interpret results adequately.

Researchers Kevin Allison, Isaiah Crawford, Ruben Echemendia, LaVome Robinson, and Dave Knepp's (1994) research shows that training opportunities in working with diverse populations have been limited in applied psychology programs. Few respondents in their sample indicate feeling competent to provide services to individuals in most of the ethnic and diverse groups studied. Graduates report limited access to courses in cultural diversity and restricted opportunities for working with clients from specific cultural groups. Martha Bernal and Felipe Castro, researchers at the Hispanic Research Center at Arizona State University (1994), also indicate that training in the area of cultural competency is seriously limited, basing their conclusions on comparisons of data collected in 1979–80 and 1990–91 that examined the training status of clinical psychologists for service research with ethnically diverse populations.

Clinical psychologist Laura Brown (1994) acknowledges that during the first twenty years or so of feminist therapy, the contributions of therapists and theorists of color, working-class and poor therapists, and other scholars from marginalized groups were underrepresented. Literature that focused on multiply oppressed people was considered "special interest" topics—of interest only to those therapists who chose to work with "special populations." Consequently, it has only been since the late 1980s that feminist therapists in the dominant culture have been more proactive in seeking information about and collaborating with culturally diverse people. And even this only resulted from challenges by those marginalized groups who demanded that feminist therapists live up to their professed standards of antioppression and inclusion.

CONCLUSIONS AND RECOMMENDATIONS

Although feminism is theoretically based on an ideology that opposes social oppression, the guiding philosophy does not necessarily include opposition to racist and class-biased tenets and beliefs. Feminist theories in and of themselves do not offer protection to women of color against oppression that is a function of race nor to women in poverty. Indeed, much of feminist literature may be interpreted as instrumental in promulgating divisive ideology. To ignore racism by assuming that all women have universal concerns based on gender alone has been to perpetuate a power imbalance between White women and "other" women. Similarly, ignoring the oppression of poverty is as insidious as neglecting gender differentials in society. Middle- and upper-class White women continue to hold a position of privilege in U.S. society and White feminist theory must acknowledge this position and the inherent power it affords. Avoidance of this issue will only deepen the divide between women representing the dominant culture and "other" women.

Only a few White feminist writers have honestly and openly acknowledged the failings in feminist theory. Brown (1994), for example, writes,

> While any feminist theory should reflect all forms of human diversity, this standard has rarely been met. White writers on feminist therapy have too often only given lip service to the importance of diverse and complex visions of human behavior. They have tended to develop theories by and about women of European heritage and then simply comment in passing that what they have said probably applies to people from other oppressed groups as well. (Brown, 1994, p. 69)

As researchers and feminist theorists, psychologists (both male and female) must adopt as a goal construction of new ways of examining and understanding women of diverse backgrounds. In recent years standards for nonsexist research have been adopted by most authors and editors. Now, adoption of nonracist and nonclassist standards must follow. The inclusion of information about the ethnicity of participants in research studies must be required along with explanations for the use of single ethnic or racial populations.

While feminist psychology continues to develop, and as researchers explicate further the ways in which women know and experience their worlds, it is essential for this research to be embedded in a philosophy that recognizes both the "universal" experiences of women and the "unique" experiences of women: being physically challenged or otherwise "able"; having an ethnic and cultural heritage and racial history that uniquely distinguish one from all other women; being economically disadvantaged and set apart from the privileged of society;

being sexually oriented to one's same sex; and experiencing all of these unique attributes *while* being a woman in a patriarchal society. Without this understanding, we stand the risk of continuing oppression and perpetuating ignorance in the guise of conducting scientific inquiry.

REFERENCES

Allison, K. W., Crawford, I., Echemendia, R., Robinson, L., & Knepp, D. (1994). Human diversity and professional competence: Training in clinical and counseling psychology revisited. *American Psychologist, 49* (9), 792–796.

Allport, G. (1954). *The nature of prejudice.* Cambridge, MA: Addison-Wesley.

Belenky, M. F., Clinchy, B. M., Goldberger, N. R., & Tarule, J. M. (1986). *Women's ways of knowing: The development of self, voice, and mind.* New York: Basic Books.

Bernal, M. A. & Castro, F. G. (1994). Are clinical psychologists prepared for service and research with ethnic minorities? Report of a decade of progress. *American Psychologist, 49* (9), 797–805.

Boyd, J. A. (1990). Ethnic and cultural diversity: Keys to power. In L. Brown & M. P. P. Root (Eds.), *Diversity and complexity in feminist therapy.* New York: Harrington Park Press.

Breuer, J., & Freud, S. (1893/1959). On the psychical mechanism of hysterical phenomena: A preliminary communication. In E. Jones (Ed.) *Sigmund Freud: Collected papers* Vol. 1, 24–41. New York: Basic Books.

Breuer, J., & Freud, S. (1895/1955). *Studies on hysteria.* New York: Basic Books.

Brown, L. (1990) The meaning of a multicultural perspective for theory-building in feminist therapy. In L. Brown & M. P. P. Root (Eds.) *Diversity and complexity in feminist therapy.* New York: Harrington Park Press.

Brown, L. (1994). *Subversive dialogues.* New York: Basic Books.

Burt, C. (1959) Class differences in general intelligence. *British Journal of Statistical Psychology, 12,* 15–33.

Burt, C. (1961). Intelligence and social mobility. *British Journal of Statistical Psychology, 14,* 3–24.

Chodorow, N. (1978). *The reproduction of mothering.* Berkeley: University of California Press.

Collins, P. H. (1991). *Black feminist thought: Knowledge, consciousness and the politics of empowerment.* New York: Routledge.

Combahee River Collective. (1982). A black feminist statement. In G. T.

Hull, P. B. Scott, & B. Smith (Eds.), *But some of us are brave*. New York: The Feminist Press.

Combahee River Collective. (1994). The Combahee River Collective Statement. In A. C. Hermann & A. J. Stewart (Eds.), *Theorizing feminism: Parallel trends in the humanities and social sciences*, 26–33. Boulder, CO: Westview Press.

Davis, A. Y. (1981) *Women, race, and class*. New York: Vintage.

Delmar, R. (1994). What is feminism? In A. C. Hermann & A. J. Stewart (Eds.), *Theorizing feminism: Parallel trends in the humanities and social sciences*, 5–25. Boulder, CO: Westview Press.

Dutton-Douglas, M. A., & Walker, L. E. (1988). Introduction to feminist therapies. In M. A. Dutton-Douglas & L. E. Walker (Eds.), *Feminist psychotherapies: Integration of therapeutic and feminist systems*. Norwood, NJ: Ablex.

Erikson, E. (1950). *Childhood and society*. New York: W.W. Norton.

Essed, P. (1991). *Understanding everyday racism: An interdisciplinary theory*. Newbury Park, CA: Sage.

Freud, S. (1905/1962). *Three essays on the theory of sexuality*. New York: Basic Books.

Freud, S. (1924). The passing of the Oedipus Complex. In E. Jones (Ed.), *Sigmund Freud: Collected papers* Vol. 2, 269–276. New York: Basic Books.

Freud, S. (1925/1959) Some psychological consequences of the anatomical distinction between the sexes. In E. Jones (Ed.), *Sigmund Freud: Collected papers* Vol. 5, 186–197. New York: Basic Books.

Galton, F. (1869). *Hereditary genius: Its laws and consequences*. London: Macmillan.

Galton, F. (1889). *Natural intelligence*. London: Macmillan.

Gilligan, C. (1982) *In a different voice*. Cambridge, MA: Harvard University Press.

Graham, S. (1992). Most of the subjects were white and middle class. *American Psychologist, 47* (5), 629–639.

Greene, B. (1986). When the therapist is white and the patient is black: Considerations for psychotherapy in the feminist heterosexual and lesbian communities. *Women & Therapy, 5*, 41–66.

Greene, B. (1994). Diversity and difference: Race and feminist psychotherapy. In M. P. Mirkin (Ed.), *Women in context: Toward a feminist reconstruction of psychotherapy*, 333–351. New York: Guilford Press.

Goldberger, N. (in press). Women's constructions of truth, self, authority and power. In H. Rosen & K. Kuehlwein (Eds.), *Constructing realities: Meaning making perspectives for psychotherapists*. San Francisco: Jossey-Bass.

Guthrie, R. V. (1976). *Even the rat was white: A historical view of psychology*. New York: Harper & Row.

Guthrie, R. V. (1991). The psychology of African Americans: An historical perspective. In R. L. Jones (Ed.), *Black Psychology* (3rd ed.), 33–45. Berkeley, CA: Cobb & Henry.

Hayes, W. A. (1991). Radical Black behaviorism. In R. L. Jones (Ed.), *Black Psychology* (3rd ed.), 65–78. Berkeley, CA: Cobb & Henry.

hooks, b. (1989). *Talking back: Thinking feminist, thinking Black.* Boston: South End Press.

hooks, b. (1981). *Ain't I a woman: Black women and feminism.* Boston: South End Press.

Horner, M. (1968). *Sex differences in achievement motivation and performance in competitive and noncompetitive situations.* Doctoral dissertation, University of Michigan, University Microfilms #6912135.

Horner, M. (1972). Toward an understanding of achievement related conflicts in women. *Journal of Social Issues, 28,* 157–175.

Hurtado, A. (1994). Relating to privilege: Seduction and rejection in the subordination of white women and women of color. In A. C. Hermann & A. J. Stewart (Eds.), *Theorizing feminism: Parallel trends in the humanities and social sciences,* 136–154. Boulder, CO: Westview Press.

Jensen, A. R. (1969). How much can we boost I.Q. and scholastic achievement? *Harvard Educational Review, 39,* 1–23.

Kohlberg, L. (1969). Stage and sequence: The cognitive-developmental approach to socialization. In D. A. Goslin (Ed.), *Handbook of socialization theory and research.* Chicago: Rand McNally.

Kohlberg, L. (1966). A cognitive developmental analysis of sex roles concepts and attitudes. In E. Maccoby (Ed.), *The development of sex differences,* 82–173. Stanford: Stanford University Press.

Moynihan, D. P. (1965). *The negro family: The case for national action.* Washington, DC: Office of Policy, Planning and Research, U.S. Department of Labor.

Piaget, J. (1965). *The moral judgment of the child.* New York: Free Press.

Rave, E. (1990). White feminist therapists and anti-racism. In L. S. Brown & M. P. Root (Eds.), *Diversity and complexity in feminist therapy,* 313–326. New York: Harrington Park Press.

Reid, P. T. (1984). Feminism versus minority group identity: Not for Black woman only. *Sex Roles, 10* (3/4), 247–253.

Reid, P. T. (1993). Poor women in psychological research: Shut up and shut out. *Psychology of Women Quarterly, 17,* 133–150.

Reid, P. T. & Flores, R. (in press). Homelessness as a point on the continuum of poverty.

Reid, P. T. & Kelly, E. (1994). Research on women of color: From ignorance to awareness. *Psychology of Women Quarterly, 18,* 477–486.

Reid, P. T. (1995). *Gender, ethnicity, class and culture in the developmental psychology class.* Paper presented at the sixty-first biennial meeting of the Society for Research in Child Development, Indianapolis, IN.

Root, M. P. P. (1990). Resolving "other" status: Identity development of biracial individuals. In L. S. Brown and M. P. Root (Eds.), *Diversity and complexity in feminist therapy*, 185–205. New York: Harrington Park Press.

Rotella, E. J. (1990) Women and the American economy. In S. Ruth (Ed.), *Issues in feminism: An introduction to women's studies*. Mountainview, CA: Mayfield.

Schneir, M. (1972). *Feminism: The essential historical writings*. New York: Vintage Books.

Scott, P. B. (1982). Debunking Sapphire: Toward a non-racist and non-sexist social science. In G. T. Hill, P. B. Scott, & B. Smith (Eds.), *But some of us are brave*. New York: The Feminist Press.

Sherif, C. W. (1994). Bias in psychology. In A. C. Hermann & A. J. Stewart (Eds.), *Theorizing feminism*, 117–135. Boulder, CO: Westview Press.

Shockley, W. (1966). Possible transfer of metallurgical and astronomical approaches to the problem of environment versus ethnic heredity. Quoted in A. Thomas & S. Sillen (1972). *Racism and psychiatry*. Secaucus, NJ: Citadel.

Thomas, A. & Sillen, S. (1972). *Racism and psychiatry*. Secaucus, NJ: The Citadel Press.

Thompson, C. M. (1941). The role of women in this culture. In J. Strouse (Ed.), *Women and analysis*, 245–277. New York: Grossman.

Thompson, C. M. (1950). Some effects of the derogatory attitude toward female sexuality. In C. M. Thompson, M. Mazer, & E. Witenberg (Eds.), *An outline of psychoanalysis*, 409–418. New York: Modern Library.

PART II

New Directions:
Connected
and Collaborative Knowing

Connected and Separate Knowing

Toward a Marriage of Two Minds

BLYTHE MCVICKER CLINCHY

IN WOMEN'S WAYS OF KNOWING (WWK, 1986) Mary Belenky, Nancy Goldberger, Jill Tarule, and I described an epistemological position we called *procedural knowledge*, which took two forms, encompassing two "procedures" that many of the women we interviewed seemed to use in searching for truth; we called them "separate" and "connected" knowing. In the ensuing years, observing the varied and often surprising meanings assigned to these notions by some who have befriended them and the abuse that has been heaped upon them by some of their foes, I have occasionally felt like the character played by Woody Allen in the film *Annie Hall,* who, returning to childhood as an invisible presence, observes his parents engaged in one of their customary and (to him) imbecilic arguments. Incensed by the absurdity of both their positions, he shouts, "You're both wrong!" but his shouts are inaudible. In this chapter I want to make my views on separate and especially connected knowing audible.

Connected knowing was originally a serendipitous discovery. We did not ask the women we interviewed to tell us about it; they did so spontaneously, and from their comments we constructed the procedure as a sort of "ideal type." Since then, I have been attempting through systematic research and conversations with colleagues (alive and dead, in person and in print) to ascertain how the two procedures (or various versions thereof) play out in actual practice. My colleague Annick Mansfield and I (1992) developed an interview designed to elicit the ways in which men and women define the two procedures; how they feel about them; what they see as their benefits, drawbacks, and purposes; when and where and with whom they do and do not use each procedure; and how their use of them has changed over time. A number of researchers, including my own students, as well as other investigators at various institutions working with widely varying populations, have also used some version of this interview. Drawing on this work, I shall try in this chapter to clarify and complicate the concepts of separate and connected knowing, and, along the way, contest misreadings of the two modes that seem to me especially pernicious.

BELIEVING AND DOUBTING

Let me begin by defining the two orientations as we intended to define them in WWK. If you approach this chapter as a separate knower, you examine its arguments with a critical eye, insisting that I justify every point. In the writer Peter Elbow's terms you "play the doubting game" (1973), looking for flaws in my reasoning, considering how I might be misinterpreting the evidence I present, what alternative interpretations could be made, and whether I might be omitting evidence that would contradict my position. The standards you apply in evaluating my arguments are objective and impersonal; they have been agreed upon and codified by logicians and scientists. You need not be a person to apply these rules; you could be a cleverly programmed computer.

If, on the other hand, you take a connected approach to this chapter, you read it with an empathic, receptive eye. Instead of inspecting the text for flaws, you play "the believing game" (Elbow, 1973): if something I say seems to you absurd, you do not ask, "'What are your arguments for such a silly view as that?' but rather, 'What do you see? . . . Give me the vision in your head. You are having an experience I don't have; help me to have it?'" "The focus," Elbow writes, "is not on propositions and validity of inferences but on experiences or ways of seeing" (1986, p. 261). In asking, "Why do you think that?" connected knowers are not demanding logical or empirical justification; they are asking, "What in your experience has led you to that point of view?" They are concerned not with the soundness of the position but with its meaning to the knower; their aim is not to test its validity but to understand it.[1] Given our present primitive grasp of the "rules" for connected knowing, it would be impossible to program a computer to practice it, and given its "personal" character, it may never be possible.

In fact, of course, you will probably approach this chapter with a mixture of the two orientations. Although for the sake of convenience I will cast separate and connected knowing into dualistic terms, I do not mean to suggest that the two modes are mutually exclusive. "Separate knowers" and "connected knowers" are fictional characters; in reality the two modes can and do coexist within the same individual. Later in the chapter I will try to deconstruct the dualities and complicate the picture. But for the moment, to paraphrase Virginia Woolf (1929/1989), let these lies flow from my lips, and remember that they are lies.

In separate knowing one takes an adversarial stance toward new ideas, even when the ideas seem intuitively appealing; the typical mode of discourse is argument. In WWK we used the following excerpt from an interview with a college sophomore to illustrate the orientation, and we have used it in research and in workshops to stimulate discussion of separate knowing:

> I never take anything someone says for granted. I just tend to see the contrary. I like playing the devil's advocate, arguing the opposite of what somebody's thinking, thinking of exceptions, or thinking of a different train of thought.

People often use images of war in describing separate knowing. Consider, for example, a young man we call Mel,[2] who espouses a sort of Patriot missile epistemology: "If I could get a job shooting holes in other people's [ideas]," he said, "I would enjoy my life immensely."

> If somebody explains [his or her position] to me and I can . . . shoot holes in it, then I won't tend to believe it, and if they can explain away every misgiving that I have about the [position], then I'll tend to believe it. . . . [And] if they seriously believe in something which you think is very wrong, if you—if you shoot enough holes in what they're saying, they'll start doubting it themselves. It could happen to you too. It happens the other way around.

In contrast, in connected knowing one tries to embrace new ideas, looking for what is "right" even in positions that seem initially wrongheaded or even abhorrent. An excerpt from another college sophomore illustrates this approach:

When I have an idea about something, and it differs from the way another person is thinking about it, I'll usually try to look at it from that person's point of view, see how they could say that, why they think that they're right, why it makes sense.

As an undergraduate we call Cecily said, "If you listen to people and listen to what they have to say, maybe you can understand why they feel the way they do. There are reasons. They're not just being irrational." Virginia Woolf, posing the question "How should one read a book?" (1932/1948), advises the reader to "try to become" the author, and Cecily agrees:

When I read a philosopher I try to think as the author does. It's hard, but I try not to bias the train of thought with my own impressions. I try to just pretend that I'm the author. I try to really just put myself in that person's place and feel why is it that they believe this way.

Connected knowers act not as adversaries, but as allies, even advocates, of the position they are examining. Become the author's "fellow worker," his "accomplice," Woolf says, and Sheila, one of our research participants, tells us that in counseling undergraduates she is "usually a bit of a chameleon": "I try to look for pieces of the truth in what the person's saying instead of going contrary to them. Sort of collaborate with them."

Some of our research participants and some of our readers perceive the separate knower's argumentative style as a pig-headed attempt to bully the opponent into submission, but I regard this as a primitive or degenerate form of separate knowing. Properly practiced, the procedure requires that one hold one's views loosely, remaining open to competing positions. For Mel, other people's ideas are fair game, but so too are his: "It happens the other way around too," he says. "It could happen to you." For mature separate knowers, the doubting game is a fair game.

Whereas separate knowers are sometimes perceived as stubbornly attached to their own opinions and deaf to the views of others, connected knowers are sometimes perceived as excessively open-minded—indeed, as having no minds of their own, like the "over-empathizers" characterized by the psychologist Robert Hogan as "equivocating jellyfish" (1973, p. 224). But the picture of the connected knower as merely a jellyfish, clone, chameleon, or wimp, like that of the separate knower as merely a bully, is a caricature. It portrays, perhaps, a primitive or regressive form of connected knowing, but it grossly distorts more mature forms. Sheila, one of our most proficient connected knowers, describes herself as only "a *bit* of a chameleon," and is careful to distinguish between understanding a point of view and agreeing with it. She is not gullible. She does not believe everything she hears—at least not for long. She "believes" in a point of view only in order to understand it. "Believing" is a *procedure* that guides her interaction with other minds; it is not the *result* of the interaction.

CONNECTED KNOWING AS PROCEDURE

Notice the recurrence of the word *try* in the descriptions connected knowers give of their approach; Cecily, for instance, uses it four times in four sentences. Although some people exhibit a proclivity toward connected knowing that appears to be "natural," those who really seem to understand and use the approach rarely describe it as effortless and often allude to its difficulties. The philosopher Elizabeth Spelman refers to the "strenuousness of knowing other people, even people very much like ourselves" (Spelman, 1988, p. 181), and the poet Adrienne Rich, in a brilliant essay recounting her attempt to enter the mind and heart of Emily Dickinson by journeying to the poet's home, depicts herself as "an insect, vibrating at the frames of windows, clinging to the panes of glass, trying to connect" (Rich, 1979, p. 161). True connected knowing is neither easy nor natural. As the anthropologist Clifford Geertz says:

> Comprehending that which is, in some manner of form, alien to us and likely to remain so, without either smoothing it over with vacant murmurs of common humanity, disarming it with to-each-his-own indifferentism, or dismissing it as charming, lovely even, but inconsequent, is a skill we have arduously to learn, and having learnt it, work continuously to keep alive; it is not a connatural capacity, like depth perception or the sense of balance, upon which we can complacently rely. (Geertz, 1986, p. 122)

In WWK we defined connected knowing as a rigorous, deliberate, and demanding *procedure*, a way of knowing that requires *work*. Contrasting it with the epistemological position we called "subjectivism," we said, "It is important to distinguish between the effortless intuition of subjectivism (in which one identifies with positions that feel right) and the deliberate imaginative extension of one's understanding into positions that initially feel wrong or remote" (*WWK*, 1986, p. 121). Many of our readers—friends and foes alike—have ignored the distinction, conflating connected knowing with subjectivism by treating it more as a reflex than as a procedure; *connected* and *procedural* become antonyms (*procedural* apparently being synonymous with *separate*), thus seeming to render connected knowing nonprocedural. The philosopher Lorraine Code makes this error, when, in discussing *WWK*, she describes people behaving "connectedly or procedurally" (Code, 1991, p. 261), and so does a member of my own household, who has read, apparently with care, every draft of everything I have written on this topic.

My immediate reactions to such misreadings are decidedly oppositional: like Mel, I prepare to launch a few verbal missiles. But then I seem to hear Cecily's voice whispering in my ear that perhaps our readers and my housemate are "not being irrational"; perhaps "there are reasons" for their "silly ideas." I resolve to use connected knowing procedures to try to understand why people are unable to see connected knowing as a procedure, why they persistently confuse it with subjectivism. Utilizing one of my favorite defense mechanisms, I transform a source of irritation into a subject for research.

In qualitative research, as methodologist Grant McCracken says, "the investigator serves as a kind of 'instrument' in the collection and analysis of data:" "Detection proceeds by a kind of 'rummaging' process. The investigator must use his or her experience and imagination to find (or fashion) a match for the patterns evidenced by the data" (McCracken, 1988, pp. 18, 19). I did not need to rummage very deeply before coming up with a couple of matches, two occasions on which I had interpreted as subjectivist, and dismissed as relatively mindless, behavior that I now believe might have exemplified connected knowing.

First match: I began teaching at a women's college while still attending graduate school at Harvard, where class discussions followed the ballistic model favored by separate knowers. Although I sometimes found it hard to breathe in this atmosphere, I also found it stimulating, and it became for me the mark of a "good class." When I tried to create the same atmosphere in the classes I was teaching, however, I met with considerable resistance from students like Sue, who said to her interviewer, "In class, when you want to say something, you just want to have it float out in the air and just, you know, stand. You don't want to have it, like, shot down." My students spoke their piece and listened politely as others spoke theirs, but they would not take issue with one another, and, in my opinion, they spent far too much time exchanging anecdotes about their personal experiences. In *Professing Feminism*, Daphne Patai and Noretta Koertge speak scornfully of women's studies groups in which everyone agrees with everyone else, "and everybody feels validated and cozy" (Patai & Koertge, 1994, p. 174). That is how I regarded these classes: It is embarrassing to recall that in a piece written at the time, I dismissed them as "sewing circle classes." (How's that for gender stereotyping?)

A second "match" drawn out of the compost of memory came from a longitudinal study that preceded and overlapped with the WWK research in which my colleague Claire Zimmerman and I (Clinchy & Zimmerman, 1982, 1985) were using William Perry's (1970) "scheme" (largely derived from and illustrated by interviews with Harvard males) to trace the epistemological and ethical development of a sample of undergraduate women. Some of the questions we asked were designed to ascertain whether the students had reached a position in Perry's scheme that involves critical thinking. Some clearly had. For instance, during the first year of the project a student made a comment we would now consider prototypical of separate knowing: "As soon as someone tells me his point of view, I immediately start arguing in my head the opposite point of view. When someone is saying something, I can't help turning it upside down." The next year, we converted this response into a stimulus and asked the students to respond to it.[3] To our dismay, most of them said that they didn't much like that approach and they didn't use it much. Grace, for instance, said that even when she disagreed with someone she didn't start arguing in her head; she started trying to imagine herself in the person's situation. She said, "I sort of fit myself into it in my mind and then I say, 'I see what you mean.'" She said, "There's this initial point where I kind of go into the story, you know? And become like Alice in Wonderland falling down the rabbit hole." Search as we might, we could find no place in Perry's scheme for falling down rabbit holes, and so we interpreted Grace's comment as evidence not of a particular way of thinking but of the absence of any kind of thinking. We saw it, as our critics often see connected knowing, as a sort of naïve credulity: Grace, we concluded, was the sort of person who would fall for anything.

It took me a long time to see that people like Grace and the students in those sewing-circle classes might be following some sort of (admittedly tacit) procedure, rather than simply wallowing in subjectivity. Because connected knowing has much in common with subjectivism, the difference can be difficult to discern. Both subjectivists and connected knowers show respect for views that differ from their own: they seem to listen and refuse to criticize. Both value the sort of knowledge that emerges from firsthand experience, and both draw on feelings and intuition as sources of information. In each of these respects, however, connected knowing does not simply incorporate features of subjectivism; it builds on them, and the resulting construction is quite different.

VALIDITY, UNDERSTANDING, AND TRUST IN THE KNOWER

Incidents of miscommunication between men and women like the ones the sociolinguist Deborah Tannen (1990) recounts in *You Just Don't Understand* often come about because the men are operating out of a separate knowing perspective, while the women are operating out of a connected knowing perspective. For instance, a wife listens intently and nods encouragingly as she draws from her husband his reasons for wishing to buy a new car; the next day he turns up with the new car and is hurt and astonished by her angry reaction. The husband has taken the wife's uncritical acceptance as evidence of her agreement and approval; the wife, however, was merely trying to understand. Miscommunications between the authors of WWK and their readers take a similar form, especially when the readers are schooled in philosophy, a discipline founded on adversarial reasoning (Moulton, 1983) and, according to the philosopher Richard Rorty, preoccupied with questions concerning the validity of knowledge.[4] This is the separate knowing perspective. Connected knowing is concerned with matters that, as Rorty (cited by Bruner, 1986, p. 12) says, Anglo American philosophy does not often address, questions about the meaning of experience. Lorraine Code believes, as do we, that in dealing with the formula "S knows that P," philosophers have paid too little attention to S, to characteristics of the knower and her situation that can affect what is known, but she argues that we go too far in the other direction, focusing exclusively on the knower—on how she knows—and ignoring *what* she knows, the content and validity of her views.

We invite that charge, I think, by using the word *know*[5] instead of, say, *believe* or *think* or *feel*. For most philosophers, to "know" something is to make some claim to validity. I may believe that Martians are filling my cellar with poison gas, but surely I do not "know" it. Although we were aware that the word *know* was ambiguous and possibly misleading, we decided, nonetheless, to use it, because it seemed the connected thing to do: we wanted as much as possible to hear the women in their own terms, and "knowing" seemed to come closest to what most of them meant. We rejected "thinking" because, given the dichotomy in this culture between cognition and affect, we were afraid that "thinking" might imply absence of feeling, and for many of the women feeling was intimately involved in "knowing." We rejected "belief" because although some of the women we interviewed distinguished between believing and knowing, others did not: in subjectivism, for example, the terms are synonymous. The literary theorist Patrocinio (Patsy) Schweickart (see her chapter in this volume) writes, "One cannot assert meaningfully that something is true or valid only for oneself." This, of course, is precisely what subjectivists do assert. "Everyone's opinion is right for him or her," they say, and, although such a statement may not be meaningful in some discourse communities, it is meaningful to them. Schweickart goes on, "I have beliefs, prejudices, or presuppositions; but I *make* validity claims" (Schweickart, 1988, p. 299). Again, although this is a sensible distinction, it is not one that subjectivists make: "Anyone's interpretation is valid, if that's the way he or she sees it. I mean, nobody can tell you that your opinion is wrong, you know."

In interviewing the women and poring over transcripts of their interviews, we relied predominantly on connected knowing, suspending judgment in an attempt to make sense of the women's of making sense of their experience. Code regards connected knowing as "epistemologically problematic" (Code, 1991, p. 253) because it precludes evaluation, and she notes with disapproval a presumption shared by subjectivists and connected knowers that, as one student said, "A person's experience can't be wrong." Although she is aware of the damage done in the past by "experts' telling women what they are really experiencing" (Code, 1991, p. 256) and acknowledges that our "quasi-therapeutic" techniques may be useful in "empowering women who have been 'damaged by patriarchal oppression'" (Code, 1991, p. 252), Code argues that our "acritical acceptance" of the women's autobiographical accounts "is not the only—or the best—alternative" (Code, 1991, p. 256). For us, however, at the data-collection stage of our research, there was no alternative. In order to hear a person in her own terms, the listener must suspend judgment. We may object to the lessons a woman has drawn from her experience. We may feel that she is a victim of "false consciousness," that she has been brainwashed by her oppressors, and that the terms in which she casts her experience are not "her own" but have been foisted on her by the patriarchy. Nevertheless, we must put these thoughts aside and accept her reality as her reality, not only accept it but collude with her in its construction. As the social scientist Stephanie Riger says,

> In contrast to traditional social science in which the researcher is the expert on assessing reality, an interpretive–phenomenological approach permits women to give their own conception of their experiences. Participants, not researchers, are considered the experts at making sense of their world. . . . The shift in authority is striking. (Riger, 1992, p. 733)

Psychologist Jill Morawski and literary theorist R. S. Steele show how in traditional psychological research "the power of the psychologist is increased at the cost of the subjects" (Morawski & Steele, 1991, p. 112), offering as an illustration the psychologist Walter Mischel's (1969) pronouncement that while "subjects" perceive continuities in their personality traits over time, statistics prove them wrong.

> According to [Mischel], in so far as the subjects are numbers on "IBM sheets," that is, objects of scientific reductionism, they are reliable. However, as sentient subjects, that is, beings capable of self-reflection and of constructing a personal history, they are untrustworthy. (Morawski & Steele, 1991, p. 113)

Distrust of the "subject" also permeates accounts of traditional psychoanalytic psychotherapy. After perusing this literature, the psychoanalyst Evelyne Schwaber concluded that "analytic listening remains steeped in a hierarchical two-reality view" (Schwaber, 1983a, p. 390), "the one the patient experiences, and the one the analyst 'knows'" (Schwaber, 1983a, p. 386):

> My first supervisor listened by sifting the material through her own perspective—that is, from the vantage point of the analyst's reality—in trying to aid the patient's observing ego to recognize the distortions in her perceptions. The second supervisor sharpened the focus from *within* the patient's perspective, to see in it a certain plausibility, however outlandish, unrealistic, entitled, it may have seemed to the outside observer. (Schwaber, 1983a, pp. 379–380)

Schwaber, like the "constructed knowers" in WWK, sees value in the more separate as well as the more connected approach and uses elements of both in her work, but she firmly rejects the notion that the analyst's view is more accurate than the patient's: the two realities, she says, are "relative" rather than hierarchical (1983a, p. 390).

Like the males in Tanner's anecdotes, readers sometimes interpret our "acritical acceptance" of the women's stories as implying approval of their views. To refrain from criticism, however, means to refrain from approval as well as disapproval. (Good critics, after all, illuminate the merits as well as the faults of the things they examine.) Connected knowing shares with subjectivistm an appreciation of subjective reality, but it does not adhere to the subjectivist doctrine of "subjective validity," the view that all opinions are equally valid and "everyone's opinion is right for him or her."[6] Connected knowing does not imply relativism in this sense. When one is using techniques of connected knowing, as in the initial stages of our research, issues of validity are simply irrelevant.

Although both subjectivists and connected knowers might say that "experience can't be wrong," they mean different things when they say it. Subjectivists *are* unmitigated relativists. They do believe that whatever truths have emerged from a person's firsthand experience are valid for that person. They do believe that these truths are unambiguous, in the feminist philosopher M. E. Hawkesworth's (1989) terms, "transparent" and "unmediated" by personal or cultural preconceptions. Asked how she decides what a poem means, a student speaking from this perspective replies, "Whatever you see in the poem, it's got to be there." Although her teacher may feel that such a student has ignored the words on the page, treating the text as a mirror or an inkblot onto which she projects the contents of her own mind, to the student the meaning is simply there on the page. Much (although not all) of Hawkesworth's critique of feminist positions based on intuition can be applied to subjectivism:

> The distrust of the conceptual aspects of thought, which sustains claims that genuine knowledge requires immediate apprehension, presumes not only that an unmediated grasp of reality is possible but also that it is authoritative. Moreover, appeals to intuition raise the specter of an authoritarian trump that precludes the possibility of rational debate. Claims based on intuition manifest an unquestioning acceptance of their own veracity. . . . Thus, intuition provides a foundation for claims about the world that is at once authoritarian, admitting of no further discussion, and relativist, since no individual can refute another's "immediate" apprehension of reality. Operating at a level of assertion that admits of no further elaboration or explication, those who abandon themselves to intuition conceive and give birth to dreams, not to truth.[7] (Hawkesworth, 1989, p. 545)

Code (1991, p. 258, n. 74), persisting in reading WWK as an endorsement of subjectivism, quotes this passage from Hawkesworth in criticizing what she interprets as our position. In fact, we could have written the passage ourselves, and we nearly did, in describing Minna, a Hispanic woman enrolled in a community college who, in our view, was beginning to struggle out of subjectivism into procedural knowledge. Deserted by her husband and left with an eight-year-old daughter, no money, no employable skills, and no friends, Minna saw now that as Hawkesworth puts it, in abandoning herself to intuition she had "conceived and given birth to dreams, not to truth." "I was confused about everything," she said. "I was unrealistic about things. I was more in a fantasy world. You have to see things for what they are, not for what you want to see them.

I don't want to live in a dream world." Now, she says, "I think everything out, and I want to make sure I understand exactly what's going on before I do anything" (WWK, 1986, p. 99). Code warns that "a subjective knower's 'gut' often lets her down," and subjectivism is not necessarily "conducive to empowerment" (Code, 1991, p. 254). This is not news to Minna, nor to the authors of WWK.

Unlike the feminist scholars who are the objects of Hawkesworth's critique, Sue, the student who wished that her words might float out into the air and just stand, does not *choose* to rely on private, intuitive truth; she has not yet developed an alternative method. Encapsulated in her own world, she can only assert her own truth. For many women who speak from a subjectivist perspective conversations, especially with like-minded people, are a source of great pleasure, but for Sue "discussion" in English class is futile: "Because I know I can't see where they're coming from, so why, you know, why keep trying at it if it doesn't feel comfortable to you, but you have your own thoughts that feel right?" With the advent of procedural knowing, epistemological isolation comes to an end, and collaborative construction of knowledge through discussion becomes not only possible but, because truth is now problematic rather than transparent, essential. Separate knowers can engage in "rational debate," rather than mere assertion and counterassertion, in order to adjudicate truth claims. And connected knowers can obtain vicarious experience through mutual "elaboration and explication" of personal narratives.

This is the sort of interchange, I now believe, that was struggling to be born and may occasionally have emerged, although I could not hear it, in those sewing circle classes I perceived as utterly unproductive. It is easy to misperceive active listening as passive and polite, hard to see it as a genuine procedure, a "skill requiring arduously to be learned." Anyone who has tried to teach (or to learn) the art of connected interviewing,[8] however, knows how difficult it is to learn to listen "objectively," in the connected sense, that is, to hear the other in the other's own terms, to become "an observer from within" (Schwaber, 1983b, p. 274).

AFFIRMING THE KNOWER

In connected knowing it is essential to refrain from judgment "because," as the psychologist Carl Rogers says, "it is impossible to be accurately perceptive of another's inner world if you have formed an evaluative opinion of that person" (Rogers, 1980, p. 152). If you doubt that assertion,

Rogers says, try to describe the views of someone you believe is definitely wrong in a fashion that the person will consider accurate. "In the believing game," Elbow writes, "the first rule is to refrain from doubting" (Elbow, 1973, p. 149). For her undergraduate honors thesis, Carolyn Rabin (1994) analyzed interviews on separate and connected knowing with undergraduates from the Massachusetts Institute of Technology and Wellesley College collected in the Clinchy–Mansfield project. She noted that for many of the MIT men this is what "connected knowing" meant—to refrain from criticism—and this is all it meant; they had not progressed beyond the first rule of the game. I argue, however, that fully developed connected knowing requires that one "affirm" or "confirm" the subjective reality of the other, and affirmation is not merely the absence of negative evaluation; it is a positive effortful act. Affirmation of a person or a position means, as Elbow says, "to say Yes to it" (Elbow, 1986, p. 279), rather than merely offering sympathetic understanding. Confirmation means, in the philosopher Martin Buber's wonderful phrases, to "imagine the real," to "make the other present" (Buber, quoted by Friedman, 1985, p. 4). It involves "a bold swinging . . . into the life of the other" (Buber, quoted by Kohn, 1990, p. 112), and as Alfie Kohn says, this other, for Buber, is a particular other, not an "interchangeable someone" (Kohn, 1990, p. 112), and the knower is "not merely avoiding objectification but affirmatively invoking, . . . addressing the other's status as a subject, . . . an actor, a knower, a center of experience" (Kohn, 1990, p. 100).

This "bold swinging into the life of the other" is a far cry from polite tolerance or "to-each-his-own indifferentism," but it is also not to be confused with approval or agreement. It should be obvious that, as Geertz puts it, "Understanding what people think doesn't mean you have to think the same thing" (Geertz, quoted in Berreby, 1995, p. 4). "'Understanding,'" Geertz writes, "in the sense of comprehension, perception, and insight needs to be distinguished from 'understanding' in the sense of agreement of opinion, union of sentiment, or commonality of commitment. . . . We must learn to grasp what we cannot embrace" (Geertz, 1986, p. 122). From the connected knowing perspective, of course, we must first try very hard to embrace it.

Conversations involving mutual confirmation are not to be confused with the "relatively harmonious situations" described by Patai and Koertge and mentioned earlier, in which "everyone feels validated and cozy" (Patai & Koertge, 1994, p. 174). If "everyone feels validated" in this situation, it is not because they have been told they are right; it is because they have been heard. As one young woman said, "When people [are] interested in why I feel the way I do and why it makes sense to me, . . . I feel that what I have to say might mean something and has some impact." This sort of validation is especially welcome to procedural knowers. Whereas subjectivists are confident that they can arrive at the truth (the truth for them) simply by reading it off from experience (whatever you see in the poem, it's got to be there) or attending to their infallible guts, procedural knowers have no such assurance. Separate knowers need to know whether their views can survive the scrutiny of an outsider's critical eye, and connected knowers need to know whether their thoughts can "mean something" to someone else, even, perhaps, "an attentive stranger" (Ruddick, 1984, p. 148).

In swinging boldly into the mind of another, truly saying yes to it, two perversions of "connected knowing" are prevented. One is to "use it as a weapon," as one woman said, as "when people say, 'Well, I can see how you would say that given your background,' . . . referring to my background as some wacky thing that nobody else has ever experienced." In this patronizing version, known, I am told, as "the California fuck off," one distances one's self from the other's experience, in effect saying "No" to it. A second perversion is to say yes too quickly, to assume without reflection that others feel as we do or as we would feel in their situation, that is, to assimilate the other to the self: "I know just how you feel!" we say, having, in fact, very little idea or quite the wrong idea.

THE SELF AS INSTRUMENT

Whereas separate knowing requires "self-extrication," "weeding out the self," in Elbow's terms, connected knowing requires "self-insertion" or "projection in the good sense" (Elbow, 1973, p. 149) or, to use a more feminine image, "receiving the other into [the] self" (Noddings, 1984, p. 30). Procedures for minimizing "projection in the bad sense" (Elbow, 1973, p. 149), or, as developmental psychologist Jean Piaget puts it, "excluding the intrusive self" (Piaget, 1972, quoted by Keller, 1983b, p. 134), have been well developed and are known to be effective, although of course not perfectly so. For instance, the effects of "bias" are reduced if observers in an experiment are "double-blinded," unaware of both the hypothesis being tested and the treatment to which the subjects have been assigned. Procedures for using the self as an instrument of understanding are less well developed, but practitioners of the increasingly prevalent "new paradigm" research have made considerable progress in developing and articulating them.

This is not the place to inventory these techniques, but I have already mentioned the procedure by which the investigator rummages through her experience in search of a "match." "The diverse aspects of the self," McCracken says, "become a bundle of templates to be held up against the data until parallels emerge" (McCracken, 1988, p. 19). "To understand a poem, an undergraduate said, "You must let the poem pass into you and become part of yourself, rather than something you see outside yourself. . . . There has to be some parallel between you and the poem." This is an active procedure: we must construct the parallels, by conjuring up "metaphorical extensions, analogies, associations" (Elbow, 1973, p. 149), and we need not simply wait for a poem or a person or a patient to strike a chord, for by "fine tuning" (Margulies, 1989, p. 16) the instrument of our subjectivity we can increase the likelihood of its "empathic resonance" (Howard, 1991, p. 189). Instead of simply "letting" the other in, we can prepare our minds to receive it by engaging in arduous systematic "self-reflection." McCracken advises, for instance, that in preparation for qualitative research, the investigator should construct a "detailed and systematic appreciation of his or her personal experience with the topic of interest. . . . The investigator must inventory and examine the associations, incidents and assumptions that surround the topic in his or her mind" (McCracken, 1988, p. 32), thus "preparing the templates with which he or she will seek out 'matches' in the interview data. The investigator listens to the self in order to listen to the respondent" (McCracken, 1988, p. 33).

In conducting the interview, too, one uses the self as an instrument of understanding. The sociologist Marjorie DeVault, who has forcefully urged us to "analyze more carefully the specific ways that interviewers use personal experience as a resource for listening," describes her own procedure as focusing "on attention to the unsaid, in order to produce it as topic and make it speakable." It "involves noticing ambiguity and problems of expression in interview data, then drawing on my own experience in an investigation aimed at 'filling in' what has been incompletely said" (DeVault, 1990, p. 104).[9]

In using the self to understand the other, we risk imposing the self on the other; projection in the good sense can easily degenerate into projection in the bad sense. Patti Lather, a sympathetic practitioner of new paradigm research, worries that "rampant subjectivity" could prove to be its "nemesis" (Lather, 1986, p. 68). How are we to distinguish between the psychoanalyst Heinz Kohut's "empathy," defined as "the recognition of the self in the other" (Kohut, 1978, quoted by Jordan, 1991, p. 68), and the subjectivist's "Whatever you see in the poem, it's got to be there"?

How do we ensure that we are not treating the other as a mirror or a blot of ink, a mere receptacle for our own subjectivity? As the psychologist Alfred Margulies says, "Because empathy is by definition the 'imaginative projection of one's own consciousness into another being,' we will unavoidably find ourselves reflected within our gaze toward the other. I look for you and see myself" (Margulies, 1989, p. 58).

Clinicians and qualitative researchers agree that the matches one pulls from one's own experience should serve only as "clues" (DeVault, 1990, p. 104), "merely a bundle of possibilities, pointers, and suggestions that can be used to plumb the remarks of a respondent" (McCracken, 1988, p. 19). "Imagining how one would feel — or actually has felt," says Alfie Kohn, should be regarded as only a "provisional indication" (Kohn, 1990, p. 133), or as Margulies puts it, "a map constructed second-hand from another life's travels, a map that undergoes constant reworking, revision (re-vision), and clarification" (Margulies, 1989, p. 53). One must remain open to "subtle surprises," to emerging discrepancies between the map and the patient's "inscape." Qualitative researchers devise strategies for inviting surprise, often enlisting the cooperation of participants in reworking the map. Indeed, one must move beyond matching to achieve true understanding. In Kohn's terms we must move beyond "imagine-self" to "imagine-other." If we assume that we have reached full understanding once we run out of matches, we are indeed assimilating the other to the self. The psychiatrist Maurice Friedman calls this truncated procedure "identification":

> [T]he therapist resonates with the experiences related by the client only to the extent that they resemble his or her own. It says, in effect, "I am thou," but misses the Thou precisely at the point where its otherness and uniqueness takes it out of the purview of one's own life stance and life experience. (Friedman, 1985, p. 197)

I, THOU, AND IT

Some of our readers and research participants conceive of connected knowing as useful only in dealing with people. At worst, they describe it as a way of "being nice," "getting along with people," and "keeping the peace"; at best, they see it as a way of understanding directed only at live and present people. In WWK, however, we said, "When we speak of separate and connected knowing we refer not to any sort of relationship between the self and another person but [to] relationships between knowers and the objects (or subjects) of knowing (which may or may not be persons)" (WWK, 1986, p. 102). We said that "the mode of knowing is personal, but the object of knowing need not be," citing Cecily's comment (WWK, 1986, p. 121) that in reading a philosopher she "tries to think as the author does," and the comment of another student, who said that "you shouldn't read a book [in this case, Dante's *Divine Comedy*] just as something printed and distant from you, but as a real experience of someone who went through some sort of situation" (WWK, 1986, p. 113).

In connected knowing, the "it" is transformed into a "thou," and the "I" enters into relationship with the thou.[10] Scientists use this procedure. The biologist Barbara McClintock says, in words that have grown familiar, that you must have the patience to hear what the corn "has to say to you" and the openness "to let it come to you" (Keller, 1983a, p. 198), and the pseudonymous biochemist portrayed by June Goodfield in *An Imagined World* says, "If you really want to understand about a tumor you've got to *be* a tumor" (Goodfield, 1991/1994, p. 226). According to the psychologist Seymour Papert, even toddlers are capable of a sensorimotor version of connected knowing. Before the age of two, he says, he "fell in love with gears"; indeed, he became a gear. "You can *be* the gear," he writes. "You can understand how it turns by projecting yourself into its place and turning with it" (Papert, 1980, pp. vi–vii). Papert and his colleague Sherry Turkle found that some of the students they observed learning to construct computer programs—especially girls and women—also "reasoned from within" their programs. Anne, for instance, "psychologically places herself in the same space as the sprites" (the objects whose movements she is programming). "She is down there, in with the sprites. . . . When she talks about them her gestures with hand and body show her moving with and among them. When she speaks of them she uses language such as 'move here'" (Turkle & Papert, 1990, p. 144).[11] Anne treats the computer rather like "a person" (Turkle, 1984, p. 112), "allowing ideas to emerge in the give and take of conversation with it" (Turkle, 1984, p. 104).

Our research participants often describe their way of reading in similar terms. "You should treat the text as if it were a friend," a student said, and she meant, as Schweickart means, not just to treat it nicely, but to regard it as "not a mere object, like a stone, but the objectification of a subject" (Schweickart, 1989, p. 83). Adrienne Rich, Schweickart writes, aims to make the poet Emily Dickinson "live as the substantial palpable presence animating her works" (Schweickart, 1989, p. 50), to "make

[her] present" as Buber (quoted by Friedman, 1985, p. 4) would say. Connected reading is an intersubjective procedure: "The reader encounters not simply a text, but a 'subjectified object': the 'heart and mind' of another woman. She comes into close contact with an interiority—a power, a creativity, a suffering, a vision—that is *not* identical with her own." Schweickart contrasts this feminist version of reader response theory with one put forth by literary theorist Georges Poulet. Poulet also takes a personal approach: "To understand a literary work . . . is to let the individual who wrote it reveal [herself] to us *in* us" (Poulet, 1980, p. 46, quoted by Schweickart, 1986, p. 52). But he portrays reader and author as opponents in a zero-sum game. The reader "becomes the 'prey' of what he reads. . . . His consciousness is 'invaded,' 'annexed,' 'usurped.' . . . In the final analysis, the process of reading leaves room for only one subjectivity" (Schweickart, 1986, pp. 52–53).

In the feminist version of the theory (we call it "connected reading"), on the other hand, there is a "doubling" of subjectivity: "One can be placed at the disposal of the text while the other remains with the reader." Schweickart warns, however, that ultimately, because the reader constructs the meaning of the text, "there is only one subject present—the reader. . . . The subjectivity roused to life by reading, while it may be attributed to the author, is nevertheless not a separate subjectivity but a projection of the subjectivity of the reader" (Schweickart, 1986, p. 53). Projection in the bad sense is a very real danger when the author, being absent, cannot speak for herself.[12] Schweickart:

> In real conversation the other person can interrupt, object to an erroneous interpretation, provide further explanations, change her mind, change the topic, or cut off conversation altogether. In reading, there are no comparable safeguards against the appropriation of the text by the reader. (Schweickart, 1986, p. 53)

The best that can be done in connected reading is to encourage absent authors to speak and to join them in a semblance of collaboration. The writer and critic Doris Grumbach recounts a midlife change in her ways of reading that sounds like a transition from a relatively separate to a relatively connected approach. "It is hard work to read more slowly," she says. "But when I slow down, I interlard the writers' words with my own. I think about what they are saying. . . . I dillydally in their views" (Grumbach, 1991, p. 15). Reading becomes a kind of conversation, and the reader apprentices herself to the writer. "Reading in the new way now, I learn. Before, I seemed to be instructing the book with my superior opinions" (Grumbach, 1991, p. 15).[13] ("Do not dictate to your author, try to become him" [Woolf, 1932, p. 282].)

"Subjectivist theories of reading," Schweickart says, "silence the text" (Schweickart, 1989, p. 83). This applies to the informal subjectivist theories of ordinary readers as well as to members of the lit-crit community: "We're all allowed to read into a poem any meaning we want," and "Whatever you see in the poem, it's got to be there," whether the poet likes it or not. Objectivist readings, on the other hand, such as the ones offered by people adhering to the epistemological position we call *received knowing*, silence the reader: to find out what a poem means, "you'd have to ask the poet; it's his poem." For connected readers it is different: A poem does not belong solely to its author. "Poems are written," a student explained, "but you also have to interpret them." A poem is not something "that sits there and does nothing. It has to be interpreted by other people, and those people are going to have their own ideas of what it means." Those ideas, however, must be grounded in the text: interpretation is "a two-person activity," involving the poet as well as the reader.

In sharing with the text the task of interpretation, instead of claiming it as solely their own, connected readers might seem to possess less authority than subjectivist readers. But the authority of subjectivism is, in fact, derivative, and, being derivative, it is fragile. Who is it who "allows" us to interpret poetry for ourselves, and if They have the power to allow it, might They not also have the power to take away the privilege? ("My English teacher lets me have my own opinions," a student said, but she worried that next semester's teacher might be less lenient.)

Authority in subjectivism is limited, as well as tenuous. In one of our studies, we asked students to tell us how they assessed the merits of a poem. "To me," one woman replied, "what makes one poem better than another one is that I can get something from it as a person. That says nothing about the poem itself. I mean, I have no authority." I hear in this comment an appropriate humility, a refusal to lay down the law and speak for the text. But I hear, too, a poignant diffidence: The student is saying that she has no public voice, that, although she is free to make her own judgments, there is no reason for anyone to listen to her. Her judgments have no objective value. They say nothing about the poem—they are just about her; there is no "it" here; subjectivist reading is a one-person activity.

In granting some voice to the text, the connected reader actually increases the power of her own voice. Although acknowledging that the authority of her interpretation is qualified, she asserts that it does have *some* authority, and, because she constructed the interpretation herself, no one can take it away (although she herself may decide to abandon it). Like the subjectivist, the connected reader speaks "as a person," but, because her words concern the poem as well as herself, they are comprehensible to others and worthy of attention. And, far from silencing the author, by speaking as a person the connected reader leaves space for the text to speak. Schweickart astutely observes that although Rich's "use of the personal voice . . . serves as a reminder that her interpretation is informed by her own perspective," it also "serves as a gesture warding off any inclination to appropriate the authority of the text as a warrant for the validity of the interpretation" (Schweickart, 1986, p. 54). Like the subjectivist, the connected reader does not presume to speak for the text, but, unlike the subjectivist, she does not speak only to herself; she assumes that her words might "mean something, and have some impact" on other readers.

THINKING AND FEELING

To adopt the perspective of the other requires thinking (reasoning, inference) as well as empathy. Indeed, although the term *empathy* has come to connote merely an affective "feeling with," the German word from which it was translated, *Einfühlung*, meant, literally, "feeling into," and referred, according to the psychologist M. F. Basch, to "the ability of one person to come to know first-hand, so to speak, the experience of another"; "inference, judgment, and other aspects of reasoning thought" were as central to its meaning as affect (Basch, 1983, p. 110). The loss in translation of these cognitive aspects can be seen as an instance of the Western tendency to treat thinking and feeling as mutually exclusive, the same tendency that has led readers of WWK to assume that because separate knowing involves reasoning, and connected knowing differs from separate knowing, then connected knowing must involve merely feeling. A tendency to place a "separate spin" on essentially connected notions is also evident here. To "feel with" seems to preserve the autonomy of knower and known: their feelings are parallel but not fused. "Feeling into," in contrast, suggests a more intimate relation. In any case, connected knowing and *Einfühlung*, in its original meaning, seem to be close relatives, if not twins.

Kohn writes that "without imagining the reality of the other, empathic feeling is ultimately self-oriented and thus unworthy of the name" (Kohn, 1990, p. 131), and imagining the reality of the other requires responding to its cognitive content as well as its affect. Kohn recalls an incident from his student days when he raised a concern with his instructor, a psychiatrist, about some aspect of the course. "I can see you're angry," the instructor said. Up to that point, Kohn says, he had not been angry, but the instructor's response did anger him, because "it referred only to what he believed was my mood, effectively brushing aside the content of what I had expressed. His exclusively affective focus felt dismissive, even infantalizing, rather than empathic or understanding" (Kohn, 1990, pp. 311–312).

Subjectivism is especially prone to this "noninferential empathy" (Flavell, 1985, p. 139). "I'm very empathic," a student told us, "very sensitive to other peoples' emotions, even if I don't know them. Somebody could be depressed across the room, and I'll be depressed all day because that person's depressed who I don't even know." Emotional contagion is not sufficient for mature connected knowing (although it may constitute a rudimentary basis for it),[14] nor is "situational role-taking," Kohn's "imagine-self," meaning, What would *I* do, given *my* background, personality, values, and so on, in *his* situation? In connected knowing one must "imagine-other" (my rephrasing of Kohn's "imagine-him"), put one's self into the head and heart, as well as the shoes of the other. Kohn:

> The issue is not just how weepy I become upon learning that your spouse has died; it is also whether I am merely recalling and reacting to a comparable loss in my own life or whether I am resonating to your unique set of circumstances—the suddenness of the death, the particular features of this person you loved that are especially vivid for you, your rocky marital history and the resultant prickles of guilt you are now feeling, the way your initial numbness is finally giving way to real pain, the respects in which your unconscious fears of being abandoned are about to be freshly revived by this event, the relationship that you and I have had up to now, and so on. (Kohn, 1990, pp. 132–133)

It is this intense concentration on the unique aspects of the object that characterizes the objectivity of connected knowing. If you act as the author's accomplice, Woolf says, "if you open your mind as widely as possible, then signs and hints of almost imperceptible fineness, from the twist and turn of the first sentences, will bring you into the presence of a human being unlike any other. Steep yourself in this, acquaint yourself with this." In separate knowing one regards the object as an instance of a category (a type of person, say, or a genre) and measures it against objective standards. In connected knowing, the focus is on the object in itself, in all its particularity of detail. Once having constructed a complex constellation of specific circumstances peculiar to the particular worlds of the novelist or the next-door neighbor, or who- or whatever, connected knowers are forced to acknowledge disjunctions between these worlds and their own, and the danger of imagining the other as the self is sharply diminished.

"Nonempathic inference" (Flavell, 1985, p. 139) seems as problematic as noninferential empathy. Kohn asks us to "imagine a continuum: on one side are universal experiences, where imagine-self will do (burning hand); on the other side are things one has not personally experienced, where imagine-him is obviously required (giving birth)" (Kohn, 1990, p. 134). ("Him" seems an odd choice of pronoun in this context.) "The interesting cases," Kohn writes, "are in the middle (death of spouse). One can get away with treating that example as a generic grief, but only at a considerable cost to the integrity of the empathic response" (Kohn, 1990, p. 134). It seems likely that we are especially prone to assimilation to the self concerning the "things in the middle," those "universal" events that appear to be similar but are experienced differently, like the ones listed by the philosopher Elizabeth Spelman: "birth, death, eating, cooking, working, loving, having kin, being friends" (Spelman, 1988, p. 179). Fully to "imagine-other" in these situations seems to me to require feeling as well as thinking, but the MIT men do not seem to think so: in delineating their versions of "connected knowing," not one of them—even among those who claimed to use the procedure—referred to empathy or, indeed, made any mention of affect, whereas many of the Wellesley women did. The difference is rooted not in gender but in epistemology (which, although related to gender, is not synonymous with it). Women who are predominantly separate knowers also practice nonempathic inference, and, perceiving their ideas as autonomous, independent of their persons, they wish that others would do the same with them. Roberta, for instance, said that although she welcomed the opportunity to defend her carefully constructed opinions, when people tried to delve into the experiences behind the opinions instead of treating them on their own merits, she tended to "push [them] away:" "I feel like they're belittling me. . . . Why don't they just ask me straight out why I think my idea, because I've thought my idea through. They don't have to like, beat around the bush about it" (Mansfield & Clinchy, 1992).

To people like Roberta, who present themselves as heavily tipped in the direction of separate knowing, it is especially important that people respond to the impersonal cognitive content of their ideas; they tend to be suspicious of more personal approaches, experiencing them as Kohn experienced his instructor's noninferential empathy, as "belittling" (Roberta), as "infantalizing" and "dismissive" (Kohn). People who present themselves as oriented toward connected knowing, on the other hand, are wary of *impersonal* approaches: like the women in Tannen's accounts, they feel bereft when their listeners (in Tannen's account, men) offer analyses and solutions to the painful problem they have recounted, instead of resonating to their pain. Some adolescent males, observing this response in girls of their acquaintance, have formed a theory about it. "Girls don't want you to fix their problems," eighteen-year-old David Constantine writes to *Parade* magazine. "They just want to talk about them, and they want you to listen. They don't want you to say, 'What do you care?' or 'It's nothing to worry about.'" David infers correctly that girls don't want their worries dismissed, but his grasp of empathy seems limited: "Girls want you to say things like, 'Hmmm . . .' and 'Really?' and 'Wow, I don't blame you.'" According to David, girls just want to feel validated and cozy. "A good 'Hmmm . . .' and a feigned interested look is more important to them than the greatest answer we could come up with to all their troubles" ("What Bothers Me about Girls," 1994). David would claim, as have several of our students and colleagues who appear to be oriented separate knowing, that it is not necessary to feel what a person is feeling in order to understand him. From the connected knowing perspective, however, thinking cannot be divorced from feeling. Those who practice fully developed connected knowing, like those who practice Kohn's fully developed empathy, "truly experience the other as a subject." Kohn uses the word *experience* rather than *understand*—and so, I think, should I—"because something more than an intellectual apprehension is required. . . . [T]he connection . . . must be felt viscerally" (Kohn, 1990, p. 150).

CONNECTED KNOWING WITH THE SELF

I first read the words "[T]he connection . . . must be felt viscerally" after teaching an especially intense session of my seminar, and they seemed to me just right, but the next phrase brought me up short: "The connection must be felt viscerally *as surely as one's own humanness and uniqueness are felt*" (Kohn, 1990, p. 150). Whoa. Was Kohn asserting that knowledge of the self is prerequisite to knowledge of others, that we experience others as subjects only by analogy to our experience of ourselves as subjects? My fifteen seminar students had asserted that afternoon with nearly perfect unanimity that they found it far easier to understand other people's

beliefs and values and desires than to know their own. They would agree
with Addie, an interviewee who said, "It's easy for me to see a whole lot
of different points of view on things and to understand why people think
those things. The hard thing is sitting down and saying, 'Okay, what do *I*
think, and why do *I* think it?'" When in our research we asked young
women to "describe themselves to themselves," they said things like "I'm
about average" and "My ideas are just sort of like the norms." They
seemed often to respond not as compassionate observers from within, but
as stern judges from without: "I'm too fat . . . fairly good with people . . .
pretty smart . . . not as tolerant as I should be." Psychologists Lyn Brown
and Carol Gilligan describe how in adolescence girls who come up
against "a wall of shoulds" (Brown & Gilligan, 1992, p. 97); they "come
to a place where they feel they cannot say or feel or know what they have
experienced" (Brown & Gilligan, 1992, p. 4). For many adult women,
the wall remains in place; they cannot seem to connect with their own
humanness and uniqueness. Muttering aloud, I reported all this to Kohn,
interlarding my words with his, and apparently he heard me, for he went
on: "[T]his last formulation gives us pause. . . [I]t is not clear that everyone does experience his or her own subjectivity" (Kohn, 1990, p. 150). It
is crystal clear from research results (as well as ordinary observation) that
many do not.

In our interviews, Annick and I tried to determine whether our respondents used separate knowing with themselves. We asked, "Do you ever
use this approach with yourself—with your own thinking? Play devil's
advocate with yourself, or argue with yourself?" Almost all said that they
did, some describing the internal critic as a destructive antagonist, others
drawing a more benign picture of "a friend behaving as an enemy" (Torbert, 1976), like the one inhabiting the philosopher Alice Koller's head,
"thinking up the strongest possible arguments against my own position"
in order to "find the flaws in my reasoning, the blunt edges of the ideas
I'm trying to sharpen" (Koller, 1990, p. 27). No one was baffled by our
question; everyone could make some sense of it.

One day Annick happened to notice that we asked no comparable
question about connected knowing, whereas in every other respect we
had constructed parallel questions about the two approaches. Although
we wanted to repair the omission, we were uncertain how to phrase such
a question, or even whether such a question made sense. It seemed non-
sensical to ask whether people tried to step into their own shoes; surely
they were already in them. Bewildered, we asked our friends, "What
would it mean to use connected knowing with yourself?" Ann Stanton
(see her chapter, this volume) instantly replied, "It means to treat your

mind as if it were a friend." This seemed to make sense. After all, we had ample evidence that the women we had interviewed found it hard to befriend their ideas, hard to "believe" them, to "say yes" to them. And so we added to the interview a question that, after repeated rephrasing, emerged (still a bit awkwardly) as "Do you ever use this approach with yourself? Try to see why you think what you do, what's right about it?" Our respondents had as much trouble answering the question as we had had in formulating it. "Huh? What? What do you mean? I don't get it." Often, they heard the question as asking about not a friend but an enemy in the head: "Oh, yeah," they said. "I'm forever second-guessing myself." Not one of our research participants managed to articulate with much clarity a practice of connected knowing with the self.

For most of the women we interviewed, then, connected knowing with the self was at least as difficult to achieve as connected knowing with the other, and possibly more so. These women were like the patient described by the psychotherapist Judith Jordan who, before therapy, "did not seem able to take her own inner experience as a serious object for interest and attention." "I care for others sometimes like a sheepherder," the woman said. . . . "I put myself in their place and I understand. With myself, though, I used to be like a lion tamer with a bull whip" (Jordan, 1991, p. 78). The clinical literature suggests that "intrapsychic empathy" (Schafer, 1964, p. 251) is a skill arduously to be learned, requiring discipline and practice, usually under the guidance of some sort of tutor (a therapist, perhaps, or a Zen master).

The psychoanalyst Joanna Field tells a compelling story of her own efforts to achieve intrapsychic empathy. Feeling "utterly at sea as to how to live my life," thinking second-hand thoughts, and "whipping" herself in pursuit of second-hand goals, she developed over a period of years her own "method" of "active passivity" that enabled her, ultimately, to step inside her own shoes, to "see through [her] own eyes instead of at second hand." The method requires that one take an active stance toward one's thoughts and feelings, rather than simply letting them run on as a sort of "unconscious monologue" in the background of one's mind, but the activity is the sort practiced by midwives rather than taskmasters. "I began to see," Field writes, "that I must play the Montessori teacher to my thought, must leave it free to follow its own laws of growth, my function being to observe its activities, provide suitable material to enchannel them, but never to coerce it into docility" (Field, 1936/1981, p. 7). The process has much in common with the modes of fostering growth used by the public leader Mary Belenky in her chapter in this volume. Field writes,

By continual watching and expression I must learn to observe my thought and maintain a vigilance not against "wrong" thoughts, but against refusal to recognize any thought. Further, this introspection meant continual expression, not continual analysis; it meant that I must bring my thoughts and feelings up in their wholeness, not argue about them. (Field, 1936/1981, pp. 204–205)

Field found that one way of bringing her thoughts and feelings up in their wholeness was to let them "write themselves" into the friendly pages of her journal. The journal turns the "I" into an "it," objectifying the knower's subjectivity, and in perusing the journal the knower turns the "it" into a "thou," in effect practicing connected knowing with herself.

But it is difficult to penetrate the wall of shoulds and speak truly, even in the privacy of one's journal, and in public it is even harder. The novelist Mary Gordon says that in striving to develop her own voice as a writer she was haunted by "bad specters" who infused her with a fear of being "trivial" (Gordon, 1980, p. 27), two famous male poets, perhaps, peering over her shoulder as she sat at the typewriter, and murmuring, "Your experience is an embarrassment; your experience is insignificant" (Gordon, 1980, p. 28). "Do you talk much in class?" we asked an undergraduate. "It's hard," she said. "I think—I always think, 'Do I really want to say this or not? Is it important enough to say?'"

Given the presence of strangling self-doubt, most of us find it impossible to achieve intrapsychic empathy on our own. Lacking the skill and stamina to serve as Montessori teachers to ourselves, we depend on external "teachers"—friends and colleagues, as well as certified teachers—who help us to say what we want to say (WWK, 1986, p. 218), reading our early drafts as "sympathetic allies," "trying to see the *validity*" in what we have written, and telling us "the ways in which [it]makes sense" (Elbow, 1986, p. 287).

It is reasonable to argue that without intimate knowledge of one's self one cannot enter into intimacy with another, that one "who is essentially a stranger to himself is unlikely to forge an affective connection to someone else" (Kohn, 1990, p. 152). Without self-knowledge we cannot exploit genuine similarities between self and other, using "templates" in the self to guide us to "matches" in the other. Without self-knowledge we cannot preserve the otherness of the other; he, she, or it becomes a creature of our projections. But how *well* must we know ourselves before we can know another, and must self-knowledge always come first? After all, as the philosopher Iris Murdoch says, "Self is as hard to see justly as other things" (Murdoch, 1970, p. 67)—harder, for people like Addie.

FEAR OF FUSION

Addie reports that when she entered her friends' subjective frames of reference, she lost touch with her own: "I felt, 'My God, I'm becoming—I'm not me anymore. I'm not thinking my own ideas anymore.' I was becoming very affected by other people's opinions and ideas." Writers on empathy seem to live in dread of such an event; anxiety over the possibility of "fusion" pervades the literature, expressed at times in hyperbolic terms and seeming to my mind to reach near-phobic proportions. "What happens to the self when it feels into the other?" Kohn asks, and he answers, apparently in an effort to quell anxiety that I was not experiencing, "All is not lost" (Kohn, 1990, p. 153). Kohn reports that Buber rejected the word *empathy* because it connoted "loss of the self in the process of experiencing the other" (Kohn, 1990, p. 153), and Buber was at pains to emphasize that one could experience the other "without forfeiting anything of the felt reality of his [own] reality" (Buber, 1947, p. 62). Schweickart assures us that Adrienne Rich does not "identify" with Dickinson, but merely "establishes an affinity" (Schweickart, 1989 p. 64). Steele warns that "the reader must claim her or his independence as a subject, not allowing her or himself to be subjugated by the text" (Steele, 1986, p. 259). Carl Rogers advises therapists "[t]o sense the client's world as if it were your own, but without ever losing the 'as if' quality" (Rogers, 1961, p. 284). Kohn asserts that empathy does not require that "the self become submerged in the other" or that "its subjectivity be demolished" (Kohn, 1990, p. 153), and Elbow reminds players of the believing game that "it's only a game"; they can quit at any time (Elbow, 1973. p. 174).

Although of course there is truth in the view that the empathic self can (indeed, must) maintain its integrity and need not (indeed, must not) allow itself to be consumed by the other, these statements raise the specter of reducing a paradox—"the paradox of separateness within connection," as Jordan defines it (Jordan, 1991, p. 69)—to a dichotomy: "seeing the self as *either* distinct and autonomous *or* merged and embedded" (Jordan, 1991, p. 72). Words like *forfeit, claim,* and *allow* seem to partake of a "justice" orientation, common among those who conceive of themselves as "separate" rather than "connected" in relationships (Lyons, 1983). Formulations of empathy seem often to begin from a premise of distance and difference—"strain[ing]" after similarity" (Barber, 1984, p. 175) across a divide over an "abyss" (Buber, 1947, p. 175)—rather than solidarity and similarity. Perhaps it is possible to "leave the self *intact* but also leave the self *transformed*" (Kohn, 1990, italics added) if *intact* is defined as "unimpaired," but the word carries traces of its root meaning of "untouched," and so in this context connotes an impregnable self. Indeed, if empathy is defined as projection into the other, as it is in the *Oxford Universal Dictionary* among many others, one may even detect a whiff of castration anxiety in forebodings of fusion.

The women we interviewed used images of reception rather than projection in describing connected knowing (*WWK*, 1986, p. 122). The biographer Elizabeth Young-Breuhl puts it this way:

> Empathizing involves . . . putting another person *in yourself*, becoming another person's habitat, without dissolving the person, without digesting the person. You are mentally pregnant, not with a potential life but with a person, indeed, a whole life, a person with her history. So the person lives on in you and you can, as it were, hear her in this intimacy. But this depends upon your ability to tell the difference between the subject and yourself, to appreciate the role that she plays in your psychic life. (Young-Breuhl, as quoted by Breslin, 1994, p. 19)

For Young-Breuhl "the other is incorporated as other" (Breslin, 1994, p. 19). There is a "doubling" of subjectivity, as in Schweickart's account of reading, in spite of the (paradoxical) fact that "there is only one subject present" (see my earlier discussion and Schweickart's chapter, this volume). In "caring," says the philosopher Nel Noddings, "I become a duality. . . . The seeing and feeling are mine, but only partly and temporarily mine, as on loan to me" (Noddings, 1984, p. 30). In this "receptive" conception of empathy one need never leave home, and so, perhaps, the risk of being stranded, like Addie, behind the eyes of the other, is diminished.[15] Although Buber's concept of "inclusion" (explicated by Friedman) contains images of moving out ("bold swinging into the life of another"), in (paradoxical) fact, it does not require that one leave one's home ground: "Inclusion . . . does not mean at any point that one gives up the ground of one's own concreteness [or] ceases to see through one's own eyes" (Friedman, 1985, p. 199) Inclusion means "making present." Through "mutual confirmation," Friedman says, "partners" make each other present in their "wholeness, unity, and uniqueness"[16] (Friedman, 1985, p. 4). In this context, connected knowing with the other and connected knowing with the self are reciprocal rather than oppositional processes: neither partner disappears into the other; each makes and keeps the other present.

KNOWING COMMUNITIES

Both separate and connected knowing achieve their full power when practiced in partnership with other like-minded knowers. Separate knowers benefit from partnership with friends willing to behave as enemies. Francis Crick, one of the discoverers of the structure of DNA, says, "A good scientist values criticism almost more highly than friendship; no, in science criticism is the height and measure of friendship. The collaborator points out the obvious, with due impatience. He stops the nonsense" (Crick, quoted by Bruffee, 1981, p. 178). An MIT student supplied a moving illustration of this process and, incidentally, of the detachment that is, for me, the heart and soul of separate knowing. Ed was one of several summer student interns working in a hospital laboratory on various projects. Each week the students met with the dozen or so scientists who were the "brains of the group," to present their problems and their ideas.

> I would say something like, "You know, we had this spike in the frequency plot here, and I think it's because of this," and before you could blink an eye one of the big older guys would go, "No, no, that's wrong." And I'm like— "Uh, okay." I mean, like, for three or four days I've been thinking that it was this thing. And I thought I was so clever for figuring it out. And the guy will— in—in five seconds shoot it down and say, "No, that's absolutely wrong because of this." And of course he's right.
>
> It took me a good part of the summer to realize how much it wasn't malicious. And that all these gentlemen were there for the purpose of science and for engineering. And they didn't mean anything personal, when they shot you down right away. But it was—the way they saw it is, they were dismissing a wrong proposition so it wouldn't have time to—They would—they would just take care of it right away.
>
> I thought it was real neat. To see that happen—I mean, some of these doctors are some of the best doctors or bioengineers around. And they were able to—they didn't see ideas as *possessions*. They saw ideas as ideas. [pause] And ideas were sort of like the group's ideas. You sat there and you formulated something for a project that the group was working on. So it was a group idea. [pause] It just continues to amaze me.[17]

Collaboration may be more essential to connected than to separate knowing. We are better at playing solitaire in the doubting game than in the believing game, Elbow thinks, because we've had more practice at it (Elbow, 1973, p. 175), and certainly the women we've talked with seemed more adept at doubting than believing themselves. It is easier to internalize a partner in the doubting game, because the rules of that game are codified within discourse communities, and anyone who knows the rules will do: the partner, to borrow a phrase from Kohn, is an "interchangeable someone" (Kohn, 1990, p. 112). Psychologists Marvin Berkowitz and Fritz Oser (1987) found that once adolescents reached the highest stage of skill in argumentation, achieving the ability to integrate a partner's argument with their own and to anticipate weaknesses in both, the partner became "superfluous . . . because one can now fully anticipate the other and take a more objective perspective on one's own reasoning, critically examining it as if from an outside perspective" (Berkowitz & Oser, 1987, p. 9).[18]

Because the partners in connected knowing are not interchangeable someones, but particular persons whose unique perspectives cannot be anticipated and so cannot be internalized, connected collaboration would seem to be minimally a two-person activity, although, of course, the external collaborator need not be a real and present person. Jill Tarule examines processes of connected collaboration in detail in her chapter in this volume. Here, I offer only one example, drawn from a famous short story, "A Jury of Her Peers," written by Susan Glaspell and published in 1917. Ed's story illustrates the power of detachment in the collaborative construction of knowledge; Glaspell's story shows how attachment can be an equally powerful force.

In the story, Mrs. Wright, a farmer's wife, has been taken off to jail on suspicion of murder, after apparently tying a rope around her husband's neck and strangling him in his sleep. Mrs. Hale, a neighbor who knew Mrs. Wright as a girl, but has rarely visited her in recent years, and Mrs. Peters, the sheriff's wife, are collecting household articles to take to Mrs. Wright in jail, while their husbands search the bleak homestead for clues to the motive for the crime. It is the women who come upon two crucial clues: a birdcage with its door hinge ripped apart, suggesting that "someone must have been—rough with it" (Glaspell, 1917, p. 273), and a strangled canary, laid in a pretty box. "'She liked the bird,'" Mrs. Hale says. "'She was going to bury it in that pretty box.'" Mrs. Peters, recapturing feelings she has trained herself to disown, remembers, "'When I was a girl . . . my kitten—there was a boy took a hatchet, and before my eyes—before I could get there—. . . If they hadn't held me back I would have—'—hearing the men's footsteps overhead she finishes "weakly,"— 'hurt him.'" "'Wright wouldn't like the bird,'" Mrs. Hale says, "'a thing that sang. She used to sing. He killed that too.'" Thinking of the bleak, childless, cheerless household, dominated by the chilly presence of the stern and silent Mr. Wright, which she has loathed to visit, and recalling

Mrs. Wright as "Minnie Foster, when she wore a white dress with blue ribbons and stood up there in the choir and sang" (Glaspell, 1917, p. 278), Mrs. Hale says, "'If there had been years and years of—nothing, then a bird to sing to you, it would be awful—still—after the bird was still.'" Glaspell writes, "It was as if something within her not herself had spoken, and it found in Mrs. Peters something she did not know as herself." "'I know what stillness is,' she said, in a queer, monotonous voice. 'When we homesteaded in Dakota, and my first baby died—after he was two years old—and me with no other then—'" (Glaspell, 1917, p. 278).

The empathic interchange seems to involve not just a "doubling" but at least a tripling of subjectivities: Each woman achieves greater understanding of herself and the other, and both come to understand a crime that had seemed initially inexplicable, especially to Mrs. Peters, a woman who is, after all, "married to the law." Digging down deep, the women find a commonality of experience that dissolves the distance between them and leads to the construction of knowledge. Although Glaspell is aware of distinctions among the three women, it is the similarities she emphasizes. Mrs. Hale says, "'We live close together and we live far apart. We all go through just a different kind of the same thing! If it weren't,—why do you and I *understand?* Why do we *know*—what we know this minute?'" (Glaspell, 1917, p. 279).

TRANSFORMATION OF SELF AND OTHER

Theories of empathy that stress preservation of an intact self seem irrelevant to Glaspell's story. They connote a conception of the self as "finished" as well as separate—a sort of packaged self that one carts about from one relationship to the next. My (partially) postmodern mind is more comfortable with a notion of selves-in-process, being coconstructed and reconstructed in the context of relationships, and this is the story Glaspell tells: Mrs. Peters, in particular, is transformed by the visions Mrs. Hale shares with her and by her own "retrospective self-empathy" (Blanck & Blanck, 1979, p. 251). Friedman's notion of "mutual confirmation" (adopted from Buber) does seem to imply such a conception: he says that "mutual confirmation is essential to becoming a self" (Friedman, 1985, p. 119), and confirmation, in Buber's terms means "accepting the whole potentiality. . . . 'I accept you as you are' [means that] I discover in you just by my accepting love . . . what you are meant to become'" (Buber, 1966, pp. 181 ff., quoted in Friedman, 1985, p. 136).

In highly developed forms of connected knowing with the other, it becomes possible to view the self from the perspective of the other. As Kohn says, "[i]n order to make the *other* into a subject by taking her perspective, one must . . . make the self into an object . . . come to see ourselves from the outside, the way others see us" (Kohn, 1990, p. 150). Schwaber describes how in becoming a more "connected" (my term) therapist, she moved from a traditional conception of the "transference" as "a phenomenon arising from internal pressures within the patient, from which the analyst, as a blank screen, could stand apart and observe, to that in which the specificity of the analyst's contribution was seen as intrinsic to its very nature" (Schwaber, 1983. p. 381). Taking the patient's reality seriously, "believing" it, forced her to see herself as the patient saw her, and to own (take seriously) her own response, instead of seeing it as merely a reaction to the patient's view, as is implied in the term *counter-transference.*

In one sense, it is not easy to objectify the self, to see one's self as others see us, especially, as Spelman points out, if it means entertaining the view of those whom we have oppressed of ourselves as oppressors (Spelman, 1988, p. 178). (Oppressors objectify the oppressed, of course, in order to prevent such revelations.) In another sense, however, women often find it all too easy to turn themselves into objects: the critic in their heads speaks from a distance, and it speaks in "shoulds," telling them how they ought to be and preventing them from seeing who they are and how they want to be. "Healthy self-objectification," Kohn says, consists of allowing one's self to be "watched and weighed" (Kohn, 1990, p. 151), an uncomfortable experience, but one that can be borne by "someone confident in her subjectivity, unafraid of being object to another." Many of our research participants, however, confess that they are not confident in their subjectivity, and, given the unhealthy objectifications to which they have been subjected in the past, perpetrated by not-so-friendly enemies within and without, they are understandably wary of being "watched and weighed." It is true that we need to face up to friends acting as enemies, but we also need friends acting as friends (Marshall & Reason, 1993), people who will view us with a compassionate rather than a critical eye, and who will invite us to do the same with them. *Subjectification*—joint subjectification—seems a better term than *objectification* to describe this process.

Spelman contrasts people (such as Schwaber) who actively seek out another person's viewpoint, "taking seriously how it represents a critique" of their own, with people who practice mere "tolerance" (Spelman, 1988, p. 183). The former are open to transformation; the latter are not. The subjectivist's spontaneity, her tendency to trust her own judgment and "go with her gut," are sources of genuine power, but they may limit her capacity for transformation. She is likely to emerge from "interactions" with ideas with her own prior positions intact. Asked how she decides among competing interpretations of a poem, a student replied:

> I usually find that when ideas are being tossed around I'm usually more akin to one than another. I don't know—my opinions are just sort of *there.*. . . It's almost more a matter of liking one more than another. I mean, I happen to agree with one or identify with it more.

In connected learning, on the other hand, both the learner and the subject matter are, Elbow says, "deformed":

> Good learning is not a matter of finding a happy medium where both parties are transformed as little as possible. Rather, both parties must be maximally transformed—in a sense deformed. There is violence in learning. We cannot learn something without eating it, yet we cannot really learn it either without being chewed up. (Elbow, 1986, p. 147)

Subjectivism is a form of what the psychologist David Perkins (Perkins, Farady, & Bushey, 1991) calls "makes-sense epistemology." A makes-sense epistemologist "believes that the way to evaluate conclusions is by asking whether they 'make sense' at first blush" (Baron, 1991, p. 177). The person

> only has to get to the point of telling one story about the situation that weaves together the facts in one way, from one point of view, congruent with the person's prior beliefs. Then the model "makes sense." When sense is achieved, there is no need to continue. (Perkins et al., 1991, p. 99)

Both separate and connected knowing are procedures that transcend makes-sense epistemology and meet the criteria for Perkins's "critical epistemology." Both procedures contain the premise that "it is not enough for a particular story to match one's prominent prior beliefs" (Perkins et al., 1991, p. 100), and "it is not enough for a particular story about a situation to hang together. One must consider what other, rather different stories might also hang together" (Perkins et al., 1991, pp. 99–100). In separate knowing one generates arguments that compete with a given position—another person's or one's own—and looks for flaws beneath the apparently sensible surface. In connected knowing one enters into stories beyond the bounds of one's own meager experience, and attempts to make meaning out of narratives that "at first blush" make little sense. Players in the believing game, Elbow says, are anything but credulous.

> The credulous person really suffers from *difficulty* in believing, not ease in believing: give him an array of assertions and he will always believe the one that requires the least expenditure of believing energy. He has a weak believing muscle and can only believe what is easy to believe. . . . The fact that we call this disease credulity when it is really incredulity reflects vividly our culture's fear of belief. (Elbow, 1973, p. 183)

Perhaps it was my own fear of belief, and my addiction to doubt, that made it so hard for me to see that when Grace told us of "falling down the rabbit hole, like Alice in Wonderland," she might be describing a hard-won ability, rather than an involuntary swoon; that an uncritical way of knowing might qualify as a critical epistemology; and that "going into the story" could be a powerful strategy for discovering how "other stories, rather different" from one's own, "might also hang together."

A part of me would like to end this chapter here, leaving you with a picture of connected knowing as a tough-minded, counterintuitive way of knowing, a critical epistemology that is in some sense the absolute opposite of the subjectivist makes-sense epistemology with which it is so often confused. This is how Elbow presents the believing game, as a way of achieving "distance" from one's spontaneous beliefs. And this is how we represent connected knowing in our research: "When I have an idea about something, and it *differs* from the way another person is thinking about it." But I cannot leave it at that. Neither Elbow's concept of the believing game nor the quotation we use in our research captures the full meaning I would like the concept to have.

Although it is important to distinguish the connected knower from the makes-sense epistemologist who accepts without further exploration whatever appears at first blush to be true, it is also important to remember that what appears to be true may in fact *be* true and should not be dismissed out of hand. This is a notion that frightens academicians, who greet with suspicion books like WWK and Gilligan's (1982) *In a Different Voice* precisely because the stories they tell "resonate so thoroughly" with the experience of women readers that they are accepted without further exploration as true and may serve to reinforce sexist stereotypes (Greeno & Maccoby, 1986, p. 315).

Of course it is dangerous to accept without further exploration ideas that seem intuitively right, but it is equally dangerous to dismiss out of hand knowledge gleaned from experience that fails to meet conventional standards of truth. That is what women and other groups marginal to the academy have done for years. We have been taught, to paraphrase Gilligan, "to forget what we know." It is well, I think, to remember what we know, or think we know; to preserve rather than abandon the respect for one's own intuition that is at the heart of subjectivism. Of course, what feels right may be wrong, but it may be right; "They" may be wrong. And although I agree that it is important to subject apparent truths to further exploration, I believe it is important to do so along connected as well as separate paths.

It took me a long time to recognize that there was a connected path. Separate knowing came easily to me, as I believe it does for most academic women, our proclivities in this direction being part of the reason we became academics: we like to argue and, as academics, we're allowed to. I first drifted into graduate school in search of the tough-minded reasoning I had known in college and had found largely missing during the years since college, spent mainly in the company of children under the age of eight and their mothers. I knew I had come to the right place when, at one of the first class meetings, the professor said, "Whenever an idea rings a bell with me, seems intuitively true, I'm immediately suspicious of it"—critical epistemology in a nutshell, and, to mix a couple of metaphors, just my cup of tea!

Like Sara Ruddick (this volume), I too have had a love affair with reason. The affair has endured, and although, as is often the case in long-term relationships, I have grown less starry-eyed and idealistic about this lover than I once was; like Ed, the MIT summer intern, I still find it "real neat" that a group of scientists can treat ideas "not as possessions" but "as ideas." On the twenty-fifth reading, Ed's story still sends thrills down my spine. I want my students, too, to fall in love and stay in love with separate knowing.

Once upon a time, this was my only wish. My pedagogical duty, as I saw it, was to stamp out any sign of reliance on firsthand experience and intuition, and instill a reliance on hard-headed critical thinking. For instance, when, objecting to my pronouncement from on high that males proved to be more adept on tests of spatial intelligence than females, a student in development psychology argued that she had a terrific sense of direction, whereas her brother couldn't find his way out of a paper bag, I would explain, patiently, through gritted teeth (accompanied, sometimes, by a sickly smile, but it's hard to do both at once), that of course there were exceptions, that psychological laws were merely proababilistic statements—saying to the student, in effect, "Your experience is irrelevant; your experience is embarrassing." In a sense, of course, I was "right," but so, in another sense, was she. Elsewhere, I have told how an African American student taught me, before the psychologist Diana Baumrind (1972) did, that parental practices defined as "authoritarian" might have a different meaning and different consequences in African American than in White families (Clinchy, 1995). Experiences such as these have led me to see that my job is not to suppress the lessons students have gained from firsthand experience, but to help them build on them. The other day, a colleague said, "Anecdotes are not data." "Nonsense," I replied, in characteristically connected fashion. "Of course they are."

As this essay attests, my relationship with connected knowing has become a full-blown affair. The procedures that Glaspell's Mrs. Hale and Mrs. Peters bring to bear on their problem are as exciting to me as the ones Ed's bioengineers bring to bear on theirs, and the knowledge they construct is just as powerful; indeed, as Mary Belenky's chapter (this volume) suggests, the Mrs. Hales and Mrs. Peterses might even transform the world.

I now bring to my teaching a polygamous epistemology, and I find that far from disrupting the first marriage, the second has stabilized it: the two are complementary. My students and I are amenable to argument, if we know that people are really listening. We are willing to dilly-dally in one another's embryonic notions, aware that with careful cultivation, these notions might blossom into powerful ideas—possibly even testable hypotheses to be subjected to the rigors of the doubting game. And, whereas once I hoped only that my students might achieve competence in the skills of separate knowing, now I wish for them what has meant so much to me—a marriage of two minds.

NOTES

1. Connected knowing differs in this respect from the believing game, the ultimate purpose of which is to test validity.
2. Unless otherwise indicated, quotations are from participants interviewed in various research projects, and names are pseudonyms.
3. In this research we frequently adopted responses given in one year as stimuli the next year, in an attempt to conduct a sort of quasi conversation among students across the period of the study.
4. Although there have always been less adversarial strains in philosophy and in social science (notably *verstehen*), they have not been dominant.
5. I thank my friend Margaret Osler for helping me to understand this.
6. We may invite misreading by careless use of the terms *subjective knowledge* and *subjectivism*, sometimes using them interchangeably, as Code (1991, p. 255) points out.
7. Subjectivists are not "authoritarian" in the usual sense, however; they make no claim that what is true for them should be true for others or that, as some standpoint theorists assert, their own views are privileged. They are honestly unmitigated relativists.
8. Separate (adversarial) interviewing also has its place, of course, and also requires skill, of a different sort.
9. In another instance of the perhaps inevitable failure of understanding across disciplinary divides, Code speaks of WWK's researchers as taking their respondents' words "literally," "from the surface" (1991, p. 256), a characterization that scarcely does justice to the sort of procedures DeVault describes, nor, indeed, to the complexity of any decent qualitative research procedure.
10. I have borrowed the phrase "I, thou, and it" from the philosopher of science David Hawkins (1967), who uses it in a different but related fashion in discussion of primary education.
11. These "body syntonic" (Turkle & Papert, 1990, note, p. 144) forms of connected knowing should be explored further. Some cultures, Nancy Goldberger says (see her chapter in this volume), support these ways of knowing, but the computer culture does not. Turkle and Papert tell of a fourth-grade boy who, overhearing a classmate speaking of "getting

down inside the computer," sneered: "That's baby talk." Instructors in a Harvard programming course were no more hospitable to these "primitive" modes.

12. Spelman (1988), following Jean-Paul Sartre, points out that the danger is not eliminated even when the subject is present. We can "imagine" the person sitting next to us instead of really trying to make her acquaintance.

13. Grumbach's description is reminiscent of Schwaber's account of the shift in her perspective as therapist from external expert, instructing the patient with her superior opinions, to "observer from within," dillydallying respectfully in their views.

14. In observations of very young children, psychologist Carolyn Zahn-Waxler and her colleagues found that "self-referential behaviors" such as "pointing to one's own injury when another is injured" and reproducing or imitating others' affective experiences" predicted later "empathic concern" (Zahn-Waxler, Radke-Yurrow, Wagner, & Chapman, 1992, pp. 133, 134).

15. Although this is sheer—perhaps wild—speculation, both "doubling" and the emphasis on receptivity versus projection may have precursors in early childhood. Doubling is reminiscent of the "double-voiced discourse" in which one attends simultaneously to one's own and one's playmates' agendas, observed by sociolinguist Amy Sheldon (1992) among preschoolers, especially girls. The spontaneous stories of preschool girls are often structured around domestic harmony, whereas boys' stories involve venturing forth into an often frightening and chaotic unknown (Nicoloupoulo, Scales, & Weintraub, 1994).

16. In my view, of course, the partner need not be a person.

17. I thank the student who conducted this interview as part of her work for a seminar I teach. The student must remain anonymous in order to protect Ed's identity, but she knows who she is.

18. "I have always had in my head an adversary," Piaget says (1972, p. 222). Piaget's adversary, usually a logical positivist, seems to me to have been something of a pushover.

REFERENCES

Barber, B. R. (1984). *Strong democracy: Participatory politics for a new age.* Berkeley: University of California Press.

Baron, J. (1991). Beliefs about thinking. In J. F. Voss, D. N. Perkins, & J. W. Segal (Eds.), *Informal reasoning and education,*169–186. Hillsdale, NJ: Lawrence Erlbaum.

Basch, M. F. (1983). The concept of self: An operational definition. In B. Lee & G. Noam (Eds.), *Developmental approaches to the self.* New York: Plenum Press.

Baumrind, D. (1972). An exploratory study of socialization effects on black children: Some black-white comparisons. *Child Development, 43,* 261–267.

Belenky, M., Clinchy, B., Goldberger, N., & Tarule, J. (1986). *Women's ways of knowing: The development of self, voice, and mind.* New York: Basic Books.

Berkowitz, M. W., & Oser, F. (1987, April). *Stages of adolescent interactive logic.* Paper presented at the Biennial Meeting of the Society for Research in Child Development, Baltimore, MD.

Berreby, David. (1995, April 9). Unabsolute truths: Clifford Geertz. *New York Times Magazine.*

Blanck, G. & Blanck, R. (1979). *Ego psychology II: Psychoanalytic developmental psychology.* New York: Columbia University Press.

Breslin, James, E. B. (1994, July 24). Terminating Mark Rothko: Biography is mourning in reverse. *The New York Times Book Review, 3,* 19.

Brown, L. M., & Gilligan, C. (1992). *Meeting at the crossroads: Women's psychology and girls' development.* Cambridge, MA: Harvard University Press.

Bruffee, K. A. (1981). The structure of knowledge and the future of liberal education. *Liberal Education, 67,* 177–186.

Bruner, J. S. (1986). Actual minds, possible worlds. Cambridge, MA: Harvard University Press.

Buber, M. (1947/1965). *Between man and man.* (Ronald G. Smith, Trans.). New York: Macmillan.

Buber, M. (1966). *The knowledge of man: A philosophy of the interhuman.* New York: Harper & Row, Torchbooks.

Clinchy, B. (1995). A connected approach to the teaching of developmental psychology. *Teaching of Psychology, 22,* 100–104.

Clinchy, B., & Zimmerman, C. (1982). Epistemology and agency in the development of undergraduate women. In P. Perun (Ed.), *The undergraduate woman: Issues in educational equity.* Lexington, MA: D. C. Heath.

Clinchy, B., & Zimmerman, C. (1985). Growing up intellectually: Issues for college women. *Work in Progress,* No. 19. Wellesley, MA: Stone Center Working Papers Series.

Code, L. (1991). *What can she know?* Ithaca, NY: Cornell University Press.

DeVault, M. L. (1990). Talking and listening from women's standpoint: Feminist strategies for interviewing and analysis. *Social Problems, 37,* 96–116.

Elbow, P. (1973). Appendix essay: The doubting game and the believing game—an analysis of the intellectual enterprise. In *Writing without teachers.* London: Oxford University Press.

Elbow, P. (1986). *Embracing contraries.* New York: Oxford University Press.

Field, J. (1936/1981). *A life of one's own.* Los Angeles: J. P. Tarcher, St. Martin's Press.

Flavell, J. (1985). *Cognitive development* (2nd ed.). Englewood Cliffs, NJ: Prentice Hall.

Friedman, M. (1985). *The healing dialogue in psychotherapy.* New York: Jason Aronson.

Geertz, C. (1986, Winter). The uses of diversity. *Michigan Quarterly Review,* 105–123.

Gilligan, C. (1982). *In a different voice.* Cambridge, MA: Harvard University Press.

Glaspell, S. (1917). A jury of her peers. Reprinted in E. J. O'Brien (Ed.) (1918), *The best short stories of 1917 and the yearbook of the American short story,* 256–281. Boston: Small, Maynard.

Goodfield, J. (1991/1994). *An imagined world: A story of scientific discovery.* Ann Arbor: University of Michigan Press.

Gordon, M. (1980). The parable of the cave or: In praise of watercolors. In J. Sternburg (Ed.), *The writer on her work,* 27–32. New York: W. W. Norton.

Greeno, C. G., & Maccoby, E. E. (1986). On *In a different voice:* An interdisciplinary forum: How different is the "different voice"? *Signs, 11,* 310–316.

Grumbach, D. (1991). *Coming into the end zone: A memoir.* New York: W. W. Norton.

Hawkesworth, M. E. (1989). Knowers, knowing, known: Feminist theory and claims of truth. *Signs, 14,* 533–557.

Hawkins, D. (1967). *I, thou, it.* Reprint of a paper presented at the Primary Teachers' Residential Course, Loughborough, Leicestershire. Cambridge, MA: Elementary Science Study, Educational Services, Inc.

Hogan, R. (1973). Moral conduct and moral character: A psychological perspective. *Psychological Bulletin, 70,* 217–232.

Howard, G. S. (1991). Culture tales: A narrative approach to thinking, cross-cultural psychology, and psychotherapy. *American Psychologist, 46,* 187–197.

Jordan, J. (1991). Empathy and self boundaries. In J. V. Jordan, A. G. Kaplan, J. B. Miller, I. P. Stiver, & J. L. Surrey (Eds.), *Women's growth in connection: Writings from the Stone Center,* 67–80. New York: Guilford Press.

Keller, E. F. (1983a). *A feeling for the organism.* New York: Freeman.

Keller, E. F. (1983b). Women, science, and popular mythology. In J. Rothschild (Ed.), *Machine ex dea,* 131–135. New York: Pergamon Press.

Kohn, A. (1990). *The brighter side of human nature: Altruism and empathy in everyday life.* New York: Basic Books.

Kohut, H. (1978). The psychoanalyst in the community of scholars. In P. Ornstein (Ed.), *The search for the self: Selected writings of Heinz Kohut,* Vol. 2, 685–724. New York: International Universities Press.

Koller, A. (1990). *The stations of solitude.* New York: William Morrow.

Lather, P. (1986). Issues of validity in openly ideological research: Between a rock and a soft place. *Interchange, 17,* 63–84.

Lyons, N. (1983). Two perspectives on self, relationships, and morality. *Harvard Education Review, 53,* 125–145.

McCracken, G. D. (1988). *The long interview. Qualitative research methods series* (vol. 13). Newbury Park: Sage.

McMillan, C. (1982). *Women, reason and nature.* Princeton, NJ: Princeton University Press.

Mansfield, A., & Clinchy, B. (1992, May 28). The influence of different kinds of relationships on the development and expression of "separate" and "connected" knowing in undergraduate women. Paper presented as part of a symposium, Voicing relationships, knowing connection: Exploring girls' and women's development, at the 22nd Annual Symposium of the Jean Piaget Society: Development and vulnerability in close relationships. Montreal, Québec, Canada.

Margulies, A. (1989). *The empathic imagination.* New York: W. W. Norton.

Marshall, J. & Reason, P. (1993). Adult learning in collaborative action research: reflections on the supervision process. *Studies in continuing education, 15,* 117–133.

May, R. (1969). The emergence of existential psychotherapy. In R. May, E. Angel, & H. F. Ellenberger (Eds.), *Existence.* New York: Simon & Schuster.

Mischel, W. (1969). Continuity & change in personality. *American Psychologist, 24,* 1012–1018.

Morawski, J. G., & Steele, R. S. (1991). The one or the other? Textual analysis of masculine power and feminist empowerment. *Theory and Psychology, 1,* 107–131.

Moulton, J. (1983). A paradigm of philosophy: The adversary method. In Harding, S., & Hintikka, M. B. (Eds.), *Discovering reality*. Dordrecht, Holland: Reidel.

Murdoch, I. (1970/1985). *The sovereignty of good*. London: ARK Paperbacks, Routledge & Kegan Paul.

Nicolopoulou, A., Scales, B., & Weintraub, J. (1994). Gender differences and symbolic imagination in the stories of four-year-olds. In A. H. Dyson & C. Genish (Eds.), *The need for story: Cultural diversity in classroom and community*. Urbana, IL: National Council of Teachers of English.

Noddings, N. (1984). *Caring*. Berkeley, CA: University of California Press.

Papert, S. (1980). *Mindstorms*. New York: Basic Books.

Patai, D. & Koertge, N. (1994). *Professing feminism*. New York: Basic Books.

Perkins, D. N., Farady, M., & Bushey, B. (1991). Everyday reasoning and the roots of intelligence. In J. F. Voss, D. N. Perkins, & J. W. Segal (Eds.), *Informal reasoning and education*. Hillsdale, NJ: Lawrence Erlbaum.

Perry, W. (1970). *Forms of intellectual and ethical development in the college years*. New York: Holt, Rinehart, & Winston.

Piaget, J. (1972) *The child's conception of the world*. Totowa, NJ: Littlefield, Adams.

Poulet, G. (1980). Criticism and the experience of interiority (C. Macksey & R Macksey, Trans.). In J. Tomkins (Ed.), *Reader-response criticism: From formalism to structuralism*. Baltimore: Johns Hopkins University Press.

Rabin, C. (1994). *Separate and connected knowing in undergraduate men and women*. Unpublished undergraduate honors thesis, Wellesley College, Wellesley, MA.

Rich, A. (1979). Vesuvius at home: The power of Emily Dickinson. In *On lies, secrets and silence: Selected prose, 1966–1978*. New York: W. W. Norton.

Riger, S. (1992). Epistemological debates, feminist voices: Science, social values, and the study of women. *American Psychologist, 47*, 730–740.

Rogers, C. R. (1951). *Client-centered therapy*. Boston: Houghton Mifflin.

Rogers, C. R. (1961). *On becoming a person: A therapist's view of psychotherapy*. Boston: Houghton Mifflin.

Rogers, C. R. (1980). Empathic: An unappreciated way of being. In *A way of being* (pp. 137–163). Boston: Houghton Mifflin.

Rogers, C. R., & Farson, R. E. (1967). Active listening. In Haney, W. V. *Communication and organizational behavior: Text and cases*, 81–97. Homewood, IL: Richard D. Irwin.

Ruddick, S. (1984). New combinations: Learning from Virginia Woolf. In Asher, C., DeSalvor, L., & Ruddick, S. *Between women*. Boston: Beacon Press.

Schafer, R. (1964). The clinical analysis of affects. *Journal of the American Psychoanalytic Association, 12*, 275–299.

Schwaber, E. (1983a). Psychoanalytic listening and psychic reality. *International Review of Psychoanalysis, 10,* 379–392.

Schwaber, E. (1983b). Construction, reconstruction, and the mode of clinical attunement. In A. Goldberg (Ed.), *The future of psychoanalysis,* 273–291. New York: International Universities Press.

Schweickart, P. P. (1986). Reading ourselves: Toward a feminist theory of reading. In Elizabeth A. Flynn & P. P. Schweickart (Eds.), *Gender and reading: Essays on readers, texts, and contexts,* 31–62. Baltimore: Johns Hopkins University Press.

Schweickart, P. P. (1988). Engendering critical discourse. In C. Koelb & Victor Lokke (Eds.), *The current in criticism: Essays on the present and future of criticism,* 295–317. West Lafayette, IN: Purdue University Press.

Schweickart, P. P. (1989). Reading, teaching, and the ethic of care. In S. L. Gabriel & I. Smithson (Eds.), *Gender in the classroom: Power and pedagogy,* 78–95. Chicago: University of Illinois Press.

Sheldon, A. (1992). Conflict talk: Sociolinguistic challenges to self-assertion and how young girls meet them. *Merrill-Palmer Quarterly, 38,* 95–118.

Spelman, E. V. (1988). *Inessential woman: Problems of exclusion in feminist thought.* Boston: Beacon Press.

Steele, R. S. (1986). Deconstructing histories: Toward a systematic criticism of psychological narratives. In T. R. Sarbin, *Narrative psychology: The storied nature of human conduct,* 256–275. New York: Praeger.

Tannen, D. (1990). *You just don't understand: Women and men in conversation.* New York: Ballantine.

Torbert, W. (1976). *Creating a community of inquiry: Conflict, collaboration, transformation.* New York: Wiley.

Turkle, S. (1984). *The second self: The computer and the human spirit.* New York: Simon & Schuster.

Turkle, S. & Papert, S. (1990). Epistemological pluralism: styles and voices within the computer culture. *Signs, 16,* 128–157.

What bothers me about girls. (1994, March 13). *Parade.*

Woolf, V. (1929/1989). *A room of one's own.* New York: Harvest/HBJ Book, Harcourt Brace Jovanovich.

Woolf, V. (1932/1948). How should one read a book? In *The common reader, Series 1 and 2,* 281–295. New York: Harcourt Brace.

Zahn-Waxler, C., Radke-Yarrow, M., Wagner, E. & Chapman, M. (1992). Development of concern for others. *Developmental Psychology, 28,* 126–136.

Reason's "Femininity"

A Case for Connected Knowing*

SARA RUDDICK

WOMEN'S RELATION TO REASON is notoriously troubled. Often we have been explicitly excluded by philosophers whose task it is to determine what counts as "rational." As the philosopher Lorraine Code summarizes the sorry situation:

> The ideals of rationality and objectivity that have guided and inspired theorists of knowledge throughout the history of western philosophy have been constructed through excluding the attributes and experiences commonly associated with femaleness and underclass status: emotion, connection, practicality, sensitivity and idiosyncracy. (Code, 1993, p. 21)

For those who are excluded, performance offers no escape from stigma. As the "Negro" psychiatrist Franz Fanon puts it:

> After much reluctance, the scientists had conceded that the Negro was a human being. . . . Reason was confident on every level. . . . [But] that victory

*I am grateful to Nancy Goldberger for careful and patient attention to earlier drafts and to Lynn Phillips for a careful and valuable reading.

played cat and mouse; it made a fool of me. As the other put it, when I was present, it [reason] was not; when it was there I was no longer. (Fanon, cited by Gordon, 1995, p. 68)

Despite this near-metaphysical discouragement, many women of all races and classes, and many men and women of so-called inferior classes, set out to prove their rationality. The challenge is daunting. Vulnerable to insult, susceptible to arrogant dismissal, often enough deprived of the resources that a developing reason requires, the excluded must nonetheless convince their judges of their worthiness. The task is also barely coherent. If worth is judged by systematically exclusionary criteria, the excluded must simultaneously fulfill prevailing standards and challenge them, must satisfy judges while denying their fitness to judge.

For privileged women whose parents are already counted as reasoners, or for women who are particularly diligent, gifted, and lucky "good students," the promise of inclusion can be treacherous in particular ways. Such women are often seduced by the promise of impersonal ideals of rationality. In a story now told many times over, these women frequently encounter stubborn, lingering prejudice against women's intellect or intellectual women. More abstractly, to the extent that reason is seen to have no sex, is neuter rather than male, it tends to be opposed to all that is bodily, including sexual difference, including, therefore the female, always the different sex.[1] Persons are reasonable, women are persons, but "womanliness" remains one of reason's antagonists. To make matters more complex, women are also offered, often seduced by, a flattering conception of "womanly" minds appropriate to their domestic relationships and work. So, in the words of Immanuel Kant, an enlightened philosopher, a women who thinks might as well wear a beard. But Kant admired a woman who thinks "differently," that is, a woman whose taste, sensibility, practical sense, and feeling disqualify her for masculine argument but equip her for wifeliness and mothering.[2]

Intellectual women have adopted various strategies for coping with conflicts between reason and "femininity." Some argue that the admittedly egregious sexism and racism of some Western philosophers does not contaminate the universal standpoint of reason that they and other more enlightened philosophers advocate. Rather than excluding women, impersonal reason offers the best defense against racism, misogyny, and many sorts of misguided passion. Moreover, these women might continue, in many Western cultures, and notably in their intellectual circles, superstitions about women's minds and prejudices against their achievement are on the wane. (No one, after all, praises Kant for his insights about women.) Today women should lay claim to, rather than question, the pleasures, powers, and capacities of reason. In *Women's Ways of Knowing* (WWK) terminology, these women would probably find themselves among "procedural knowers" to whom WWK attributes the "voice of reason."

In contrast, the most alienated women, like WWK "subjectivists," "distrust logic, analysis, abstraction, and even language itself . . . alien territory belonging to men" (Belenky, Clinchy, Goldberger, & Tarule, 1986, p. 71). Others, so-called different voice theorists, temper a milder alienation from dominant ideals of rationality with a strong, positive desire to redescribe and endorse the cognitive capacities that have been labeled feminine, to bring a "different voice" into epistemological conversations. These women appear most strongly in WWK in the authorial voice, throughout the text and especially in the discussion of "connected knowers."

Many intellectual feminists move, as particular situations or intellectual tasks suggest, between endorsing and rejecting both dominant and allegedly "feminine" voices of reason. Their primary aim is to revise ideals of rationality so that they better represent and serve women. These feminists are "constructivist" in a sense akin to the WWK use of the term. They recognize that ideals of reason are socially created in particular historical circumstances whose power relations they reflect. They therefore subject these ideals to a "hermeneutics of suspicion" in order to reveal their exclusionary force, partiality, and epistemological inadequacy. At the same time they develop alternative, less partial, more inclusive, and, importantly, more "objective" ideals of reason. WWK as a whole, and in its particular praise of constructivists knowers, endorses and contributes to this revisionary work.

Although feminist strategies can be located within a *Women's Ways of Knowing* conceptual scheme, its authors are engaged in an enterprise that is distinct from most feminist epistemology in ways that are exciting for many women. The authors do not begin, as epistemologists typically do, by asking how women *should* know, how they justify their knowledge claims, but rather how they *do* know, what stances they actually take toward evidence, authority, and argument. Unlike many philosophers, even feminists, the WWK authors do not (usually) draw inspiration or authority from earlier (often white male) philosophers; WWK gathers its ideas from women.[3] The authors are white, apparently heterosexual, and to varying degrees "comfortable enough" women, but their stated aim and increasingly successful practice is to cultivate and respect diversity among the women with whom they speak. Most important they are clearly on the side of women who, because of poverty, violence, racial bigotry, or dismissive arrogance, have been deprived of the promise and pleasures of reason.

Not surprisingly, WWK evokes passionate response. Students—and I too—come to our reading with an uneasy, ambivalent, yet intense investment in reason. They are/I am promised democratic ideals of rationality that originate in, and can enhance, their own experiences of knowing. Yet despite, and partly because of, these expectations, WWK is a controversial, sometimes even a divisive text. For women's troubles with reason cannot be made simply to disappear. Indeed, despite their intentions and stated agenda, certain central aspects of the WWK conceptual framework seem to raise in new guises familiar tensions between "women's ways" and "knowing."

I will consider three such focuses of tension. First, despite their respectful relation to women in every "epistemological position," the authors engage in judgments couched in the terms of developmental theory. Claims of psychological "progress" can appear more disturbingly normative than epistemological judgments. Psychologists evaluate people whereas epistemologists (typically) propose standards that (allegedly) any person can meet. Second, some readers "accuse" WWK of "essentialism," attributing to women in very different social circumstances distinctly "women's" ways of knowing. Finally WWK appears to praise certain kinds of "womanly" knowing in a way reminiscent of Kant. It therefore raises the specter of a distinctively female domestic and domesticated mind.

DEVELOPMENT

From very early in their book to Nancy Goldberger's latest work on cultural psychology, WWK authors have denied that they are positing higher and lower stages in a developmental theory.

> We describe in this book epistemological *perspectives* from which women know and view the world. We leave it to future work to determine whether these perspectives have any stagelike qualities. (Belenky et al., 1986, p. 15)

The most they are willing to do is to "speculate about developmental sequences or trajectories," drawing on their subjects' stories of intellectual change.

Despite these explicit disclaimers, the rhetoric of the book, reinforced by its organization and the invocation of other developmental psychologists, continually evokes notions of progress from simpler to more com-

plex, less to more adequate "ways of knowing" or "epistemological perspectives." Moreover, whatever their intentions, WWK authors will be
read within the context of psychological theory and U.S. educational
institutions. The "progression" from received knowing to proceduralism
and then constructivism mirrors dominant educational ideologies. It
therefore not only gives the illusion of progress but also serves as an accurate measure of what counts as epistemological success.

The idea of "development" is intuitively both attractive and plausible.
Parents and teachers are delighted when children or students think more
subtly, comprehensively, critically, appreciatively—to use vague but
deliberately judgmental terms. It is enormously heartening to read of
Mary Belenky's work (this volume) with young, impoverished mothers
who move out of "silence" into an appreciation of their own and their
children's minds. And none of us wants to be beyond "development."

Yet I have a suspicion "in my gut" of the ideal of developmental stages
and of the developmental rhetoric of WWK. Generally speaking, I find
"stages" of development redolent of social status, educational class, and,
in a country where status and class are racialized, redolent also of racial
arrogance. International relations between more or less "developed"
states reek of imperialist arrogance and exploitation. The difficulty is not
only that the less "developed" are treated with condescension. As standpoint theorists have argued, those who are marginalized or subjugated
may see what insiders deny; their standpoint, epistemologically speaking,
may be less partial, more "objective," than that of those who enact dominant epistemologies.[4]

The idea of developmental stages has been specifically insulting to
women. I began by noting that in much of Western philosophy judgments of more adequate, "developed," rationality are shot through with
misogyny. Similarly, in many versions of psychological theory a child
develops by "separating" from the mother. Despite passionate commitment to women, there may be vestiges of misogyny even in WWK.
Received knowing and subjectivism, low in the ladder, are resonant with
"femininity"—excessive trust, passivity, conventionality, dependence on
authority among the received knowers, emotionality and self-preoccupied
self-expression among the subjectivists. On the other hand, WWK praises
connected knowing, which they at least tacitly associate with "women."
It is perhaps significant that connected knowing seems to have emerged
almost accidentally, outside the developmental scheme. "Zimmerman
and I [Clinchy] stumbled upon what we now call connected knowing
while searching for evidence of what we call separate knowing." They
first labeled connected knowing as 4F, an allusion to a similar fourth

position identified by the psychologist William Perry, joined with an F for female (F) and, by association, for the draft classification "unfit for military [epistemological] service" (Clinchy, 1995, p. 25).

I recognize that my difficulties with WWK's idea of development are partly a result of standing outside psychological disciplines. I am perhaps unduly disturbed by the psychological conception of a knowing, developing "self." Although WWK speaks of "ways of knowing," it classifies *people.* A woman doesn't know in a receptive way in respect to some subjects in certain circumstances. Rather she is a "received knower." To the extent that her way of knowing is lesser, so is she.[5] This, unlike, for example, Mary Belenky's inspiring accounts of change in previously silent women, sets my teeth on edge. When WWK does classify epistemological tendencies I am not always clear whether they are identifying ways in which women "know," attitudes toward their own and others' knowledge, or philosophical positions about the ways in which knowledge is produced and legitimated.

These discomforts often sound churlish in my own ears. I am aware that the WWK authors, unlike most epistemologists, attend to the real material circumstances of knowers. They are evidently more interested in applauding "progress" than in judging applicants. Most important, whatever the constrictions of the developmental scheme, WWK recognizes bona fide epistemological value in distinct ways of knowing, a respect that its favored "constructivists share."

Inspired by WWK's insightful and respectful attention to women, aware of my ignorance of psychological theory, I have been tempted to bypass my worries about development. But in discussions over the years, including most recently with colleagues about this essay, the idea of "developmental stages" haunts me and hinders the kinds of open reflection on epistemology that the book should inspire. I therefore repeat here certain ideas about development I used to urge on students, who almost to a woman (and to a man) also rejected developmental schemes. My aim then, as in this essay, was to defuse resistance to developmental theory so that I/we could more fruitfully discuss the book.

Briefly and dogmatically then, this is the way I understand epistemological "development." Although there are more or less complex and adequate "ways of knowing" or epistemological positions, there is no single measure of progress. Cognitive capacities are not inherently at odds. Individuals differ from each other in their ability to know receptively; engage in impersonal, rule-governed inquiry; name and tolerate emotions; to mention only three capacities prominent in WWK. Any group— family, classroom, political caucus, or neighborhood organization—

would want to include individuals who collectively express these and other cognitive capacities.

Each position or way has its virtues and defects. Nancy Goldberger (this volume) explores various cultural and positive meanings of silence at what appears to be the lowest rung of the WWK ladder. From her appreciative accounts of silence we might learn a lesson critical to white intellectuals at this moment: the ability to remain silent out of respect for what you don't understand is often an intellectual achievement and political virtue as well as a practical necessity. At WWK's top reaches, a thorough constructivist epistemology may well lack respect for the "intractable dimensions of the world ... the intransigence of material circumstances" (Code, 1993, p. 40). Less abstractly, a respect for each way of knowing within its personal or cultural context can lend itself to a tepid epistemological laissez faire.

Epistemological positions or ways of knowing are elicited in particular circumstances (see Goldberger, this volume). For example, "silence," understood solely as a negative state of not knowing, designates a conjunction of fears and passivities that can afflict any knower caught in threatening social circumstances, whatever other ways of knowing she has acquired. Similarly, a person may "feel in her gut," and respect her feelings, as I am trying to do with regard to "development," without that subjectivism's preventing "impersonal" inquiry. It may also be true that certain ways or positions may, at least for a time, characterize a *person*. So, for example, for some people subject to social or familial abuse, "silence," in its wholly negative sense, becomes a settled condition of mind. Similarly, faced with classroom divisions that I will take up later, I found myself referring to "knowers" who were "separate" or "connected," so settled did certain students seem in their epistemological ways.

A person does not "know" irrespective of the object of knowledge or the practices in which she is engaged. A mother (to take only one group WWK treats with special respect) may try to understand her child's night terrors, his nutritional needs, the social structure of her workplace, her physician's advice about her own chronic pain, and, for example, depending on her expertise, the costs and consequences of managed care, the most effective and least demeaning sales techniques, or the intricacies of immigration law. It is unlikely that she will "know" in the same way in each of these contexts; nor, if she becomes epistemologically reflective, will she likely take the same position toward authority, evidence, argument, and persuasion. On the other hand, prolonged focus on any of these kinds of inquiries may well produce cognitive capacities and attitudes that recur to different degrees in epistemologically dissimilar contexts. Thus maternal thinking, as a whole, might affect even the models of theoretical science.

Finally a "position" or "way" allows development *within* its modality. There are more or less adequate ways of "receiving," for example, as is evident from WWK remarks on "receptive rationality" in their discussion of connected knowing, or their remarks on attentive love, which is associated with constructivism. To know receptively and more adequately—with a nuanced and flexible relation to authorities, for example, or with a clearer sense of the dangers of projection—it is not necessary for a received knower to move on to another "position." She receives differently. Similarly, Blythe Clinchy urges developmental psychologists "to look for psychological development 'within rather than beyond the concrete', to begin to trace the development not *from* concrete thinking but *of* concrete thinking" (Clinchy, 1994, p.5). WWK itself could be read as advocating a more developed proceduralism, one still respectful of shared self-restraining ("impersonal") methodologies, but less adversarial, more collaborative, less imperiously judgmental of other ways of knowing, than the proceduralism practiced in U.S. universities.

With these obiter dicta I turn away from the idea of development. In closing I will introduce relational and social conceptions of knowing offered by feminist epistemologists that I believe lend support to these conceptions of development while undermining notions of context-free "progression." But I will not otherwise "justify" the conceptions I now presuppose.

WWK, "FEMININITY," AND REASON: I

Suspicion of femininity—of allegedly "feminine" ethics, epistemological ideals, or psychological identities—was pervasive in U.S. feminist and intellectual circles in the late eighties and early nineties. Not surprisingly, suspicions of femininity also arose during the several years (1989–94) that I included WWK as a text in graduate and undergraduate seminars on feminist epistemology or feminist ethics. Both public and classroom discussions had two entwined but distinct preoccupations: "essentialist" attribution of "women's" voices to women of radically distinct social circumstances and a positive estimation of "feminine" values.

The national discussion focused on "essentialism." I have found that those who know WWK only by reputation—or by its somewhat misleading title—expect that it is "essentialist." It seems to me, however, that the WWK authors are relatively free of "essentialist" generalization. They speak of "women," not woman. They identify at least five epistemologi-cal positions or "ways of knowing." Each, since the authors studied women, is ipso facto womanly; none is declared, a priori, absent from men's thinking. Hence WWK makes no claim for a single "feminine" (let alone female) way of reasoning even within the cultures they study.

The authors do suggest that women's and men's histories of knowing tend to differ. But unless the getting and making of knowledge were quite divorced from ordinary experience, we should expect that women and men would reveal somewhat different ways of knowing in a society with a long history of patriarchy where women and men continue to lead "gendered lives" (Fineman, 1994). The existence at this historical moment in this culture of a gendered dimension to epistemology does not mean that women of different cultures, all women of a given culture, or even women within a family share "ways of knowing."

More important, from the outset the WWK authors were aware of the dangers of white and privileged parochialism. They attempted to listen as widely as possible to women of various ethnicities and classes, adopting a strategy of *inclusion*, or responsible generalization, later endorsed by philosopher Jane Roland Martin in her critical discussion of the taboo of "essentialism" (Martin, 1994). In their reporting, the WWK authors attend to the particular social circumstances of the women they interview and of their families. More recently, Nancy Goldberger and her new col-laborators have engaged self-critically in multicultural research and let their subjects' stories challenge basic developmental categories of WWK.

In the years surrounding the publication of WWK, feminist theorists, especially women of color, elaborated a complex, rich account of the ways "women" are multiply burdened, multiply jeopardized, and some-times multiply empowered by race, sexual orientation, ethnicity, "native" or immigrant status, and social class. Collectively, these theorists reject claims of single, primary, or fixed identities, including the identity "women." Instead they speak of identities as "intersections" of social experiences or markers; of "multiple," sometimes conflicting, conscious-ness; of "mobile subjectivities" evoked in particular circumstances.[6] In my classes, we read some of these writings before, some after, turning to WWK. We noted the relative absence of specific references in WWK to race, sexual orientation, and class—though poverty was a weighty pres-ence. These readings by women of color also called into question the unified "self" who sometimes appears to be the subject of "develop-ment." We, like the authors themselves, realized that WWK needed mod-ification, but fears of essentializm did not prevent our open exploration of the text.

WWK, REASON, AND FEMININITY: II
AN IMPASSE

There is a second dissent from WWK's way of talking about "women," which is often subsumed under the charge of essentialist generalization but which I believe is distinct. Briefly, WWK appears to praise ways of knowing that are "feminine" and perhaps more often expressed by women than men. This flat statement does not capture the tension surrounding the possibility of this epistemological "difference."

I have found that I can best capture the emotions surrounding the idea of allegedly "feminine reason" by remembering students responses to WWK and my responses to students. What I recall as the honest, relatively untutored responses of certain students illuminate, I believe, dissensions and feelings less frankly expressed in meetings of feminists and feminist philosophers where "women's" perspectives are discussed. But a word of warning. I am not presenting bona fide research about student attitudes. I do recall vividly that in the first undergraduate seminar in which I taught WWK our discussions became almost too angry and divided for fruitful, productive exchange. But in speaking of this and other classes I am supplementing memory—perhaps even inventing. I introduce students in order to capture a *conversation* in which I myself was a confused and anxious participant. Similar conversations seem to repeat themselves in more public domains. By speaking within a conversation I approach the subject of "feminine reason" indirectly. In the final section I will step out of conversation and offer, in my own voice, certain concepts of knowing and gender that I hope defuse the anxieties I report and also provide a context in which the idea of allegedly "feminine reason" makes sense.

But now to the story. In her classic essay "A gender diary" the critic Ann Snitow (1992) writes of a "central divide" among feminists about the value of "femininity." She contrasts two women's responses to feminism. "Now I can be a woman," says one, who feels she need no longer pretend to be a man. "Now I don't have to be a woman anymore," says another, who counts on feminism to free her from constraints of gender. The first feminist attributes to women certain valuable characteristics, say "connected knowing" or an "ethics of care." She is also likely to "maximize," and often celebrate, differences between women and men. The second feminist "minimizes" differences between women and men and attributes them to social conditions that can and should be changed. Rather than celebrating women's voices, she envisions a society in which all voices are heard but gender makes no difference.

There were both kinds of feminists in my classrooms, and some who did not much count themselves as feminists at all. But all of the students tended to see the WWK authors as "maximizers." Like the philosopher Nel Noddings and the psychologist Carol Gilligan, whom they cite, the WWK authors appeared to be engaged in "different voice" theorizing, identifying and legitimating "womanly" women's way of knowing. More specifically, the students heard these authors as *praising* "connectedness," a voice of one's own, emotionality, "embodied" knowledge, and other characteristics widely understood to be "feminine."

The students did not doubt, nor were they especially excited by, the general idea that women's and men's ways of knowing differ. Nor were they disturbed when WWK noted differences between women and men that might be attributed to patriarchal oppression, if women were said to be more easily silenced than men, for example, or more subservient to, less identified with authority. But for many students women's alleged differences from men became disturbing when joined with an appreciation of the differences observed. Hence, when girls were reported to find the telephone a favorite toy, when this preference appeared as a preparation for "connected" knowing, difference became decidedly unwelcome.

The students who were most critical of WWK tended to be both minimizers skeptical of women's differences from men and, in WWK terms, impersonal, separate procedural knowers.[7] (That is, they described themselves as proceduralists when asked by me to characterize themselves in WWK terms, though they barely countenanced this kind of "psychological" classifying.) But though they recognized themselves as impersonal proceduralists, these students were critical of what they took to be WWK's negative portrayal of that epistemological position. To be sure, proceduralism seems like a "higher" stage of knowing, in both U.S. culture and the book. Yet separate, impersonal proceduralism as it is practiced in U.S. universities is more than tacitly criticized by WWK for being too adversarial, too critical, impersonal to the point of self-denial; too little collaborative and connected with others: too "masculine," too little "feminine" as these characteristics are coded.

The impersonal procedural knowers relished the very characteristics WWK attributed to them but seemed to criticize. They believed ideas could and should be divorced from person and personality. They praised methodological rigor and enjoyed adversarial argument. They liked to think of themselves as talkers who "talked back," to adapt a phrase from *Talking Back* by bell hooks, which we read in the same class (hooks, 1986). Many of them felt they were struggling, as hooks herself had, within their families and cultures to justify their intellectual, reflective, skeptical bent of mind. They saw proceduralism as offering an impartial impersonal perch to which they could invite their families (since procedures were open to all) but that also allowed them to escape and to judge those who judged them. By contrast, appeals to connectedness and relationships had been used to inhibit them, to "keep them home."

My invocation of bell hooks may seem a coded suggestion that minimizing/proceduralist students were, like hooks herself, working-class and African American or, more generally, women of color. But I do not remember this kind of reliable correlation of social position with a negative attitude toward positive femininity or with the proceduralist epistemological position. Among those who rejected WWK's appreciation of allegedly "feminine" connected knowing I vividly recall students who insistently presented themselves as working class; a woman of Irish descent and a Latina stand out. I recall also Korean Americans in several classes who found WWK's praise of connectedness an all-too-familiar source of conflict and guilt. But we were reading WWK in predominantly white classes and the voice of minimalizing sounded across evident racial, ethnic, and class boundaries. So, for instance, in the discussions of WWK, many white students and many who did not present themselves as working class identified with bell hooks. I do not mean to suggest that sexual orientation and class, ethnic or racial differences, didn't matter—they mattered to everyone. But they did not separate people along the "central divide" between feminists who were suspicious of the very idea of "feminine" reasoning and those who were eager to claim the ways of knowing that WWK praised.[8]

There were, of course, students who responded appreciatively, even gratefully, to the ideals of connected knowing as they are described in WWK. Like their counterparts among the interviewees in WWK these students did not enjoy, and they did not value, arguing, attacking, defending positions; they did value the ability to listen, to understand others, and to appreciate the objects of their study, whether the complexity of the physical world, a work of fiction, or a historical analysis. They did not believe that ideas—or epistemological positions—floated free of the people who expressed them; to understand an idea meant, for them, understanding a person in her social circumstances. When the WWK authors cited, approvingly, Nel Noddings's concepts of "generous thinking," "receptive rationality," and "empathy" free of projection, these students felt that their *minds* had been recognized. By contrast, many rejected impersonal procedural knowing, except for quite specific purposes, as too abstract and decontextualized to address the questions that most concerned them.

The students did not fall into neat groups, either as I remember them or as they "really" were. But insofar as, and on the days when, they could be classified as minimalist procedural knowers or connected knowers, they seemed each to be the inverse of the other, as they are in WWK. There was, however, an asymmetry between the two groups. Those who appreciated WWK's appreciation of connected knowing were not "maximizers" who celebrated women's differences. Unlike minimalist/proceduralists for whom epistemology and freedom from "femininity" were intertwined, the connected knowers were relatively indifferent to gender difference even in seminars labeled feminist. I remember several remarking that men too could become connected knowers given cultural encouragement. (And indeed among the men who were a tiny minority in these classes, most identified with connected knowing.) This gesture of inclusion—itself perhaps conventionally "feminine"—was neither self-consciously ashamed nor proud of its sex. I remember an African American student, a self-identified connected knower, who also identified herself as a womanist and encouraged others to assume that identity. One or two feminist graduate students were determined to bring into philosophy an oppositional, hitherto excluded feminine voice. But for the most part these students valued ways of knowing, not women. I therefore speak of these students simply as "connected knowers," identifying them with the epistemological ideals with which they identified. Connected knowers, like minimalist proceduralists, crossed ethnic and class boundaries. But they were at least as likely as their counterparts to insist on the specificity and importance to them of their cultural heritage.

In the midst of student divisions, my own sympathies were also divided. As an undergraduate I was a fervent minimizer and separator. In the absence of feminist theory, feminist philosophy, and (almost) feminists, impersonal reason had been one of my few weapons in a fight against conventional expectations of a female life. I had no desire and doubted my ability to muster the practicality, emotionality, and relational connectedness expected of women. As a teacher I retrospectively identified with and enjoyed my combative students. They cheerfully argued with me about the value of any epistemological position, including the idea that ideas are embodied and embedded in social and personal history and therefore cannot be subject to impersonal combat. But despite my pleasure in these students I found "connected knowing" epistemologically and politically promising and, though I hate to say it, in some sense "feminine."

I was, on the other hand, often frustrated by the patient, tentative narrative mode of the connected knowers among my students. Like WWK constructivists, they saw distinctive value in each way of knowing, but this sometimes seemed more to be indifferent tolerance than epistemological judgment. Moreover, they sometimes seemed impatient not only of adversarial argument but of coherence, clarity, and requests for evidence. They tended to resist my invitation to measured reflection; I resented their resistance. Nonetheless, I espoused the ideals with which these connected knowers identified. Like the combative proceduralist I remain, I wanted to defend them.

MAKING A "CASE" FOR CONNECTED KNOWING

It is difficult to step out of conversation and approach "feminine reason" more directly. Personally, I am too engaged in controversy, hear "both sides" in my head. More abstractly, given its distrust of argument and proof, "connected knowing" cannot set out to prove itself "right." What I now offer is a "case" in which connected knowing fits, which is also the beginning of a case for its epistemic virtues. First I situate WWK's artic-ulation of "connected knowing" as part of a collective epistemological project. Then I offer a general account of knowing, of gender, and of their connection. In this account connected knowing appears as an instance of "reason" and reason's "femininity" becomes nonmysterious and unthreatening.

I have been speaking of "connected knowing" as if its meaning were clear, when it is very much in the process of elaboration. From my per-spective, WWK makes a significant contribution to a *collective* project: the articulation of an "alternative epistemology" that seems appropriately labeled "connected knowing."[9] The characteristics of this epistemology are not limited to any one "position" in WWK but include elements of receptive knowing, subjective knowing, connected knowing in the nar-rower sense, and perhaps especially constructivism, the WWK alternative epistemological ideal. Articulating this alternative epistemology is very much a work in progress. Nonetheless, it is possible to identify charac-teristics that recur in the works of epistemologists quite different from each other and in WWK.

Some of these characteristics of "connected knowing" (CK, as I will label this alternative epistemology) are aspects of knowing as an activity. Knowing is not separated from feeling; emotion is not only a spur but often a test of knowledge. Knowers attend to particulars—particular per-sons, relationships, or objects; they engage in what Blythe Clinchy calls "concrete" thinking. Knowing involves a capacity to appreciate, subtly and accurately, that is as productive of truth and knowledge as the abil-ity to criticize. These and other "methods" of knowing might be thought of as CK's "procedures." Other characteristics of CK are attributes of knowers' relationships with each other. Knowers present their evidence and construct understandings through contextual and open-ended narratives in which analytic distinction, deductive argument, and replicable experiment may figure but do not predominate. Knowers take disagreement as an occasion for collaborative deliberation and communication rather than for debate.

These characteristics of knowing and relationships among knowers are not meant to constitute an exhaustive definition of "connected knowing." Rather, they begin to paint a (moving) picture of what knowing and knowers might look like. The contrast is, of course, with impersonal procedural knowing, which continuously separates knower from known and the mind's knowing from its emotional, bodily, and social life. ImpK (as I will abbreviate it) brackets and perhaps suppresses emotion, seeks abstraction, and, at least in U.S. culture, values critical over appreciative abilities. ImpK argues, proves, demonstrates, and, again perhaps especially in U.S. circles, seeks to prevail. The alternative epistemology project—CK—does not seek to eliminate, though it might reform, ImpK. ImpK remains one way of knowing necessary for many projects and dominant in some.

Recent feminist epistemologies provide a "case" into which to fit connected knowing, a general account of all knowing that allows CK to appear no less reasonable, no more constrained by gender, than ImpK. According to these epistemologies, all "ways of knowing" emerge through relationships in which knowers participate from earliest childhood throughout adult life. Ways of knowing also emerge from and are tested by the practices in which adult knowers engage. Knowledge as a public product is produced by "epistemic communities" that legitimate some but not other ways of knowing. The concepts of knowing as relational and practical and of knowledge production as social also serve to illuminate connections between knowing and gender. Gender is constructed, alongside ways of knowing, through relationships and practices. Epistemic communities often include a gender discourse that identifies and ranks "masculine" and "feminine" ways of knowing.

The idea of a relational self is familiar from feminist metaphysics and psychoanalytic theory: persons are not fundamentally separate and isolated but rather "are literally constituted by the relationships of which we are a part," "construed in and by [our] relationships to others" (Nedelsky, 1993, p. 12; Shanley, 1995, p. 77; see also Nedelsky, 1990). Relationships are as "personal" as "one" gets; a person *is* the relationships that constitute and are constituted by her. Separation and differentiation, like attachment and dependence, are ways of relating to others. But relationships are also always social. The earliest and simplest relationships—between a single parent and only child, for example—are themselves in part a creation of other relationships—with the parent's parents, for example, or his lover, or his employer. And these relations are themselves constituted within institutions that legiti·   · certain forms of fatherhood and of normal childhood that a man .. · .is child may resist but cannot ignore.

This fundamental "relationality," as I will call it, precedes both knowing and gender. A knowing self, like other aspects of selfness, is created within relationships. In the words of the psychoanalyst and philosopher Marcia Cavell, "Thinking begins in attachment to others. . . . There is thought only where there are question and answer, need and response, interpersonal activities, and communications of various sorts, . . . Love is not external to mind but its very condition" (Cavell, 1993, pp. 231, 230).[10]

The (m)other is the first presence in which a child hears herself speaking; so too (s)he is the first presence in which a child hears herself silenced. Small children inquire and explore, are tested and silenced, in relationships that structure their ways of knowing and determine the objects legitimately known. Later, a person learns ("receives") from, entrusts herself to, the "objects" of her knowledge, whether other people, texts, narratives of the past, or the natural world. Even in our technocratic culture and certainly more in cultures elsewhere, a person may consider herself in relation to, actively listening to, and receiving from the "nature" (s)he studies. WWK is one of the many feminist texts to quote the geneticist Barbara McClintock, who listened to an ear of corn, let it come to her. A distant and manipulative relation to ears of corn is, however, equally though differently relational with its own psychosocial history. Knowing is always a relationship with the known as well as with other knowers.[11]

Within the relationships through which a knowing self is constructed, gender is also, simultaneously, constructed. A knowing self becomes a (more or less) "masculine" or "feminine" self. Gender itself, as philosopher Sandra Harding points out (this volume) is a "relationship between women and men," and I would add, between boys and girls, boys and men, girls and women. These relationships of gender are created in familial and social contexts that are marked by "ethnicity," "race," "normative often compulsory heterosexuality," and economic and social "class"— abstract labels that themselves signify emotion-laden connections and disconnections with parents, siblings, extended kin, peers, teachers, and with the "world" in which these significant others create and are (re)created.

Even as gendered knowing selves are created within relationships, those relationships become some of the primary "objects" that knowers seek to understand. To paraphrase Lorraine Code, "knowing people in relationships" is at least as worthy as a model of knowledge as knowing physical objects or the various theoretical entities of the sciences (Code, 1993, p. 12). The (m)other is the first object of knowledge as well as love; it is a child's love—and hate, envy, loss, greed, and a host of other emotions—that calls out for understanding. Later, simply in their own self-interest, children and then adults turn the gaze of inquiry on the relationships in which they become curious or intimidated, articulate or "dumb." To state the point most generally, it is through knowing the relationships in which she is constituted that a person knows herself.

To say that knowledge is relational is to agree with connected knowers that ideas are embodied and embedded in someone's personal history and present psychological life. It follows that to understand ideas it is appropriate, and often necessary, to understand the relationships in which persons/ideas express themselves. But it does not follow, even if one accepts the premises of connected knowing, that ImpK knowers are "wrong" to see ideas as floating free of persons and their relationships. Rather ImpK's have developed a distanced, detached, *relationship* to (most) ideas.

The conception of knowing as practical "connects" always evolving knowers to the activities in which, as adults, they engage (Ruddick, 1995). Briefly, ways of knowing arise out of *practices*. Whoever engages extensively and intensively in a practice—farming, engineering, mothering, or psychotherapy, for example—will acquire distinctive ways of thinking provoked by that practice. It is within a practice, and in accordance with its aims, that people judge which questions are sensible, which "methods" are suitable for addressing them, which answers are appropriate to them, and which criteria distinguish better or worse answers.

The knowing that arises out of practices is also gendered. To the extent that women and men engage more extensively and intensively in certain practices than others the thinking that arises out of these practices will have a masculine or feminine aspect. Conversely women's and men's thinking will, to a degree, be marked by their undertaking certain practices. Thus the "receptive rationality" of which Nel Noddings speaks arises, in her view, in large part from practices of caregiving that have shaped and been shaped by women, who have disproportionately undertaken the labors of care. When men care as intensively and extensively as women, both they and the rationalities of care will change. Similarly, separate proceduralist knowing, as WWK describes it, has been largely the creation of men practicing epistemology. Impersonal procedural inquiry may therefore be marked by "masculinity" and in turn mark the

men who engage in it, though proceduralism and men (and for that matter women) will change when its practice is equally shaped by women
and men.

Finally, knowledge *about*, for example, farming, psychotherapy, or
mothering is produced by "epistemic communities." As philosopher
Lynn Hankinson Nelson expresses this point:

> The knowing we do as individuals is derivative, . . . your knowing or mine
> depends on *our* knowing, for some "we." . . . Studies of how knowledge is
> generated [should] begin from the histories, social relations, and practices of
> communities; from the contexts and activities in and through which ontolo-
> gies are developed, standards of evidence and methodologies are adapted,
> theories are constructed, and others are abandoned or excluded. (Nelson,
> 1993, pp. 124–126)[12]

Epistemic communities include practitioners to varying degrees and
with varying respect. Knowledge about mothering, for example, has
often been constructed with minimal respect for maternal thinking that
arises out of maternal practices. Epistemic communities also include
nonpracticing "experts" whose expertise is constructed in overlapping
communities.

The idea that all knowledge is socially produced by "epistemic communities" enables us to ask how criteria of rationality are negotiated in
particular circumstances. Several feminist philosophers have pointed to
ways in which these negotiations are entwined with assumptions or
charges of masculinity and femininity. Stated generally, epistemological
communities are typically structured by what Carol Cohn, a feminist
critical theorist, has called "gender discourse" (Cohn, 1993).[13] A *gender
discourse* is a symbolic system that dichotomizes human characteristics
such as thought and feeling, mind and body, confrontation and accommodation, and systematically associates the first and valued set of characteristics with masculinity, the second, and opposite set with femininity.

Carol Cohn has employed the idea of gender discourse to understand
the particular epistemic communities of defense analysts and strategists.
Briefly, within this largely white and middle-class community a general
cultural devaluation of the feminine is intensified by a specific military
professional identification with "masculinity." Masculinity in turn is
expressed in—and requires—an "objective," abstract style of thinking so
deeply rooted as to appear "natural." In this "epistemic community," gendered discourse positions males and females, and equally, ideas and emotions, as "masculine" or "feminine." Some ideas, emotions, questions are

rendered "masculine" and legitimate; others become "feminine" and despised. The entrenched superior status of masculinity and the pervasiveness of abstract objectivity and denial make it "extremely difficult for anyone, female or *male*, to express concerns or ideas marked as 'feminine' and still maintain his or her legitimacy." Women and men are limited by a *system* that makes it difficult to think in a "voice" that is both "different" and credible. So, for example, among defense intellectuals, empathy, the desire to accommodate, horror of concrete suffering, interest in the enemy, and a range of other attitudes are "feminine"; they cannot enter into "reasonable" discussion. Or, to describe the matter as WWK might, connected *knowing* is a contradiction the system cannot allow.

I see WWK and similar alternative epistemologies as disruptive interventions in epistemic communities marked by insistently separate, impersonal procedural knowing that is labeled and legitimated as "masculine." Defense analysts have created a particularly visible, unusually lethal, but finally also familiar form of such a community's thinking. The WWK authors and the women they interview are at best marginal to such "masculine" communities. They attempt to make audible a voice that is difficult even for them to hear: a voice of *reason* that is cast as "feminine."

Reason arises in relationships, develops in practices, and speaks or is silenced within epistemic communities. Reason's "femininity" or "masculinity" arises alongside reason itself, a creation of the same relationships, practices, and gendered discourse. This general epistemological view pertains no less to ImpK than to any other way of knowing. But it contrasts with a view of knowing as individual and separable from contexts of its discovery that is usually presumed by ImpK. And it makes a conceptual space for an alternative epistemology that recognizes, studies, and values relationships among knowers and between knower and known.

This story of connected knowing does not constitute a *justification*. "One" can always ask, Why listen? Why and how do capacities such as empathy and attention to particulars bear the fruits of knowledge? How does emotion further and test inquiry? Why should "one" seek to communicate rather than prevail? Why are contextual narratives the favored—though by no means the only—forms of communication?

In an influential paper, the philosopher Annette Baier questioned the hegemony in ethical theory of a Kantian or Rawlsian theory of justice that strongly influenced the developmental theory of Lawrence Kohlberg. The epistemological analogue to this moral theory is impersonal proceduralism. "Whether the supposed blindspots of [either] outlook are due to male bias, or to nonparental bias, or to early traumas of powerlessness or to early resignations to 'detachment' from others," Baier remarked, "we need first to be persuaded that they *are* blindspots before we will have an interest in their cause and cure." We must, conversely, be persuaded that the illuminating powers of connected knowing *are* powerful and illuminating (Baier, 1995).[14]

This is an ongoing task for me and others. But I want to close with two more obiter dicta. As I said many pages ago, a more limited proceduralism and a more developed connected knowing will allow of more, rather than less, "objective" truths. WWK is sometimes criticized for lacking a "doctrine and practice of *objectivity*" (Code, 1991, p. 253). But the dream of objectivity that transcends connection, of proof without dialogue, is not only impossible of fulfillment but dangerous. Not that I am content to rest with "cultural difference." I long for ways to see "truly," long for ways to see what children "really" need, for example, or whether, how, and when humiliation and corporal punishment "really" damage them. But such "truths" emerge in the midst of conflictual conversations, not despite them. Universal truths—however we might wish for them—have a way of turning out to be the truths of a few that cannot be imposed on others—the parents of assaulted children, for example—or are imposed only with an imperialist and often self-defeating harshness.

Finally, in my understanding, connected knowing will be judged by ethical as well as epistemological ideals. I evaluate ways of knowing and the knowledge they produce in the "light of" the good to which they lead and that they yield. So, for example, there are many ways and capacities for knowing that go into the ability of a community, or a hospital, to keep a person alive. Many treatments can be learned, tested impersonally, and methodically delivered. But finally I look for ways of knowing and counting knowledge that would judge these treatments in the light of the pleasures they offer, the love they make possible, the care they provide, and the justice they observe. There are many kinds of knowing how and knowing that, many uses of received, procedural, and connected capacities, required for building a bridge. I want to know where the bridge will lead, who can make use of it, what goods are brought over and how they are distributed, who if anyone is permitted to bomb the bridge, and who can stop the bombing. These are the kinds of questions defense intellectuals hear as feminine and so do not hear at all. I too hesitate to write them out. But this connection between epistemological ideal and moral result seems to me central to the feminist epistemological enterprise and to WWK.

NOTES

1. I am paraphrasing Genevieve Lloyd (1993). In this essay, Lloyd is developing, with particular attention to metaphor, ideas she put forward in *Man of Reason: Male and Female in Western Philosophy* (1984), the first attempt to offer a careful, textual reading of philosophy's gender.

2. Genevieve Lloyd (1984), chapters 4 and 5, cites Kant and also gives an excellent succinct account of the idea that women's reason complements men's.

3. WWK seems to be more indebted to the work of William Perry than I had admitted (see Nancy Goldberger, introduction, this volume, as well as WWK, introduction). So far as I can gather, their indebtedness to Perry is partly responsible for aspects of the developmental scheme that trouble me: the placing of "subjectivism," the inclusion of "connected knowing" as a kind of procedural knowing, and the general idea of stage sequencing.

4. According to standpoint theorists, the superiority of standpoints derives both from the social position of "outsiders" and from the labor in which they engage, or more generally from the lives that they lead. "Outsiders," the subordinate, powerless, or marginal, see more clearly than the powerful; often they see from the double consciousness of the "outsider within," as in Patricia Hill Collins's (1986) noted example of the domestic worker who sees herself and the families she works for more clearly than they see themselves or her. In the version of standpoint theory first and strongly developed by Nancy Hartsock (1983) people who engage in caring labor, for example, in mothering, also develop distinctive and superior ways of knowing. Sandra Harding (1986, 1991) has interpreted and defended standpoint theories for many years, including in this volume.

5. This identification of self with ways of knowing seems to be partly at least a methodological artifact. The WWK authors classified *women*, then identified ways of knowing, then tested each way of classifying against the other. They described subjects' attitudes to evidence and authority, for example, without respect to what they were trying to

"know" — another person's feelings, a performance of *The Tempest*, the workings of DNA, the rules and effects of the welfare system.

6. Over the several years I taught WWK, students and I learned from several feminist theorists. Among the most valuable writers we considered were, first, Elsa Barkley Brown (1989) Deborah King (1988) and Aída Hurtado (1989), then Kimberle Crenshaw (1991) and Angela Harris (1991), and finally Patricia Williams (1991) and Kathy Ferguson (1993).

7. A point of terminology. For the most part, I refer to WWK's "separate" procedural knowing as "impersonal" procedural knowing. *Impersonal* suggests to me an epistemological aim — to bracket the personal. *Separate* suggests a psychological tendency — to separate knower from known, mind from body and emotion, individual from social group. I also often refer, in a shorthand way, to proceduralism. Blythe Clinchy (this volume and in agreement with WWK) insists that connected knowing employs "procedures." I do not doubt this. But the role of procedures and the ways in which they are taught and agreed on are so different in impersonal proceduralism and connected knowing that I would prefer to use distinctive terms.

8. Of these socially marked "mobile subjectivities" lesbian identity was most often explicitly invoked in discussions of positive "femininity" or "feminine" reason. But on these matters, certain lesbian-identified students were often in explicit, sometimes strongly felt disagreement.

9. I take the term *alternative epistemology* from Walker (1995), who cites three characteristics: attention to particulars, contextual narration, and communicative deliberation.

10. Also Cavell (1993, p. 230): "Thought itself is more passional than we sometimes take it to be. The human infant requires something extrinsic or external to it . . . before it can have or be anything we call as self. A crucial part of this external world is other creatures to whom the child is libidinally attached. Through its interactions with them the child learns a language and comes by its sense of Self and Other, acquires the capacities to generalize, to frame scientific hypotheses as well as more homely everyday generalizations, to formulate maxims and moral principles."

11. The original account of McClintock's relation to the object of her study appeared in Evelyn Fox Keller (1983, 1986).

12. The view that knowledge is social is connected with feminist and other critiques of science, particularly with the now-familiar claim that observation is theory-laden, evidence is selected according to standards that are of "our own making," and theories are undetermined by data. Hence claims about what we see, as well as what we infer, emerge through "negotiation."

13. For examples of this sophistication, in Antony and Witt (1993) see Lloyd (1993) and Scheman (1993). In Alcoff and Potter (1993) see Potter (1993), Dalmiya and Alcoff (1993). In gender discourse neither mas-

culinity nor femininity is a simple category. In Carol Cohn's words: "There are many specific discourses of gender, which vary by race, class, ethnicity, locale, sexuality, and other factors. The masculinity idealized in the gender discourse of new Haitian immigrants is in some ways different from that of sixth generation white Anglo-Saxon Protestant business executives, and both differ somewhat from that of white-male defense intellectuals and security analysts. One version of masculinity is *mobilized* and *enforced* in the armed forces in order to enable men to fight wars, while a somewhat different version of masculinity is *drawn upon* and expressed by abstract theoreticians of wars" (Cohn, 1993, p. 238, my italic).

14. A fine example of a critique in its own terms of adversarial proceduralism is Janice Moulton (1989).

REFERENCES

Alcoff, L., & Potter, E. (1993). *Feminist epistemologies*. New York: Routledge.

Antony, L., & Witt, C. (1993). *A mind of their own*. Boulder, CO: Westview Press.

Baier, A. (1995). The need for more than justice. In V. Held (Ed.), *Justice and care: Essential Readings in Feminist Ethics*, Boulder, CO: Westview Press.

Bartlett, K. T., & Kennedy, R. (Eds.) (1991). *Feminist legal theory*. Boulder, CO: Westview Press.

Belenky, M., Clinchy, B., Goldberger, N., & Tarule, J. (1986). *Women's ways of knowing*. New York: Basic Books.

Brown, E. B. (1989, Summer). African-American women's quilting: A framework for teaching African-American's women's history. *Signs, 14*, 941–969.

Cavell, M. (1993). *The psychoanalytic mind: From Freud to philosophy*. Cambridge, MA: Harvard University Press.

Clinchy, B. (1994). *Is interconnected thinking really thinking?* Annual Symposium of the Piaget Society, Chicago. Manuscript courtesy of author.

Clinchy, B. (1995). Commentary. *Human Development, 879*.

Code, L. (1991). *What can she know*. Ithaca, NY: Cornell University Press.

Code, L. (1993). Taking subjectivity into account. In L. Alcoff and E. Potter (Eds.), *Feminist epistemologies*. New York: Routledge.

Cohn, C. (1993). War, wimps and women. In M. Cooke and A. Woolacott (Eds.), *Gendering war talk*. Princeton, NJ: Princeton University Press.

Collins, P. H. (1986). Learning from the outsider within: The social significance of black feminist thought. *Social Problems, 33*.

Crenshaw, K. (1991). Demarginalizing the intersection of race and sex: A black feminist critique of antidiscrimination doctrine, feminist theory and anti-racist politics. In Bartlett & Kennedy (Eds.)

Dalmiya, V., & Alcoff, L. (1993). Are old wives tales justified? In L. Alcoff & E. Potter (Eds.), *Feminist epistemologies*. New York: Routledge.

Ferguson, K. (1993). *The man question in feminism*. New York: Routledge.

Fineman M. (1994). *The neutered mother, the sexual family and other twentieth century tragedies*. New York: Routledge.

271

Garry, A., & Pearsall, M. (Eds.) (1989). *Women, knowledge and philosophy.* Boston: Unwin Hyman.

Gordon, L. R. (1995). *Black faith and antiblack racism.* Highlands, NJ: Humanities Press.

Harding, S., & Hintikka, M. (1983). *Discovering reality.* Utrecht: D. Reidel.

Harding, S. (1986). *The science question in feminism.* Ithaca, NY: Cornell University Press.

Harding, S. (1991) *Whose science, whose knowledge?* Ithaca, NY: Cornell University Press.

Harris, A. (1991). Race and essentialism in feminist legal theory. In K. T. Bartlett & R. Kennedy (Eds.), *Feminist legal theory.* Boulder, CO: Westview Press.

Hartsock, N. (1983). The feminist standpoint: Developing the grounds for a specifically feminist historical materialism. In S. Harding & M. Hintikka (Eds.), *Discovering reality.* Utrecht: D. Reidel.

Held, V. (1995). *Justice and care: Essential readings in feminist ethics.* Boulder, CO: Westview Press.

Hirsch, M., & Keller, E. F. (Eds.) (1992). *Conflicts in feminism.* New York: Routledge.

hooks, b. (1986). *Talking back, thinking feminist, thinking black.* Boston: South End Press.

Hurtado, A. (1989) Relating to Privilege: Seduction and rejection is the subordination of white women and women of color. *Signs, 14* (4), 833–855.

Keller, E. F. (1983). A feeling for the organism: *The life and work of Barbara McClintock.* New York: Freeman.

Keller, E. F. (1986). *Reflections of gender and science.* New Haven: Yale University Press.

King, D. K. (1988). Multiple jeopardy, multiple consciousness: The context of a black feminist ideology. *Signs, 14* (1), 42–72.

Lloyd, G. (1984). *Man of reason: Male and female in Western philosophy.* Minneapolis: University of Minnesota Press.

Lloyd, G. (1993). Maleness, Metaphor and the Crisis of Reason. In L. Antony & C. Witt (Eds.), *A mind of their own.* Boulder, CO: Westview Press.

Martin, J. R. (1994) Methodological essentialism, false difference, and other dangerous traps. *Signs, 19,* 630–657.

Moulton, J. (1989). A paradigm of philosophy: The adversary method. In A. Garry & M. Pearsall (Eds.), *Women, knowledge and philosophy.* Boston: Unwin Hyman.

Nedelsky, J. (1990). Law, boundaries and the bounded self. *Representations, 30.*

Nedelsky, J. (1993) Reconceiving rights as relationships. *Review of constitutional studies, 1* (1).

Nelson, L. H. (1993). Epistemological communities. In L. Alcoff & E. Potter (Eds.), *Feminist epistemologies.* New York: Routledge.

Potter, E. (1993). Gender and epistemic negotiation. In L. Alcoff & E. Potter (Eds.), *Feminist epistemologies*. New York: Routledge.

Ruddick, S. (1995). *Maternal thinking*, Boston: Beacon Press.

Scheman, N. (1993). If this be Method there is Madness in it. In L. Antony & C. Witt (Eds.), *A mind of their own*. Boulder, CO: Westview Press.

Shanley, M. (1995). Fathers' rights, mothers' wrongs. *Hypatia, 10* (1), 74–103.

Snitow, A. (1992). A gender diary. In M. Hirsch & E. Fox Keller (Eds.), *Conflicts in feminism*. New York: Routledge Press.

Walker, M. U. (1995). Moral understanding: Alternative "epistemology" for a feminist ethics. In V. Held (Ed.), *Justice and care: Essential readings in feminist ethics*. Boulder, CO: Westview Press.

Williams, P. J. (1991). *Alchemy of race and rights*. Cambridge, MA: Harvard University Press.

9

Voices in Dialogue

Collaborative Ways of Knowing*

JILL MATTUCK TARULE

We read *Women's Ways of Knowing* with interest and found much there that resonated with our students' tales of being silenced and struggling to believe in their own intelligence. (Stenitz & Kanter, 1991, p. 138)

Many of these students try to tell the truth about their experience as women, as they try to construct and reconstruct themselves as subjects of knowledge through language. Coming to voice is a central epistemological metaphor for intellectual development, as [the authors] show in *Women's Ways of Knowing*. Many of my students, however, have been silenced or, at best, discouraged from expressing themselves, not only by the all pervasive mutings of education and socialization, but also by sexual violence. (Gannett, 1992, p. 178)

*In conducting this research on classrooms, specifically collaborative learning classrooms, I am indebted to my coresearcher, Bill Whipple. In addition, I am indebted to Mary Kay Tetreault, who appointed me as a visiting scholar at California State University—Fullerton and gave me the opportunity to do action research on classroom strategies with the College of Human Development and Family Studies faculty. Earlier forms of this work and my thinking were helped immeasurably by a collaborative study group with Blythe Clinchy, Nona Lyons, Frinde Maher, Jane Martin, Muffy Paradise, and Phyllis Silberman. More recently, Rob Tarule and Anne Stanton along with the Muddy Waters study group—Holly Busier, Kelly Clark, Rebecca Esch, Corinne Glesne, and Yvette Pigeon—have been sources of invaluable support and dialogue.

274

> For the last two decades, feminist teachers committed to creating education that would also be a "practice of freedom" for students, especially for women, have attempted to promote more egalitarian classrooms responsive to differences not only of gender, but also of class, race, sexual preference, ethnicity, and age. Crucial to this goal of developing new pedagogues that are participatory, experiential and non-hierarchical . . . have been concepts like "empowerment," "student voice," "dialogue," and "critical thinking," concepts that entail a new understanding of the nature and roles of "knowledge" in teaching and learning." (Finke, 1993, p. 7)

The way we discussed voice in *Women's Ways of Knowing* (WWK) has captured the attention of many who write about the experience of becoming a learner and about teaching. As the preceding excerpts illustrate, voice has come to signify rather different meanings ranging from the capacity to speak "in a different voice" about moral and ethical development (Brown & Gilligan, 1992; Gilligan, 1982; Lyons, 1983) to being "empowered" to speak out of silence about being marginalized or about being abused (Finke, 1993; Gannett, 1992; Lewis, 1990). The metaphor of developing a voice, and of joining with other voices in dialogue, has become central in the literature about emancipatory pedagogy (Ellsworth, 1989; Maher, 1987; Weiler, 1991)' and about other approaches in college classrooms such as learning communities and collaborative learning (Kadel & Keechner, 1994; Gabelnick, MacGregor, Matthews, & Smith, 1990; Romer, 1985; Romer & Whipple, 1991; Trimbur, 1989; Weiner, 1986; Whipple, 1987). The best understanding and definitions of voice seem to be drawn from inquiry based on women's experience, as we learned while writing WWK, because women emphasize relationships in their development, an emphasis that stresses voice, listening, and talking as the medium for connecting with others.

During our years of inquiry analyzing the WWK interviews, it was profoundly moving to me to hear our informants (or what I would now call our collaborators) telling us that their sense of self and of knowing were intimately linked with their assessment of being able to speak about what mattered to them. We described voice, then, as a metaphor, and we often heard women talk specifically about the power of a speaking voice in their lives: about "speaking up," "speaking out," "being silenced," "really talking," "saying what you mean," "listening to be heard." We came to understand that "the development of a sense of voice, mind, and self were inextricably entwined" (WWK, p. 18). But, a "sense of voice," I would now argue, does not quite capture the importance of language in human development. Nor does pairing the notion of listening and speaking capture the epistemological importance of conversation or of dialogue.

After the book came out, my colleagues and I were frequently asked to present our work to college and university faculty. Over about a four-year period, I ran workshops or gave talks, often with Blythe, Nancy, or Mary, to thirty or more groups of faculty. Frequently these presentations became conversations about helping students to participate in discussions. How could we help them to know what they thought and to feel comfortable enough to speak so they might engage more in learning? Those conversations helped to clarify my own questions about how the WWK work could inform teaching in higher education. I especially wondered how it could contribute to transforming practices so that marginalized groups, that is, women and others, would be more likely to experience themselves as competent, more likely to excel.

To undergird this growing inquiry, it became critical in my research and teaching to expand my understanding of the relationships between epistemological development and the nature of voice and dialogue, the former referring to speech and the individual, the latter to speech among individuals. And I wanted to expand the study, as much as I could, to examine experiences in classrooms specifically in order to emphasize contexts where learning and dialogue supposedly occur.[1]

This chapter grows out of that work. I first explore the voice as an indispensable aspect of knowing and thinking. I then discuss what happens when voice moves into conversation by "illuminating" (Hoshmond, 1989) the role of dialogue as a way of knowing. In the latter part of the chapter, I look at classes in which instructors were developing collaborative learning strategies. These classrooms are what I have called "dialogue-rich" (Tarule, 1992) sites in which voice, dialogue, relationships, and learning intersect. Finally, I discuss how the analysis of these intersections suggests a shift not only in how knowledge is defined, but also in the role of "expert" in classroom teaching and knowledge construction.

VOICE AND THINKING

Two grandfathers of developmental psychology, Jean Piaget and Lev Vygotsky, posit language as central and indispensable in human development, but they differ significantly in their analysis of the development of language and its relation to learning. In *WWK*, we alluded to Vygotsky's theory that speech develops in social interaction: first the child acquires language by internalizing the external voice of caregivers; later an inner language and voice of one's own develops. We were drawn to this analysis of the development of thought as concurrent with the development of language and the ability to speak because it emphasizes the role of interaction with others as central to human growth, just as our interviewees had emphasized the importance of relationships in developing a voice and in learning.

In Piaget's theory understanding is built as the individual undertakes action on objects and reflects on the results of those actions. Understanding precedes language, which is therefore developed after the fact to describe and report on the newly apprehended world. Relationships and social interaction were "never critical to Piaget's theory" (Rogoff, 1993, p. 125).

For "Piaget, cognitive development is an individual process that *may* be influenced by social interaction" (Rogoff, 1993, p. 125, emphasis added). In contrast, Vygotsky posits that "cognitive development is a socio-cultural process" conducted in "participation and communication" with others (Rogoff, 1993, p. 125).

Piaget and Vygotsky were contemporaries. A Russian, Vygotsky was embedded in a sociocultural context that emphasized the social and communal as early tenets of communism. The Swiss Piaget was embedded in the Euro-American focus on the individual as a sole and autonomous actor who makes his or her way often in spite of social constraints. It seems reasonable to presume that in developing their divergent theories, each was influenced by these rather different social, historical, and political contexts.

Moreover, the two approaches are quite reminiscent of separate and connected knowing (Clinchy, 1995). As in separate knowing, Piaget's emphasis is on how knowledge develops through interaction with the objective world. Vygotsky's emphasis, as in connected knowing, is on how thinking and knowledge are mediated through interaction with others. The first leads to a kind of dialogue that values the ability to pronounce or "report" one's ideas, whereas the second values a dialogue that relies on relationships as one enters meaningful conversations that connect one's ideas with others' and establish "rapport" (Tannen, 1990). The progress, content, and nature of the conversation in the two approaches may differ significantly. But in both approaches language, voice, thinking, and the construction of knowledge are inextricably entwined.

"I know what I think when I hear what I say," one woman student said, describing how her thought is linked to her ability to speak about it, but linked in a very particular way. Without talk, she is not sure she is thinking.

Vygotsky (1986) did not see thought and language as the same. Rather, the meaning of words is always changing because the relationship between word and thought is constantly shifting. Moreover, inner speech and external speech link differently with thought:

> Inner speech is not the interior aspect of external speech — it is a function in itself. It still remains speech, i.e. thought connected with words. But while in external speech, thought is embodied in words in inner speech words die as they bring forth thought. Inner speech is to a large extent pure meaning. It is a shifting, unstable thing, fluttering between word and thought, the two more or less stable, more or less firmly delineated components of verbal thought. Its true nature and place can be understood only after examining the next plane of verbal thought, the one still more inward than inner speech.
>
> That plane is thought itself. As we have said, every thought creates a connection, fulfills a function, solves a problem. The flow of thought is not accompanied by a simultaneous unfolding of speech. The two processes are not identical, and there is no rigid correspondence between the units of thought and speech. This is especially obvious when a thought process miscarries — when, as Dostoevski put it, a thought "will not enter words." (p. 249)

Like Dostoevski, students often complain that their thought is not amenable to spoken or written language. They allude to inner speech as a presence and stress how much this feels like an evolving, intrapsychic process. Sarah, commuting by car to college an hour each way, recalls her experience of inner speech as her ruminations flutter between thought and word:

> A lot of times I turn off the radio and I talk to myself, out loud, like I'm talking to you. . . . I know it seems like . . . sometimes I babble, but I never really say anything until I have really gone over it . . . that's my style. . . . Sometimes my internal discourse gets so harried [laughs] that I *do* go to someone and say, you know, this is the situation, this is how, what I've been doing, but it's getting a little too much for me to handle. I need to bounce some ideas off of you, and give me feedback.

Inner speech for Sarah has a "harried," shifting quality. Yet, this process provides her with an orientation to her ideas: what might be called a prenarrative or predialogue "voice." Eventually Sarah turns to "external speech" to stabilize the fluttering — her babbling inner speech—and it allows her to "know what [she] thinks" (John-Steiner & Suberman, 1978). To speak, as one of my students recently put it, is to know.

In this theory, voice is an integral component in the thinking process, in knowing. Out loud or silently, voice animates thinking, produces thought, and enables the thinker to stabilize and expand her thought.

But the monologue can get to be "a little too much . . . to handle." There is a "need to bounce some ideas" around with others. It is not enough to speak to an empty car. What animates both voice and listening in "the space between us" (Josselson, 1992) is dialogue, and it is dialogue that helps to create and solidify thought.

DIALOGUE AS A WAY OF KNOWING

> When I read it, it's like, well, big deal. [laughs] But whenever you talk about it, it's a different thing. Then it, then it, for me it brings meaning.

This student asserts that although ideas are somehow inserted in her thinking as she reads alone, it is no "big deal." Words fail to animate or inform her thinking until she is able to participate in a dialogue. It is dialogue that "brings meaning." The student's description echoes how the educational philosopher Nicholas Burbules (1993) defines dialogue as representing "a continuous developmental communicative interchange through which we stand to gain a fuller apprehension of the world, ourselves, and one another" (p. 8).

Dialogue may be "idealized as a relation between two participants, it can also be used to characterize some forms of group discussion" (Burbules, 1993, p. 9). It is unclear to me why Burbules describes a dyadic dialogue as idealized, although it is reminiscent of what political scientist Jean Bethke Elhstein (and philosopher Jürgen Habermas before her) identified as an "ideal speech situation" (WWK, p. 145; see Schweikart, this volume). Burbules may mean to signal his intent to depersonalize the interpersonal interchange—the "relation between two participants"— which he further defines as playing a "Dialogue Game," a game with agreed-on rules and moves. The game has four genres: dialogue as instruction, as conversation, as debate, and as inquiry. The emphasis on a game and on objective and distant procedures for a conversation invokes a separate knowing approach to understanding and analyzing dialogues.

Kenneth Bruffee (1993) invokes a definition of dialogue more like connected knowing by telling a story about his own discovery of the role of conversation in relationship with significant others as the site for constructing knowledge. Bruffee reports being assigned, as a young English professor, the job of developing a writing program for Brooklyn College, just as the City College of New York (CCNY) system had gone to open enrollments in the sixties. Mourning his "pellucid lecture notes on Wordsworth and the English Romantics, yellowing away in a drawer, unthumbed, unreferred to, unapplauded" (pp. 15–16), Bruffee turned in desperation to other colleagues, who, like him, were struggling to teach speaking and writing to students whom they referred to as "underprepared." This group began to meet for Saturday discussions, sometimes about their students and teaching, sometimes about something they had read. They became "a small transitional community," which is also Bruffee's definition of a classroom. The dialogue of Bruffee and his peers took on a particular form:

> The language we had begun to use literally constituted the small transition community of which we were now increasingly devoted members. Learning, as we were experiencing it, was not just inextricably related to that new social relationship among us. It was identical with it and inseparable from it. To paraphrase Richard Rorty's account of learning, it was not a shift inside us that now suited us to enter new relationships with reality and with other people. Learning *was* that shift in our language which constituted relations with others. (p. 18)

Dialogue is making knowledge in conversation. Emily, a student participant in a team-taught collaborative learning class, a pedagogy based on promoting learning in "language-constituted" relationships, describes how her learning, too, was expanded and directed by conversation. She acknowledges that she knows the professors had information and "were fun to pull from," but she contrasts that extraction with the ways she has learned in other classes: "It felt like we were all in it together," she says. That collaborative class had become a "small transition community" of both students and faculty in which ideas could be explored together. Sarah describes the same class, observing that the

> class [was] more . . . a discussion, you know, a conversation between all of us. Um, I didn't feel, I felt like whenever [the teachers] offered [their] opinion, interpretation, whatever you want to call it, that that's just how it was supposed to be taken, as what [the teachers] thought, not as this is true, this is the way it is. And if we disagreed, fine. If we agreed, fine . . . it was just a really, like a racquetball court where all these different—where all of our

opinions were just being bounced around in a very benign sort of way and it wasn't threatening or anything.

Like Burbules, Sarah positions dialogue in a game, the racquetball court where the ball bounces off all the surfaces, just as in a group conversation ideas bounce around. They may seem to emerge from left field or from nowhere as all ideas are included, debated, contested, expanded. It led to interpretation and to the development of Sarah's ideas. It created learning. But she stipulates that the dialogue had to be nonthreatening for her participation and learning to flourish. This stipulation highlights what are for many women the relational requirements for a productive dialogue, an emphasis that reverberates with the relational emphasis in human development (Chodorow, 1978; Gilligan, 1982; Jordan, Kaplan, & Miller, 1991; Lyons, 1983; Brown & Gilligan, 1992; Ruddick, 1986).

We heard the same emphasis in many of the WWK women's stories as they asserted the importance of relationships in their framing of their worldview, their values, their ethical stance, their view of themselves. In WWK, we locate an examination of the role of relationships in analytic thinking specifically and knowledge construction generally in the discussion of the procedural connected knowers' learning (see Blythe Clinchy's chapter, this volume). However, locating the relational emphasis in knowing in this particular position may obscure what Bruffee asserts about all learning: that these dialogue-rich, language-constituted relations *are* the way learning occurs and knowledge is constructed.

DIALOGUE AND WOMEN'S WAYS
OF KNOWING POSITIONS

To examine further the idea of knowledge construction in "language-constituted relations," Bruffee (1993) turns to William Perry's (1970) work on Harvard students' development and reexamines the students' words, looking not for evidence of cognitive developmental positions in how the students make meaning, but for evidence of how they describe dialogue as a socially constructed process that is their learning. Revisiting Perry's excerpts from students' statements, Bruffee asserts that "the real importance of Perry's book . . . is not the mythic mental 'forms' he infers but the evidence of the social construction of knowledge which his students generously provided him" (pp. 160–161).

Bruffee is not a developmental psychologist and seems not to have benefited from constructing knowledge in dialogue with anyone who is.

He seems unable to imagine a dialectical definition of development and learning in which both schemata and dialogue create and shape knowing. Learning and development can exist in both our language-rich relationships and "mental forms" or schemata, just as language exists in both inner and external speech.

Nonetheless, I still found Bruffee's analysis of Perry's students intriguing. And given that the analysis of our collaborators/informants' developmental positions was so influenced by Perry's early work, it was intriguing to return to those women's words to see whether they, too, had "generously provided" us with "evidence of the social construction of knowledge" in their learning. Were there times when they were telling us that their learning was in a conversation? Was there evidence in the WWK excerpts that could be reframed to emphasize when the women appeared to assert that their learning and conversations were indistinguishable?

Bonnie, a young mother who appeared in the chapter on silence, describes such a conversation with her baby:

> I never used to listen to her cries. I used to pick her up and put a bottle in her mouth. I thought that's all babies wanted. . . . That was before I kind of realized that there's more than just a bottle. . . . For some reason, I never thought about changing her diapers. . . . It never clicked in my head. . . . There are some things that just wouldn't click in my head. (WWK, p. 27)

"Now," she says, "I think of all those nights I could have just changed her diaper" and, presumably, gone back to sleep herself a good deal sooner! In the excerpts, we only hear that Bonnie's thinking changed in a dialogue with her baby's cries as she began to hear those cries as differentiated communication. As may be the case for many silent knowers, it is a conversation without language, perhaps "shifting and unstable, fluttering between thought and words." Nonetheless, Bonnie locates her "new apprehension"—the "click"—in this dialogue with her baby. Here the learning is the conversation with her new child, and it is learning that is grounded in and furthers the relationship between them.

Another unnamed WWK woman elaborates on words and thought in her highly valued relationship with a "special" aunt to whom she could tell "anything and everything."

> We don't get nervous talking to each other. We think alike. Like you can talk to somebody about how you feel and they feel the same way you do. . . . It's really strange. . . . We think the same things. (WWK, p. 38)

In a dialogue that is not, as Sarah put it, "threatening or anything," one discovers that both parties think (and feel) "the same things." This could be heard as receiving validation for one's "mental forms," but it can also be heard as thought emerging from a "communicative interchange."

Anna Jean says it more direct: "Reading books is not enough, I really want to talk to people" (p. 74). As it does for the student quoted earlier, talk "brings meaning," and the absence of talk may mean that thought cannot be formulated in any stable way. We originally heard Anna Jean's notion as a "distrust of books and the written word in favor of learning through direct sensory experience" (p. 74), what we called *subjective knowing*. That may well be the epistemological schemata that Anna Jean has available, but she also is emphasizing that learning occurs in conversation. Moreover, both women quoted enter into a dialogue with fairly undifferentiated "feeling," and emerge with more stabilized thought, suggesting a process in which they move from direct sensory experience and undifferentiated feeling to language and thought as a way of knowing (Tarule, 1978, 1980). Bruffee describes a similar progression in his story of how his emotional experience of disappointment and dislocation as a new professor was transformed when he entered the conversational relationship with valued colleagues who we can imagine were, like the cherished aunt, struggling with the same experience he was and thinking "the same things" about it.

Another subjective knower, Inez, describes how emerging from and leaving forever her abusive families, one of origin, the other of choice, she began to attend self-help groups and later entered therapy, finally learning through a relationship with a new boyfriend that she had "intuition, instinct—what I call my gut" (WWK, p. 57). In the WWK case study of Inez, we do not hear her speak directly about how her learning might be lodged in conversation. However, it is reasonable to imagine that her participation in self-help or twelve-step groups may well have provided her with the "language-constituted relations" of learning.

Twelve-step groups provide very particular rules for language-constituted relations: the principle of anonymity and no "cross-talk" (Campbell, 1994). The anonymity—using only one's first name and agreeing not to reveal the identity of anyone who is present at meetings—provides the opportunity to participate in a selfless conversation, a dialogue in which the words are what matter as together the group creates an understanding of their addiction. Requiring "no cross-talk" assures individuals that their process of moving from internal to external speech will not be hindered by challenge or debate, which can be threatening and can still thought. The no-cross-talk rule is intended to preserve group conversation and to prevent the dialogue from disintegrating into a two-person debate. Both the cross-talk and anonymity rules for what Burbules (1993) might call the game of dialogue-as-conversation create the conditions to "shift from individual to group as the agent of meaning," such that the learning is now lodged in the conversation (Campbell, 1994, p. 17).

A particularly poignant example of this approach to learning occurred with Inez early in the WWK project. Mary, Blythe, Nancy, and I were scheduled to present our work at a particular college. We discovered that Inez was attending the presentation, and, although we had permission to quote from her interview, we still had considerable concern about how she would react to hearing her own words read as an example of subjective knowing. We worried too about how she would feel, hearing herself lodged in the middle of a developmental progression that we had learned was often interpreted as a dimension of more rudimentary and inadequate thought to more complex and adequate cognitive structures (the "Is higher better?" question we often heard raised in these presentations).

Before the presentation Inez assured us that she was comfortable with having her words used. Still, we were uneasy as the workshop began. At the end of the workshop as people milled around the room, Inez approached Blythe with excitement. She was thrilled that her words had been able to teach other people about something; she was pleased to have them intermingled with the presentation. Whereas our concerns had centered on what we thought Inez might hear as a negative judgment about the social and cognitive adequacy of "her" subjective knower position, she had emphasized the "learning in the conversation." Perhaps as a result of Inez's experience of twelve-step groups, she didn't emphasize the power of her individual contribution but shifted emphasis to the power of her thought as part of a "group consciousness" in which individual meaning is given up to a conversational process and "each participant takes on the character and power of the process as a whole" (Campbell, 1994, p. 26). Rather than hearing the presentation as "inscribing" (Olesen, 1994) the developmental positions, Inez recasts it as providing a site for socially constructing knowledge.

Dialogue as learning seems to be even more evident in the interview excerpts from the women we coded as capable of procedural and constructed "mental forms." Here, conversation can take different forms. One woman describes how she likes "playing the devil's advocate, arguing the opposite of what someone is saying" (WWK, p. 101), because it sharpens how she is thinking about an issue. Although she clearly is describing what we called procedural separate knowing, she also reveals that the knowing is dependent on a conversation. A procedural connected knowing peer describes her first year at college as "just sitting around and talking" with "all kinds of people. . . . That really made me start listening to people and comparing and contrasting views" (WWK, p. 114; see Clinchy's chapter, this volume).

These two women describe approaches to analysis, but approaches that position them differently for the academy: for engaging in debate, for adopting a voiced position in the "master narratives" (Greene, 1992), and for feeling thus enabled and empowered to enter various realms of discourse. Other women we quoted described different ways of feeling entitled to participate in dialogue, sometimes as listener only, sometimes as speaking tentatively, sometimes seeking what those coded as constructive knowers called "real talk," talk that creates an optimum setting in which "the half baked or emergent idea can grow" (WWK, p. 144).

All of these excerpts provide evidence of particular cognitive structures that influence, in part, the kinds of dialogue that are possible. But in addition, as Bruffee noted with Perry's subjects, all the WWK women emphasize that the roots of their thinking are nourished by conversation and that dialogue is how they apprehend new understanding and reinterpret their thinking and their ideas.

Not all dialogues, discourses, or interpretations, however, are created equal. If "we think because we can talk" (Bruffee, 1993), then the kind of thinking possible is constrained or enhanced by the nature of the community. Mary Belenky, Lynne Bond, and Jackie Weinstock (in press) explored problem-solving conversations between mothers and their children, differentiated by the mothers' epistemological positions. There were vast differences in the nature of the conversations. Mothers coded as silent and received knowers focus on completing the task with minimal talk and minimal involvement of the child. Mothers coded as subjective knowers encourage their children to be expressive, but they struggle to not take over the completion of the task. Mothers coded as procedural knowers engage their children in a conversation in which they together consider the nature of the problem, generate alternative procedures, and share in completing the task together. These mothers experience the dialogue with their children as stimulating their own thought.

In the social constructivist revisionist vocabulary, the developmental positions are *interpretative communities,* and the capacity to think mirrors the quality of the discourse in those communities. Analysis of development in this context must include the "contextual web" in which individuals exist (Fisher & Todd, 1986). "Rather than viewing individuals, their social partners, and the socio-cultural context as independent influences or factors of development [analyses must integrate] the differing angles of an integrated process" (Rogoff, 1990, p. 26). Focusing on discourse communities as a site for promoting and enhancing development maintains the web.

This brief examination of the WWK women's learning in dialogue gives us a different angle on cognitive developmental theory, which emphasizes different assumptions about learning and knowing by contrasting what Bruffee (1993) calls "foundational" knowledge with "nonfoundational" knowledge. Representing two sides of a boundary, the former is a "community constituted in the foundational language of cognition," the latter is a "community constituted in the language of nonfoundational social construction" (p. 165):

> When we see students learning judgment in groups better and faster than individually . . . when students tell us they learned more, faster and better in the dorm talking with their peers than in their professors' classes; and when we see infants learning in collaboration with mothers and mother-surrogates to do things we never imagined they could do, we have difficulty accounting for what we see. (Bruffee, 1993, p. 171)

To account for this learning, we must "[liberate] ourselves from [foundational] language and assumptions of cognition" (p. 170) in order to allow the nonfoundational language and assumptions of socially constructed learning to emerge.

Although I would still argue that both sides of the boundary have explanatory power, there is no doubt that redefining learning in a way that integrates individual learning, the role of others as social partners in dialogue, and the importance of the context make it possible to view the production of knowledge as a communal project.

DIALOGUE AND DISCOURSE COMMUNITIES

The primary assertion about nonfoundational knowledge is that all knowledge is produced and modified in community and communication. So far, this assertion has been used primarily to revise epistemological assumptions about how knowledge develops within academic disciplines (Bruffee, 1986; Geertz, 1983; Resaldo, 1986). *Discourse* or *interpretative communities* are defined as sites in which knowledge is produced, reproduced, and contested. In this way, knowledge production, like dialogue, becomes a shifting and unstable process. Knowledge is "common property of the community" (Kuhn, quoted in Bruffee, 1986, p. 3), negotiated through language and dialogue among informed peers.

The two terms for community—discourse and interpretative—are used fairly interchangeably (Bruffee, 1986; Damrosch, 1995); the former is most often attributed to Richard Rorty (1979), the latter to Stanley Fish (1980). Together they demarcate the major features of these communities. The task of the community is to interpret material and, through discourse or dialogue, to arrive at what one faculty member described as "an odd truce," referring to how he and his coteacher developed a syllabus together. These uneasy truces are a momentary consensus about meaning, agreements about what matters in a particular discipline as well as about acceptable procedures for developing those meanings. The progress of meaning making occurs through discourse, which may refer to a spoken conversation among scholars or a written text. Understanding grows in these communities through dialogue and through reading, the latter making library stacks "not a repository" but "a crowd" (Bruffee, 1993, p. 20).

When WWK introduced the notion of connected teaching, we added a new dimension to interpretive communities by emphasizing the influence of relationships in this process of constructing knowledge. This emphasis has not been explored much in the literature that examines a nonfoundational epistemology, which focuses only on the conversation as an object or a site for the production of ideas (see P. Schweikart's chapter, this volume).

Scholars in what we might call the feminist pedagogy discourse community have elaborated on the dimension of relationships as critical in the construction of knowledge. Some have been drawn to this perspective because it captures the power of relationships in learning (Lewis, 1990); some because it helps to define a dialogic community in which the individual's social and political "positionality" in relation to learning and knowledge production is acknowledged (Lather, 1992; Maher & Tetreault, 1994; Steinitz & Kanter, 1991); some have missed the point altogether and see the connected learner and the connected dialogue as a "laissez-faire, feel good," psychologically oriented conversation devoid of substance or subject (Freire & Macedo, 1995).

Christine Hoff Sommers (1994) exemplifies the latter perspective. She examines separate and connected knowing and feminist theories about the phases of curriculum transformation as processes that, according to her, attempt to describe a reconstructed academy. Yet she hears these analyses as "more lyrical than informative" about what the "transformed academy will actually look like." In six pages of her book, Sommers names a crew of theorists—Peggy McIntosh, Catharine Stimpson, Marilyn R. Schuster and Susan R. VanDyne, Linda Gardiner, Evelyn Fox Keller, and the WWK collaborators—as "feminist critic(s)" who are "more ingenious at finding male bias in a field than in proposing an intelligible alternative way to deal with its subject matter" (p. 71). Sommers wants to dis-integrate the "contextual web" of individual development, pedagogy, social context, and subject matter. Decrying the messy nonfoundational, intersubjective discourse of the social constructionist interpretation, she yearns for the disciplinary discourse community to be reinserted as foundational. Quoting Margarita Levin—"One still wants to know whether feminists' airplanes would stay airborne for feminist engineers" (p. 73)—Sommers reverts to a Piaget-like dependence on learning as action on objects. She fails to understand that the discourse and interpretative communities of the academy have been constructed systematically to eliminate certain authors, certain voices, particular emphases in analysis, and even historically situated "facts"—a construction that suggests that curricular designs, core curriculum, and the canon itself are themselves part of the problem (Greene, 1992; Maher & Tetreault, 1994; Martin, 1985; Finke, 1993).

Other members of the feminist pedagogy discourse, who do not suffer from Sommers's failures of "apprehension" and imagination, pose important and interesting elaborations on the function of both voice and connected knowing in nonfoundational approaches to disciplinary or interdisciplinary inquiry and curriculum. For them, the role of relationships and the ability to put one's understanding and learning into language cannot be ignored pedagogically, nor in the construction of knowledge.

Feminist teachers use "the vast differences in the worlds experienced by men and by women to expose and explore the political and social construction of all knowledge" (Maher & Tetreault, 1994, p. 8). The history of subjugation, violence, and marginalization in womens' lives becomes a "standpoint" (Haraway, 1988), a position, which one analyzes and from which one joins a conversation and interprets knowledge: "The political struggle over meaning must be seen as the focus of our pedagogical project" (Lewis, 1990, p. 470). This stance no longer sees pedagogy as mere technique for presenting material, but requires a relatively unique level of involvement of learners and teachers together in the pursuit of knowing. Learning becomes a "conversation," an identifier that appears often in writing about both feminist pedagogy and other pedagogical approaches like those in the discourse communities on teaching writing (Bruffee, 1986, Gannett, 1992, Trimbur, 1989, Weiner, 1986), on learning communities (Gablenick et al., 1990), and on collaborative learning (Goodsell, Maher, & Tinmto, 1992; Kadel & Keechner, 1994; Landa & Tarule, 1992; Romer, 1985; Romer & Whipple, 1991; Whipple, 1987). All are grounded in an assumption that knowledge is nonfoundational, and all include an insistence that creating classrooms as sites of discourse and interpretation requires attention to the nature of voice and dialogue, and (to a lesser extent for some) the role of relationships in learning.

DISCOURSE COMMUNITIES
AND POSTMODERN PEDAGOGIES.

As I finished the Women's Ways project, my ear and attention had turned more and more to these emerging dialogues about alternative approaches to teaching. It was becoming increasingly clear that the new thinking about the nature of disciplines and the role of dialogue in learning and knowledge production was a Trojan horse. Once it had been admitted, teaching practice had to change. I was teaching a developmental psychology class for thirty counseling master's degree students when the Trojan horse metaphor hit me. We were a few weeks into the course, discussing a theory I can no longer recall. We had read an English therapist and an American theorist on the topic, and the dialogue began to lumber toward interrogating the applicability of the theory to groups other than the white middle class in America. That interrogation quickly became the dominant discourse in our discussions. I dropped my planned syllabus and invited students to form work groups. These groups would interview people from a variety of racial and ethnic groups, balanced for gender; analyze their data together; and present their findings in what we came to call the class's Mini-Conference on Diversity in Developmental Psychology. The dialogue flourished as we grew more skilled at interrupting theory from our diverse perspectives, leading to questions about the nature of the self, attachment, cognitive development, and so on (see Goldberger and Bing & Reid chapters, this volume, on diverse perspectives in psychology). The learning was in the conversation for all of us. Although I would teach the course four more times, it was, to my delight, altered irrevocably.

I, like Bruffee, began seeking a dialogue with others who seemed to be having the same experience. In dialogue with people concerned with the particulars of feminist pedagogy (the political and positionality agenda), of writing (the voice agenda), and of learning communities (the interdisciplinary curriculum agenda), my emphasis centered on what is currently called *collaborative learning*, an agenda of experimenting with and examining new ways to construct classrooms as discourse and interpretive communities, inviting students and teachers to engage in what educational theorist Paulo Freire (Freire & Macedo, 1995) has called "dialogic meaning making." Within collaborative discourse, my particular concerns were integrating notions about relationships and the creation of classroom communities that transformed not only the conventional disciplinary boundaries, but also the ways students and faculty experience themselves as knowers.

The emphasis in collaborative learning is on the social context of the classroom as a site for constructing knowledge. The accompanying pedagogical emphasis is on creating the conditions in which a particular kind of dialogue can flourish: a dialogue of definition, exploration, experimentation, and inquiry that constructs and reconstructs apprehension and understanding of the discipline(s) being studied. Thus, collaborative learning involves a distinct epistemology and pedagogy. It produces distinct outcomes and creates a distinctly different classroom culture than that of other more traditional approaches (Whipple, 1987). Collaborative learning "assumes . . . that knowledge is a consensus among the members of a community of knowledgeable peers—something people construct by talking together and reaching agreement" (Bruffee, 1993, p. 3).

This dialogue, "talking together," leads to a revision of the nature of disciplinary knowledge. It admits what the anthropologist Paul Rabinow (1986) calls "corridor talk." "For many years" he writes,

> anthropologists informally discussed fieldwork experiences among themselves. Gossip about an anthropologist's field experience was an important component. . . . but such matters, were not until recently, written about "seriously." It remains in the corridors and faculty clubs. (p. 16)

Observing that through corridor talk "we learn a good deal," he suggests that moving corridor talk into "the production of anthropological knowledge [and] out of the domain of gossip . . . would be a step in the right direction."

Rabinow's "gossip" is not the same gossip we explored in WWK, although it does capture the collaborative process and dialogue among us four authors—what we came to call "pajama party scholarship." But all of these are forms of dialogue in which knowledge is constructed but not admitted into what constitutes the mainstream of the discourse or the interpretation. These dialogues in what WWK called the "bywaters" of the mainstream have long been part of learning environments—the study groups that students put together to support their learning, for example. And consistently, the academy has required these to be outside "regular" class time, relegating them to the corridors and coffee shops and ensuring that although they may support individuals' learning, they are not designed intentionally as part of the classroom discourse.

Collaborative learning attempts to alter that balance and to foster corridor and study group conversations as integral to classroom learning. Of her hopes for this process as she thought about coteaching her first collaborative learning class, one of the faculty members of the aforementioned "odd truce," says:

> This was supposed to be a course with students [who] get real involved and talk a lot and go out and, you know, and do interviews and bring them to class and we'd all discuss them. . . . So by the end it should be a real group thing. I had these visions, I'm getting really excited.

Courses are not often "a real group thing," but are instead a teacher's construction of the knowledge delivered through syllabus, lectures, even facilitated discussions. The boundaries of knowledge are predefined. An example of the prevalence of this emphasis in teaching is that, until very recently, studies of classrooms focused on teachers' questions and students' responses (Carlsen, 1991), ignoring what college professors Kris Gutierrez, Betsy Rymes, and Joanne Larson (1995) call the "underlife" of student dialogue in classroom conversations. When the underlife and the teacher's questions begin to coincide, they create a "third space" through a "dialogic pedagogy," which "means more than bringing students into the teacher script—that is, 'giving students voice.'" Such a pedagogy requires the inclusion and critique of the teacher's and students' stories at both the "intrapsychological and interpsychological level" (p. 453).

When corridor, discipline-based, interpsychological, and intrapsychological narratives are all admitted into a collaborative discourse, the site for and the content of meaning making shift. Sarah, a student in the course described as a "real group thing," defines the outcomes from that discourse:

> I feel like together we came out with some pretty neat things and some pretty big insights. It wasn't just one person. Somebody would say, "like the dog." Somebody else would say "and the cat." Somebody else would say, "ran to the. . . ."

Her metaphor for the dialogue in the class is the group's uttering a single sentence together. For her, no other class had produced this sense of

learning in dialogue, nor had she seen herself as a knowledge and meaning maker in her other classes. Relationships also flourished. In the next
semester, Sarah and two other participants designed and completed a
collaborative undergraduate thesis.

Such collaborations are rare in the culture of the academy. Study
groups are acceptable, but talking or working together during a test is
cheating. Professors' scholarship is frequently collaborative (Ede &
Lunsford, 1990), but there is a value-laden hierarchy about the accept-
ability of the practice. Cowritten articles may count for less in tenure
decisions, and applicants are frequently required to assess their specific
contribution to the work. Citation practice adopted by the American Psychological Association dictates that if two people collaborate, they should
both be cited. Beyond two, convention requires the first citation of a
work to list all authors; subsequently only the name of the first author is
listed with the rest collapsed into the "et al." In the case of work by more
than four authors, only the first name is ever cited (APA Style Manual).
Convention asserts, thus, that more than four cannot collaborate equally.

Students and faculty alike learn these rules for discourse, classrooms,
and scholarship as part of the process of acculturation to the academy.
When collaborative procedures are introduced, they are not simply new
"tricks" for teaching; they disrupt the basic assumptions about how learning progresses and who gets to be a knower.

When collaborative classrooms work, the discourse usually moves
through two phases: a first in which a "vocabulary" that may include specific disciplinary terms is established and always includes a more
inchoate vocabulary of how conversation will proceed, and a second in
which the learning becomes lodged in the discipline and the discourse
(Bruffee, 1993; Tarule, 1992). In the second phase, roles often shift dramatically for both the teacher and the student.

Emily, a student, remembers that she came to see the coteaching faculty as

> not really teachers, but kind of guides, in a way, especially with the research
> stuff because, you know, you guys have been doing this sort of thing and here
> this was the first time I was really exposed to a research project starting, as I
> said, from ground zero and building up.

Sarah elaborates that the teachers "were not really teachers, although
[they] were resources." The teachers knew "more about the topic," she
says, "but I felt like we were all in this together."

The role of teachers as "resources" or "guides" in a "real group thing" signaled a shift of authority in the class. Everyone had something to contribute to the discourse. And although the professors were acknowledged to know "more," what the students knew about the discipline seemed to stand on level ground. Another student from a collaborative class says, "[It] made me feel like that student–professor role wasn't . . . the stereotyped role where there's the big space in between."

However, level ground is not always a comfortable place to stand. In the conventional and foundational construction of disciplines, the relevant knowledge resides in the minds of the experts and authority. In WWK, we describe how the "teacher as midwife" helps students give birth to and nurture their own voice and ideas, and about how connected teaching emphasizes believing students' ideas over doubting them, creating conditions for development that do not rely on competition or conflict to promote individuals' thought.

Certainly taking students' ideas seriously is critical to collaborative discourse, but often that focus is described in terms of the teacher/student relationship, ignoring both the "third space" and underlife in the classroom. Collaborative learning practices, though involving the connected teaching qualities of trust, intersubjectivity, and respect, move the dialogue into the "third space" of the whole class: student to student during in-class study groups, students and teachers in classroom dialogues. These dialogues interpret and contest what may be "accepted truths."

In WWK, we describe an incident of this kind of classroom discourse that one student reported she had left feeling she had "accomplished something." The class discussion surfaced ideas the professor had "not thought about." It led to "a whole different way" of understanding the book they were studying. By the next class, the professor "returned to the podium" (p. 220). Conversation died. The student was disappointed. We can imagine that perhaps the professor was relieved to have regained authority and to have reinstated himself as the best knower in the room.

Groups led by a guide are different from groups led by an authority. The authoritative voice is no longer held by only one person; it is lodged in the discourse. Nora, an honors engineering student who could certainly design planes that fly, compares her learning from a professor at the podium with her learning when the authority is lodged in the conversation. In the collaborative discourse, she says:

> We finally had some professors that were willing to let the conversation go as it would or let the thought flow as they would. . . . I really did like the fact that

the class was like open and casual and that the participation was so spontaneous. That's what stands out to me most about the class, not so much what
we studied as the fact that it seemed to pertain, everything seemed to have an
importance.

"Does [the collaborative class] stand out against other [discussion-
based] classes?" the interviewer asks.

It, to me it stood above the other classes. But I would put [the discussion-
based] classes next and then the ordinary classes next and some of the ordinary classes way to the bottom. I mean . . . the freshman classes where [there
are what] looks like a hundred people in a big auditorium and the professors
a dot down there speaking into a microphone. . . . That is a waste, a total
waste. I wound up reading the book, trying to memorize a few facts so I could
regurgitate them back on the exam and get through. . . . I would almost take
notes verbatim. . . . I couldn't even paraphrase and write it in my own
words. . . . I would even lose track of what he was saying so I would just catch
myself verbatim spilling it out there.

The way a class is structured and the role the authority takes shape not
only the discourse but the meaning this student makes; it is (or is not)
learning. When the dialogue feels "spontaneous" and learning is in the
conversation, she is engaged in both the material and what it relates to in
her other classes and her life. When the professor is a dot speaking into
a microphone from a podium, language seems to lose all meaning and
Nora is reduced to simple reproduction of the teacher's words, words
devoid of meaning.

Faculty who walk out from the podium to engage their subject in
"spontaneous" collaborative inquiry with students in discourse community classrooms experience more than a shift in their authority. They are
often troubled by a similarly profound change in their role as the
"expert" and they are startled that their voice as either authority or expert
has been muted (Ellsworth, 1989; Hollingsworth, 1994; Maher &
Tetreault, 1994; Weiler, 1991).

EXPERTS, AUTHORITY, AND THE
COLLABORATIVE DISCOURSE

Much of what is understood and described as cognitive development
emanates from defining knowledge as foundational, mediated through

the experts to the naive learner or student. The model certainly has power as an explanation for how some knowledge is acquired. But the power of the explanation diminishes in the context of learning in higher education. It especially pales as there is an increased emphasis on the social context for learning and on the creation of nonfoundational interpretations rather than the conveying of immutable truths.

For faculty, the notion of expert has been shaped and molded in their own foundational, disciplinary education. Moreover, the academy's requirements for becoming an expert by achieving disciplinary author(ity) reward the isolated, lone individual and eliminate those who understand knowledge as a nonfoundational construction mediated by and constructed in dialogue. Scholarship for both faculty and doctoral student goes on in "a community of one" and takes on "a markedly introverted cast." But regardless of how "wide the audience reached (or, more often, fantasized) the work is built out of solitude" (Damrosch, 1995, p. 85). Experts carry this work as scholarly nuggets that, if they are not to be consigned to "yellowing away in a drawer, unthumbed, unreferred to, unapplauded," are to be hurled at students from a "dot down there" behind a podium.

The role of the expert or authority who mediates knowledge to promote learning was important in our WWK inquiry. When we were interviewing the WWK women, we asked them about how they understood the relationship between experts and knowledge. We offered the interviewee the statement "In areas where the right answers are known, I think the experts should tell us what is right. But in areas where there is no right answer, I think anybody's opinion is as good as another's." And we followed it up with a probing question: "In learning something you really want to know, can you rely on the experts?"

As interviewers, we introduced for the interviewee's consideration the notion of experts as the repository of knowledge, and we suggested that foundational knowledge exists ("where right answers are known") and is the purview of the expert whereas nonfoundational knowledge ("where there is no right answer") is not associated with expertise.

Since the interview itself lodges knowledge, authority, and expertise in a collaborative dialogue, the interviewee is quite likely to have experienced the interviewer as an "expert,'" creating an infinite regression—like the man on the Quaker Oats box holding a box with a picture of a man on the Quaker Oats box, ad infinitum. As a dialogue, this is now a situation in which the person who is perceived as expert/authority is asking the "subject" about how s/he relates to and uses the thought of experts. Moreover, given the form of interview in which the interviewer is trained not to interpret nor interrupt, that is, to create not a dialogue but a question-directed monologue, the "subject" is now not only being asked to talk about experts (the interviewer) but to do so in a relative dialogue vacuum, a conversation shaped by the interviewer's questions, just as classrooms are seen to be shaped by the teachers' questions.

If one assumes that the production of knowledge and thought is lodged and constructed in the social context of dialogue-rich relationships, the social context of the interview probably had unintended influences on how we understood individuals' experience of expert, their definition of expert, and the role of the expert in their own learning and knowledge. Perhaps, like Nora, the interviewee looks for a way to reproduce "verbatim" what she understands of the interviewer's words about how experts construct knowledge. Does she look for nuggets she is to reproduce? The interviewee may be telling us more about the dialogic relationship between the interviewer and her than about her definition of expert, since "expert" was not her language in the first place. Is she describing her experience of the interviewer as expert? Is she being careful about what she says to protect the dialogue? Is she struggling to find out what the interviewer means by "expert"? Is she, as many did, simply rejecting altogether the notion of "expert" in any form?

In our research after WWK was published we abandoned the earlier questions in the interview for the more open-ended "How do you go about learning something new?" Once the expert and knowledge definition have been removed from the conversation, a large number of the people I have interviewed using this new question do *not* invoke the expert (suggesting the expert was indeed a construction of the interviewer), but instead answer that what they do is "ask someone," or "talk to a friend." When you want to know something, you seek a dialogue about it; learning is in the conversation. Maybe it is a question, or maybe it is a long dialogue. Maybe, like Sarah's it starts alone in your car while you practice what it is you want to engage others in thinking about. But in all cases and regardless of apparent developmental position, experts do not seem naturally to spring up as either the first or only source of knowledge. They may not appear at all. These "subjects" tell us that their cognitive development—our theories and constructs aside—is furthered through dialogue with colleagues perceived, mostly, as peers.

However, in the culture of the academy, the expert question still pertains. "In a lecture," one student says, "the only ideas being exchanged [are] the professors' . . . it's just one way." But in a collaborative class, she says, learning is "two-way . . . between the students and the professor and the students and the students." Students and faculty alike have been acculturated to believe that knowledge flows from expert faculty to student, not between student and student nor, even, between faculty and student in a coconstruction.

As the definition of both expert and authority shifts, so do definitions about learning, about what constitutes information and knowledge. One student says that her course "wasn't like, here's the information, don't touch it but know it." In most of the classes in this large university, a setting we did not explore in WWK, learning is "just recollection . . . just memorize this list, repeat that on the bubble sheets, just fill in the bubble." Being asked to "touch" the information, the students in the collaborative class on motivation

> would actually manipulate information. You would actually use it and try to combine a little of this, a little of that, come out with a new statement, which may have already been developed but you kind of led yourself into that theory . . . which was nice.

"You had to think," this student says, "and that's not a requirement in all my classes."

However, being required to think and to do so with peers can be stimulating or frustrating, just as listening to a lecture can sometimes be experienced as an exhilarating "conversation" that engages one's thinking or as a disheartening conversation that deadens one's thought. One's collaborating peers may not be "really thinking about the question or they just seem[ed] to be kind of tossing the ideas off their head." Even in a brainstorming session, one of the university students says, she sometimes felt her peers were not "digging into what I thought the question was asking or not getting in deep enough . . . and I would get frustrated."

Faculty frustration with the process can be equally acute. Honing in on the issue of power by exploring work between student and faculty as "Collaboration Across the Power Line," collaborative learning theorists Karen Romer and Bill Whipple (1991) report that one faculty member responded to the idea of collaborative learning, "Are you telling me that I should forgo my authority in the classroom?" (p. 68).

These theorists pick up on the voice metaphor described at the beginning of this chapter and find "similarities between our use of authority and the concept of voice." In collaborative learning situations, faculty members need to become conscious of the difference between "organic authority rooted in knowledge and inherent in one's person and the authority of power that the condition of being learned gives one over others" (p. 68; see also Maher & Tetreault, 1994, pp. 128ff.). It is the latter, they say, that is constantly negotiated in the collaborative classroom.

Authority is not abandoned but "silenced" to allow for "absorbing the authority of another or while constructing a new group authority (see Clinchy, this volume, on "absorbing" others' thought)." It is a "a dialogue of authority" that takes place in the truly collaborative classroom. The role of both authority and expert is lodged in the conversation just as the construction of knowledge is.

This may mean abandoning knowledge as constructed and outlined in the syllabus. Sandra Hollingsworth (1994) describes a two-year collaborative conversation she had with beginning teachers, a conversation that she thought would expand on her early instruction to them on the subject of teaching reading. The group took the conversation elsewhere. "As hard as I tried," Hollingsworth writes, "I could not get the conversation to focus on my interest in their subject-matter learning" (p. 380). Abandoning her expert "organic authority," she revised her role and helped the group to construct an authority lodged in the dialogue. As she did so, both the process and the outcome were transformed. Experiencing "people making meaning together" (p. 387), she and her collaborators began to appreciate their roles as professionals and as knowledge makers. "[T]he continuous cycles of critique, knowledge construction and social action were both method and result." When the making of knowledge together goes "deep," as the student quoted earlier said, the learning that results goes equally deep. The distinction between content and process blurs. The dialogue creates a pedagogical "space" for transforming voices and revising the role of authority. The result reconstructs knowing and the nature of knowledge.

DIFFICULT DIALOGUES AND THE FUTURE

In WWK, we understood the importance of learners' feeling they could speak about what they knew and of learning environments that valued students' connections to the subject of study, to the teachers, as well as to alternative forms for analysis such as connected knowing. Classrooms that supported this process were rich, "yeasty" environments in which the students' ideas could flourish.

Still, at that time, our emphasis was on the individual's ability to emerge from her education with a sense of efficacy, even authority, instead of a sense of being silenced and a damaged self-esteem. We knew that educators could often better support the individual student by promoting collaboration and making learning meaningful by connecting with students' experience and procedures for constructing knowledge.

We knew educators needed sometimes to adopt silence over imposition (*WWK*, p. 229).

Examining the epistemic significance of dialogue in the social construction of knowledge shifts the emphasis from the individual student or faculty member, generally struggling alone "in a community of one" (Damrosch, 1994), to emphasize learning as a "profoundly social" (John-Steiner & Souberman, 1978) endeavor conducted through dialogue.

As the emphasis moves to community and collaboration, the possibilities for the kind of learning that may result expand. There is a current plea, a social imperative, that we learn quickly how to create contexts in which neither a single view nor a single voice—master or otherwise—dominates. Creating college classrooms that reify and reproduce patterns of dominance is not only an obsolete methodology, it is destructive.

College professors, along with others, need to construct contexts that promote dialogue as indispensable in students' learning. As participants in these contexts begin to experience how those dialogues *are* their learning, they seek ways to engage their learning and teaching in new ways. Most often, these new ways include what Beverly Guy-Sheftell (Albert, 1991; Guy-Sheftell, 1994) has called the "difficult dialogues," dialogues that seek to construct knowledge within a complex multicultural and diverse context, dialogues that interrogate knowledge from diverse perspectives and measure validity in relation to sociocultural contexts. These dialogues are more likely to emphasize colabor rather than dominance, to seek common ground rather than consensus (Burbules & Rice; 1991; Weisbord, 1992). Clearly these revised practices are required of all participants if we are to successfully address the challenge to transform the academy into a culture where all students can learn, and all humans—students and faculty alike—can develop and flourish.

NOTES

1. Excerpts about collaborative classrooms are drawn from a research project I did collaboratively with Bill Whipple. Most are from a study in which we interviewed faculty and students who had completed a semester-long honors course, Gender and Thought, team taught at a small, mostly undergraduate public university campus in the South. Additional interviews are from a graduate and adult baccalaureate level psychology of women course in a small private college in the East, and an undergraduate motivation course at a large eastern public university.

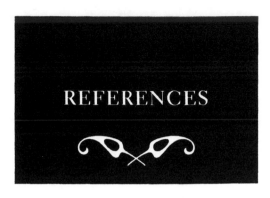

REFERENCES

Albert, L. (1991). Difficult dialogues. *AAHE Bulletin, 43,* 3–5.

Belenky, M. F., Bond, L. A., & Weinstock, J. S. (in press). *A tradition that has no name: Public homeplaces and the development of people, families, and communities.* New York: Basic Books.

Belenky, M. F., Clinchy, B. M., Goldberger, N. R., & Tarule, J. M. (1986). *Women's ways of knowing: The development of self, voice, and mind.* New York: Basic Books.

Brown, L. M. & Gilligan, C. (1992). *Meeting at the crossroads: Women's psychology and girl's development.* Cambridge, MA: Harvard University Press.

Bruffee, K. (1986). Social construction, language, and the authority of knowledge: A bibliographic essay. *College English, 48,* 773–790.

Bruffee, K. (1993). *Collaborative learning: Higher education, interdependence, and the authority of knowledge.* Baltimore: Johns Hopkins University Press.

Burbules, N., & Rice, S. (1991). Dialogue across differences: Continuing the conversation. *Harvard Educational Review, 61,* 393–416.

Burbules, N. (1993). *Dialogue in teaching: Theory and practice.* New York: Teachers College Press, Columbia University.

Campbell, W. (1994). *The politics of creativity.* Lesley College Graduate School Qualifying Paper, Cambridge, MA.

Carlsen, W. S. (1991). Questioning in classrooms: A sociolinguistic perspective. *Review of Educational Research, 16,* 157–178.

Chodorow, N. (1978). *The reproduction of mothering.* Berkeley: University of California Press.

Clinchy, B. (1995). Commentary. *Human Development, 38,* 258–264.

Damrosch, D. (1995). *We scholars: Changing the culture of the university.* Cambridge, MA: Harvard University Press.

Ede, L., & Lunsford, A. (1990). *Singular texts/plural authors: Perspectives on collaborative writing.* Carbondale: Southern Illinois University Press.

Ellsworth, E. (1989). Why doesn't this feel empowering? Working through the repressive myths of critical pedagogy. *Harvard Educational Review, 59,* 297–324.

Finke, L. (1993). Knowledge as bait: Feminism, voice, and the pedagogical unconscious. *College English, 55*(1), 7–27.

Fish, S. (1980). *Is there a text in this class? The authority of interpretive communities.* Cambridge, MA: Harvard University Press.

Fisher, S., & Todd, A. D. (Eds.) (1986). *Discourse and institutional authority: Medicine, education, and law.* Norwood, NJ: Ablex.

Freire, P., & Macedo, D. P. (1995). A dialogue: Culture, language, and race. *Harvard Educational Review, 65,* 377–402.

Gabelnick, F., MacGregor, J., Matthews, R., & Smith, B. (1990). *Learning communities: Creating connections among students, faculty and disciplines.* San Francisco: Jossey-Bass.

Gannett, C. (1992). *Gender and the journal: Diaries and academic discourse.* Albany, NY: State University of New York Press.

Geertz, C. (1983). *Local knowledge: Further essays in interpretive anthropology.* New York: Basic Books.

Gilligan, C. (1982). *In a different voice: Psychological theory and women's development.* Cambridge, MA: Harvard University Press.

Goodsell, A., Maher, M., & Tinmto, V. with MacGregor, J. & Smith, B. (1992). *Sourcebook on collaborative and cooperative learning.* University Park, PA: National Center on Postsecondary Teaching, Learning and Assessment.

Greene, M. (1992). Foreword. In C. Luke & J. Gore (Eds.), *Feminisms and critical pedagogy.* New York: Routledge.

Gutierrez K., Rymes, B., & Larson, J. (1995). Script, counterscript, and underlife in the classroom: James Brown versus *Brown v. Board of Education. Harvard Educational Review, 65,* 445–469.

Guy-Sheftell, B. (1994). Difficult dialogues: Gender studies in the liberal arts curriculum. Keynote presented at Gender Issues in Higher Education. University of Vermont, Burlington.

Haraway, D. (1988). Situated knowledges: The science question in feminism and the privilege of partial perspective. *Feminist Studies, 14* (3), 575–599.

Hollingsworth, S. (1994). Learning to teach through collaborative conversation: A feminist approach. *American Educational Research Journal, 29,* 373–404.

Hoshmond, L. L. S. (1989). Alternative research paradigms: A review and teaching proposal. *Counseling Psychologist, 17,* 3–79.

John-Steiner, V. & Souberman, E. (1978). Afterword. In Cole, M., John-Steiner, V., Scribner, S., & Souberman, E. (Eds.), Vygotsky, L. S., *Mind in society: The development of higher education processes.* Cambridge, MA: Harvard University Press.

Jordan, J., Kaplan, A., Miller, J. B., Stiver, I., & Surrey, J. (1991). *Women's growth in connection: Writing from the Stone Center.* New York: Guilford.

Josselson, R. (1992). *The space between us: Exploring the dimension of human relationships*. San Francisco: Jossey-Bass.

Kadel, S., & Keechner, J. A. (1994). *Collaborative learning: A sourcebook for higher education*. (Vol. II). University Park, PA: National Center on Postsecondary Teaching, Learning, and Assessment.

Landa, A., & Tarule, J. M. (1992). *Collaborative learning in postsecondary education*. Cambridge, MA: Collaborative Learning Project of the Lesley College Center for Research, Pedagogical and Policy Studies.

Lather, P. (1992). Post-critical pedagogies: A feminist reading. In C. Luke & J. Gore (Eds.), *Feminisms and critical pedagogy*. New York: Routledge.

Lewis, M. (1990). Interrupting patriarchy: Politics, resistance, and the transformation in the feminist classroom. *Harvard Educational Review, 60*, 467–888.

Lunsford, A., & Ede, L. (1990). *Singular texts/plural authors: perspectives on collaborative writing*. Carbondale: Southern Illinois University Press.

Lyons, N. (1983). Two perspectives on self, relationships and morality. *Harvard Educational Review, 53*, 125–145.

Maher, F. (1987). Toward a richer theory of feminist pedagogy. *Journal of Education, 169*(3), 91–99.

Maher, F., & Tetreault, M. K. (1994). *Inside feminist classrooms: An inside look at how professors and students are transforming higher education for a diverse society*. New York: Basic Books.

Martin, J. (1985). *Reclaiming a conversation: The ideal of the educated woman*. New Haven, CT: Yale University Press.

Olesen, V. (1994). Feminisms and models of qualitative research. In N. Danzin & Y. Guba (Eds.), *Handbook of qualitative research*. Newbury Park, CA: Sage.

Perry, W. G. (1970). *Forms of intellectual and ethical development in the college years*. Cambridge, MA: Harvard University Press.

Rabinow, P. (1986). Representations are social facts: Modernity and postmodernity in anthropology. In J. Clifford & G. Marcus (Eds.), *Writing culture: The poetics and politics of ethnography*. Berkeley: University of California Press.

Resaldo, R. (1986). *Culture and truth: The remaking of social analysis*. Boston: Beacon Press.

Rogoff, B. (1990). *Apprenticeship in thinking: Cognitive development in social context*. New York: Oxford University Press.

Rogoff, B. (1993). Children's guided participation and participatory appropriation in sociocultural activity. In G. Wozniak & K. Fisher (Eds.), *Development in context: Acting and thinking in specific environments*. Hillsdale, NJ: Erlbaum.

Romer, K. T. (1985). Collaboration: New forms of learning, new ways of thinking. *Forum for Liberal Education, 8*, 2–4.

Romer, K., & Whipple, W. (1991). Collaboration across the power line. *College Teaching, 39,* 66–70.

Rorty, R. M. (1979). *Philosophy and the mirror of nature.* Princeton, NJ: Princeton University Press.

Ruddick, S. (1986). *Maternal thinking: Toward a politics of peace.* Boston: Beacon Press.

Sommers, C. H. (1994). *Who stole feminism? How women have betrayed women.* New York: Simon & Schuster.

Stenitz, V., & Kanter, S. (1991). Becoming outspoken: Beyond connected education. *Women's Studies Quarterly, 1 2,* 138–153.

Tannen, D. (1990). *You just don't understand: Women and men in conversation.* New York: Ballantine.

Tarule, J. M. (1978). *Patterns of development transition in adulthood.* Unpublished doctoral dissertation, Harvard Graduate School of Education.

Tarule, J. M. (1980). Steps toward change: The process of transition. In E. Greenberg, K. O'Donnel, & W. Berquist (Eds.), *Educating learners of all ages.* San Francisco: Jossey-Bass.

Tarule, J. M. (1992). Dialogue and adult learning. *Liberal Education, 4,* 12–19.

Trimbur, J. (1989). Consensus and difference in collaborative learning. *College English, 52,* 653–660.

Vygotsky, L. (1986). *Thought and language.* Cambridge, MA: MIT Press.

Weiler, K. (1991). Freire and a feminist pedagogy of difference. *Harvard Educational Review, 61,* 449–474.

Weiner, H. S. (1986). Collaborative learning in the classroom: A guide to evaluation. *College English, 58,* 52–61.

Weisbord, W. R. (1992). *Discovering common ground: How future search conferences bring people together to achieve breakthrough innovation, empowerment, shared vision, and collaborative action.* San Francisco: Berrett-Koehler.

Whipple, W. (1987). Collaborative learning: Recognizing it when we see it. *AAHE Bulletin, 40*(2), 3–7.

Speech Is Silver, Silence Is Gold

The Asymmetrical Intersubjectivity of Communicative Action

PATROCINIO P. SCHWEICKART

I

WOMEN'S WAYS OF KNOWING (WWK) provoked two kinds of reactions in me. The first was experiential. I set the research findings against my own experiences, observed similarities as well as differences, and tried to make sense of one in light of the other. The second reaction was theoretical. I read the epistemological model offered by WWK in light of my own preoccupations with theories of reading and discourse.

My experiential reaction to WWK was complicated. I immediately felt both an aversion to the feminine aura of its findings and a strong reluctance to regard them as applicable to me. Because, like many educated women of my generation, I had learned well to think like a man (or, to think that I think like a man), I was inclined to regard myself as a counterexample to the findings of WWK, and, in addition, to feel that the difference was to my credit. At the same time, my experience with the women's movement and with women's studies induced me to be skeptical of this reaction. I questioned WWK's findings and research methodology; I wondered whether they had misinterpreted the data or had chosen their subjects so as to skew the data in certain directions; I disputed the legitimacy of their model and noted the theoretical flaws imported from William Perry's work, and so on. But it also occurred to me that all of these questions, although legitimate enough, were really rationalizations of my aversion to femininity—a defense against being "lumped in" with other women—that was a reflex of my conventional education.[1] I first tried to resolve the conflict by acknowledging that the findings of WWK were valid and interesting to the extent that they illuminated the experience and perspectives of a significant segment (perhaps a majority) of *other* women: for all sorts of reasons, I (luckily) was different. But, as often happens, the process of self-reflection, once initiated, took an unexpected turn. I began to notice that my ways of knowing were at odds not only with the women's ways described in WWK, but also with the conventional views. Oddly enough, once I got past the obvious gender issue, I noticed that what I found most questionable from an experiential point of view was not the discussion of the distinction between "separate" and "connected" knowing, but the thematization of "silence" as the opposite of knowledge.

Two experiential strands led me to have a different intuition about silence. The first had to do with my being Filipino. WWK made me recall two proverbs from my Filipino upbringing: *Speech is silver, but silence is gold*, and *Silent waters run deep*. The popular appeal of these proverbs among Filipinos suggests that for them silence often represents cognitive activity, and that thoughtful silence is a highly valued form of agency. It is perhaps tempting to fit this valorization of silence into the stereotype of the subservient Asian child or woman. I can only say that this would be inappropriate. Filipinos expect children to be polite and respectful, but they do not subscribe to the rule that "children should be seen, not heard." Although the modest demeanor admired in women entails being soft-spoken, decorous, and courteous, they are not required to be silent or to refrain from expressing their views.

In fact, the proverbs apply to all. Filipinos are a loquacious people. The proverbs represent a collective ironic reflection on our love of talk. "Speech is silver, silence is gold" is said to inhibit the overestimation of verbal power, or to gently rebuke someone who, being too full of himself, has become overly enamored with the sound of his own voice. "Silent waters run deep" is often said in appreciation of someone who speaks infrequently but wisely. Among Filipinos, silence attends wisdom.

The other strand of experience that contributed to my respect for silence stemmed from my college and graduate education in engineering and mathematics, where periods of learning correlated with periods of sustained silence—as I listened to the professor lecturing or solving a problem on the board, or as I read the textbook and worked through sample and exercise problems. It seemed to me that to assimilate this experience into the WWK null position of "silence" or, even, into the position of "received knowing" would be to miss something important.[2] My silence in class or while working on a problem was the sign not of passivity, but of the most intense intellectual engagement. Moreover, one could not learn calculus or physical chemistry by mechanically receiving information or following instructions—one had to attain insight; one had to get the point, to figure it out for/in oneself. My silence was indicative not of my subservience to the authority of the professor or the text, but, on the contrary, of my intellectual autonomy, my independent effort to understand. The association of silence with cognitive agency during my years as a student of engineering and mathematics is reinforced by my experience in my current discipline of literary studies where reading—almost always *silent*—is the condition for the acquisition of literary knowledge.

As it turns out, my recognition of the crucial role of silence in my knowledge projects leads me back to the centerpiece of the epistemological model presented by WWK—connected knowing. What distinguishes this position from that of subjectivism (these two are often conflated; see Blythe Clinchy's chapter in this volume) is that the former associates knowledge with intersubjectivity. In this essay, I will show that intersubjectivity involves two different modes of subjective agency—the assertive mode of speaking and writing, and the receptive, silent mode of listening and reading. The attentive and thoughtful silence valued by Filipinos and prominent in my experience as a student of mathematics and engineering is a necessary moment of connected knowing.

WWK also engaged me theoretically. When it was published in 1986, it entered an intellectual environment that had been stirred by theoretical and empirical studies in several disciplines that represented gender as the locus of significant, determinate, and specifiable difference. Nancy Chodorow's *The Reproduction of Mothering* (1978) argued that psychological development follows divergent paths in men and women: because (in our society) infants are cared for primarily by women, masculine identity is formed in relation to a strongly differentiated other, but feminine identity in relation to an other that is not unequivocally differentiated; consequently, men have a greater psychic investment in individuation, women a greater investment in relatedness. *In a Different Voice* (1982), by Carol Gilligan, and *Caring* (1984), by Nel Noddings, found in women's moral reasoning evidence of a distinctively different moral point of view—an ethic of care—that cannot be fully accounted for in the dominant androcentric model of an ethic of rights. Concurrently, feminist critics were finding gender differences in writing and reading, and linguists were finding distinctive differences in language use.

I want to make several observations about the research programs I have described. First of all, they are gynocentric.[3] This means that they are concerned, in the first instance, not with gender difference, but rather, with discovering, elaborating and making sense of *women's* perspectives, interests, and experiences. Such studies are motivated, to use Sandra Harding's term, by the "strong objectivity" of "feminist standpoint epistemology." In "starting off thought" from the lives of women, they endeavor to "use history as a resource by socially situating knowledge projects in the scientifically and epistemologically most favorable historical locations" (1992, p. 441).

Second, these studies are necessarily ambivalent about the distinctive qualities they find in women. They raise not only empirical questions of whether these qualities are shared by all women and to what extent they are evident in or accessible to men, but also crucial questions of value. Are these qualities to be fostered or resisted, honored or deplored? What is their scope—are they valuable only as womanly attributes or are they valuable as well when manifested by men? To what extent are they true values, and to what extent do they stem from and promote women's subordination? The empirical questions are interesting, but in this essay I emphasize questions of value. I think that certain qualities and competencies that have been obscured and marginalized because of their association with women are, *in fact*, socially necessary, accessible to and desirable in women and men alike.

Third, it is useful, following Edwin Ardener (1975) to think of these marginalized capacities and competencies as "muted" in the sense that they are not articulated in the publicly persuasive discourses that produce and reproduce the defining values of the culture. In particular, they are not articulated in the dominant academic discourses—philosophical, epistemological, aesthetic, literary, and discursive theories—that define the "humanities." Thus, "feminine" values are not silent: they speak, they do their cultural work—we all say we ought to "care" and to "listen" and, of course, often we do. We *must*, for life becomes impossible otherwise. But from the perspective of the traditional human sciences, these feminized values are antithetical to theory, something like static—inarticulate, disorganized, incoherent, incomprehensible background noise.

Feminist researchers on women during the last decade have corroborated and reinforced each other, and their findings have come to be framed around the relational psychology identified by Chodorow and the morality of care foregrounded by Gilligan and Noddings. Although the research program of WWK is distinguished by its focus on epistemological rather than moral issues, the work of Gilligan and Noddings and the findings of WWK are two sides of the same coin—the capacities and predilections identified by Gilligan and Noddings as the hallmarks of an ethic of care are shown in WWK to be deployed by women toward cognitive ends. This becomes particularly clear when one considers the central role conversation plays in both: knowledge like morality is produced by "really talking." Taken together, WWK and research on the ethic of care underscore the mutual implication of cognitive, moral, and communicative agency.

At the time that I was encountering feminist research on women's ways of thinking, feeling, and speaking I was also reading Jürgen Habermas, whose work during the last twenty years had been devoted to showing the mutual implication of cognitive, moral, and communicative development. I was first drawn to Habermas's account of truth (1973) as something that is produced through intersubjective validation, for I saw in it a way of resolving the impasse in literary theory between objectivist and subjectivist conceptions of meaning. While the subjectivists speak for the active agency and interpretive freedom of each reader as a producer of meaning, the objectivists argue that if we deny that meaning is lodged in the verbal object, then we also have to forgo the notion of validity. In the absence of any means for distinguishing true from false interpretations, literary criticism as a knowledge project becomes incoherent. Habermas's work suggests that the way out of the impasse is to recognize that meaning resides neither objectively in the text nor subjectively in the reader, but is the product of the discursive interaction of a community of readers (see Bleich, 1986). This view has the further advantage of being more in keeping with what actually happens—we figure out whether or not an interpretation is valid by discussing it with others.

However, as much as I was convinced by Habermas's (1987, 1990, 1993) effort to put intersubjectivity in the forefront of cognitive and moral theories, I felt there was something not quite right with the "volitional-emotional tone"[4] of his work. I was particularly baffled by the counterintuitive reduction of "understanding" to "agreement" (don't we often disagree even with views we understand?). In my view, Habermas offers a stripped-down version of communication, one that has been emptied of substance in order to render it theoretically manageable. One theoretical consequence of the exclusion of "feminized" substance is a

theory that misrepresents the structure of intersubjectivity and communication. WWK recuperates the substance that has been dumped out (or
"muted") by Habermas.

II

Perhaps the most influential notion in WWK is the distinction between
separate and connected knowing, and the empirical finding that women
show significant preference for the latter and significant distaste for the
former. The idea of connected knowing has important precedents in
composition studies. WWK (p. 113) cites composition theorist Peter
Elbow's notion of the "believing game," where you

> suspend your disbelief, put your own views aside, and try to see the logic in
> the idea. Ultimately, you need not agree with it, but while you are entertain-
> ing it you must, as Elbow says, "say yes to it": you must empathize with it, feel
> with it and think with the person who created it. (Clinchy, 1989, p. 651)

Elbow is a leading proponent of the idea of writing as a process of finding one's "voice." In his view, composing a text is a way of composing
myself—a way of figuring out how I feel, how I think, what I stand for,
what I am able to speak for, a way of understanding myself. The conver-
gence between writing process theory and feminist research, has led
some to characterize the "emerging field of composition studies . . . as
feminization of our previous conceptions of how writers write and how
writing should be taught" (Flynn, 1988, p. 423; also see Lamb, 1991, and
Frey, 1990).

The connection to literary studies becomes apparent when it is
observed that the idea of a willing suspension of disbelief is one of the
tenets of traditional literary criticism.[5] The "doubting game" characterized by a "combative kind of energy that feels like clenching a muscle"
is generally considered to be the wrong approach to reading a poem or a
novel, for it is unlikely to yield a *critical*—which is to say, appreciative
and value-enhancing—understanding of the text. One of the pioneering
works of feminist criticism, Judith Fetterley's *The Resisting Reader* (1978),
was shocking because in recommending that women readers resist and
question the immasculating designs of male-centered literary works she
seemed to be recommending something tantamount to a personal attack
on authors and a desecration of their works. In literary criticism, connected knowing—defined in terms of Elbow's believing game—is not

antithetical to critical thinking, but is one of its fundamental moments. Even feminist critiques like that of Fetterley presuppose a prior appreciation of the literary qualities of the texts in question.

In this essay, I will set aside the connection of WWK to composition studies and concentrate on its link to literary criticism. I will argue that the feminine moral, cognitive, and communicative capacities that make up connected knowing are cultivated at the "lower stages" of development, where literary criticism is identified with the careful and sensitive reading of literature. However, at the "highest stage" of development of the discipline, separate knowing manifested in argumentative adversarial discourse becomes the public face of professional literary criticism. The connected knowing valued in the sensitive reader recedes to the background.

The distinction between separate and connected knowing revolves around two issues: the first has to do with the stance toward the *other* (the object to be known as well as one's interlocutors in the knowledge project), the second with the stance of the knower toward herself. Two examples cited in WWK, both about a student named Faith, illustrate these two issues.

In the first example, Faith reports on a class where the professor gave his interpretation of Henry James's *The Turn of the Screw* and then invited his class to "start ripping at it." Faith, like many women, was reluctant to "rip at" what others say, and to adopt the doubting, argumentative, adversarial stance of separate knowing (WWK, p. 105). In the second example, Faith talks about her difficulty in separating her personal opinion of Heathcliff as a person from her analysis of the literary qualities of Emily Brontë's novel.

> When Faith first read [*Wuthering Heights*] she just plain hated Heathcliff. Upon the third reading she could see how Emily Brontë had developed the character; and this, she saw, was what the teacher wanted her to write about. He did not care how she personally felt about Heathcliff as a person; he wanted her to explain how Heathcliff worked within the system of the novel. (p. 109)

In the first example, separate knowing is identified with discursive combat. When "presented with a proposition," the separate knower "immediately look[s] for something wrong—a loophole, a factual error, a logical contradiction, the omission of contrary evidence" (p. 104). "It does not matter whether you agree with an interpretation or not; you must still try to find something wrong with it . . . the more believable the interpretation is, the harder you must try to doubt it" (p. 105). In the second example, separate knowing is characterized by the demand that the knower "'weed out the self' . . . so that the flowers of pure reason may flourish" (p. 109). Whereas separate knowing requires the depersonalization both of self and of others, the connected knowing preferred by many women is predicated on a respect for knowledge that is based on personal experience, and on imaginative attachment to the other. A good metaphor for separate knowing is that of an "armed vision,"[6] for connected knowing that of a *personal* knower "really" talking *and* listening to *personal* (or personalized) others.

In these two examples, we see that literary criticism is divisible into three moments: (a) one must read the literary text; (b) one must write about it; and (c) one must engage in critical debate with others. One could think of these three moments as stages of disciplinary development: the first moment sets the stage for the second, and the second for the third. Viewed this way, the first moment, reading, is fundamental. However, as is typically the case in stage theories, the developmental order becomes a hierarchy of skills, where the lower-order skills are assumed to be preserved and incorporated in the higher-order ones. When the ability to engage in critical debate is taken to represent the highest degree of development, it is assumed that it incorporates the fullest development of reading and writing skills; as one passes from lower to higher stages, one *gains* competence; nothing of importance is left behind.

Although lip service is given to the idea that reading is fundamental, the second view described above more closely reflects reality in literary studies, where the most important index of expertise is whether or not one's interpretive and critical claims stand up to the test of critical peer evaluation. Olivia Frey read every essay published from 1975 to 1988 in *PMLA*, the premier journal of the profession, and found that "all the essays . . . with only two exceptions, used some version of the adversarial method," ranging from "a very mild adversarial stance . . . to outright hostility."

> Whether the [critical] statement is seemingly innocent and appears to be useful or whether it is obviously attacking, the goals . . . are the same—to establish cognitive authority not only by demonstrating the value of one's own idea but also by demonstrating the weakness or error in the ideas of others. At the heart of the literary critical enterprise seems to be competition, not cooperation. In my most cynical moments I have thought of our behavior as a sort of literary Darwinism, the survival of the fittest theory or the fittest scholar. (Frey, 1990, p. 512)

Although it is generally assumed that expert critical discourse involves the fullest development of reading and writing skills, I would argue that the expectation that what one writes will be contested and must "pass muster" conditions what and how one writes, and what and how one must write conditions what and how one reads. In the process, reading and writing skills are both refined *and reduced.*

The class in which the instructor presented his interpretation of James's novel and then instructed his students to rip at it models the "highest stage of development" of literary criticism, that of experts debating each other on the pages of journals or at conferences. At this level, literary criticism aspires to the ideal of philosophic discourse, that of "an impassioned debate among adversaries who try to defend their views against counterexamples and produce counterexamples to opposing views." This adversary method is presumed to be the best (indeed, the *only*) way of arriving at the truth. A claim that has survived argumentative contest is thought to be "more likely to be correct than one that has not" (Moulton, 1983, pp. 152–153).

Faith's instructor was trying to socialize the class into the dominant adversarial form of critical discourse, and to impress upon them that this is the way "opinions," "ideas," and "feelings" pass muster and become "genuine" knowledge. The exercise was designed to teach them not to take criticism "personally," to write in anticipation of questions and objections, and to be ready to defend their own views and to attack those of others. The second example reinforces the lesson. The point is not for Faith to express her feelings about Brontë's novel, but to advance a winning argument.

Blythe Clinchy (1989) reports that (in interviews she conducted with Claire Zimmerman) men speak of argument as intellectually stimulating and useful to all participants, a way of clarifying one's own thinking and of helping others to think more clearly. However, women often saw argument as a "zero-sum game," where only one side could win. They spoke of arguments as often being crippling and recalled occasions when they were reduced to silence and to tears. The same contrasting attitude is evident when one compares Jürgen Habermas, an important philosopher who gives argument the place of honor in his theory of communicative action, and feminist scholars like Frey who have serious misgivings about the cognitive and moral distortions that result when discourse is dominated by argument.

Habermas (1987, vol. 1, pp. 273–337) makes a distinction between "strategic action," which is oriented toward the successful implementation of a goal, and "communicative action," which is oriented toward coming to an understanding with another. In a discursive context, persuasion that is accomplished through force, deception, intimidation, or rhetorical manipulation would fall in the category of "strategic action." In communicative action the goal is "understanding" or "rational agreement," meaning agreement that is obtained *only* through the "unforced force of the better argument."

In Habermas's view, truth and morality are best understood not as attributes of propositions, but as claims, implicit in the *act* of making a statement, that may be tacitly accepted or explicitly questioned. Argumentative discourse in an "ideal speech situation"—where the opportunity to speak is equally distributed among the interlocutors, and where no force operates except the force of the better argument—is the *only* way we can determine the validity of any truth or morality claim. For Habermas, argumentative competence is the principal index of cognitive and moral agency, and a necessary qualification for the highest stage of cognitive and moral development.[7]

Habermas's idea that truth and morality are produced not through monologic reflection by the individual agent but through dialogic interaction with others seems at first glance to fit very well with WWK and Gilligan's finding about the importance for women of "really talking" as a vehicle for clarifying cognitive and moral issues.[8] However, whereas for Habermas, "really talking" in an ideal speech situation means argument, Gilligan and WWK as well as feminist critics like Frey question the privileged role of argument as a way of vindicating truth and moral claims, and point to forms of "communicative action oriented toward understanding" that have been obscured and marginalized as a result of the overvaluation of argument. These contrasting cognitive and moral intuitions are most clearly indicated by Habermas's view of argumentative discourse as a collaborative enterprise, and as the most civilized, humane, and just way for resolving differences and Frey's Darwinian image of the same process as a brutal contest where only the "fittest" survive.[9]

The issue of gender is relevant to Frey's finding that separate knowing (or an armed vision) is the canonical form of knowledge in professional literary criticism. Women tend to form the majority of students in undergraduate and graduate literature classes, as well as a significant number of part-time and adjunct composition and literature teachers, but as one moves up the professional ladder, one observes an increasing defeminization—increasing cognitive and professional authority appears to correlate with decreasing femininity. The price of the ticket into the professional ranks is, to use Fetterley's provocative term, cognitive and discursive "immasculation"—learning to think and to argue like a man.

Of course, an important factor in the development of literary criticism is the influence of other disciplines, in particular, of philosophy, the model for intellectual discourse in the humanities. The "rise of English" as an academic discipline may be described as a struggle to shed the burden of the femininity of its lower stages and to become as manly as philosophy.[10]

However, the progress toward manliness is problematical for literary criticism in part because of the strong presence of women in the literary tradition (both as characters and as authors) as well as in English classes, among English teachers, and even (in diminished numbers) among the ranks of the most influential critics and scholars; and in part, in my view, because the (feminized and hence muted) attitudes and competencies of the connected knower are actually essential constituents of the foundational activity of the discipline—the reading of literature. Although the expert discourse of literary criticism is dominated by masculine voices, women and their cognitive, moral, emotional, and discursive faculties and inclinations are vitally present at the level of reading. The paradigmatic literary critic may well be a man, but the paradigmatic (even, stereotypical) reader of literature (unlike that of philosophy) is arguably a woman. Novel reading, since at least the eighteenth century, has been regarded as a feminine or effeminate activity, and certainly today reading poetry and fiction (in fact, reading in general) is coded as feminine (*not* masculine), especially among children and adolescents.[11]

The example of Faith cited above illustrates the friction in the literature classroom between the manly voice of professional criticism and the womanly voice of reading. Professors encounter students (mostly, but not exclusively, women) who come with a love for reading literature, and who, in the name of this love, resist the reduction of literary discussion to the argumentative mode, who react emotionally to the texts they read, and who want to talk and write about these reactions. Professors also encounter students—men no less than women—who learn, in the words of a WWK subject, to "crank out" "bullshit" that "does not mean anything." Sheree Meyer reports that when students are required to mimic the argumentative stance of experts, they often respond by "assault[ing] the text, grabbing large chunks . . . [to be] sprinkled liberally through their essays. They did not analyze the words they quoted; after all, they were there to prove a point—one point, one citation; another point, another citation, and so on through three or five painful pages" (1993, p. 47).

Although I have set up an opposition between (womanly) reading and the (manly) discourse of literary criticism, in fact both activities involve reading—in the first case, reading literature, and in the second, reading scholarship and criticism written by other members of the interpretive community. The conventions governing how critics read one another's works are diametrically opposed to those governing the reading of literary texts. In the WWK example, the instructor offers his own interpretation of *The Turn of the Screw* to teach Faith and her classmates to take an adversarial stance toward the interpretive and critical texts of others. Although it is perfectly acceptable to read a scholarly or critical work in anticipation of "ripping at it," such an aggressive approach is generally deplored when applied to literature. It would have been shocking had the instructor asked his students to rip at James's novella.

The conventions governing the reader's posture toward a literary text are more consonant with connected than with separate knowing. With regard to a literary text, the general rule is that one must be willing to suspend one's disbelief, if only provisionally. The reader must, to use the words of WWK, strive for a "deliberate, imaginative extension of one's understanding into positions that initially feel wrong or remote," to open her "mind to the point where [she] can see what the author was all about, the *isness* of what he is trying to say" (WWK, pp. 121–122). Reading literature requires the receptive stance toward another that Keats called "negative capability"—the ability not to be always "full" of oneself, the capacity to be susceptible, to allow one's thoughts, feelings, passions, and senses to be taken up, moved by, filled with, an other.[12] This is not to say that good reading does not involve critical judgment; only that judgment must be predicated on a sensitive apprehension and a full appreciation of the text. In literature classes we often need to discourage students from making premature judgments. And far from encouraging them to rip at a literary text, we let them know that such an aggressive, argumentative attitude is epistemologically uncalled for. It may be that women students gravitate in large numbers toward English courses in part because reading literature gratifies their predilection for connected knowing. It is not surprising that they generalize their readerly competence to all texts; that they are unwilling to do to the utterances of their teachers, their classmates, and other critics what they would not do to a literary text; and that they expect discussions of the text to take a form consonant with the cognitive and communicative skills valued in the reader of literature.[13]

III

The overvaluation of argumentation gets under way with the identification of communicative action as discourse—that is, as speech. Whereas the role of the reader is culturally coded feminine, that of the speaker is culturally coded masculine, so that a speech community is customarily figured as a community of men. Thus, a theory such as Habermas's in which communicative action is identified with speech is bound to concentrate on the qualities typically valued in men speaking to other men—being able to form one's opinions and speak one's mind, respecting other men's right to speak freely, being able to wrestle fairly with other views (without committing "fouls," using only the force of the better argument), and not taking attacks "personally" as long as they are directed at one's "argument" rather than at one's "person." Clearly, the ethics of argument codified in Habermas's "ideal speech situation"—the reciprocal distribution of the free speech rights to all interlocutors, and the equal distribution of the opportunity to speak—coincide with the ethics of justice caricatured by Annette Baier (1986) as "traffic rules for self-asserters" and codified in Lawrence Kohlberg's (1981, 1984) theory of moral development, whose claim to universality has been questioned by Gilligan and others.[14]

To be sure, it is easy to be absorbed by the speaking role, and to identify agency (as even WWK does) with having a "voice." Nevertheless, it is a gross error to represent discursive intersubjectivity as that between two speakers. Communicative action does not happen in the first instance between two speakers, but between a speaker and a listener. Intersubjectivity can happen only between different subjects exercising irreducibly different modes of subjectivity.

Habermas's model stipulates an equitable alternation of speaking roles, which means also an equitable alternation in the silent position. It is presumed that the nonspeaking partner is listening, but there is no recognition of the necessity to give an account of listening as doing something. Or, to be more precise, the listener is reduced in Habermas's theory to the minimal quasi-speaking role of agreeing or disagreeing, silently *saying* yes or no to what is being said in anticipation of the next opportunity to defend himself or shoot down what the other has said. The overestimation of the assertive agency of speaking goes hand in hand with the underestimation of the receptive agency (the paradoxical "negative capability") of listening, with the overvaluation of argument, and with the reduction of the goal of "understanding" to that of "agreement."[15]

That communicative action involves a receptive as well as an assertive form of agency becomes clear when we look at written rather than oral communication. In a speech situation where speaking and listening are contemporaneous, the sound of speech masks the activity of the listener. Voice is taken to be the index of active assertion (the speaker "takes the floor," "speaks out," "articulates," "signifies," "expresses" his views). He produces something—a speech, an utterance—that can be materially preserved (transcribed or taped), handled, and circulated. By comparison, the listener appears to "just sit there," doing nothing, producing nothing. Her silence, taken only as the absence of speech, becomes the index of passive, effortless, immediate receptivity. (Of course, within the prevailing cultural codes, the active role of the speaker connotes masculinity and the apparently passive role of the listener connotes femininity.)

The importance of the receptive role becomes evident when we shift to written communication where the moment of assertion, writing, is detached from the moment of reception, reading, and both are reduced to silence, so that neither appears to be more nor less active than the other. At the moment of writing, meaning is in the custody of the writer; at the moment of reading, it passes to the custody of the reader. Writer and reader are never present to each other; a text mediates the interaction of a present subject (writer or reader) with an absent other. Thus, we do not have simply an alternation of voices as it appears in oral communication, but an alternation between two irreducibly different forms of *silent* communicative agency, writing and reading: *I write, you read; you write, I read.* To complete each instance of communication, the writer's project must be completed by the reader. "It is the conjoint effort of author and reader which brings upon the scene that concrete and imaginary object [that is, meaning] which is the work of the mind" (Sartre, 1978, p. 37).

At the moment of reading, the reader, the only human agent present, is the producer of meaning. While it is easy to think of listening as doing nothing, everyone will agree that reading often takes considerable time and effort, and that comprehension does not happen mechanically.

> The hundred thousand words aligned in a book can be read one by one so that the meaning of the work does not emerge. If [the reader] is inattentive, tired, stupid, thoughtless, most of the [signifying] relations will escape him. He will never manage to "catch on" to the object (in the sense that we see that fire "catches" or "doesn't catch"). He will draw some phrases out of the shadow, but they will seem to appear as random strokes. If he is at his best, he will project beyond the words a synthetic form, each phrase of which will

be no more than a partial function: the "theme," the "subject" or the "meaning." (Sartre, 1978, pp. 37–38)

IV

The preceding discussion of written communication brings to light what is obscured in oral communication by the contemporaneity of speaking and listening and by the immediacy of voice. The silence of the listener does not mean that she is doing nothing and producing nothing (to the extent that she is doing nothing, she is *not* listening). Like the reader, she is actively engaged in producing the meaning of the other's utterance. Although general opinion attaches communicative power to the speaker, in fact the completion of the latter's project is dependent on and vulnerable to the interpretive agency of the listener. Any argument has force as argument (rather than as an order or a threat) only to the extent that the listener is disposed to give it a fair hearing—that is, to perform the labor of understanding it and appreciating its merits. Recognizing that there are two irreducibly different but equally necessary modes of communicative action—listening and speaking—leads us to see that, contrary to Habermas, discourse involves not just the alternation of speakers but the alternation of speaking and listening: I speak/you listen; you speak/I listen. To understand the relationship between a reader and a text and a listener and the speech of another, we need an asymmetrical model of interaction between subjects in two irreducibly different roles.

Such a model can be found in Nel Noddings's construction of the caring relation. According to Noddings, caring is a relationship between one caring and one cared-for. The one caring takes an attitude of receptive attention or engrossment toward the one cared-for, and undertakes the displacement of part of her motive energy in the direction of the cared-for's project. The receptive agency of listening, like that of reading, is structurally analogous to the role Noddings attributes to one caring in a caring relation. Like one caring, the listener must care for the utterance of her interlocutor. To understand the speaker, she must reach out toward what is said in an attitude of receptive attention or "engrossment," and she must undertake the "motivational displacement" that lends a portion of her subjective resources to the project of producing the other's meaning. On the other hand, the speaker, like the cared-for, is in a position of dependency and vulnerability to the interpretive agency of the listener. A hostile, uncaring, or self-centered and self-serving listener will defeat the speaker's communicative project.

Listening and reading, like caring, involve an epistemological and moral lean toward an other. However, as Noddings stresses, this does not necessarily imply the total surrender of self typically associated with romantically infatuated women. The one caring must restrain her impulses toward self-assertion, but complete identification with the cared-for is not conducive to effective caring. One caring must maintain a dual perspective—one part devoted to the appreciation of the situation of the cared-for, another grounded in her own cognitive and moral values. Similarly, listening—in the sense of critical understanding—involves the interanimation of the "voice" of the speaker enabled by an attentive listener and the "voice" of the listener's own moral and cognitive interests.

Noddings recognizes that it is morally unacceptable for anyone to be fixed either in the role of one caring or one cared-for. In most relationships it is desirable for the participants to alternate between these two positions. However, in Noddings's view, the role of one caring is irreducibly different from that of the one cared-for, and the moral reciprocity between them cannot be defined in terms of the equivalence between gifts given and received. Caring flows from the one caring toward the one cared-for; moral reciprocity does not require the reversal of the current during a given interval of care. The one cared-for must acknowledge and accept the care given, use its enabling power to advance her own projects, and freely share accounts of her life and her activities with the one caring. To complete each instance of care, she must *accept* and make use of the care offered. It is no more appropriate for one cared-for to respond by adopting the role of one caring than for someone to respond to an appeal to be one caring by asking to be cared for herself. The cared-for must first respond as cared-for to complete the present cycle, before initiating a new cycle by adopting the role of one caring.

However one might question or wish to modify Noddings's account of the caring relation, the important point for me is that she constructs an ethical model of an inherently asymmetrical relation. As in a caring relation, the completion of each interval of communication depends on each participant performing her role—the speaker speaks and the listener listens. It would not do for you to respond to my speaking by speaking yourself; first (while I am speaking) you must listen. Nor would it do for me, as soon as I see that you are listening, to interrupt my speech in order to adopt the role of listener. I must accept the gift of your listening, and use your enabling attention to complete my speech. Then I can fulfill my obligation to listen to you as carefully as you have listened to me.

Not surprisingly, some feminists have criticized Noddings for adopting an asymmetrical relation as an ethical ideal.[16] Although such criticism may be well taken, it is important to observe how much the aversion to asymmetrical relations stems from the traditional modern Western norm codified in the ethic of rights of the symmetrical reciprocity of equivalent moral agents. The problem with this ideal is that actual encounters between self and other are often asymmetrical. Obviously, such is the case between a parent and a young child, or a teacher and a student. But even relations between peers are often characterized by moments of asymmetry—one is often asking for something (information, material, help, support) from someone (an official, a doctor, a teacher, a colleague, a friend) who is in the position to give it. These relationships can be fitted into the framework of the ideal of symmetrical self–other relations only at the cost of abstracting from, and hence, obscuring, the asymmetrical structure of such occasions.

The presupposition of equivalent and symmetrically positioned moral agents has two consequences in theories of discourse. The first is the overvaluation of the assertive agency of the speaker role, and the nullification of the receptive agency of the listener. The second consequence is the underestimation of cognitive and communicative competences associated with the ethic of care and characteristic of the receptive agency of the listener. This is evident at the highest stage of development of literary criticism, where one's status as an expert rests on being able to take one's place as a powerful speaker (or writer) able to go toe-to-toe with other powerful speakers. The hermeneutic sensitivity and receptivity valued in the listener and the reader of literature are subsumed in and overshadowed by the ability to engage in argumentative contests. The regulative ideal for such an expert discourse is an ethics of rights. The ethics of care implicit in the receptive agency of the listener and reader drops out of the picture.

The common ground between connected knowing described in WWK and the ethic of care represented in the work of Gilligan, Noddings, and others could readily be seen in the common emphasis on the crucial role of communication in the production of knowledge and of morality; in the value that is given to personal experience, feelings, and personal (rather than impersonal) interactions; in the resistance to thinking that abstracts out the particularities of the situation; and in the attentiveness to the needs of others. However, it is Noddings's particular contribution to represent the ethic of care as an ethic of inherently asymmetrical relations. It is a virtue of an asymmetrical model that it is conducive to the recognition of irreducible difference. In the caring rela tion, we have not only two different subjects, but also two different modes of being subjects. Applied to communicative action, Noddings's asymmetrical model allows us to dispense with the reduction of communicative action to the speaking role, and to see that communicative action involves not just different agents, but different modes of communicative agency—an assertive mode manifested in speaking and writing and a receptive mode that is a condition for careful listening and reading.

V

Let me now go back to the empirical evidence documented by WWK, Clinchy, and others that women do not like to argue, and let me counterpose this to the evidence that women do argue, and argue well: in fact, feminist critiques of argument—Clinchy's, Frey's, Moulton's, and my own—*are* arguments. How do we make sense of this paradox?

Let me begin by invoking ideas from Habermas. According to Habermas, linguistic assertions imply four kinds of validity claims: regarding the truth, normative correctness, sincerity, and intelligibility of the utterance. When Faith, the student in the earlier examples, speaks or writes about a novel, she does so with the presupposition (a) that what she says corresponds to the novel; (b) that it is morally or ethically appropriate; (c) that it accurately represents her views; and (d) that it is intelligible to other speakers of English. Leaving aside the issue of intelligibility, it could be argued that students like Faith, who are happy to be emotionally and intellectually engaged in the text, are uneasy with argumentative discourse because they feel that it puts them in the untenable position of speaking in such a way as to violate both the rule of normative propriety and the rule of sincerity. Argumentation forces them to treat their interlocutors uncaringly, and to write and speak in a way that misrepresents their experience of reading the text. I daresay that the more conscientious and committed she is as a reader of literature, the more her sense of communicative ethics and sincerity will be governed by the moral sensibilites associated with the ethic of care, and the more difficult it will be for her to adjust to the norms of critical disputation.

I would argue further that women's resistance to conventional argumentation stems from cognitive as well as moral concerns. According to Habermas, the warrant for truth is consensus attained under conditions of ideal speech situation, defined as a contest where claims compete with another, employing no force but the force of the better argument. women resist argumentation not only because it feels somehow to be morally disagreeable, but also because they doubt that this is the best procedure for vindicating truth claims and have no confidence that the views that emerge victorious will necessarily be valid. Taking full account of the cognitive, moral, and communicative intuitions represented in WWK and other feminist research allows us to see that the free speech conditions stipulated by Habermas are necessary but not sufficient to define the discursive conditions for the vindication of validity claims. Habermas's theory, as we have seen, is marred by the overestimation of the speaker role and the nullification of the receptive agency of the listener. To put it colloquially, how can truth emerge in a speech situation when everyone is speaking and no one is *really listening?*

What then can we say about the fact that feminist critiques of argumentation—advanced by the authors of WWK, Moulton, Frey, and me—are themselves arguments? Does this not prove that argumentation is inevitable? In engaging in argumentation, do I feel that *I* am advancing false moral and cognitive claims?

These questions point to the need for the elaboration of a theory of communicative action that takes full account of intersubjectivity as the interaction of different modes of communicative agency. For now let me say that feminist arguments against argument presuppose a different notion of discursive interaction. What is at issue is not the structure of the utterance (argument), but the structure of the privileged discursive relations (adversarial) conventionally imposed on the interlocutors. The works of feminist critics of argument are distinguished by a hermeneutic sensitivity toward other interlocutors, an effort to understand even (or especially) those with whom one disagrees. These works are rhetorically organized so as to offer evidence not only in support of specific claims, but also of the author's careful attitude as a listener and reader of the discourse of others, and of her expectation that the same care will be extended to her own work. The author's confidence in the validity of her claims stems at least in part from her confidence in her performance as a careful—i.e., connected—listener or reader. In spite of appearances, these works call for a different theory of communicative action.

NOTES

1. Teresa de Lauretis observes that critics of feminist "essentialism" often resort to "supplying a hidden premise (innate female essence) in order to construct a coherent image of feminism which thus becomes available to charges (essentialism) based on the very premise that had to be supplied" (1989, p. 13). She speculates that the motivation for the assiduous effort to construct and then exorcise such a "fantom essentialism" is "less the risk of essentialism itself than the further risk which that entails: the risk of challenging directly the social-symbolic institution of heterosexuality" (p. 32). De Lauretis's suggestion is rather cryptic, but I read her as recognizing the cultural reflex that causes me (and many other women) to recoil against being "lumped in" with other women — that is, against being situated as a woman in relation to other women.

   For a lucid recent analysis of the vexed issue of essentialism, see Charlotte Witt (1995).

2. I am pleased to see that Nancy Goldberger (this volume) recognizes the need to revise the low epistemological rating given in WWK to the positions of "silence" (equated with "not knowing") and "received knowing" (equated with passive, uncritical submission to authority). Goldberger observes that "silence" and "received knowing" have different significance and uses in different cultures. It is interesting that, in the examples she cites, the value assigned by the respondents to both positions correlates with their recognition of the importance of the discursive agency of the listener.

   Although my Filipino upbringing may have led me to appreciate silence and to associate it with wisdom and thoughtfulness, my point in this essay (underscored by the reference to my mathematics and engineering education) is more general — silence is a necessary moment of all knowledge projects. What is culturally variable is less the role of silence but the value given to it in relation to speech. Western culture and Western theories of discourse *erroneously* overvalue speech.

   I appreciate Goldberger's project of exploring cultural differences in ways of knowing. However, it is important to recognize that empirical research involving subjects from different cultures often suffer from insufficient numbers of subjects from each particular culture. One result of this situation is that the difference of these cultures from Western culture is accentuated, while their differences from one another are glossed over. For example, Goldberger cites "Issi from the Philippines, Leela from India, Mai from Burma, and Sondra from Brazil," all of whom "grew up in cultures in which they were taught to listen to elders and to their fathers and husbands" (p. 349). Speaking as a Filipino native informant, I agree with the first part of Goldberger's statement, but not with the second. Filipinos are indeed taught to respect their elders and to listen to them. Thus a Filipino woman will feel obliged to listen to her parents (the mother's moral teachings, or *pangaral*, are at least as authoritative and deserving of respect as those of the father). But this obligation does not carry over with equal force to her husband. The traditional marital ideal in the Philippines prescribes mutual respect between husband and wife. Filipinos speak rather proudly of the high regard or "respect" the culture accords women. This is not mere empty boast; it has substance to the extent that it signifies the cultural ideal, if not always actual practice.

The Filipino respondent, Issi, says: "I listen to anyone who is talking to me and I respect someone who is talking to me whether I like what I am hearing or not. And I digest it inside. . . . If the person is an expert, I have to agree with them" (p. 350). Assimilating this statement into those of others from presumably "authoritarian" cultures misses something very important about what Issi is saying. She listens to anyone—not just elders, men or authority figures—who is speaking to her. She willingly accepts the invitation, implicit in being spoken to, of taking a turn as listener. She listens, and in doing so, she suspends judgment. But, listening is agentive: she "digests [what she is hearing] inside." She reserves to herself the critical evaluation not only of what is being said, but of the credentials of the speaker. The obligation to defer to the authority of the speaker is conditioned on her judgment that he is an expert. Although Issi's statement shows her willingness to listen, we cannot conclude from it that she has abdicated her right to speak.

3. In literary studies, Elaine Showalter (1981) heralded the emergence of "gynocritics," a new and theoretically promising critical discourse devoted to the study of "the history, styles, themes, genres, and structures of writing by women; the psychodynamics of female creativity; the trajectory of the individual or collective female career; and the evolution and laws of a female literary tradition" (p. 185).

4. The term "emotional-volitional tone" is from Mikhail Bakhtin's essay (1990, pp. 30–31).

5. The phrase is from Coleridge's "that willing suspension of disbelief for the moment, which constitutes poetic faith" (*Biographia Literaria, Collected Works*, 1983, vol. 7, part 2, p. 6).

6. This startling mixed but apt metaphor comes from the title of Stanley Hyman's book *The Armed Vision: A Study of the Methods of Modern Literary Criticism* (1952). It is important to note that Hyman's book celebrates rather than deplores this armed vision.

7. Habermas explicitly presents his discourse ethics as an extension of Kohlberg's moral theory. See pp. 116–194 of *Moral Consciousness and Communicative Action* (1990) and "Lawrence Kohlberg and neo-Aristotelianism" in *Justification and Application* (1993, pp. 113–132).

8. Habermas's focus on intersubjectivity and on the inherent sociality of the self is a key element of his appeal to feminists. However, having affirmed intersubjectivity and the dialogic production of truth and morality, it matters what specific qualities characterize intersubjectivity and dialogic interaction. For feminist discussions of Habermas, see Benhabib (1992) and Meehan (1995).

9. Daniel O'Keefe (1982, pp. 3–23) draws a distinction between two senses of argument: first is to be found in "he made an argument," and the second in "we had an argument." In the first, "argument" refers to "a kind of utterance or communicative act" typically consisting of "(1) a linguistically explicable claim and (2) one or more overtly expressed reasons which are linguistically explicit." Argument, in the second, more everyday sense, refers to "a particular kind of interaction" typically characterized by "extended overt disagreement." In everyday talk, "argument" is synonymous with "tiff" "squabble," fight," "quarrel," or "dispute."

   It is apparent that women who dislike argumentation are not inclined to make O'Keefe's distinction. For them making an argument (the first sense) is a way of having an extended disagreeable interaction—"quarrel," "fight," "squabble," "tiff"—with another. They sense that linguistically expressed claims and reasons often serve to mask an aggressive, combative, domineering, even hostile disposition toward another; the drive to win an argument is, afterall, the drive to defeat other contenders.

10. The phrase is from Terry Eagleton (1983). For a history of the development of literary studies as a profession in the United States, see Gerald Graff (1987).

11. See Segel (1986, pp. 165–186) for a history of the gender polarization of childhood reading. The "universal opinion" that although girls are avid readers of boys' books, boys "did not and would not read girls' books" has led teacher education textbooks to recommend that teachers favor boys' books over girls' books (by as much as a two-to-one ratio) when choosing materials for English courses and for the library collection. "Getting boys to relate to literature is often a major problem but it can become insoluble if the literature presented is incorrectly oriented" (*Teaching English Today*, Houghton Mifflin, 1975; quoted in Segel, p. 183).

12. See Letter to George and Thomas Keats, 27 December 1917 (*The Letters of John Keats*, vol. 1, p. 193).

13. In refering to the womanly reader of literature in opposition to the manly professional critic I am not making any claims regarding *essential* feminine or masculine qualities. I qualify the reader as womanly, first of all, to underscore the strong presence (even predominance) of women among readers of literature in contrast to their relatively diminished numbers at the most exalted level of professional discourse; and secondly, to note the fact that cognitive and interactive qualities culturally coded feminine actually inform our ideas of how to approach a literary text.

In a study of the interpretive strategies of college freshmen, Elizabeth Flynn (1986) found that "male students sometimes react to disturbing stories by rejecting them or by dominating them, a strategy, it seems, women do not often employ." The study also suggests that although women are less inclined to reject or dominate texts, they also

> more frequently break free of submissive entanglement in a text and evaluate characters and events with critical detachment.... They attempt to understand [texts] before making a judgment on them.
>
> Reading is a silent, private activity and so perhaps affords women a degree of protection not present when they speak. Quite possibly the hedging and tentativeness of women's speech are transformed into useful interpretive strategies—receptivity and yet critical assessment of the text—in the act of reading. A willingness to listen, a sensitivity to emotional nuance, an ability to empathize with and yet judge, may be disadvantages in speech but advantages in reading. We may come to discover that women have interpretive powers that have not been sufficiently appreciated. (p. 286)

Theories of discourse which focus, like that of Habermas, on argumentation to the exclusion of other modes of discourse are not simply manly, but are *super*manly, for they discount capacities that are possessed by both men and women and exalt only the communicative competence typically valued in man-to-man discourse.

14. Habermas discusses Gilligan's reservations against Kohlberg's schema (see 1990, pp. 175–180). Unfortunately, the discussion is very brief and rather dismissive.

15. If everyone has the right to speak, then, it would seem, everyone has the obligation to listen. However, the meaning of the obligation to listen cannot be deduced from the recognition of another's right to speak. From the latter, one can get only the minimal negative obligation to refrain from interfering with another's speech turn, not the positive need to be responsive, to exert oneself in the effort to comprehend the other. More specifically, an ethics of rights is premised on the reciproc-

ity of symmetrical subject positions, exemplified in the ideal of dialogue as the interaction of individuals positioned in symmetrical speaking roles. However, if we recognize that every instance of communication occurs not between two speakers but between a speaker and a listener, and that the receptive agency of listening is not simply a muted version of the assertive agency of speaking, then we see that communication involves an asymmetrical intersubjectivity that exceeds the resources of an ethics of rights.

16. See Sarah Hoagland's "Some thoughts about *Caring*" (in Card, 1991, pp. 246–263). Card's disparaging comment (1991, p. 17) that the gynocentricism of Carol Gilligan is "conservative and parochial," and therefore not "feisty" enough to be included in her volume on feminist ethics is directed as well as Noddings.

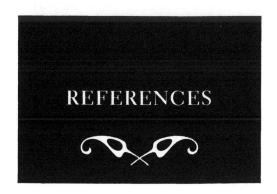

REFERENCES

Ardener, E. (1975). Belief and the problem of women. In S. Ardener (Ed.), *Perceiving women*, 1–17. London: Dent.

Baier, A. (1986). Trust and antitrust. *Ethics, 96,* 231–260.

Bakhtin, M. (1990). Author and hero in aesthetic activity. In M. Holquist and V. Liapunov (Eds.), *Art and answerability,* 4–256. Austin, TX: University of Texas Press.

Belenky, M. F., Clinchy, B. M., Goldberger, N. R., & Tarule, J. M. (1986). *Women's ways of knowing: The development of self, voice, and mind.* New York: Basic Books.

Benhabib, S. (1992). *Situating the self: Gender, community and postmodernism in contemporary ethics.* New York: Routledge.

Bleich, D. (1986). Intersubjective reading. *New Literary History, 17,* 401–421.

Card, C. (Ed.) (1991). *Feminist ethics.* Lawrence, KS: University Press of Kansas.

Chodorow, N. (1978). *The reproduction of mothering.* Berkeley: University of California Press.

Clinchy, B. M. (1989). The development of thoughtfulness in college women: Integrating reason and care. *American Behavioral Scientist, 32,* 647–657.

Coleridge, S. T. (1983). *Biographia literaria. Collected works,* Vol. 7. James Engell and W. Jackson Bate (Eds.) Princeton, NJ: Princeton University Press.

De Lauretis, T. (1989). The essence of a triangle or taking the risk essentialism seriously: Feminist theory in Italy, the U.S., and Britain. *Differences, 1,* 3–37.

Eagleton, T. (1983). *Literary theory: An introduction,* Minneapolis, MN: University of Minnesota Press.

Fetterley, J. (1978). *The resisting reader: A feminist approach to American fiction.* Bloomington, IN: Indiana University Press.

Flynn, E. A. (1986). Gender and reading. In E. A. Flynn and P. Schweickart (Eds.), *Gender and reading: Essays on readers, texts, and contexts,* 267–288. Baltimore: Johns Hopkins University Press.

Flynn, E. A. (1988). Composing as a woman. *College Composition and Communication, 39,* 423–435.

Flynn, E. A., & Schweickart, P. (Eds.) (1986). *Gender and reading: Essays on readers, texts, and contexts.* Baltimore: Johns Hopkins University Press.

Frey, O. (1990). Beyond literary Darwinism: Women's voices and critical discourse. *College English, 52,* 507–526.

Gilligan, C. (1982). *In a different voice: Psychological theory and women's development.* Cambridge, MA: Harvard University Press.

Graff, G. (1987). *Professing literature.* Chicago: University of Chicago Press.

Habermas, J. (1973). Wahrheitstheorien. *Wirklichkeit und reflexion: Walter Schulz zum 60. Geburstag,* 211–265. Pfullingen: Nesge.

Habermas, J. (1987). *The theory of communicative action,* Vol. 1 & 2. (Trans. T. McCarthy.) Boston: Beacon Press.

Habermas, J. (1990). *Moral consciousness and communicative action.* (Trans. C. Lenhardt and S. W. Nicholsen.) Cambridge, MA: MIT Press.

Habermas, J. (1993). *Justification and application: Remarks on discourse ethics.* Trans. C. Cronin. Cambridge, MA: MIT Press.

Harding, S. (1992). Rethinking standpoint epistemology: What is "strong objectivity"? *The Centennial Review, 36,* 437–440.

Hoagland, S. L. (1991). Some thoughts on *Caring.* In C. Card (Ed.), *Feminist ethics,* 246–263. Lawrence, KS: University Press of Kansas.

Hyman, S. E. (1952). *The armed vision: A study of the methods of modern literary criticism.* New York: Knopf.

Keats, J. (1958). *The letters of John Keats,* Vol. 1. H. E. Rollins (Ed.). Cambridge, MA: Harvard University Press.

Kohlberg, L. (1981). *The philosophy of moral development.* New York: Harper & Row.

Kohlberg, L. (1984). *The psychology of moral development.* New York: Harper & Row.

Lamb, C. E. (1991). Beyond argument in feminist composition. *College Composition and Communication, 42,* 11–23.

Meehan, J. (Ed.) (1995). *Feminists read Habermas: Gendering the subject of discourse.* New York: Routledge.

Meyer, S. L. (1993). Refusing to play the confidence game: The illusion of mastery in the reading/writing of texts. *College English, 55,* 46–63.

Moulton, J. (1983). A paradigm of philosophy: The adversary method. In S. Harding & M. B. Hintikka (Eds.), *Discovering reality,* 149–164. Dordrecht, Holland: Reidel.

Noddings, N. (1984). *Caring: A feminine approach to ethics and moral education.* Berkeley: University of California Press.

O'Keefe, D. J. (1982). The concepts of argument and arguing. In J. R. Cox and C. A. Willard (Eds.), *Advances in argumentation theory and research,* 3–23. Carbondale and Edwardsville, IL: Southern Illinois University Press.

Sartre, J. P. (1978). *What is literature?* (Trans. B. Frechtman.) Gloucester, MA: Peter Smith.

Segel, E. (1986). As the twig is bent: Gender and childhood reading. In E. A. Flynn and P. Schweickart (Eds.), *Gender and reading: Essays on readers, texts, and contexts*, 165–186. Baltimore: Johns Hopkins University Press.

Showalter, E. (1981). Feminist criticism in the wilderness. *Critical Inquiry*, 8, 179–205.

Witt, C. (1995). Anti-essentialism in feminist theory. *Philosophical Topics*, 23.

New Directions:
Culture, Power, and Knowing

Cultural Imperatives and Diversity in Ways of Knowing*

NANCY RULE GOLDBERGER

IN THEIR DIFFERENT VOICES, the following four Americans tell stories about living in multiple worlds and the difficulties they faced as they grew up and came to think of themselves as knowers and learners. In spite of the great disparity in their cultural backgrounds and personal histories, the common themes in their accounts of the bicultural experience and the process of coming to know are striking. With these stories, one can easily see why feminist and culture theorists, and some psychologists, argue that we must move beyond the family for understanding human development and focus in addition on the social, economic, and

*I would like to thank the interviewees who contributed the words as well as the many Fielding students who worked with me on the Diversity in Ways of Knowing research project, with a special acknowledgment to those students whose interviews I refer to or quote in the text: Mary Bassell, Chris Krebs, Carol Lambert, Jeanne Sterling, Harvey Plouffe, John Maliga, Carol Whitehill, Myrna Frank, Irene McHenry, Ann Karcher, Dan Weinberg, Wendy Lockwood, Mary Kingston, Jan Guertin, Carolyn Truesdale, Judith Win, Mary Lilly, Vernetta Hegstead, Mary Lynn Sheldon, Dawn Noggle, and Lynda Bernacki. The thoughts and perspectives of these two groups of people have enriched and informed my work.

335

political systems—"the imperatives of culture" (Cohen, 1971)—within which people live and define themselves.

Kat, a South American–born woman from a Mestiza background, is now a citizen and counselor in the United States:

> My grandmother [who was a shaman] would teach me the difference between thinking that you know something and knowing it. She would take me out into the woods and have me sense becoming things. Not just looking and describing what I saw. I had to be the tree, I had to be the rock, I was the bird. Some of that [kind of knowing] is helped with sacred medicine plants. They allow one to open up many different channels and get all the information possible. Whereas [simply] thinking about something feels like it is a very narrow band, a very narrow channel. . . . When I came to this country, I became very quiet. The silence became almost like this cage that I could not get out of. . . . In this culture, there are certain ways of knowing that are much more valued than others. So, unless one can quantify, qualify, and prove and have backup and examples, then any knowledge that doesn't fit is just not valid—or society doesn't see it as valid.

Born in the United States, Christine, a Chinese American businesswoman and entrepreneur, says:

> I was living in a seminary, working in the black community, and taking a Chinese philosophy course at the university. And the ways of thinking just crashed. I got sick. I was emotionally exhausted from these conflicting worlds. . . . It was the different realities that I operated in at different times and with different people. It was different ways of knowing. . . . I'm always thinking of many sides, but I can't explain to people that I know where I stand when I take those sides. . . . I work for synthesis. Some of that is the Chinese–Asian side of me that says how do we get to some harmony here? How do we get to some peace?

Having lived her early life in a Native Alaskan fishing community before leaving to attend school, Allaq is now a health worker back in her Inuit village:

> As a child, I learned a lot just listening to the elders. They talked about the way of living, yuyarag, the way of living of the Yupik people. . . . Knowledge is part of the soul. You have to learn it spiritually in every aspect of life—spiritually, mentally, emotionally, physically, socially, as a whole person. Yuyarag is passed through generations. . . . The white society has tried to assimilate and accultur-

ate us through education. We had to hang up our nativeness outside the door and come in and think like white people in the classroom. . . . I became very, very angry. And when I was real angry I couldn't listen and I couldn't learn. . . . You know, in the Caucasian world, everything is systematic, everything is categorized. Where in my world, everything is interrelated. Everything interrelates.

Toshi, an African American woman, has recently gained tenure in the college where she teaches:

Black people have a different way of relating to the world. Even intellectually active black people. And that way is more experientially related than cognitively related. We think less about something but react more. I like being able to go from my experience, rather than having to think about it. As a black person, I don't have to hold it in. I can express it. . . . But if you want to be successful in this country, the United States of America, you have to be able to function in a white world. You have to give up a lot of who you are to make it through the system. It makes you crazy to do it in a way that's not natural to you. You do it "their way" which is not a bad way, it's just a different way. But, at some point, you have to come back to yourself—I'm talking about being a bicultural individual—you have to come back and reunite these two ways and make some peace for yourself.

Throughout these short stories (actually, excerpts from much longer interviews) are echoes of many of the issues that any student of culture and human difference will encounter and hear debated today in the academy and in the popular press. These stories touch on the pain and anger and confusion that accompany acculturation; on the power of dominant cultures to impose ways of being and ways of knowing on individuals from minority cultures and immigrant groups; on the paths of resistance or accommodation to assimilation forces; on what it means to be "an American"; on the personal losses and the gains as one learns to take on a new culture, different language, alien mores; on what it feels like to live as a bicultural[1] individual with dual consciousness, dual realities, and dual allegiances.

My own story began many years ago in the segregated American South, where, as a white girl of privilege, I came to be aware of, first, the not easily negotiated boundaries of class that kept one side of my family insulated from the other. Later, as an adolescent, I tried to forge my own identity disembedded from the dictates of southern protocol and definitions of southern womanhood. Bolstered by the critical distance provided by a northern education, I came to discover—literally to "see"—the others in my southern world who had been invisible to me in my childhood: people of color,

Jews, the Appalachian poor. My world, my reality, my self changed with the discovery that I had lived side by side with people hidden from me by the shields of class, religion, culture, and race. The nature of reality and truth, the coexistence of worlds, and the possibility and problems of "oppositional" identity (defining the self as what one is not) became enduring preoccupations for me. Although the manifestation of these preoccupations has taken different shapes throughout my professional career, they were the primary impetus behind my involvement with my colleagues on the Women's Ways of Knowing project. They drive my work today.

In this chapter, I weave together the questions I bring from my past with the culture tales (Howard, 1991) and accounts of ways of knowing (Belenky, Clinchy, Goldberger, & Tarule, 1986) gathered from various women and men now living in different corners of America. But not only individuals spin culture tales. Mair has argued that members of a profession as well as members of the culture "live in and through stories. . . . We are lived by the stories of our race and place" (Mair, 1988, p. 127). George Howard (1991), following Miller Mair's analogy of psychology as storytelling, extends the argument that scientific theorizing is an instance of storytelling and story refinement. The epistemological scheme my colleagues and I presented in *Women's Ways of Knowing* (WWK) is itself a culture tale, bounded and limited by our cultural lens and social positionality, by the historical era in which our initial work was done, and by the language and constructs available to us at the time as we organized and made meaning of our observations. My intent in this chapter is to

- raise questions about strategies and ethics of researching people very different from oneself;

- use the stories from culturally diverse individuals to raise questions about the intersection of knowledge, knowing, and culture;

- consider the original ways of knowing schema (presented in WWK)[2] as a culture-bound tale that requires a retelling when data from culturally diverse people are examined.

RESEARCHING DIFFERENCE: THE DIVERSITY IN WAYS OF KNOWING PROJECT

Pamela Trotman Reid (1993; also see her chapter with Vanessa M. Bing, this volume), among others, has argued that the poor and culturally marginalized people have been "shut up and shut out" of psychological research. Their voices have been silenced in the construction of psychological knowledge. Equally importantly, the special knowledge perspectives and knowledge production of individuals who are members of multiple "marked" or stigmatized groups (for instance, poor black women) have been relatively undocumented (see the chapter by Aída Hurtado, this volume).

The claim by researchers of difficulties in access to ethnic minority or working-class communities has resulted in samples of convenience; as a result, white middle-class researchers have tended to stick with white middle-class informants, who are closer at hand and certainly more familiar to them. Furthermore, even when researchers turn their attention to the study of difference, rather than letting the "others" speak for themselves, they have tended to assume the platform of "expert" as if the outsider's "objective" knowledge is privileged over the insider's "subjective" knowledge (Goldberger & Veroff, 1995, p. 16). Within the positivist paradigm that has dominated American psychology in the twentieth century, research has been something done on "subjects" for the sake of obtaining data to support or refute the researcher's hypotheses. Recently, however, narrative interview-based methodology that emphasizes storytelling, listening, and dialogue has supported postpositivist, new paradigm studies of the subjectivities of people marginalized in our society—and allowed researchers to begin to reflect on their own subjectivity and the space between them and their so-called subjects (Oakley, 1981; Mischler, 1986; Personal Narratives Group, 1989; Lykes, 1989; Nielsen, 1990; Reinharz, 1994). Slowly, psychological researchers are taking off their ethnocentric blinders and learning how to see the world from the "perspectives of experiences and lives that are not theirs" (Harding, 1992).

After the publication of WWK, and stimulated by the many questions people asked me about whether we meant to imply that there were essential differences between men's and women's ways of knowing, I began to think more carefully and explicitly about the roles of history, situation, class, and culture as factors that influence the ways people know. In the past, by and large, psychologists, including me, only paid lip service to the proposition that personal theories of knowledge and experiences of gender and self are culturally and class embedded. Exactly *how* one shapes and is shaped by one's class and cultural context has not often been a focus of psychological study. It is only over the past two decades or so that identity development and meaning making (including how one thinks about knowledge and truth) have been recognized as both intrapsychic and sociocultural phenomena.

We all grow up in families, communities, and cultures that affect the definitional boundaries for "male" and "female," but each of us also constructs narratives of self and other, gender, family, authority, and truth that evolve as we encounter new ideas and situations and new outlooks on life. For bicultural individuals who live at the junction of two cultures, just as for all women and men who are born into a genderized, racist, and classist society, identity development is complicated by divided loyalties and "double consciousness" (DuBois, 1961) or even "multiple consciousness" (King, 1988). As Bing and Reid (this volume) and Hurtado (this volume) point out, gender or class or race alone can not provide an adequate lens for understanding the ways of knowing and self-definitions of people who are multiply stigmatized in a society; women of color, for instance, experience race, class, and gender oppression simultaneously. As I will argue later, only by addressing structural oppression and social power can one begin to understand the vicissitudes of an individual's development, ways of knowing, and life choices.

My research focus, consequently, over the years since WWK was published, has shifted away from exclusive study of women (although I still am especially interested in women's experience) to study of biculturalism, cultural diversity, and ways of knowing—and the subjectivities of women and men who are culturally "unlike me." Some years ago, as part of a qualitative research training seminar at the Fielding Institute, my students and I began collecting ways of knowing interviews and life stories from people of different cultural backgrounds—many, in fact, who lived in ethnic and immigrant pocket communities across the United States. Before beginning the interviews, the students and I discussed the limitations and advantages of different research epistemologies and practices (especially those associated with positivism) and the challenges for those interested in the study of the diversity of human experience. We came to ask, Can we know someone who is very unlike us? Can or should academics research and presume to interpret the experiences of unfamiliar "others"? Are there some research strategies and practices that are more respectful of the individuals one is trying to understand? In trying to understand others whose lives seem remote from our own, are there precautions to be taken that will reduce the distance between us, acknowledge if not reduce the power differential between the researcher and the researched, and establish the research interview as a collaborative, even emancipatory, act? Although these questions are and will continue to be asked and argued among feminists, philosophers of science, and culture theorists, they have no simple answers. "Resolving other status," as the psychologist Maria Root has forcefully argued (1990), is a challenge for nonoppressive psychological theory that aims to take into account the sociocultural and political, as well as familial, influences shaping the individual experience of ethnic and racial identity. At best, it seems important—at least it did for me and my students—to keep these questions at the center of an ongoing reflexive process throughout all stages of research on difference.

Members of the Fielding research team came from diverse cultural backgrounds and lived and worked in different parts of the United States.[3] The level of experience of various team members with, and access to, ethnic, immigrant, and working-class communities enriched and informed our discussions of interview data. The interviewees themselves were neighbors, work acquaintances, and friends of friends who volunteered to be interviewed. Potential interviewees were told that we (the Fielding research team) were interested in hearing their stories about what it was like to grow up and/or live in a culturally diverse America; about their experiences of difference and feeling different; about how they came to think of themselves as knowers and learners; and, for most of the interviewees, the meaning of silence in their lives.[4] Because the interview questions did not originate with the interviewees (as they do in true participatory action research), we tried to develop a sense of collaboration and trust in spite of power imbalances and assure them of our interest in hearing their experience in their own words. We emphasized the control they retained over the interview process: they chose the location of the interview; they chose their own aliases/code names;[5] only after they had given permission did we record and transcribe the interviews; at the end of the interview, they could tell us about their interview experience (both immediately and several days later in a follow-up interview) and question us about goals and outcomes; they were given copies of their transcribed interviews and invited to add or make changes to them.

Over the course of four years, various students and I have collected interviews with approximately sixty bicultural individuals, primarily but not exclusively women,[6] all living in the United States. Each student in my seminar interviewed at least one person who was culturally unlike her (or him). Although, as researchers, we have not been immune to limited vision and have occasionally been startled to discover how we impose meaning on the interview narratives based on our own assumptive worlds, we have struggled to keep ourselves open and self-conscious, constantly exploring our own assumptions and cultural biases. It helped to have the words of the people we interviewed before us.

DIVERSITY IN WAYS OF KNOWING:
CULTURE TALES

In the four stories that introduced this chapter, we heard bicultural individuals describe their experience of the normative American culture and
ways of knowing; they experienced the acculturation process as prescribed rather than freely chosen, coercive and exclusive rather than
expansive and inclusive. In the effort to educate new populations (immigrants) and marginalized groups in the mainstream culture—that is, to
hasten the assimilation process and turn people into "true" Americans—
educators and other social interventionists have neglected, even negated,
the wisdom and intellectual competencies that these groups carry with
them from their own cultures. As the anthropologist Clifford Geertz
(1983) and the psychologist Howard Gardner (1984) have pointed out,
cultures differ enormously in the forms of knowledge valued. Indigenous
or local knowledge systems set the limits on what is known and who can
know.[7] Education and learning within a culture, "no matter how well
motivated, are based on implicit assumptions about *what* knowledge is
and *how* it should be transmitted" (Gardner, 1984, p. 239). Gardner goes
on to point out that these assumptions may differ greatly in the minds of
the persons with the invested power to plan and implement the educational programs and those who are the presumed beneficiaries of the programs. The psychologist Jerome Bruner (1990) in his treatise on "folk
psychology" (which is rooted in a culture's shared conceptual structure
that encompasses beliefs, desires, and commitments) has discussed how
the high valuation in the United States of science and scientific thought
has played a role in keeping other ways of knowing marginalized and
devalued. As Bruner says: "Scientific psychology insists . . . on its right to
attack, debate, and even replace the tenets of folk psychology. It insists
upon its right to deny the causal efficacy of mental states and of culture
itself."

By turning to the ways of knowing interviews that my students and I
have collected with culturally diverse people, I will look at issues of culture, knowing, and the knowledge perspectives first described in WWK,
choosing excerpts from stories that best illustrate points I wish to make.
The names attached to particular excerpts are the code names that each
person selected for himself or herself. I will highlight those aspects of the
individual stories that reveal the "cultural imperatives" (Cohen, 1971)
that bind persons to the assumptive worlds they live within and the strategies for knowing that they embrace. In some cases, these stories concern
the gradual process of adaptation to a new or majority culture; in others,

they reveal paths of resistance to majority culture norms—and the psychological consequences resistance carries with it. As I reflect on the perspectives on knowing of these culturally diverse people, I will emphasize the tension between accommodation and resistance to the culturally endorsed routes to "right answers" and expertise that gives each story its dramatic twist.

UNDERNEATH SILENCE

In WWK, we described *Silence* as a position of "not knowing" and as a way women protect themselves and hide from dangerous authority. We drew on the stories of women who called themselves deaf and dumb, who were unable to speak for fear of revealing their lack of understanding, who were literally unable to find the words to communicate with others around them. Although we acknowledge that women at other knowledge perspectives also described moments, even long periods, of silence in their lives, we decided to call this one particular group the Silent Women because the absence of voice was as striking as the fragile and hidden sense of self.[8]

I have felt for some time that silence is a much more complicated phenomenon than we initially described in WWK. Because of my special interest in the topic, I intentionally built into the culture interviews a section on personal experiences of silence in order to look at the intersection of culture, knowing, and individuals' sense of personal efficacy and authoritative voice. Under what conditions and situations does a person fall silent? Is silence chosen or imposed? What are the functions and meanings of silence in one's culture?[9]

The Native American and Canadian women and men, perhaps more than any others from the culture sample, best expressed how culturally determined silence can be. Allaq, the Inuit woman quoted earlier; an adolescent boy, Hard Rider, from the Canadian West Coast Dtidaht band; and Wanda Flask, an Ojibway, who is a doctoral student in anthropology, all speak of silence as something taught within their tribal groups. As Indian children growing up, they learned that one should not waste time in foolish talk. Allaq remembers the "nice silence" of many children in a room, listening as the elders told stories. Hard Rider, struggling to learn from his grandfather how to be a tribal leader, had already recognized the advantages of silent and respectful listening rather than confrontation and physical strength. Wanda, conflicted over being stereotyped a "stoic Indian" as she has gained status and earned the right to "break the silence," nevertheless recounts the story of picking up an Ojibway elder who needed a ride. For six hours they rode in silence. "Politeness," Wanda says, "is to be quiet and to let people have their space and just wait."

Learning when *not* to speak is basic to the production of culturally appropriate behavior. Particularly in collectivist cultures (Triandis, 1989) that stress interdependence and social connections rather than individualism and personal autonomy (Markus & Kitayama, 1991), the rules of speech tend to be more tightly regulated by relationships and statuses (e.g., one keeps one's place in the social hierarchy and does not speak out of turn). The anthropologist Keith Basso (1970), commenting on the paucity of cross-cultural studies on silence, showed in his research with the Western Apache that there is even "a fierce reluctance to talk." The educational literature is replete with data that characterize the Native American child as reluctant to speak or answer questions in the classroom. Even though such studies as Basso's have shown that silence has culturally specific meanings,[10] too often Native American silence and interpersonal passivity have been interpreted as manifestations of a cultural "disposition" or a nonverbal, nonanalytic learning style (McCarty, Wallace, Lynch, & Benally, 1991). Education that caters to these conventional characterizations, McCarty and his colleagues argue, can perpetuate patterns of learned dependence in the classroom and extend to the "reproduction of structural relations within the wider society" (p. 42).

Wanda, Judith (of mixed Native American and Caucasian heritage), and Allaq—all adult women at the time of the interview—remember and report on feelings of inauthenticity during their early (Western) school years: feelings of being "colonized," "invalidated," and stereotyped. Wanda, who has risen almost to the peak of her academic career as a graduate student in anthropology, still finds the issue of "to talk or not to talk" a sensitive one, particularly because it affects how she is viewed within her department. Speech versus silence, for her, is "wrapped up in identity and racism" (inside her Native community, she is considered a big talker; outside the community, she is seen as quiet and "not enormously verbal"). If quiet, she is stereotyped as the stoic Indian; if voiced, she becomes the "mouthy militant."

The complexities of silence are revealed not just in the stories of Native Americans and other indigenous people, but in those belonging to other U.S. ethnic and racial minorities. In a memorable and influential article on black women's silence and voice, Signithia Fordham (1993) analyzes how "loudness" has become a major metaphor for African American women's contrariness and resistance to cultural images of their "nothingness." In a culture that has normalized definitions of femaleness as white, middle-class womanhood, black women are in double jeopardy (Beale, 1972; King, 1988) as they face the dual discriminations of racism and sexism—and, one can add, as Deborah King (1988) and Wendy Lutrell (1993) have, classism. Becoming one of "those loud black girls" (first so-named by social activist Angela Davis in 1971, then elaborated by Grace Evans in 1980) is a route of resistance for a cohort of young women who refuse to conform to standards of good school behavior and who flaunt academic regulations in their search for a safe cultural space to define themselves (also see Collins, 1990). Although some of these feisty young women succeed academically, more often they are academic underachievers. To become an academic success, Fordham argues (1993), requires adopting silence as a strategy. High-achieving black females are taught not to speak out and draw attention to their female selves. They learn "gender-passing" (Fordham, 1993), from parents, teachers, and male peers, that is, how to behave in ways typically associated with white femaleness: silent and passive.

One African American student we interviewed, Vicki, who as a child had brought people in her church to tears by speaking "from her heart" about racism and sexism and who as a grade schooler had considered a career as a public speaker, was silenced in the predominantly white, middle-class elitist high school where she entered as a scholarship student. She told us:

> I was the only minority and one of the few women in my class and they weren't interested in hearing my experiences. There, silence was encouraged. "Don't be different, be quiet." It was never exactly told to you, but you felt it.

Vicki, like Toshi, who recently achieved tenure in her department, has learned to speak quietly and to "speak white" as long as it yields professional rewards.

Tactical or strategic silence was mentioned by a number of other interviewees (also see Hurtado, this volume), particularly by bicultural individuals who were negotiating life in white communities or workplaces. Betty, an African American single mother, poor and undereducated, told us of finding a place for her daughter in a world different from the one she grew up in, that is, in a mixed ethnic community and school. She wants her daughter to "grow away from her" so that she will not experience the same fears, the racism, the limits with which her mother grew up. Betty feels intimidated by the better educated parents in her daughter's school but finds the strength and pride to assert: "I refuse to talk with anyone who won't listen. . . . It's silence that we travel in until we find that person that makes us feel we can share who we truly are without crying or feeling ashamed."

Seekay, a graduate student from the West Indies who grew up in an expressive culture and a household in which everyone got to speak, has learned to bury her emotions and voice in the United States. In her words, she has learned to adopt "a good WASP mask" in order to survive. She uses silence to pull away from external input and sort things out internally. She prefers to be silent around knowledgeable people so that she can absorb their "pearls of wisdom" as well as their style of thinking. She aims to use silence as a tool in difficult workplace negotiations, to wait, and watch how others respond before revealing herself.

James Chan, a Chinese American business administrator, learned to be humble and self-effacing from his Chinese mother. Although in many ways an American product who can assert himself and confront others, he finds that he silences himself at work in order to fit into his organization.

All of these culture tales about the meaning of silence demonstrate the importance of understanding both the immediate (familial, community) and the distant (cultural, political) contexts for silence and speech. To communicate verbally is essentially the outcome of a decision-making process. In unfamiliar societies and situations, the newcomer must learn what kinds of speech are used in what kinds of situations with what kinds of people. Growing up, one also learns about the meaning of silence in one's own community and the social repercussions in a dyad or a group when someone falls silent. Even living within strict cultural rules, most people claim a choice about when and where they speak what they know.

It is only those who are silenced by oppressive and demeaning life conditions who feel powerless, mindless, and truly without words. The sense of choice about whether to speak or not to speak is missing for such women and men, as is their sense of knowing. For this reason, it seems important to distinguish this category of people (those who fell into the original WWK category Silence) from individuals who resort to strategic or culturally and ritually endorsed silence, but who may have other well-developed ways of acquiring, even constructing, knowledge. My coauthor Mary Belenky has suggested that we refer to the former group (in WWK, the Silent) as "Silenced," a characterization that more accurately reflects how some people may be driven to a defensive posture of passivity and silence out of fear and threat. The several bicultural individuals I have described thus far, though they may be silent at times, are clearly engaged as active contributing knowers in their communities.

EXTERNAL AUTHORITY
AND RECEIVED KNOWLEDGE

In retrospect, in WWK we did not examine closely the realities of people living within close religious or authority-based communities in which the wisdom of elders/ancestors/spiritual beings/God guides human activities (we did not have the kind of data that would have drawn our attention to these issues). Thus, our original description of Received Knowing emphasized an orientation to external authority, status, and power hierarchies that is automatic and unreflective. The persons we categorized as Received Knowers tended to be overly obedient and passive students or individuals living primarily by externally prescribed social roles and duties. Yielding to authorities external to oneself is often characterized in Western culture, which values autonomy and independent judgment, as "childlike," "passive," or "dependent." Received Knowers are subject to such characterization—and are often considered to be low on the developmental ladder. However, receiving knowledge from external authorities is not necessarily unreflective and automatic; at times one may choose to listen and receive knowledge from others. Relying on experts or yielding to the knowledge of others is not necessarily indicative of the narrowly defined version of Received Knowing we present in WWK. For instance, persons we categorize as Constructed Knowers may seek out, open up to, and enjoy "expert" knowledge without fear that their own perspectives are being compromised; the WWK Subjective Knowers may describe receiving knowledge from favored experts as long as they are very much like them. It is the way in which a person "constructs" authority and expert that helps us understand more fully his or her epistemological stance.

Particularly informative in examining variations on and value of received knowing are the stories of African Americans about the importance of religious faith and the Black church. Although they emphasize in their stories the importance of receiving support and accepting guidance from God, their construal of God as authority is more one of Collaborator and Coknower than Dictator.[11] The sociologist Patricia Hill Collins (1990) has written extensively about those aspects of the African American experience, including the black church, that support and define an epistemology that she considers Afrocentric and feminist—that is, one that emphasizes concrete personal experience, dialogue, the ethic of caring, and the ethic of personal accountability (an amalgam of characteristics that is suggestive of a constructivist way of knowing as we describe it in WWK). In Collins's analysis, black women, as cultural workers, have been active in preserving Afrocentric conceptualizations of community that empower their people and provide a safe haven for personal development in a society that is racist and sexist. Especially important in twentieth-century African American history are the black church, the black women's club movement, labor union "centerwomen," and community "othermothers" (Collins, 1990, p. 223). My colleague Mary Belenky, in her new work, is also drawing attention to black women's community-based activities as examples of what she calls "public homeplaces." She argues (in this volume) that a constructivist epistemology, emphasizing connected knowing and collaborative construction of knowledge, best describes the style of these women. But, to return to my point, knowing by *receiving* from, as well as sharing knowledge with, others is also prominent in these collaborative communities.

To illustrate: A number of the African American women interviewed in my culture sample spoke of the centrality of God or church in their lives and the importance to them of the church community. Probing in the interviews led me to understand that, although African American women speak about their faith and their trust in the ultimate authority of God, there is a sense of God as someone who *listens* as well as directs and dictates, who *frees* as well as expects obedience. Furthermore, God is experienced as "in me" (not external); thus, the person's voice can be God's voice. The orientation to God as authority coexists with a strong sense of self, experienced as a distinct and particular person who can and should be known by God and by other people on her own terms.

Deloris, for example, who directs an outreach ministry in her church, expects that

> If I am talking with someone with authority, I would ask that they not forget that I am me, to try to really get to know me, know me and my feelings, not to go by some book.

Deloris expects this of God as well—that He[12] know her, talk to her, and listen to her almost as if she were speaking of a relationship of equals. For Deloris, it is quid pro quo: if God listens to her, she will listen to him. She has a God *within* her who affirms her and is on her side.

Another African American woman we interviewed, Aunt Margaret, a wry and outspoken ninety-year-old community activist, has no trouble explaining the place of God in her life. Her interview reveals a willingness to yield to God's authority because of her strong and enduring faith in God's guidance and wisdom; she allows God to override her own personal authority.[13] Nevertheless she, like Deloris, turns for truth to the God inside, to the Christ-like side of herself.

> I don't count on my gut to tell me the truth—the truth for me. I count on a higher power. A spiritual higher power that is greater than I. I do this by meditating and generally I'd come up with the truth. I found I connected with this way most when I was trying to make sense of racism. I had to believe in something beyond me to make any sense of it. . . . We are Christ-like as a race because we have suffered. At times, all we had was our spirituality.

For Aunt Margaret, and other African American women we interviewed, the Black church provides a sense of belonging and security in a world where there are reasons to distrust others. The mutually supportive "call and response" mode of interaction in the Black church represents an affirmation of personal voice (Collins, 1990). Faith in God as authority coexists with faith in the community and a sense of responsibility for becoming the author of one's own life.

Some of the interviews with persons formerly from collectivist cultures (Triandis, 1989) cast another kind of light of the meaning and utility of received knowledge. A number of people in the culture sample were immigrants from countries and cultures in which strict adherence to external authority (parents, church, elders, and, for women, husbands) is expected and culturally enforced. In their interviews, several of these people talked about the move to the United States, where independent thought and personal voice are valued. The double consciousness for these bicultural individuals was marked by the conflict between the old culture's norms of receiving knowledge from sanctioned others and new Western cultural norms that sanction personal authority and independent thought.

Issi from the Philippines, Leela from India, Mai from Burma, and Sondra from Brazil all grew up in cultures in which they were taught to listen to elders and to their fathers and husbands. Leela conformed to her parents' wishes in order to please them: "You know, freedom is not possible in that society. The whole is more important than the parts." And, as Issi says, "I listen to anyone who is talking to me and I respect someone who is talking to me whether I like what I am hearing or not. And I digest it inside. . . . If a person is an expert, I have to agree with them."

The double consciousness of such immigrants to the United States

may have serious psychological repercussions. Mai and Issi both feel
that they do not think as well as the "smart" people in America and
report being baffled by expectations in American schools. They are
beginning to suspect that perhaps they should learn to be more open
and less preoccupied with what others say. Leela feels that one day she
may be able to get "out of the boundaries and be free" because "in the
U.S., thinking is like a buffet—you can choose." However, Leela is a
forty-year-old Indian woman transplanted by marriage to the United
States, living by the dictum that, after you are married, you "never
think." She remembers with nostalgia the Indian households in which
each person knew his or her place and "everything flowed. . . . [In
India], you don't have to think about tomorrow because it's going to be
the same as today."

Sondra, who is also living with an American husband in the United
States, was brutally taught in her home country in South America that
to question authority is dangerous. Her authoritarian father killed her
mother, who, after sixteen years of marriage, had "gotten strength from
her age and maturity" and initiated separation proceedings; similarly a
gentle teacher–priest Sondra knew spoke out against official authority
and was assassinated. In the United States, Sondra feels safer, gets more
respect from others, and is now taking karate classes, even though she is
still somewhat timorous and insecure in her own opinions. Like Sondra
(and several women from our original sample in WWK), other people we
interviewed had had past experience with violence that had short-
circuited their growth and voice and had seemingly locked them into a
passive receptiveness and resignation in which fearfulness of authority
led to their keeping their reflective and defiant selves underground (not
unlike what WWK associates with Silenced women).

Lily, a Russian Jew who came to the United States many years ago to
escape pogroms, keeps her thoughts hidden. She may question things in
her mind and has a great desire for knowledge, but she says she "would
never question authority." It is not a matter of fighting back, she told us.
"It is just a matter of being unable to speak" since she assumes there is
nothing she can do about authority over whom she has no power. Thus,
she keeps silent and remains deferential before external authorities in
spite of all she may "know inside myself."

Nekko provided an unusual story about knowing, deference, and the
experience of living between two cultures. As a Japanese exchange student in the United States, she has become argumentative in defense of
her own opinions and proud of holding her ground, even though she
feels she still doesn't "explain much, or ask much, or talk much." She has

recognized that when speaking English, it is easy to express her feelings and ideas. However, she realizes that in Japan and *in the Japanese language* she falls back into a conformist and passive received mode. She says that a friend has told her that when she speaks Japanese

> my facial expression is different and my voice changes and my attitude changes. . . . In Japan, of course, when you talk to your teachers, your parents, or someone in a higher position than you, you behave like you are a failure. . . . When I speak English, I'm really aggressive and very independent.

Received knowing, then, is not as simple nor necessarily as passive as we initially described, especially when one factors in cultural meanings of deference to external authority. It can be situationally determined. The Asian scholar Francis Hsu (1985), in an analysis of the self in cross-cultural perspective, examines the strict regulation of superior–inferior relationships (*iemoto*) in Japan and the equally powerful kinship and authority relationships in China that govern what Hsu calls "psychosocial homeostasis." Deference, though prescribed in the Japanese and Chinese collectivist cultures (Triandis, 1989), is basic to the conceptions of self. Similarly, as the Native American women, Allaq and Wanda, emphasized in their discussion of the role of deference to elders, the cultural emphasis is on "never losing anything." One should listen to the wisdom of the elders, open and prepare oneself to be ready to receive, and pass the wisdom on. The Asian and Native American cultural arrangements and regulations of interactions with authority contrast greatly with the American or Western requirements for adulthood (and psychosocial homeostasis), in which individuals (men, at least) can be expected to overthrow authorities and rely on their own judgment and evaluations for direction.

As I suggested earlier, enforced deference to authority that is part of the history of slavery and terrorist political regimes may have different personal epistemological outcomes, depending on the culture of origin. African Americans have cultivated at least one strategy of endurance and resistance that combines deference to an ultimate authority—that is, God—with a strong sense of an authoritative, yet community-oriented self. In contrast, persons who grow up in political dictatorships, in threatening families (for instance, abusive), or oppressive communities (for example, anti-Semitic)—and who do not have other supportive community resources—may forever be damaged psychologically, subject to internalized dangerous Authorities (with a big A, as psychologist William Perry says), and utterly passive as knowers.

BODY KNOWLEDGE:
A KIND OF SUBJECTIVE KNOWING?

One aspect of knowing that we did not explore in any depth in WWK pertains to a kind of knowledge that is grounded in bodily cues and experiences. We did notice and emphasize how Subjective Knowers use body metaphors as they speak about personal authority and convictions: "My gut always knows what is right." However, the culture sample interviews focused my attention anew not only on body metaphors for knowing, but also on a kind of knowing similar to what Mark Johnson (1987) calls nonpropositional embodied knowledge. Whether or not these rich and complex body-based approaches to knowing (that I will describe later) should be categorized as a kind of Subjective Knowing is doubtful. Although they are experienced as primarily internally derived states of knowing, a number of the informants emphasize the disappearance of self boundaries and a merging with nature in order to arrive at "truths." In addition, the persons who adhere to this kind of knowing often are quite articulate about the procedures and/or processes of such an approach; thus they are unlike Subjective Knowers, who tend to eschew thought and reflection as central to knowing and are unable to articulate how they "just know."

First an example of body metaphors for knowing: Nouvelle, a nurse in her midthirties, linked her preferred way of knowing to her African American roots and "world sense." Her emphasis on concrete practical knowledge and on the body as an instrument for knowing is reminiscent of Collins's analysis of black feminist epistemology (1990) and also psychologist John Ogbu's "ghetto theory of success" (1981). Her acknowledgment of visceral or "gut knowing" is also reminiscent of the descriptions of Subjectivist Knowers in WWK. Nouvelle attempted to describe what was meant by street sense among Black Americans:

> I think that growing up as a person of color in this society, you develop something more instinctual and survival like. It's a different kind of smart and a different kind of sense . . . more homey, more comfortable. . . . It almost defies description. It's much more visceral, it's much more down here [points to stomach].

Nouvelle links knowing not only to cultural imperatives, but to what she perceives as gender differences. Earlier in the interview, reproducing the ancient sexual stereotypes of men and women, Nouvelle had insisted on gender differences in ways of knowing, since, she believes, black or white, "men are men regardless of their upbringing." Men adhere to a "traditional linear way of thinking . . . which for some reason has been adopted by the world." Women, she added, are more experiential, more attuned to pain and trauma, more likely to incorporate through their senses and to trust their gut. "I'm not saying that men are more intelligent," sh , 'ens to add. "I'm saying that's where the difference lies."

Such attribution of essential gender differences embedded in a mind–body dualism has a long history. The split between mind and body emerged first with the philosopher Plato, then arrived full force with the eighteenth-century Enlightenment embrace of rationality and objectivism that promised to free Western man (but not perhaps woman) from the hegemony of superstition and ecclesiastical authority. In the aftermath of the Enlightenment, in establishment circles and institutions, reason came to prevail over emotion, rationality over bodily experience, and logic over "baser" instinctive impulses and intuitions. Some have argued (for example, Ortner, 1974; Sampson, 1978; Keller & Grontkowski, 1983; Harding, 1986) that along with the Enlightenment, and the patriarchy that fueled it, came an equation of man with reason–mind and woman with nature–body, initiating a two- to three-century-long genderized division of labor, separate sphere ideologies, and reverence for a masculinist ideal of a disembodied, abstract, universal reason.[14] Women, manual laborers, and the peasant class, "primitives," — indeed almost all people involved in the grit and grime of daily existence and bodily functions — came to be seen as excluded from what followers of the French psychoanalyst Jacques Lacan (Lacan, 1977) call the *Symbolic Order* and from what are presumed to be the "higher" (developmentally and ontogenetically) levels of thought, which include abstract thought and propositional knowledge (Johnson, 1987).

Reclaiming the centrality of the body in meaning making and putting the body back into the mind have in recent years become a project for a number of philosophers, feminists, psychologists, and culture theorists. The scientist-turned-philosopher Michael Polanyi (1958, 1966) moved from the premise that "we know more than we can tell" to a description of what he called "tacit knowledge" and an assertion that "our body is the ultimate instrument of all our external knowledge" (1966, p. 15).[15] In more recent years, R. M. Zaner (1971); Mark Johnson (1987), who coined the phrase "the body in the mind;" and Drew Leder (1990), among others, have argued that all human knowledge and language are embodied, that is, tied to bodily orientations, experiences, and interactions in and with our environment.

The French feminist psychoanalyst Luce Irigaray (1985), observing that women are trapped in a system of meaning (the Symbolic Order and "Law of the Father" of Jacques Lacan) that serves only the masculine subject, has argued for a feminine discourse that reclaims the female body and sexuality. Psychologist Claudia Zanardi (1995) contrasts the "corporal language" of Sigmund Freud and Jacques Lacan—the language of the father—with Irigaray's attempts to give voice to women's bodies—the language of the mother. Other feminists in the United States, especially Carol Gilligan and her colleagues (Gilligan, Brown, & Rogers, 1990; Debold, 1991; Tolman, 1990), have argued for a place for both body and culture in personality theory and theories of the mind (they call for a "psyche embedded" in both body and culture).

Very few psychologists have discussed or analyzed the impact of culture on the recognition and valuation of body knowledge. In the past psychology tended to see body experience (cast as preverbal, prelogical, and prior to culture) as an impediment to rational thought. The Italian cognitive therapist Vittorio Guidano (1987) points out, however, that, even though higher semantic levels of information processing gradually replace global "here-and-now" tacit apprehensions of the world, the two modes function autonomously but in dynamic interaction throughout the life cycle. Guidano argues that there are large and persistent individual differences (and, one might add, cultural differences) in the relative importance of tacit (unconscious and body-based) and explicit (abstract and propositional) knowledge. Psychologist Howard Gardner (1984), in his work on multiple intelligences and the acquisition of culture, stresses that cultures and subcultures choose to highlight certain intelligences or competencies while minimizing or negating others. Bodily–kinesthetic competence, valued in our culture for athletes and dancers, is even more highly valued in cultures in which the body is seen as a vehicle or vessel for spiritual communion.

Judith, a Native American woman in her forties, claims that the "Christian world and Christian thinking almost killed me." After years of experiencing a kind of intellectual shame in Anglo schools, she now embraces body-based knowing—a way of knowing that she identifies as Indian. She goes into the desert wilderness to "listen with her skin." From knowledge acquired through her body arise "the words that I write, the paintings that I do, the beadwork that I do."

The Peruvian woman Kat also insists that her knowing has a deeper source than her intellect. An articulate and highly reflective woman (whom we coded ultimately as a Constructed Knower), Kat argues for the centrality of visceral knowing that is more than "just words."

When I know something, it is just this inward sense of like listening with all of me. And when it comes out it does not come out in parts, it is like this big picture. This is like what I think intuition is—the brain's more efficient way of being able to process all this amazing information from everywhere, from the whole universe, and bring it into this kind of full-blown moment, of like ah-ha.

Recall from Kat's story at the beginning of this chapter that her grandmother, a shaman, taught her to go into the woods and *be* the tree, the rock, the bird. She taught her a "greater way of knowing"—to "attune yourself, to tune the body, to turn on all the senses." By opening the body, Kat claims, you lose the sense of self-importance, so nothing gets in the way of that which you are trying to know. It is a sense of knowing that does not have to have words.

The body knows. Dreaming for me is just as real as waking life. I think the body is constantly sending messages that get comprised in this experience that we call the dream. In fact I almost think that the body is in a constant dream. . . . It is amazing that we can carry on so many different processes— electrochemical, hormonal—that is all a knowingness. The body seems to know how to send messages when something needs to change—or you manifest it through a symptom of the body. There is a much greater intelligence than I will ever be able to be conscious of.

Not all of the women and men we interviewed were as descriptive of the process of body knowing as Judith and Kat, even though people from different cultural backgrounds—in particular, East Indian, African American, and Native American—demonstrated a proclivity for body metaphors as they described their minds and ways of knowing. One might ask whether body metaphors are for some individuals only "skin deep," primarily reflecting only a cultural idiom or transient linguistic convenience rather than a preferred, heuristic, and deeply embodied knowledge perspective. However, if we take seriously arguments that metaphors are powerful tools for organizing, articulating, and communicating human experience (Lakoff & Johnson, 1980; Martin, 1987), even worldviews (Pepper, 1942), then close attention to the metaphorical dimension of human utterances is well warranted. Whether body knowing is construed as simply a linguistic convention, a kind of Subjective Knowing; an aspect of a more complex and fluid way of knowing typified by Constructed Knowers; or a new category of knowing not captured by WWK, bringing the body back into the mind becomes an important item for psychology's agenda if it is to be responsive to culturally diverse populations.

CONSTRUCTED KNOWING, SITUATIONAL KNOWING, AND RESPONSIBLE KNOWING

The description in WWK of the last knowledge perspective, Constructed Knowing, was in some ways the least detailed and most tentative. In part, this was due to our realization that our original sample of women whom we coded as Constructed Knowers was limited to white college-educated women—a narrow and, we thought, probably skewed sample. Many of the women we assigned to this category were among the youngest in our sample. Where were the wise older women, we wondered, since we intuitively expected to find them in this group and knew of such women in our communities, from our travels, and from our reading. Some reviewers, after the publication of WWK, suggested that what we called Constructed Knowing might have been an artifact of good fortune, higher education, and the power and privilege associated with the dominant culture (Hoffman, 1986; Harding, 1987; also see Harding, this volume); they wondered whether the inclusion of marginalized, less privileged, yet politically involved women might not have revealed other ways of knowing that shape and are shaped by community work and social action.[16] My new research, as well as that of Mary Belenky (in this volume) and my former student Dawn Noggle (1996), casts light on this point.

My culture interviews (and those of Belenky and Noggle) reveal that people of color, immigrants, and members of the working class can (though not all do) develop a way of knowing that seems to evolve through their marginality and life struggles, not exclusively through higher education. Their way of knowing is truly contextual and constructed in that they have learned firsthand how situated and power-related ways of knowing can be. Knowledge and knowing are, for them, a matter of strategy and survival—a point made by several contributors to this volume, who describe multiple consciousness and social "standpoint" or "positionality." What is distinctive about most of these particular knowers is that they are not trapped in or paralyzed by relativism (some critics of relativist epistemologies claim that value relativity undermines moral commitment and the possibility of moral action); they seem rather to be committed to a moral and political life and the "beloved community" (see Belenky, this volume, for a more extended discussion on this point). These knowers are exemplars of what Perry called "commitment within relativism" (Perry, 1970), that is, the struggle toward finding a basis for (moral) action in spite of one's awareness of the shifting nature of truth and its co-optation by those in power. As both Noggle and Belenky argue, it is the collectivity of knowers that empowers individuals. A life devoted to political action and social justice may promote a kind of knowing that includes connection, the collaborative construction of knowledge, and conviction. As we described them, even ten years ago in *WWK*, Constructed Knowers hold that an opinion is more than an exercise of the intellect; it is something to live by (*WWK*, p. 149). It is from the position of constructed knowing that a person can, if she chooses, reflect on the personal and communal construction of meaning, make informed choices and commitments, take action, and conceive of her life and acts as political.

Reading the culture interviews again and again, I have come to understand that constructed knowing is much more than the understanding that knowledge is contextual and situated and that the knower is always a part of the known. Such knowing also entails a *flexibility* in approaches to knowing and *ability to assess the appropriateness and utility* of a particular way of knowing given the moment, situation, cultural and political imperatives, and relational and ethical ramifications. In other words, constructed knowing is flexible, responsive, and responsible knowing as well. Nevertheless, one may find constructed knowers who emphasize or value one knowing perspective over another for certain purposes and situations (for example, the body-based knowing of Kat or the received knowing of Aunt Margaret, both of which supplement the more objectivist or rationalist approaches that they also employ and embrace). I believe, however, that once one attains a constructed knowing perspective the world can never look the same. Once one understands that questions and answers grow out of contexts, there is no turning back to naive objectivism or subjectivism—even though at times in one's life the gut and inner voice (so vivid and primary for the Subjective Knower) or the convictions of external authorities (vital to the Received Knower) may override tempered or complex thought or judgment.

Some stories, such as Christine's, illustrate the fluidity of approaches to knowing as well as the cultural and situational specificity of knowing. They raise the question of whether members of certain cultures may be better equipped to adjust to new and unfamiliar ways of knowing as they move between cultures. Christine, the third-generation Chinese woman and entrepreneur mentioned earlier, feels both Asian and American. She claims she "thinks in contradictions" and has "multiple selves."

> As an Asian, I think of the whole picture and the circle of things, but as an American or a Western thinker, I understand the linear path. . . . For all my convictions, I do see other sides—and it makes it real hard for me to say that it's just my idea or it's your idea. I can always say, it's our idea. It's your side and my side, but then let's come to a synthesis. I work for that synthesis. Again it's that Chinese–Asian side [of me] that says how do we get to some harmony here? . . . Probably I'm not able to stand in one place for people. And yet, I think that people think I do.

Because she is so aware of context and situation, and how she shifts to accommodate, she has a chameleonlike feel to her except for the fact that, throughout her interview, there is a core solidity and self-assurance in her self-presentation that prevail. She says she always tells people that "the Chinese word for think includes the character for heart." For Christine, "the heart and the mind are not separate." My students and I coded Christine's approach to knowing as constructivist.

Although one should be cautious about generalizations about culture groups, it appears that the Chinese and Japanese individuals whom we interviewed (in this admittedly very small sample), of all the culture groups, seemed most unsurprised by and ready to accept multiple ways of knowing. Their epistemology changed more easily with a change in geography. Francis Hsu and many other anthropologists and psychologists who have written about various Asian cultures have described an Asian situational self that is embedded in relationships; they question "the stranglehold of the Western ideal of individualism" (Hsu, 1985) and Western assumption of a bounded autonomous self. Hsu addresses the concept of the Chinese word jen (in Japanese, jin), which connotes "the place of the individual in a web of interpersonal relationships, while his wishes, predilections, and anxieties are judged according to whether they contribute to or destroy his interpersonal relationships" (Hsu, 1985, p. 33). Other theorists and researchers have followed the lead of Hsu and the anthropologists Clifford Geertz (1975, 1983) and Richard Shweder (1982) by describing construals of the self that differ from the Western individualistic self—for instance, collective versus individual self (Triandis, 1989), interdependent versus dependent self (Markus & Kitayama, 1991), and indexical versus referential self (Landrine, 1992). Shweder (1991) has explicitly related cultural concepts of the person to modes of thought (ways of knowing). He observes that "a tendency *not* to abstract a concept of the inviolate personality free of social role and social relationship" is associated with a style of thinking that is "concrete, contextualized, and nonabstractive" (1991, p. 122). It may be that what my colleagues and I have described in *WWK* as a tendency of some female knowers to resist automatic abstraction and decontextualized thought (in favor of knowledge grounded in personal experience, inclusiveness, and situation) is an extension of this notion of Shweder's. As Christine says:

> The word "understanding" is key in my world. . . . It is based on a fundamental premise — namely the interrelationship of things. I think that not only women try to interrelate things, but in the Asian context, interrelationships are so key. And that is what gives me a sense of knowing — that I can relate everything to something else.

A striving for inclusiveness and comprehensiveness was also vividly described by other people from my culture sample who think out of a constructed knowing perspective. Kat from Peru, while discussing her openness to multiple sensory input and information, insists that thinking per se is a "very narrow band, a very narrow channel" in the spectrum of knowing. In her move to the United States and in her acquisition of linear abstract thinking skills, she feels she is in danger of losing access to "spontaneous knowledge" that can "arise and be used in the moment." She feels there must be a way one can accommodate a new culture without fully giving up the old, even though she knows she cannot go back. For the moment, she is trying to find ways of merging and integrating the two worlds and approaches of knowing even though for her they are very much in conflict.

The Native American woman Wanda describes herself as a "walk-around thinker"; that is, she says she both literally and figuratively needs to walk around (circle and see from multiple vantage points) ideas and facts with which she is trying to come to terms. Although she recognizes the advantages of Western abstraction and propositional knowledge, she, like those in her Native American community, also absorbs concrete details around her and values "dreams, intuitions, what's out there in the environment" in the process of knowing. She feels she now holds on to a cultural identity and ways of knowing tied to her Indian heritage, whereas in the past she had trouble with the question "Am I keeping faith with my traditions if I am in Anthropology at the university?"

Adelita, a Mexican American single mother and political activist from a farm family background, has developed a way of knowing that she feels best serves her community and her political activities (see Noggle, 1996, for an in-depth study of Adelita and other working-class activist women and their ways of knowing). Adelita feels that her triple marginalization as a poor, female person of color has led her to a life devoted to social change and social justice and a commitment to collective action. As a community advocate, she has worked in the past with monolingual, undocumented men as well as women. And she has come to "learn a lot about communicating and negotiating and representing these individuals." For her, knowing and learning should be flexible and responsive to the people you are with. She uses logic, analysis, and devil's advocacy as a way of challenging herself and others in group problem solving. Respect for others rather than arguments for a personal position guides her use of confrontation and challenge. Most importantly, Adelita stresses connection and listening as a way of "breaking down barriers" between people. Dialogue is at the center of her knowing. Knowing and learning are, for Adelita, a matter of collaboration and networking— communicating with people, calling, writing, getting together, maintaining close relationships. When speaking, Adelita often substitutes the collective *we* for the personal *I*. As for authority, she says:

> We always think of authority as the system, but they only have as much authority as we allow them to. So it's a term that doesn't frighten me.

In many ways, Adelita exemplifies in her personal development and her political objectives what social theorist Paulo Friere calls a "critical consciousness"—an ability to live both inside and outside systems (or different worlds) while retaining a conscious critical awareness of the costs and consequences of moving across the barriers between the two. Her approach to knowing, so centered in political action and community problem solving, is also an excellent example of cooperative inquiry and coconstruction of knowledge (Reason & Heron, 1995).

CONCLUSIONS

How have these culture tales challenged the five original ways of knowing categories? Do our five WWK categories collapse under the weight of testimony from culturally diverse people? Are they useful in understanding the lived experience of the bicultural people we interviewed? Do the tales suggest a need for modification and/or elaboration of the ways of knowing scheme?

The ways of knowing scheme, as we initially presented it, was focused more on the descriptions of *persons* whom we sorted into types of knowers than on *types or ways of knowing* that persons used for different purposes and at different points in their lives. Consequently, our emphasis tended to be on the commonalities (for example, in life issues and priorities, nature of relationships, concepts of self) across persons within each knowledge perspective, stripped of their ethnic and class identities. This emphasis contributed to the tendency (ours and others') to refer, for example, to "Received Knowers" or "Subjective Knowers" as if the person were the category. Furthermore, our understanding and original interpretation of the knowledge positions were limited by the persons we included in our *WWK* sample. Our presentation of our person-focused observations and interpretive scheme precluded an extensive discussion of class or race or stigmatization in general as a factor in knowing; it directed our attention away from discussion of individuals as persons embedded in communities and cultures (as Maher and Tetreault this volume, say, "as occupants of a certain place in this world"). We unwittingly were acting like the person-focused psychologists we had been trained to be—overly committed to our story of the development of individual self (a white feminist version of the Western self) and relatively insensitive to the centrality of power, positionality, community, and culture as factors in knowing and identity development. Our only discussion of the *contexts* of individual lives centered on how the social institutions of family and school facilitated or hindered individual development. It was this singular focus on individual psychology and development (rather than on individuals-in-social–cultural-contexts) that limited our vision and reveals our original scheme as culture-bound.

Implicit in our original work is the premise that the research task is, first, to fit individuals into one of the five person typologies; then, second, at least to speculate about (or determine with longitudinal data) the developmental shifts in knowing and say something about the person's "growing edge."[17] Many people have assumed that we intended our scheme to be a developmental stage theory, a movement "upward" across the five ways of knowing in the order in which we discussed them (Silence, Received, Subjective, Procedural, Constructed). Inevitably people who have used our scheme (particularly in educational settings) have viewed the "earlier" or "lower" positions in the sequence as "less developed" or "less mature." When typologies or positions are constructed, it is difficult to resist seeing "ideals," or stagelike progression through the positions that imply "higher is better." Our original data,

indeed even our own thinking, have not been immune to such misleading readings. The four WWK authors disagree somewhat on
whether the five original knowledge positions can or should represent a
developmental sequence. In this chapter, I have presented an argument
that, if one takes culture and context into account, the stages make little sense. However, if one is investigating the acquisition of cognitive
competence that accompanies socialization into the dominant current
American culture, values, and educational objectives (and, according to
most psychological theory, requires a shift from passive to active knowing, from dualism to relativism, from concrete to abstract thought), then
the five positions are arranged from less to more adequate—and can be
read as developmental. However, it should be kept in mind that this
ideal "progression" in cognitive competence has been defined and studied by Western psychologists who are themselves embedded in the scientific epistemology of the West (see Harding, this volume). Other cultures would define the development of cognitive competence very
differently (Gardner, 1984).

Although in WWK we resisted calling our five knowledge perspectives
developmental stages, we did imply that the fifth position, Constructed
Knowing, was somehow a superior epistemology in that it encompassed
multiple approaches to knowing and avoided overvaluation of any one
way of knowing. This is a debatable point since it has not been verified
that constructed knowing is suited to all environments and cultures,
some of which may require a less complex and less fluid approach to
knowing in favor of a more absolutist and predictable approach that supports community solidarity and consensus; some cultures may intentionally teach giving up analytic thought and objectivity in order to promote
communion with nature and the spirit world.

When context is factored into the study of knowing, one begins to see
the advantages of thinking of the five categories as *strategies* for knowing
(rather than person types). Thus, persons may "prefer," "be trained for,"
"be assigned to," "revert to," "call on," or "spiral through" different strategies for knowing, depending on social position, cultural practice, situation, political objective, personal (even unconscious) motives. Any individual's way(s) of knowing would be the constellation of various strategies
in her repertoire, some perhaps more prominent or commonly used.
Aunt Margaret and Kat are examples of persons with multifaceted, contextualized, flexible ways of knowing (that we would characterize as constructed knowing), who also value particular ways as strategies that often
work for them. To the extent that a person's strategy for knowing adheres
to a single strategy that is static or rigidly applied, then one can ask what

are the contextual factors that limit or inhibit alternative strategies. An example here would be Lily, whose experience with pogroms resulted in a telescoped and limiting strategy of received knowing characterized by passivity and fearfulness.

An additional advantage in this reframing of knowing as strategy rather than person is that it allows us to talk about different manifestations or uses of or even meanings (constructions) of a particular way of knowing. Thus, received knowing can be passive, unquestioned, chosen, or embraced; it can be infantilizing, soothing, honored, or considered dangerous. How a culture construes external authority, the self, God, elders, shamans, and so forth, affects the force and personal meaningfulness of received knowing. In a similar vein, situational and cultural factors can dictate individual "strategic" silence; culturally endorsed power differentials can lead to "structural" silence and the silencing of a group of people based, for example, on gender, class, or race membership. Silence, then, will be experienced differently depending on the culturally assigned meaning and the sense of choice in the matter.

As I have also noted, some cultures endorse body-based knowing and nonideational communion with spirits and nature, thus rendering this kind of knowing a normative and educational ideal. In Western technological cultures, this kind of knowing is considered aberrant. In the United States, we do not have a well-developed language for or conceptual understanding of knowledge acquisition that proceeds without rational thought and analysis. As I have pointed out, even our category of subjective knowing does not capture the essence of what some culture groups describe as body knowledge.

My focus on the bicultural experience has brought to the forefront the importance of understanding power and the politics of knowledge. All of us—whether members of the dominant culture, immigrants, or members of stigmatized groups—learn to negotiate power relationships within and across groups. Gender relations, as well as race and class relations, are central to these negotiations since how one knows and what one is allowed to know differ according to cultural assignments (by gender, race, class) and social power differentials. Although my interviews with culturally diverse people living in the United States provided a route into a broader look at issues of domination and power in this country, only further study and analysis of ways of knowing within cultures will illuminate whether the ways of knowing discussed in this chapter are adequate for understanding power and genderized knowledge specific to a given culture and to classes within that culture. Learning, for instance, about the shifting ways of knowing of an educated privileged Chinese

American woman such as Christine who is accommodating herself to life in the United States tells us little about how educated Chinese women in China think and know relative to educated Chinese men or to uneducated peasant class men or women. This kind of work and understanding lie ahead of us.

NOTES

1. I use the definition of *bicultural* provided by LaFromboise, Coleman, and Gerton (1993) citing R. E. Park (1928) and E. V. Stonequist (1935). Marginalized bicultural people are those who live "at the juncture between two cultures and can lay a claim to belonging to both cultures, either by being of mixed racial heritage or born in one culture and raised in a second." *Marginalization* arises when "two or more cultures share the same geographical area, with one culture maintaining a higher status than another."
2. In the following pages, I will adopt the convention of using capital letters when referring to one of the five ways of knowing perspectives as we originally described them (e.g., Silence, Received Knowing, Subjective Knowing, Procedural Knowing, Constructed Knowing).
3. Were it not for the structure of the Fielding Institute — a distance learning, electronically linked doctoral program for midcareer adult students — I doubt I could have succeeded in the particular form of interview-based, multisite research that I ultimately mounted. Working alone, I would never have had the mobility and money (or courage?) to travel to such far reaches of the United States. Fielding students are scattered throughout the United States and have access through their jobs, families, and friends to a wide variety of ethnic minority communities and individuals. Although I live in and work out of the Northeast, I am in touch with students, not only face to face at national and regional meetings, but via Fielding computer e-mail and bulletin boards. Thus, my students and I have been able to work together as a nationally dispersed research team during the interview collection and analysis stages of an ongoing study of diversity in ways of knowing.
4. Since the Women's Ways of Knowing project, I have been particularly interested in the relationship between perspectives on knowing and experiences of silence — whether they be negative in the sense of feeling silenced, ignored, negated, or without words to speak out, or positive in the sense of peaceful retreat and self-renewal, self-editing, or strategic silence. The many meanings of silence and voice are, as we have pointed out in WWK, related to experiences of self, mind, and authority.

5. In fact, they were given the choice of whether to keep the interviews confidential and their identity disguised or openly share their stories with whoever is interested. As M. Brinton Lykes (1989) discovered in her research with Guatemalan women, her informants felt that they had already negotiated a trusting relationship before agreeing to participate. The requirement of signed informed consent forms and assurances of confidentiality was experienced by them as an intrusion into the relationship.

6. The fact that approximately 80 percent of the interviews were with women was not planned, but was an artifact of leaving the choice of gender of the informant to the student interviewers. There are undoubtedly a number of reasons why this gender imbalance occurred. Some of the students were drawn to the project because of my initial work on women's ways of knowing and wanted to extend it; or it may have been that women were more available as interviewees. The gender imbalance is unfortunate since additional male voices would have further enriched my discussion of the intersection of culture and knowing as it is manifested in various men's and women's lives.

7. See the chapter by Sandra Harding in this volume for an extended discussion of gender and local knowledge systems.

8. Mary Belenky, in her new research (in this volume), has elaborated on the life experiences and prospects for personal growth and change in such a group of silent, isolated rural women (primarily white and poor).

9. A recent article by Shulamit Reinharz (1994) describes how an ethnography of voice and silence could further our understanding of the concepts of disenfranchisement and oppression, especially since individuals may not necessarily identify themselves as oppressed or powerless even though researchers label them as such. As we reported in WWK, people easily describe their experience of knowing and authority using the metaphors of voice and silence.

10. Keith Basso's research identifies, for instance, several reasons why an Apache individual may "give up words": (1) to resist the power or influence of an unfamiliar person who may want to teach something or want something; (2) to wait to see just how changed or judgmental a child or friend might be who has been away from home for some time; (3) to prevent stirring up a person who seems enraged or crazy; (4) to be courteous with people who are sad or ritualistically transformed (as in tribal ceremonies); (5) to prevent revealing one's stupidity in uncertain or ambiguous situations. In no cases does Basso imply that silence is dispositional; it is situational and relational.

11. I thank my colleague Mary Belenky for alerting me to this distinction.

12. Deloris herself referred to God as "He."

13. Most persons' approach to knowing is complex and dynamic and cuts across two or more categories. Although one perspective usually pre-

dominates at the time of the interview, others seem to be more secondary and represent both remnants from past perspectives and developing perspectives that may become dominant in the future. Aunt Margaret, for example, perhaps with the experience of age, had developed a wise and unique voice of her own; she was coded as Constructivist with received knowing prominent.

14. Thomas Nagel (1986) has called the objectivist's postulation of the disembodied mind "the view from nowhere." Susan Bordo (1990), in a bow to Nagel, has called the postmodernist "fantasy of transcendence" of mind over body and the deconstruction of subjectivity a "new imagination of disembodiment: a dream of being everywhere" (p. 143).

15. One should acknowledge the role of the body in Freud's theory. A centerpiece of his theory of psychic development is what he calls the "body ego" (Freud, 1960/1989). His postulation of psychosexual stages of development that are grounded in body zones (oral, anal, phallic, genital) reveal him as a theorist who gives great weight to the role of the body in psychic development. According to some feminists, however, this aspect of his theory locates him as a biological determinist who believes that "anatomy is destiny." They also argue that, because of Freud's perplexity over female sexuality and development, his story of human development is decidedly masculinist in its focus on the male body, the phallus, and male psychic experience.

16. As Bing and Reid point out in their chapter in this volume, poor women and women of color are more likely to spend time working politically for civic causes and the betterment of all people in their communities than white women who espouse narrower "white" feminist objectives of equality of opportunities and empowerment for women alone.

17. Actually we rarely coded someone in only one knowledge category. Most people are better described, and actually reveal in their life stories a more dynamic, shifting epistemology as their situation in life and their understanding of themselves in the world evolve. Coding a person's ways of knowing, then, becomes a matter of trying to capture a person's history and future; what has been, was is now, and what might be. Tying a person to a particular category or categories should be recognized as simply taking a convenient snapshot of a person in a moment in time.

REFERENCES

Basso, K. H. (1970). "To give up on words": Silence in Western Apache culture. *Southwestern Journal of Anthropology, 26*(3), 213–230.

Beale, F. (1972). Double jeopardy: To be black and female. In T. Cade (Ed.), *The black woman: An anthology,* 90–100. New York: New American Library.

Belenky, M., Bond, L., & Weinstock, J. (in press). *A tradition that has no name: Public homeplaces and the development of people, families, and communities.* New York: Basic Books.

Belenky, M. F., Clinchy, B. M., Goldberger, N. R., & Tarule, J. M. (1986). *Women's ways of knowing: The development of self, voice, and mind.* New York: Basic Books.

Bordo, S. (1990). Feminism, postmodernism, and gender-skepticism. In L. Nicholson (Ed.), *Feminism/postmodernism.* New York: Routledge.

Bruner, J. (1990). *Acts of meaning.* Cambridge, MA: Harvard University Press.

Cohen, Y. A. (1971). The shaping of men's minds: Adaptations to the imperatives of culture. In M. L. Max, S. Diamond, & F. O. Gearing (Eds.), *Anthropological perspectives on education.* New York: Basic Books.

Collins, P. H. (1990). *Black feminist thought: Knowledge, consciousness, and the politics of empowerment.* Cambridge, MA: Unwin Hyman.

Davis, A. (1971). Reflections of the black woman's role in the community of slaves. *Black Scholar, 3,* 2–16.

Debold, E. (1991). The body at play. In C. Gilligan, A. Rogers, & D. Tolman (Eds.), *Women, girls, and psychotherapy: Reframing resistance.* Binghamton, NY: Haworth Press.

DuBois, W. E. B. (1961). *The soul of black folks: Essays and sketches.* New York: Fawcett.

Evans, G. (1980). Those loud black girls. In D. Spender & E. Sarah (Eds.), *Learning to lose: sexism and education.* London: Women's Press.

Fordham, S. (1993). Those loud black girls: Black women, silence, and gender "passing" in the academy. *Anthropology and Education Quarterly, 24* (1), 3–32.

Freud, S. (1960/1989). *The ego and the id.* New York: W. W. Norton.

Gardner, H. (1984). The development of competence in culturally defined domains: A preliminary framework. In R. A. Shweder & R. A. LeVine (Eds.), *Culture theory: Essays on mind, self, and emotion.* Cambridge: Cambridge University Press.

Geertz, C. (1975). From the native's point of view: On the nature of anthropological understanding. *American Scientist, 63,* 47–53.

Geertz, C. (1983). *Local knowledge.* New York: Basic Books.

Gilligan, C., Brown, L. M., & Rogers, A. (1990). Psyche embedded: A place for body, relationships, and culture in personality theory. In A. I. Rabin, R. Zucker, R. Emmons, & S. Frank (Eds.), *Studying persons and lives.* New York: Springer.

Goldberger, N. R., & Veroff, J. B. (Eds.) (1995). *The culture and psychology reader.* New York: New York University Press.

Guidano, V. F. (1987). *Complexity of the self: A developmental approach to psychopathology and therapy.* New York: Guilford Press.

Harding, S. (1987). Struggling for self-definition. *Women's Review of Books, 4* (6), pp. 6–7.

Harding, S. (1992). Subjectivity, experience, and knowledge: An epistemology from/for Rainbow Coalition politics. *Development and Change, 23*(3), 175–193.

Hoffman, N. J. (1986). Feminist scholarship and women's studies. *Harvard Educational Review, 56*(4), 511–519.

Howard, G. S. (1991). Culture tales: A narrative approach to thinking, cross-cultural psychology, and psychotherapy. *American Psychologist, 46,* 187–197.

Hsu, F. L. K. (1985). The self in cross-cultural perspective. In A. Marsella, G. DeVos, & F. L. K. Hsu (Eds.), *Culture and the self.* London: Tavistock.

Irigaray, L. (1985). *This sex which is not one* (C. Porter, Trans.). Ithaca, NY: Cornell University Press.

Johnson, M. (1987). *The body in the mind: The bodily basis of meaning, imagination, and reason.* Chicago: University of Chicago Press.

Keller, E. F., & Grontkowski, C. R. (1983). The mind's eye. In S. Harding & M. Hintikka (Eds.), *Discovering reality,* 207–224. Dordrecht, Holland: Reidel.

King, D. H. (1988). Multiple jeopardy, multiple consciousness: The context of a black feminist ideology. *Signs: Journal of Women in Culture and Society, 14*(11), 42–72.

Lacan, J. (1977). *Ecrits: A selection* (A. Sheridan, Trans.). New York: W. W. Norton.

LaFromboise, T., Coleman, H. L. K., & Gerton, J. (1993). Psychological impact of biculturalism: Evidence and theory. *Psychological Bulletin, 114,* 395–412.

Lakoff, G., & Johnson, M. (1980). *Metaphors we live by.* Chicago: University of Chicago Press.

Landrine, H. (1992). Clinical implications of cultural differences: The referential versus the indexical self. *Clinical Psychology Review*, *12*, 401–415.

Leder, D. (1990). *The absent body*. Chicago: University of Chicago Press.

Luttrell, W. (1993). "The teachers, they all had their pets": Concepts of gender, knowledge, and power. *Signs: Journal of Women in Culture and Society*, *18* (3), 505–546.

Lykes, M. B. (1989). Dialogue with Guatemalan Indian women: Critical perspectives on constructing collaborative research. In R. K. Unger (Ed.), *Representations: Social constructions of gender*. Amityville, NY: Baywood.

Mair, M. (1988). Psychology as storytelling. *International Journal of Personal Construct Psychology*, *1*, 125–138.

Markus, H. R., & Kitayama, S. (1991). Culture and self: Implications for cognition, emotion, and motivation. *Psychological Review*, *98* (2), 224–253.

Martin, E. (1987). *The woman in the body: A cultural analysis of reproduction*. Boston: Beacon Press.

McCarty, T. L., Wallace, S., Lynch, R. H., & Benally, A. (1991). Classroom inquiry and Navajo learning styles: A call for reassessment. *Anthropology and Education Quarterly*, *22*, 42–59.

Mishler, E. (1986). *Research interviewing: Context and narrative*. Cambridge, MA: Harvard University Press.

Nagel, T. (1986). *The view from nowhere*. Oxford: Oxford University Press.

Neilsen, J. M. (1990). *Feminist research methods*. Boulder, CO: Westview Press.

Noggle, D. (1996). *Women activists of diverse backgrounds: A qualitative study of self-perceived developmental influences and values*. Unpublished doctoral dissertation, The Fielding Institute, Santa Barbara, CA.

Oakley, A. (1981). Interviewing women: A contradiction in terms. In H. Roberts (Ed.), *Doing feminist research*. Boston: Routledge & Kegan Paul.

Ogbu, J. U. (1981). Origins of human competence: A cultural–ecological perspective. *Child Development*, *52*, 413–429.

Ortner, S. B. (1974). Is female to male as nature is to culture? In M. Z. Rosaldo & L. Lamphere (Eds.), *Woman, culture, and society*. Stanford, CA: Stanford University Press.

Park, R. E. (1928). Human migration and the marginal man. *American Journal of Sociology*, *5*, 881–893.

Pepper, S. C. (1942). *World hypotheses: A study in evidence*. Berkeley: University of California Press.

Perry, W. G. (1970). *Forms of intellectual and ethical development in the college years*. New York: Holt, Rinehart, & Winston.

Personal Narratives Group (Ed.). (1989). *Interpreting women's lives: Feminist theory and personal narratives*. Bloomington, IN: Indiana University Press.

Polanyi, M. (1958). *Personal knowledge.* Chicago: University of Chicago Press.

Polanyi, M. (1966). *The tacit dimension.* New York: Doubleday.

Reason, P. & Heron, J. (1995). Co-operative inquiry. In J. A. Smith, R. Harre, & L. Van Langenhove (Eds.), *Rethinking methods in psychology.* Thousand Oaks, CA: Sage.

Reid, P. T. (1993). Poor women in psychological research: Shut up and shut out. *Psychology of Women Quarterly, 17,* 133–150.

Reinharz, S. (1994). Toward an ethnography of "voice" and "silence." In E. J. Trickett, R. J. Watts, & D. Birman (Eds.), *Human diversity: Perspectives of people in context.* San Francisco: Jossey-Bass.

Root, M. P. P. (1990). Resolving "other" status: Identity development of biracial individuals. *Women and Therapy, 9,* 185–205.

Sampson, E. E. (1978). Scientific paradigm and social value: Wanted—a scientific revolution. *Journal of Personality and Social Psychology, 36,* 1332–1343.

Shweder, R. A. (1982). Does the concept of the person vary cross-culturally? In A. J. Marsella & G. M. White (Eds.), *Cultural conceptions of mental health and therapy.* Dordrecht, Holland: Reidel.

Shweder, R. A. (1991). *Thinking through cultures: Expeditions in cultural psychology.* Cambridge, MA: Harvard University Press.

Stonequist, E. V. (1935). The problem of marginal man. *American Journal of Sociology, 7,* 1–12.

Tolman, D. (1990). *Just say no to what? A preliminary analysis of sexual subjectivity in a multicultural group of adolescent females.* Paper presented at the American Orthopsychiatric Association, Miami.

Triandis, H. C. (1989). The self and social behavior in differing cultural contexts. *Psychological Review, 98,* 506–520.

Zanardi, C. (1995). The maternal in psychoanalysis: From mind/body to body/mind. *Psychoanalysis and Contemporary Thought, 18* (3), 419–454.

Zaner, R. M. (1971). *The problem of embodiment.* The Hague: Martinus Nijhoff.

Strategic Suspensions

Feminists of Color Theorize the
Production of Knowledge*

AÍDA HURTADO

WOMEN'S WAYS OF KNOWING (WWK) (Belenky, Clinchy, Goldberger, & Tarule, 1986) broke important conceptual ground on how knowledge is produced, comprehended, and ultimately internalized. Not surprisingly, although often undocumented, women go about these processes differently than men. The variations lie not in the biological differences between women and men but in the division of labor and the value attached to those divisions in our society. However, the value attached to one's labor is not determined only by gender but also by other important categorical group memberships, like class, race, and ethnicity (Hurtado, 1996). Being poor, of Color, and also a woman results in daily experiences that create a systematically different relationship to knowledge (including its production, comprehension, and integration). This unique relationship—these special ways of knowing—has gone largely undocu-

*I thank the following people for critically reading this work: Craig Haney, Tomás Almaguer, and Pattye Crespo. I also would like to acknowledge the support of the Chicano/Latino Research Center, University of California, Santa Cruz, Professors Norma Klahn and Pedro Castillo, Co-Directors.

mented in academic writings. Until feminists of Color began writing about these issues, there was not a paradigm—other than madness—to comprehend fully how multiple consciousness is produced and how individuals with this ability make sense of their daily lives. In this chapter I examine the special mechanisms of knowledge production and knowledge acquisition that have been identified in the writing of feminists of Color. As I will show, some of these mechanisms overlap with those identified in WWK, whereas others—because they arise out of a particular structural experience that interacts with multiple group memberships—do not.

MULTIPLE IDENTITIES

Often when psychologists write about multiple identities, the phenomenon remains undefined. Consequently, for many academics, multiple identities seem akin to schizophrenia or some form of mental illness that further rarefies the experience of women of Color. The fact is that all of us have multiple identities when we make the important distinction between *personal* and *social identity*. Schematically, the difference between social and personal identity follows from the definition of each of these concepts and where is it that we derive meaning for each one of them (see figure on page 374). Tajfel and others posit that *personal identity* is an aspect of self that we think of as being composed of psychological traits and dispositions that give us personal uniqueness, whereas *social identity* consists of those aspects of an individual's self-concept that derive from one's knowledge of being part of categories and groups, together with the value and emotional significance attached to those memberships (Tajfel 1978, 1981; Tajfel & Turner 1979). Social identity by its very nature is derived from society and culture and therefore largely socially constructed and fluid, whereas personal identity is derived from intrapsychic influences, many of which are socialized within family units (however they are defined). From this perspective, we have a great deal in common as human beings precisely because our personal identities comprise certain universal processes such as loving, mating, raising children, and doing productive work. These processes are universal components of the concept of self. Personal identity is much more stable and coherent over time than social identity. Most individuals do not have *multiple personal* identities, nor do their personal identities change from social context to social context. Social identity, on the other hand, is highly variable and susceptible to structural forces like race, class, and gender. Structural forces have such an important influence on the development of social identity precisely because not all social groups are valued equally and not all groups are allocated the same amount of material resources, like education, jobs, and choices for determining one's life. The constriction of choice and opportunity and the ways in which group memberships are used to allocate power and privilege constitute the focus of the work of social psychologists. The differences in value attached to significant group memberships to a large extent determines what access individuals have to knowledge, what is considered knowledge, and ultimately how it is that one comes to perceive oneself as knowledgeable in spite of one's group memberships.

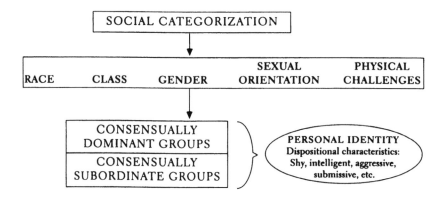

The difference in how social identity and personal identity are constructed

The concept of multiple social identities does not imply that individuals change from extroverts to introverts or that they actually "become another person" but rather that individuals are made accountable to different expectations and behaviors because they belong to certain significant social groups that have been socially categorized in our society into a specific, well-defined set of expectations. Multiple social identities are not problematic if they are not stigmatized. A White professional man can and, in fact, is expected to let his hair down at a football game, act silly, even wear a chicken on his head (if that is the team's mascot) without contradiction when he returns to his judicial bench the next morning. His social identity as a professional is completely congruent with his social identity as a Roosters' fan. According to Tajfel (1981), social identities have real consequences, especially for knowledge production and reception, only when those social identities are stigmatized—that is, when they are used to allocate differential amounts of social and economic power. Therefore, being a woman, being poor, and being Puerto Rican produce conflict that *has to be negotiated,* because we do not value *equally* all those group memberships. Because feminists of Color write from a position of negotiation because of their multiple group memberships, they have particular importance in documenting the maneuvers necessary to obtain and generate knowledge.

Because of the emphasis in this country on a monocultural social and personal identity (although it really has never existed in the United States) and the philosophical and political underpinnings of rugged individualism, the very notion of multiplicity has been conceptualized as deviant or pathological. The dominant paradigm emphasized in mainstream scholarship for understanding "biculturality" is the pain and stress of transition from one "cultural world" to another. In fact, most of us come to terms with more than one social and intellectual world most of the time. Besides *marginality, alienation, acculturation stress,* and so on, feminists of Color have written about the unique knowledge that can be gleaned from the interstices of multiple and stigmatized social identities. That is the essence of this chapter. I choose not to emphasize the pain, struggle, and submission that arise from the difficult task of managing several stigmatized identities. This more typical emphasis inadvertently reinforces the notion that nonconflictual and monocultural social identities are superior and desirable. That is, if being a member of several groups is problematic, then one of the solutions is to abandon one or several of those groups and avoid the pain of multiculturalism. In fact, that is the dominant hegomonic belief about ethnicity in the United States— assimilation into the dominant (often undefined) mainstream is the desired path for ethnically and racially diverse populations. Rather, my focus is on the ways successful individuals deal with the inevitable cognitive transitions that result from multiple group memberships and the ways knowledge is generated within the restrictions defined by these memberships to rise above them, often to offer us unprecedented and brilliant insights—knowledge that could not be generated except from this outsider's perspective (Collins, 1990).

My aim in this chapter is to elaborate how *positionality* (see the chapters by Harding and by Maher and Tetreault in this volume) is manifested in the writings of feminists of Color. The mechanisms I address have been collated from diverse feminists of Color and draw their similarity from these writers' *positions* in society, which result from their stigmatized multiple group memberships. Although postmodern feminists call into question all "universal categories" as "totalizing identities," this is more of a theoretical concern for academics than a practical misrepresentation of the social and structural world in the United States. Postmodern feminists are correct in proclaiming that all identities are socially constructed and therefore the outcome of context-specific relationships. And yet, these social contexts are not independent of a ruthless, relentless, and pervasive social structure that still uses gender, race/ethnicity, class, and sexual orientation (as crude as these categories are) to enforce privilege and subordination, privilege and subordination that are largely mediated through the production and distribution of knowledge. *Successful marginality*, although not without pain, allows for the generation of knowledge that we as a society have systematically eclipsed at the expense of attaining a more complex and just social world.

Writing from diverse disciplines in the humanities, social sciences, and performing arts, feminists of Color of different ethnic/racial origins have articulated several mechanisms as essential to the generation and comprehension of knowledge. In this chapter I examine five of the specific mechanisms that recur in this literature: anger, silence/outspokenness, withdrawal, shifting consciousness, and multiple *lenguas* (tongues).

> Nothing in the world made me angrier than inaction, than silence. The refusal or inability to do something, say something when a thing needed doing or saying, was unbearable. The watchers, the head shakers, the back turners made my skin prickle. (Davis, 1974, pp. 93–94)

ANGER

Children are able to recognize the major social identities of sex, race, ethnicity, and class at different developmental stages. However, they do not necessarily recognize at the same time that certain group memberships are more desirable than others. For example, children are able to recognize whether they are boys or girls at the age of two (a process called *identification* by Gurin, Miller, & Gurin, 1980). They also become aware of their race fairly early in their development, around four years old. The recognition of gender and race happens early for children because both concepts are largely based on concrete physical facts—the implied presence of sex-specific genitalia, in the case of gender (West & Zimmerman, 1987), and skin color and phenotypic attributes, in the case of "race." Not surprisingly, ethnicity is much more difficult for children to recognize and they usually do so much later, between five and ten years of age (Hurtado & García, 1995). Gender, race, and ethnicity *constancy* also has the same developmental sequence: Children know that they will *remain* boys or girls, Black or White earlier than they know that they will *remain* Chicano or Asian regardless of the situation (Knight, Bernal, Garza, & Cota, 1993).

A class identity seems to develop as an integral part of other social identities, mostly race and ethnicity (for example, "African Americans are poor"; "Latinos are poor"), rather than a distinct social identity that is used to assign power, independent of other group memberships. This developmental sequence, not only of the process of identification but more importantly of the stigma attached to certain social identities, leads women of Color to an awareness of how they are derogated because of Color and, later, how that derogation is related to gender. The stigma, which in many ways manifests itself as a direct attack on women of Color, causes many of these women to experience anger very early in life. Audre Lorde (1984), Cherrie Moraga (1981), Gloria Anzaldúa (1987), among others, have given us eloquent testimony that, as children, they discovered the hate reserved for women of Color both in public spaces and within their own families. As Audre Lorde (1984, pp. 147–148) so eloquently states:

> I don't like to talk about the hate. I don't like to remember the cancellation and hatred, heavy as my wished-for-death, seen in the eyes of so many white people from the time I could see. . . . I had not tools to dissect it, no language to name it.
> The AA subway train to Harlem . . . a woman in a fur hat. . . . She jerks her coat closer to her . . . she has communicated her horror to me. . . . When I look up the woman is still staring at me, her nose holes and eyes huge. And suddenly I realize there is nothing crawling up the seat between us: it is me she doesn't want her coat to touch. . . . No word has been spoken. I'm afraid to say anything to my mother because I don't know what I've done. . . . Something's going on here I do not understand, but I will never forget it. Her eyes. The flared nostrils. The hate.

The stigma suffered by women of Color also comes from the restrictions imposed by members of their own group. Gloria Anzaldúa expresses its manifestation since childhood:

At a very early age I had a strong sense of who I was and what I was about and what was fair. I had a stubborn will.... *Terca* [stubborn]. Even as a child I would not obey. I was "lazy." Instead of ironing my younger brothers' shirts or cleaning the cupboards, I would pass many hours studying, reading, painting, writing. Every bit of self-faith I'd painstakingly gathered took a beating daily. Nothing in my culture approved of me. *Había agarrado malos pasos* [I was following the deviant road]. Something was wrong with me. *Estabá más allá de la tradición* [I was beyond tradition]. (Anzaldúa, 1987, p. 16)

When the environment and the state intervene in your everyday life, there develops an intuitive sense of danger that is primarily kept at bay through anger. Putting a "bit" on anger is of primary importance for survival for many women of Color. To "know" logically necessitates, temporarily, through an enormous amount of discipline and grit, the strategic suspension of anger. What privileged White men learn at the university—that all truth is relative—is quickly learned by many women of Color, whose portrayal in different spheres of society never quite "jibes" with their internal reality. Most women of Color know that they are not as valued as most White women, as most White men, and even as much as most men in their ethnic/racial groups. They know that hegemonic standards of beauty and femininity also place them at a disadvantage in relation to most White women. Many women of Color learn that these social evaluations of their stigmatized group memberships are context dependent. As a graduate student recently told me, "I'm either a very beautiful light-skinned African American woman or a mediocre-looking White woman." The nuanced social evaluation of multiple group memberships makes many women of Color "relative knowers"—they understand how knowledge is not fixed and is largely socially and politically constructed. For many women of Color *not* to assume the role of "knower" invites disaster and potential annihilation. "To know" is not the problem; the challenge is "to know what you know" *and* to be able to circumvent the consequences of that knowledge while being true to yourself.

The consistent experience of anger since childhood as a result of group memberships can block as well as facilitate access to knowledge for many women of Color. That is, when anger is not effectively managed, it results in reactance that does not allow many effective use of their talents to access knowledge. When it is effectively used, however, *anger* becomes one of their most effective weapons.

I have confronted these dilemmas about the destructive/productive use of anger in myself. Having grown up in the brutal racial atmosphere of South Texas (which we jokingly referred to as South Africa), I learned early that my mouth was my most powerful weapon. As a child I learned that to survive the most racist and sexist arguments hurled at me—not only by Whites but by men and the authority figures in my own community—meant that I had to develop a "mouth." In my small undergraduate state school I developed such a reputation that professors feared having me in their classes. A usual argument in class started when a professor said that people educated in a language other than their first language would forever be deficient because they could not conceptualize higher-order concepts. So, for example, children who grew up with Spanish in the home (true of about 95 percent of the students sitting in class) and then learned English in school, if asked to sort fruit and vegetables into higher categories, would organize them by color rather than by fruit versus vegetables simply because they were cognitively incapable of doing otherwise. I would then attempt systematically to dismantle this argument, while keeping my anger at the argument's implications in check. For example, I would raise my hand and begin by saying, "How many people in this class started speaking Spanish in the home before they started school?" Usually slightly less than the 95 percent would raise their hands for fear of where this was going. Then I would say, "So did I. So Professor so and so, you are saying that all of us are therefore cognitively deficient and that regardless of how much we achieve we will forever be damaged?" And the response of the professor would usually vary according to how belligerent she or he wanted to be. Some would say, "Yes, that is what the research shows." In which case, I would respond, "So, we are cognitively deficient because we are bilingual and we have achieved so much already, so if we had grown up like you, knowing only one language, imagine what geniuses we would all be!" At this point there would be laughter and I would grin and be quiet for the rest of the class. Whenever I had these kinds of confrontations I would make it a point never to get less than a perfect score in all of my exams. (The fact that I rarely had confrontations with my professors of physical education—which in Texas we were required to take—is what prevented me from getting a perfect 4.0!) The point here is that humor, logic, belligerence, outspokenness, and direct confrontation became absolute prerequisites for survival. These mechanisms were not unique to me, although they are not the mode for women of Color. They are mechanisms of highly successful outliers who stand in strong contrast to what we read about in White feminist theory.

The challenge for me, and perhaps for many other feminists of Color, was to bridle the anger and outspokenness—in a sense to tame it—

because of its potential to destroy the person using it or to harm those who did not deserve to be hurt. My feminist consciousness, unlike that of many White women, was to *tame* my argumentativeness, to be a kind listener, to withhold the sarcasm, not to point to all illogical arguments — even when the speaker was weaker than I was — in other words to become more like a White woman with the characteristics of hegemonic femininity.

The unbridled ferociousness I sometimes see in young women of Color does not often allow itself to be channeled into academic success or effective challenges to institutional oppression (Fordham, 1993). I saw it in a fifteen-year-old Puerto Rican woman standing in line at the ticket counter at the Boston airport on my way back to California from a conference on gender differences held at Radcliffe. She was with two other young women who appeared to be her sisters and each had a small child of her own. An older brother was also with them. Phenotypically they looked African American and they were wearing clothes that are usually associated with inner city youth — baggy jeans, black sweatshirts. The women also wore dark lipstick and eye shadow, large gold hoop earrings, and pulled-back hair. The young woman who appeared to be the one to be taking the trip had a large suitcase, which she wanted to carry on board. The ticket agent refused and she started to argue loudly. The agent kept repeating in a monotonous voice, "I'm sorry, we can't take a suitcase past a certain size." The young woman burst into screams, called her a "bitch," and told the agent she was disrespecting her; the other two women joined and the brother just stood back. As a result of the commotion, the supervisor was called; he tried to reassure her that the ticket agent was treating her fairly and that it was simply a regulation. The young woman would have none of it; she continued to argue her point and outline exactly why she needed to do what she needed to do, and finally the supervisor (a young White male) became exasperated and told her either she complied or she couldn't get on. She told them they were racist fools and that she would go to the gate and figure something out or take another airline.

I was stunned. I admired her passion, her ability not to be corralled in by expectations of propriety, and her ability to argue that other passengers' unreasonable requests are accommodated if they are White or privileged (much of which was true, as exhibited by a very rich family in front of me with thirty pieces of luggage; the woman had just talked the agent into bending regulations to accommodate her special requests). I also felt sad because this courageous, obviously smart, and extremely articulate young woman would probably never have the opportunity to use her verbal and analytical skills to defy authority for the collective good. Indeed, if she had been a White young man from an upper-middle-class background, all of the characteristics she exhibited would probably have led to success in a variety of productive arenas—law, business, politics, to name a few. Even progressive scholars have labeled individuals like this as having "oppositional identities," being "alienated," not having "cultural capital." All of these concepts bypass the thornier issue of which individuals are allowed to act as this young woman did and not be punished but, in fact, rewarded for their reactive behavior. Instead of having an "oppositional identity," they are labeled as being "aggressive," "competitive," "driven," "motivated." The differences in labels for similar behavior escape neither dominant group members nor members of subordinated groups. The awareness of the relativity of merit leads to anger and to intergroup conflict and almost simultaneously to *extreme* intragroup solidarity. For women of Color, the anger they feel much of the time may lead to an exaggerated solidarity with their own ethnic/racial group that blinds them to the abuse they may suffer with men in their own ethnic/racial groups.

Familial and sexual relationships between women of Color and men of Color comprise the area in which feminists of Color have made fewer inroads. A partial explanation is that these writers are not as free to use their very well-honed skills to detect oppression from the men in their groups because intergroup ethnic/racial conflict creates the need for little-questioned solidarity in order to survive. The awareness that all knowledge and self-worth, and most behavior are filtered through unequal power relations based on race makes it difficult to criticize, in productive ways, the internal functioning of the ethnic/racial group even on issues that negatively affect women in these groups, such as sexism, incest, and battery.

Our weapon was the word. (Davis, 1974, p. 80)

SILENCE/OUTSPOKENNESS—TALKING BACK

Throughout *Women's Ways of Knowing* (WWK) is a concern for women's developing their own voices. For women of Color, this is a central concern, which becomes even more complicated because it requires them to develop *multiple voices*. Women of Color have many communities, based on solidarity created by their stigmatized identities, within which

they have to talk. Developing a "voice" is not based on individual assertion or individual identity; it is not even based on an identity solely as a
woman. Many women of Color struggle to develop a voice that is representative of the complexity of all the groups they belong to because,
unlike many middle-class White feminists, they do not wish to reject
their communities of origin. Their struggle is to make congruent all
those "voices" while being true to themselves. Two strategies, silence and
outspokenness, are outlined by many feminists writers of Color to represent the different communities to which many women of Color hold
allegiance.

Silence is a powerful weapon when it can be controlled. It is akin to
camouflaging oneself when at war in an open field; playing possum at
strategic times causes the power of the silent one to be underestimated.
Rollins (1985) and Romero (1992) in their studies of women of Color
who work as maids brilliantly document that more is going on in these
women's minds than their employers ever come to realize. Furthermore,
strategic silence allows the employee to learn about power without the
employer's ever suspecting that he or she is being studied. Henley (1986)
also discusses how White women have learned a great deal about White
men by silently observing them. Unfortunately, the silence has cost many
White women a great deal: In many instances it has cost them their identities and senses of self as human beings because they did not have a strategy for the silence or a political goal for the knowledge they were glean-
ing through their silence (Ostrander, 1984; Hurtado & Stewart, 1996).
Many women of Color use silence with a specific goal in mind and
return to their own safe communities to share what they have learned
and to verify the accuracy of their observations (Hurtado, 1989a). Ultimately, the knowledge obtained by remaining silent is like a reconnais-
sance flight into enemy territory that allows for individual and group survival.

Outspokenness is the complement of the strategy of silence. Knowing
when to talk and just exactly what to say is especially effective if individuals are not expected to talk. It is the surprise attack that has the most
impact. Feminists of Color have written extensively about how they are
more outspoken, or ferociously outspoken, than many White feminists
(Sandoval, 1990). Elsewhere I have argued that it is partly because of the
distance between many feminists of Color and White men (usually the
ones in charge of protecting structural privilege) and partly because of
different socialization patterns that result from class differences (White,
working-class feminists are also more likely not to be as afraid of anger
and/or outspokenness) (Hurtado, 1989b). The result is that feminists of

Color many times violate the notions of hegemonic femininity because of their verbal style. However, the exercise of their verbal abilities allows many of them to test their knowledge, to practice their ideas, and ultimately to sharpen their debating skills in ways that many White feminists advocate for their constituencies.

These two strategies for the acquisition and display of knowledge, silence and outspokenness, are central to understanding how many women of Color negotiate private and public knowledge.

WITHDRAWAL

The structure of social life in communities of Color allows many women in these groups to withdraw to smaller, predominantly female, networks. For men of Color, the segregation of the labor market (Zavella, 1987; Segura, 1986; Pesquera, 1985), marital break-up (Ortíz, 1995), death at a much earlier age, the devastating rate of incarceration, and selective immigration and migration all have trained many women of Color to live without men (Zavella & Cruz Takash, 1993). These structural conditions have allowed them to learn how to withdraw from men without necessarily fearing for their own existence. They also allow for the psychological distance to withdraw from men when tactically it is more efficient to do so. This does not mean that feminists of Color desire relationships with men any less, but that these relationships are less available to them because of structural factors.

The distance from men (Henley, 1986) also allows many women of Color to develop their own sense of authority (Collins, 1991). The harsh economic conditions that many groups of Color have to withstand (Hurtado, 1996) also catapult women in these groups into the public sphere of work, where they are away from the protection of men in their communities and where they have to develop their own resources for survival. In my own family, my first such memories are attached to my paternal grandmother. At the turn of the century she migrated from her rural Mexican village to the city of Tampico and began working at age thirteen in a tortilla factory owned by a wealthy businessman. At the age of fourteen my grandmother Lázara began supporting her family after being abandoned by her own father. My great-grandmother Agustina (her mother) helped by raising pigs and selling them at market. My own mother, separated from my father, left my brother and me with my grandmother, when she came to the United States in 1956 as an undocumented worker. In 1962, she was able to achieve legal status by getting a job as a licensed vocational nurse and at that time brought my brother and me to the United States. She was twenty-eight years old. By the time I was in college in the United States, my grandmother Lázara, now in her sixties, had become a successful entrepreneur by transporting goods from the United States on the bus and taking them to Tampico (a major city six hours from the U.S.–Mexican border) and selling them at a higher price. She had successfully raised five children, had ten grandchildren, owned one of the biggest houses in the neighborhood where she lived all her life, and still did not know how to read or write. My favorite activity as a teenager was to accompany her on shopping trips in the U.S. border town of McAllen, Texas, and have her ask me how much things cost—she couldn't read numbers—and I would say, "Ten dollars" and then, mentally, she would multiply the dollars times the going rate in Mexican *pesos* plus adding the necessary percentage to make a profit. Inevitably she would always do it quicker in her head than I did with a pencil. Although there were many men in our family, when I think of knowledge, skills, and strength, I usually remember the women. Mostly I remember the men as the members of our family whom we, as women, needed to take care of, not as those who protected us. Even my father recognized this. When I received my bachelor of arts degree in 1975, he took my face into his hands as I walked off the stage with my magna cum laude diploma and said, "Now you don't ever have to depend on a man!" He looked the proudest I have ever seen him. Again, these adaptations are not without cost, but rarely have we examined them for the strengths they provide for those women who successfully negotiate their obstacles.

My story is not uncommon among feminist writers of Color (Harris, 1993; Davis, 1974; Anzaldúa, 1987; Moraga, 1981), or even among academically successful women of Color (Gándara, 1994). What is uncommon is the integration of these stories into our feminist theory and method (Hurtado & Stewart, 1996; Harding, this volume).

SHIFTING CONSCIOUSNESS

The notion of shifting consciousness was first fully presented with the benchmark publication of *This Bridge Called My Back* (Moraga & Anzaldúa, 1981). A *shifting consciousness* is the ability of many women of Color to *shift* from one group's perception of social reality to another, and, at times, to be able simultaneously to perceive multiple social realities without losing their sense of self-coherence. *This Bridge Called My*

Back also reflected how the very structure of knowledge generated by a shifting consciousness can be expressed only through mixing and even creating new genres of writing. The book contains essays, poems, short stories, stream-of-consciousness works, and art. The restriction of disciplinary boundaries is abandoned because they do not adequately allow the expression of a shifting consciousness. Inherent in the concept is that women of Color have knowledge for which there is no language or apparatus through which to express their thoughts accurately. Alternatively, in the concept of shifting consciousness is the notion that knowledge not only is cognitive but is derived through overall sensory as well as unconscious and conscious processes. Unlike radical feminists who argue that it is through "women's intuition" versus "men's rationality" that knowledge is obtained, shifting consciousness is more structural and political. Women of Color cannot express their knowledge because it is *subjugated knowledge*—not the central aspect of our language, emotion, or social structures. It is like when an artist tries to express an internal vision previously uncaptured, but, unlike the artist, who at least may have a palette, a piece of charcoal, or a blank canvas, women of Color have *literally* no conceptual instruments. At the same time, they know that the expression of the yearning *in itself* generates thought (hooks, 1990). Audre Lorde (1984, p. 37) tells us that "Poetry is the way we help give name to the nameless so it can be thought," or Elba Sánchez (1992) "gives birth to herself" through the process of dismantling the webs that have previously constrained her consciousness. Chela Sandoval (1991, p. 14) also calls shifting consciousness a "differential consciousness" and makes it akin to an automobile's clutch system that allows an individual to "select, engage, and disengage gears in a system for the transmission of power."

> Por eso necesitamos muchas voces. Porque una sola voz nos mata a las dos. [That's why we need many voices. Because one voice alone kills us both.] (Lugones & Spelman, 1983, p. 573)

MULTIPLE *LENGUAS*

The ability to shift consciousness has also caused women of Color to have multiple voices (or multiple *lenguas* [tongues]) by developing the ability to talk to different audiences without losing a sense of coherence (in WWK known as *contextual relativists*).

Many women of Color are able to be the bridges that connect opposing views because they can see both sides of the argument simultaneously (Moraga & Anzaldúa, 1981; Anzaldúa, 1990; Anzaldúa, 1987; A. P. Harris, 1990; duCille, 1994; C. I. Harris, 1993). In the writings of feminists of Color there is direct advocacy for not granting a privilege to certain views over others or for ranking "truths" into some logical scheme based on how effectively opposing parties can drum up evidence for their point of view. Instead, many feminists of Color see knowledge as *relational* and recognize that what is true in one context is not necessarily true in another (A. P. Harris, 1990; C. I. Harris, 1993). But unlike radical feminists who do not take social structure into their analysis, feminists of Color view knowledge as firmly rooted in the material conditions of life (hooks, 1984; Davis, 1981). Simultaneously, however, they refuse to objectify those in power but rather see them as part of a system of oppression that persists regardless of the individual players (Anzaldúa, 1987). Furthermore, feminists of Color believe in redemption—the ability of individuals to be educated and change to become more humane regardless of their group memberships (hooks & West, 1991).

CONCLUSIONS: TEACHING TO TRANSGRESS

In *Teaching to Transgress*, bell hooks (1994) reminds us that the transmission of knowledge can be revolutionary. Here, too, feminists of Color have made an enormous theoretical contribution to how and to what purpose we transmit knowledge. One contribution has been the democratization of the teaching process—that previously derogated groups are holders of knowledge that do not fit our traditional paradigms and that these individuals have a right to be an integral part of how they want to use knowledge (Gutiérrez, 1990). From this perspective, knowledge is more participatory and collective.

WWK's discussion of knowledge is divided into five major epistemological categories: *silence, received knowledge, subjective knowledge, procedural knowledge,* and *constructed knowledge.* Although women of Color swim in and out of this epistemological scheme, there is a sixth dimension that may be called *subjugated knowledge,* which is their second important contribution to our understanding of how we acquire and use knowledge. *Subjugated knowledge* is knowledge that is temporarily suspended or subjugated to resist structures of oppression and to create interstices of rebellion and potential revolution. It is often referred to as a "border consciousness" or as existing in the "limen"—the in-between and betwixt existence (Lugones, 1992; Moraga & Anzaldúa, 1981;

Anzaldúa, 1987) that multiple stigmatized identities create. Successful negotiators use the limen to gain even a deeper truth than is available through intuition or logic. Successful negotiators avoid the bifurcation (the either/or of intuition or logic) that has been documented in the psychological literature as being the cornerstone of the differences between women and men. Feminists of Color, however, added other dimensions to the bifurcation based on sex because of their stigmatized group memberships. When the explanations for differences in learning styles are largely based on sex, they lend themselves to an essentialist explanation of "difference" as biologically based. The statement "Biology is destiny" has no actors but instead is a "natural" unfolding of predetermined, unchangeable biological mechanisms. There is also an implied benevolence in the statement because, if certain people are "naturally" weaker (women), then the "stronger" people (men) should take care of them. Biological essentialist explanations bypass the political nature of creating group "differences" especially because other group memberships than sex are more difficult to prove scientifically to be solely the outcome of biological differences (for example, race and class—especially class in the United States, which prides itself on complete class mobility based on individual merit, Haney & Hurtado, 1994).

Most feminists of Color have circumvented the nature-versus-nurture debate and have proclaimed the social construction of group memberships as solely based on the enforcement of political power (C. I. Harris, 1993). Therefore, all knowledge is political, and, from this assertion, the generation of counterknowledge is a political act. Feminists of Color refer to the transmission of knowledge to create resistance as *tactical subjectivity* (Sandoval, 1991, p. 14)—that is, the ability of many women of Color to "recenter depending upon the kinds of oppression to be confronted" (Sandoval, 1991, p. 14). Similarly, other feminists of Color refer to *tactical subjectivity* as being akin to guerrilla warfare, where the transmission and expression of knowledge is not codified but learned through everyday battle with the state apparatus (Hurtado, 1989a; Moraga, 1981). Moraga (1981, p. xix) clearly states the reflexive nature of this kind of knowledge where each social interaction requires the assessment of what is said, to whom, and how it is said. Every tactical judgment involves risk because each interaction requires assessment of who can be an ally, a friend, or an enemy regardless of a person's skin color, sex, or sexuality. The transmission and use of knowledge, therefore, are not neutral, as a male Western tradition has claimed historically, nor are they bifurcated by sex differences between women and men, but instead, the creation and use of knowledge are political acts. It is the use of knowledge that has replaced the everyday use of force (exclusively) to create social, economic, and political hierarchies. Feminists of Color, together with White feminists, have made revolutionary inroads toward the deconstruction of our man-made (Spender, 1980) categories, ones that serve to mystify the basis of knowing and the status of "knower," and prevent the dismantling of existing knowledge-based privilege.

REFERENCES

Anzaldúa, G. (1987). *Borderlands/La frontera: The new mestiza.* San Francisco: Spinsters/Aunt Lute.

Anzaldúa, G. (1990). *Making face, making soul/Haciendo caras: Creative and critical perspectives by women of Color.* San Francisco: Aunt Lute.

Belenky, M. F., McVicker, B., Goldberger, N. R., & Tarule, J. M. (1986). *Women's ways of knowing: The development of self, voice, and mind.* New York: Basic Books.

Bem, S. L., & Bem, D. J. (1984). Homogenizing the American woman: The power of an unconscious ideology. In A. M. Jaggar & P. Rothenburg Struhl (Eds.), *Feminist frameworks* (2d ed.), 6–28. New York: McGraw-Hill.

Collins, P. H. (1986). Learning from the outsider within: The sociological significance of black feminist thought. *Social Problems, 33* (6), 14–32.

Collins, P. H. (1989). The social construction of black feminist thought. *Signs: Journal of Women in Culture and Society, 14* (4), 745–773.

Collins, P. H. (1990). *Black feminist thought: Knowledge, consciousness, and the politics of empowerment.* New York: Routledge.

Davis, A. Y. (1974). *With my mind on freedom: An autobiography.* New York: Bantam.

Davis, A. Y. (1981). *Women, race and class.* New York: Random House.

DuBois, E., Dunlap, M., Gilligan, C., MacKinnon, C. & Menkel-Meadow, C. (1985). Feminist discourse, moral values, and the law—a conversation. *Buffalo Law Review, 34,* 11–87.

duCille, A. (1994). The occult of true black womanhood: Critical demeanor and black feminist studies. *Signs: Journal of Women in Culture and Society, 19,* 591–629.

Fordham, S. (1993). Those loud black girls—(black) women, silence, and gender passing in the academy. *Anthropology and Education Quarterly, 24* (1), 3–32.

Gándara, P. (1994). Chicana high achievers across two generations: A working paper. In A. Hurtado & E. E. García (Eds.), *The educational achievement of Latinos: Barriers and successes,* 121–147. Santa Cruz, CA: University of California, Santa Cruz, Latino Eligibility Study.

Gurin. P., Miller, H., & Gurin, G. (1980). Stratum identification and consciousness. *Social Psychology Quarterly, 43,* 30–47.

Gutiérrez, L. M. (1990). Working with women of color: An empowerment perspective. *Social Work,* 149–153.

Haney, C., & Hurtado, A. (1994). The jurisprudence of race and meritocracy: Standardized testing and "race-neutral" racism in the workplace. *Law and Human Behavior, 18* (3), 223–248.

Harris, A. P. (1990). Race and essentialism in feminist legal theory. *Stanford Law Review, 42,* 581–616.

Harris, C. I. (1993). Whiteness as property. *Harvard Law Review, 106* (8), 1709–1791.

Henley, N. (1986). *Body politics: Power, sex, and nonverbal communication.* New York: Simon & Schuster.

hooks, b. (1984). *Feminist theory from margin to center.* Boston: South End Press.

hooks, b. (1990). *Yearning: Race, gender, and cultural politics.* Boston: South End Press.

hooks, b. (1994). *Teaching to transgress: Education as the practice of freedom.* New York: Routledge.

hooks, b., & West, C. (1991). *Breaking bread: Insurgent black intellectual life.* Boston: South End Press.

Hurtado, A. (1989b). Relating to privilege: Seduction and rejection in the subordination of white women and women of color. *Signs, 14* (4), 833–855.

Hurtado, A. (1989a). Reflections on white feminism: A perspective from a woman of color. In S. Chan (Ed.), *Social and gender boundaries in the United States,* 155–186. Lewiston, NY: The Edwin Mellen Press.

Hurtado, A. (1996). *The color of privilege: Three blasphemies on race and feminism.* Ann Arbor: University of Michigan Press.

Hurtado, A., & García, E. E. (1995). Becoming American: A review of current research on the development of racial and ethnic identity in children. In A. Jackson & W. B. Hawley (Eds.), *Towards a common destiny: Improving race and ethnic relations in America,* 163–184. San Francisco: Jossey-Bass.

Hurtado, A., & Stewart, A. (in press). Through the looking glass: Implications of studying whiteness for feminists methods. In M. Fine, L. Powell, L. Weis, & M. Wong (Eds.), *Off white: Readings on society, race and culture.* New York: Routledge.

Knight, G. P., Bernal, M. E., Garza, C. A., & Cota, M. K. (1993). A social cognitive model of the development of ethnic identity and ethnically based behaviors. In M. E. Bernal, & G. P. Knight (Eds.), *Ethnic identity: Formation and transmission among Hispanics and other minorities,* 213–234. Albany: State University of New York Press.

Lorde, Audre. (1984). *Sister outsider.* Trumansburg, NY: Crossing Press.

Lugones, M. C. (1992). *Structure/antistructure and agency under oppression.* Unpublished Manuscript, Carleton College.

Lugones, M. C., & Spelman, E. V. (1983). Have we got a theory for you! Feminist theory, cultural imperialism and the demand for the "woman's voice." *Women's Studies International Forum, 6* (6), 573–581.

Moraga, C. (1981). La guerra. In C. Moraga & G. Anzaldúa (Eds.), *This bridge called my back: Writings by radical women of Color,* 27–34. Watertown, MA: Persephone Press.

Moraga, C., & Anzaldúa, G. (Eds.) (1981). *This bridge called my back: Writings by radical women of Color.* Watertown, MA: Persephone Press.

Ortíz, V. (1995). The diversity of Latino families. In R. E. Zambrana (Ed.), *Understanding Latino families: Scholarship, policy, and practice,* 18–39). Thousand Oakes, CA: Sage.

Ostrander, S. (1984). *Women of the upper class.* Philadelphia: Temple University Press.

Pesquera, B. (1985). *Work and family: A comparative analysis of professional clerical, and blue-collar Chicana workers.* Unpublished doctoral dissertation, University of California, Berkeley.

Rollins, J. (1985). *Between women: Domestics and their employers.* Philadelphia: Temple University Press.

Romero, M. (1992). *Maid in the U.S.A.* New York: Routledge.

Sánchez, E. (1992). *Tallos de luna/moon shoots.* Santa Cruz, CA: Moving Arts Press.

Sandoval, C. (1981). Feminism and racism: A report on the 1981 National Women's Studies Association Conference. In G. Anzaldúa (Ed.), *Making face, making soul/Haciendo caras: Creative and critical perspectives by women of color,* 55–71. San Francisco: Aunt Lute.

Sandoval, C. (1991). U. S. third world feminism: The theory and method of oppositional consciousness in the postmodern world. *Genders, 10,* 1–24.

Segura, D. (1986). *Chicanas and Mexican immigrant women in the labor market: A study of occupational mobility and stratification.* Unpublished doctoral dissertation, University of California, Berkeley.

Spender, D. (1980). *Man made language.* London: Routledge, Chapman & Hall.

Tajfel, H. (1978). *Differentiation between social groups: Studies in the social psychology of intergroup relations.* London: Academic Press, European Monographs in Social Psychology.

Tajfel, H. (1981). *Human groups and social categories: Studies in social psychology.* London: Cambridge University Press.

Tajfel, H., & Turner, J. (1979). An integrative theory of intergroup conflict. In W. G. Austin & S. Worchel (Eds.), *The social psychology of intergroup relations,* 33–47. Pacific Grove, CA: Brooks/Cole.

West, C., & Zimmerman, D. H. (1987). Doing gender. *Gender and Society, 1* (2): 125–151.

Zavella, P. (1987). *Women's work and Chicano families: Cannery workers of the Santa Clara Valley.* Ithaca, NY: Cornell University Press.

Zavella, P., & Cruz Takash, P. (1993). Gender and power: Reconstructing Latino ethnography. *Urban Anthropology, 22* (3–4), 231–236.

Public Homeplaces

Nurturing the Development of People, Families, and Communities*

MARY FIELD BELENKY

ALL THE WHILE Blythe Clinchy, Nancy Goldberger, Jill Tarule, and I were working on *Women's Ways of Knowing* (WWK) I kept thinking about the women we had interviewed who did not think they could think. One question kept presenting itself to me: Is it possible to support such women to become active thinkers, consciously cultivating the power of their minds to confront and solve the problems facing them, their families, and their communities? The question seemed urgent as these women were often quite voiceless in the face of many inequities and the most demeaning life circumstances.

Of the five ways of knowing described in WWK, only the outlooks we called Silenced and Received Knowledge were held by people who had little conscious awareness that human beings can and do construct

*As always, my thinking and writing for this chapter developed in conversations with patient friends who read draft after draft and shared their thoughts with me. The long list includes Blythe Clinchy, Nancy Goldberger, Jill Tarule, Lynne Bond, Jackie Weinstock, Larry Parks Daloz, William Gamson, Zelda Gamson, Anita Landa, Sharon Daloz Parks, and Ann Stanton. Undoubtedly Bob Belenky has been the most forbearing of all.

393

knowledge by reflecting on experience.[1] Women who held the Received Knowledge perspective, for instance, believed they can only get knowledge from listening to authorities. They presume that everyone else, even the authorities, also learn this way. Needless to say, this way of knowing is very likely to be reinforced by authorities who believe people ought to take directions from others and remain in subordinated positions. The Silenced see words more as weapons than as a means of passing meanings back and forth between people. They do not believe themselves capable of understanding and remembering what the authorities or anyone else might say to them; they do not feel capable of articulating their own thoughts and feelings to others. A woman we interviewed linked the problem with the battering she received from a man for ten long years:

> You know, I used to hear only his words, and his words kept coming out of my mouth. He had me thinking that I did not know anything. But now, you know, I realize I'm not so dumb. . . . My own words are coming out of my mouth now. (Belenky, Clinchy, Goldberger, & Tarule, 1986, p. 30)

Without the most basic tools for dialogue the Silenced feel voiceless and excluded from the social life of their community.

The women we interviewed who operated out of the Silenced and Received Knowers perspectives had somewhat similar backgrounds. More often than not, they had grown up in poverty. They and their families were often stigmatized by stereotypes that marked them as different and deficient. All described their families as hierarchically organized; their parents as highly authoritative, if not authoritarian. The women we called Silenced were living especially isolated lives amid a great deal of violence. Undoubtedly, some of these patterns were a function of the fact that the women with minimal educations came into the WWK sample through social agencies serving clinical populations. If we had reached women with little formal education through other means we could have seen very different life circumstances associated with these epistemological frameworks.

THE INVISIBLE COLLEGES

All of the Silenced, most of the Received Knowers, and a few Subjective Knowers entered the study sample through one of the three social agencies serving mothers of young children living in rural poverty. We named these programs the "invisible colleges" to distinguish them from the degree-granting institutions we studied. One program paired teenage mothers with a volunteer, another mother close in age, who would serve as a mentor. The second was a local chapter of a national self-help network for parents working to overcome a history of child abuse and family violence. A children's health program that saw the support of mothers as central to the health care of children was the third.

The invisible colleges were, for the most part, women-led organizations designed for women by women. We thought that the inclusion of social institutions shaped by women who held the perspectives and values of women in the highest regard might help us see what is typically left out of institutions founded and run by men. We were also interested in the invisible colleges as they were reaching out to poor mothers—one of the more isolated, unsupported, and demeaned groups in contemporary society. We thought that their inclusion in a study of women attending degree-granting colleges would broaden our vision. Indeed, it did.

For one, the interviews we conducted suggested that the invisible colleges were enabling many marginalized women to gain a voice, claim the powers of their minds, and begin democratizing their families. Excited by that, I went back and reinterviewed some of these women several more times—although that was not part of the original research agenda. I thought that by continuing the conversation I could understand more about the paths that were leading young mothers out of silence, and how the staff and programs at the invisible colleges were facilitating this progress.

In one way or another, the mothers kept saying that the invisible colleges were making a difference because the people involved regularly drew each other out and listened to one another with care and respect. Relationships there were consistently characterized by dialogue, reciprocity, and mutuality. Most of the "faculty" provided excellent examples of what we described in WWK as connected teaching. Connected teachers, we argued, used the skills of connected knowing to enter into the perspectives of their students to view the world through their eyes, with the hope of understanding each in his or her own terms. Like midwives, connected teachers worked to draw out their students' fledgling thoughts and foster the growth of their ideas. They focused their attentions on a person's strengths and mirrored what they saw. By naming and celebrating the strong points, they helped the women become more aware of what was already in place to build on. In WWK we called practices like these "playing the believing game" (Elbow, 1970). When a woman's thinking seemed partial or contradictory, the connected midwife teacher would struggle especially hard to take her perspective, trying to imagine why she might think that way. Such an effort requires a kind of empathic role taking that would be greatly hampered if one were to point out the contradictions and correct the errors in the woman's thinking. Because the faculty of these invisible colleges often attained such a good sense of these women, their experience of the world, and their dreams for the future, they were able to join them at the places where they were starting out.

The invisible colleges also stressed other practices common to most self-help or mutual aid groups. Individuals were supported in their personal development *and* were expected to support the development of others. Helping others was clearly an empowering experience for women with a long history of feeling dependent and helpless.

All of the invisible colleges sponsored ongoing discussion groups where the women could talk with one another as equals about the problems facing them and their families. Being one among equals was a watershed experience for most. All too often they had been confined to the bottommost rungs of one social hierarchy or another. In these discussion groups the women helped each other develop an analysis of their situation, solve problems, and imagine alternative ways to live. They often spoke of their amazement that others were coping with similar problems. This was of the greatest importance to the women; it suggested that many of their problems were a function of the social arrangements that devalued and excluded women (especially mothers) and the poor. Previously, the women assumed the difficulties they faced were due to their personal inadequacies—a paralyzing assumption that left most without a sense of hope.

As I read and reread the women's interviews and thought about the time I spent talking with them and their children I made several observations. The invisible colleges seemed to be enabling women to claim their powers of mind, and this could be documented by tracing changes in their ways of knowing. Women who had a better sense of the power of their own minds seemed more likely to think of their children as active, thinking people who struggle to make better meaning of their experience in the world and better life choices. These women influenced their children's behavior by engaging them in reflective dialogue, drawing out their problem-solving abilities. By contrast, the women who did not see themselves as thinkers seemed much less aware of their children's thinking processes. They relied almost exclusively on authoritarian, power-oriented child-rearing techniques. Many were in relationships with men who used similar techniques on them. If these observations were correct—that invisible colleges and connected midwife teachers do empower women to gain a voice and claim the powers of mind—these programs might well lead to more democratic families and the ripple effect will be felt down through the generations.

THE LISTENING PARTNERS STUDY

As the WWK project drew to a close I began looking for a community of colleagues near my Vermont home who would help me explore these issues. I soon teamed up with Lynne A. Bond at the University of Vermont. She is a developmental psychologist who had already instituted a range of projects enabling families and educators to support children to become more active constructors of knowledge.

Lynne seemed to have the deepest understanding of the ideas I was groping toward. I now believe I understand why. Although she had attended the requisite number of degree-granting colleges and universities, she grew up in an invisible college. Both of her parents had been leaders in the Settlement House movement, a national network of invisible colleges for new immigrants and other inner city dwellers. This movement had been set in motion by Jane Addams at the beginning of our century (Addams, 1910; Seigfried, 1996). (For an important intellectual history comparing Addams's work with that of the social scientists who gained control over the academy, see Deegan, 1978.) Like her contemporary John Dewey (1916), Addams was confident in the ability of ordinary men and women to participate in the democratic process. Addams and Dewey both saw education based on involvement in the democratic process as a form of liberation. When people take responsibility for governing themselves and their communities they learn to understand complex issues, to articulate their dreams, and to back up their positions well; the society becomes more life-enhancing and more democratic. Addams thought that dramatic alterations in American society could be accomplished by providing a meeting place where two very different groups—highly educated women and impoverished immigrants—could bridge their differences and grapple together with the problems facing them and their city. Both groups were extremely marginal to the political process at that time: women could not vote and immigrants were facing the devastating effects of industrialization and urbanization in a strange and unwelcoming society. Addams picked one of the most stressed areas in the city of Chicago and built a place she called Hull House. The women moved in and opened the doors of their home to the immigrants living in the neighborhood. Both groups worked together studying the problems facing their community; they made and presented art that reflected on and communicated the condition of their lives. Social science action research, theater, music, and fiction writing all thrived at Hull House. A museum was built to display the immigrants' traditional crafts and honor the arts and industries the people had developed in the Old World.

Together Lynne and I designed an invisible college for isolated mothers with preschool-aged children living in rural Vermont, not far from the Canadian border. The area had extremely high rates of poverty and social disorganization because of the precipitous decline of family farms and an agrarian way of life. We called the project "Listening Partners" to highlight the qualities of dialogue, reciprocity, and mutuality we thought essential for supporting the development of silenced and marginalized women. We framed the project with a rather elaborate research component to see (1) whether the program could enable women to develop more complex ways of knowing and (2) whether a woman's ways of knowing are related to her conception of her child as a knower and to her child-rearing practices.

Lynne and I were joined by Jackie Weinstock, who was beginning her doctoral work at the University of Vermont in developmental psychology. As an undergraduate, Jackie had conducted a number of research studies using William Perry's scheme of intellectual and ethical development (a theoretical framework that had provided a starting place for the WWK study). Jackie wanted to pursue this line of research and had a strong commitment to the project's overall goals. She would work on all aspects of the research process.[2] Ann Dunn, Jean Lathrop, and Laura Latham Smith joined the Listening Partners staff as discussion group facilitators. All three had been involved in developing and running some sort of invisible college for people living at the margins of society. All were skilled at connected midwife teaching. We located the project at the Lamoille Family Center, sensing that this woman-run organization would feel comfortable to the isolated women we hoped would join the project. At the time, the Family Center was being run on a shoestring out of a dingy village storefront located in the middle of the rural area we wanted to serve. It was a lowkey, nonbureaucratic operation that stressed prevention, self-help, and mutual aid. It felt like an invisible college. (For more complete accounts of the Listening Partners project see Belenky, Bond, & Weinstock, in press; Bond, Belenky, & Weinstock, 1991; Bond, Belenky, Weinstock & Cook, 1996).

We invited low-income, isolated mothers of preschool children living in the area to meet in small discussion groups of twelve or so (including two group facilitators) one morning a week over an eight-month period. We provided transportation and a play group for the children. Although we stressed many of the values and practices emphasized by the midwife teachers from the invisible colleges there were a number of differences. We focused more intentionally and intently on the participants' ways of knowing than did the staff of these other programs. We also taught problem-solving skills building on the work of Shure and Spivack (1978). We encouraged women to look at the problems they were facing as challenges to be worked out over long periods, as their concerns were usually complex and not amenable to quick fixes. We supported them to work collaboratively whenever possible, as many of the issues they were working on were shared problems. We tried to think of these projects as experiments that could be revised and repeated. If something did not work, we would go back to the drawing board (for a fuller description of the problem-solving approach see Rogoff, 1990).

We made a special effort to document and mirror the women's words, especially when they spoke of strengths, successes, and problems solved. Most of the women were remarkably unaware of their strengths and perceived all their weaknesses and failures (real and imagined) in the greatest detail. As we tape-recorded all of the weekly meetings we could transcribe and edit the tapes whenever we saw someone breaking through to new ground. In this way we created quite an extensive collection of "growth stories" that we would then take to the group for further discussion, reflection, and, of course, celebration of the breakthrough. A dramatic illustration of the growth stories we documented is provided by a painful account contrasting a participant's response to two different rapes:

I Sat and Figured It Out on My Own:
It Took a Lot of Understanding

Then I was raped again, by another man. Again I couldn't talk to anybody. I felt like I was used, like a piece of trash that was thrown away.

But I had really changed. This time I went back and faced him. I went down there to ask him why he done it. He told me that I had asked for it. I said, "Don't tell me this bullshit!! I was sound asleep!!"

I didn't have a counselor that told me how to do this. I sat and figured it out on my own. I went and did it on my own.

The way I faced it myself was this. I sat alone in a room with no one around. I listened to music. The only one that was there was my dog. She was always a comfort to me. It took a lot of facing. It took a lot of understanding to understand what had happened to me and why it happened. I didn't ask for it. It was nothing that should have ever happened.

He never touched me again. He put me down, but he didn't win. He respects me to this day as a person.

The author of this story considered at length the mistreatment she had suffered from a person who held considerable power over her. She determined in her own mind that he was wrong and that she herself had done nothing to cause this behavior. She presented him with her judgment and asked him to account for himself. When he tried to put the blame back on her, she backed up her arguments with facts he could not dispute. The man accepted her judgment and altered his subsequent behavior.

On hearing this story we realized this was the first time we were aware that the author saw herself as a person who could create new knowledge by reflecting on her own experience. This achievement is emphasized by the title we chose from a line embedded in the story.

All too often people at the margins see themselves only as they are reflected in the negative stereotypes. By carefully documenting the women's strengths we encouraged them to see themselves and their potential in a new light. As the women discussed and reflected on a number of these "growth stories," they began recognizing and naming other strengths, strategies, and accomplishments that had previously gone unnoticed. The process of meticulous naming of what had gone unnamed was arduous, challenging, and exciting to all of us. Sometimes we left these meetings feeling we had unearthed some amazing truths.

The project's research component allowed us to assess the effectiveness of activities like these for promoting the women's development; it also enabled us to investigate the relationship between their ways of knowing and their parenting. One hundred and twenty women participated over a period of two years. Half joined the weekly discussion group meetings for eight months; the other half were followed as a comparison sample. We interviewed the women when they entered the project and at the conclusion of the weekly peer-group sessions. We conducted a third round of interviews almost a year later to see whether any effects were long-lasting. Among other things, the transcribed interviews assessed the women's ways of knowing, their conceptions of friendships, their conceptions of their child as a knower, and their philosophy of child rearing.

Almost 80 percent of the women were utilizing the frameworks of Silenced and/or Received Knowledge almost exclusively when they entered the project. Comparing the participants' and the nonparticipants' ways of knowing at the three different periods, we concluded that it was indeed possible to create environments that sponsor women in gaining a voice and claiming their powers of mind. These gains were the greatest for those who entered the program with the least awareness of their intellectual powers. The gap between the participants' and nonparticipants' performances on many of the measures used continued to grow in the postprogram period. This was strong evidence that the participants' increased capacity for self-reflection, dialogue, and making friends had provided the women with the "motor" and "tools" for continued development.

The research interviews also demonstrated that the women who saw themselves as active thinkers who learn from dialogue and reflection on their own experiences were more likely to imagine their children as having these abilities. These women were more likely to teach their children by engaging them in dialogues that encouraged active reflection by everyone. The women who did not think of themselves as thinkers were more likely to rely on authoritarian, power-oriented child-rearing practices.

A woman we will call Rachel illustrates the changes that can occur in the life of a person who decides she has the right to use the power of her good mind. This is how Rachel responded to some of our questions when she first joined the project:

Can you think of a time when you had to make a decision, but you just weren't sure what was right?

I don't know. [long pause]

A big decision. It could be recent, it could be anytime in the past.

Hmmm, I don't know. [long pause]

Did leaving school seem like a big decision?

No, not really.

It just sort of happened?

Yea.

Did having your daughter seem like a big decision?

No. [laughs] Because it wasn't a decision, it just happened.

What about moving in with your boyfriend?

Uh-huh. We've been together for over three years; it will be four years.

Was that a decision?

No. [both laugh]

Well, that's interesting! What's your life going to be like in the future, say a year from now?

I don't know for sure. I don't like to think about things. I don't expect anything to change.

At the time of this first interview, Rachel was highly accomplished as a Received Knower. That is, she thought that listening to authorities was *the only* way one could acquire knowledge ("How can you learn if the teacher isn't telling you?"). Rachel knew she was smart because she had found it easy to remember what the teachers were telling her and could answer their questions quickly, succinctly, and correctly.

Even so, Rachel was incapacitated as a knower when we first knew her. Not only was she unaware of her abilities to gather knowledge from reflecting on her own experiences in the world, she did not think she had a "right" to be smart. Conforming to the social norms of her rural community that presume females will subordinate themselves to males and the poor are less able than the well heeled, Rachel had done what she could to disconnect herself from the power of her own good mind. As a child she had been an outstanding student in her small rural school. As she approached adolescence she was feeling increasingly "out of place" as "a really smart person." Generally her accomplishments made her feel disloyal to her nonachieving friends—a problem common to children of the underclass in black ghettos and elsewhere (see Goldberger, this volume). Rachel "solved" the problem by dropping out of school. She was thirteen years of age.

By the time Rachel finished the Listening Partners project it was abundantly clear to her that (1) she was smart, (2) she had as much right as anyone else in the world to use the power of her good mind, and (3) that listening to the words of authorities was only one way of gathering knowledge. Rachel had become a full participant in a community of women who were constantly reflecting on their own experiences in the world, discussing and comparing their emerging ideas and insights. Together the women came up with a whole range of understandings they could never have achieved simply by listening to authorities.

The impact that these changes had on Rachel is reflected in her second interview almost a year later:

Okay, Rachel, how would you describe yourself to yourself?

[laughs] Ah, more ambitious. Very confident.

More confident, mmm-hmmm.

More confident in when I'm speaking. Yeah . . . I speak up more than what I used to. I'm more open and tell what I feel and [long pause].. . . Like it has been nothing but a battle with my boyfriend.

Describe it.

I tell him what I want from him, . . . what I want and what I feel and what I expect from him. . . . Asking him to move out was an important decision for me. I had to make him realize that I wasn't going to live that kind of life with him if he kept up the drinking. I gained a lot of confidence in myself and was able to do something for myself, get something going so I could have a career. . . . I have changed. I have a better outlook on life. Knowing what I want out of life. What I want to do. I've made a lot of decisions and I'm going to go through with them. I had to figure out how I wanted to live my life.

When women like Rachel begin to realize that they have a mind of their own and can learn from their experience, insight, and intuition they exude images of liberation, rebirth, agency, and self-direction. They can question the authorities (and anyone else) who would have them believe they have neither the right nor the capacity to think for themselves. When the Rachels of this world understand they have the capacity and the right to have a say in the running of their own lives, they begin solving the many problems that have buffeted them and their families at every turn.

THE PUBLIC HOMEPLACE STUDY

As we talked with people around the country about the Listening Partners project they told us of other projects sponsored by women that were bringing an excluded group into voice. It seemed that a study of such ongoing organizations could reveal important factors about empowerment of people that could not be understood from an experimental design and a short-term project like ours. I was particularly drawn to several of these organizations. Although they were similar to Listening Partners in many ways, there were important differences. They were ongoing projects that had been evolving for twenty years or more, whereas Listening Partners was a short-term experiment. They also supported their members to develop a public voice, that is, to cultivate a commitment to the common good, a critical stance toward social arrangements

that keep people silenced and isolated. (For discussion of public dialogue see Tarule's and Harding's chapters, this volume. For a full
account of the Public Homeplace study see Belenky, Bond, & Weinstock, in press.)

I chose four of these organizations to study. Two of them, the Mothers' Centers movements in Germany and the United States, had nearly
identical names and missions but were formed independently. In both
countries women decided to do something about the isolation and devaluation they were experiencing as mothers. Both movements developed a
national network of Mothers' Centers where women from different walks
of life could meet on a regular basis, supporting each other's efforts for
making public spaces more responsive to the needs of women, children,
and families.

A seed was planted for the third organization I observed, National
Congress of Neighborhood Women, when an interracial, intercultural
grass-roots group of women began dealing with the problems plaguing
their divided and declining urban neighborhood in Brooklyn, New York.
Neighborhood women went on to build a wide variety of programs
including one of the first shelters for battered women in the state of New
York, a child care program, and a center for the elderly. When the
women realized that few of them had the credentials to fill the jobs they
were developing they created a college program located in the neighborhood and focused the curriculum on the rejuvenation of urban communities. Using their local project as a model for continued experimentation, the neighborhood women teamed up with grass-roots women
around the country engaged in similar efforts. This culturally and racially
diverse group of women formed the National Congress of Neighborhood
Women to support the leadership of women who struggle to make their
communities more responsive to the needs of women, families, and children. They are now extending this network to include women leaders
from developing countries around the globe.

The fourth organization—Center for Cultural and Community
Development (CCCD)—grew out of the work of African American
women from the deep South who call themselves "cultural workers."
Since the middle passage and slavery times black women have been cultivating a style of leadership dedicated to drawing out and uplifting the
community. Such leadership has enabled many generations of African
Americans to overcome the devastation inflicted by the dominant group
(Payne, 1995). The cultural workers look to the traditions passed down to
them by their foremothers as they cultivate their leadership promoting
the development of people and their communities. They work with the

community to cultivate other arts and traditions of the African diaspora that strengthen and uplift.

The cultural workers went on to establish the Center for Cultural and Community Development as a national network to support local leaders from different cultural groups around the country who sponsor the development of people and communities denigrated and excluded by the larger society.

I interviewed the founders of these four programs and spent a good deal of time with their organizations to see how their philosophies were being played out in action. I interviewed people who were involved in the earliest phases of the organizations as well as many of the current participants. Comparing the experiences of the founding and the current members, we could see a remarkable continuity and stability of goals and practices in all of the organizations over a twenty-year span.

I could sense that these highly diverse organizations had many things in common even though they were on the surface so different. If there were commonalities that could be named and studied, we might learn a lot about the kinds of social institutions that actually sponsor people to develop themselves as individuals committed to the common good.

At first I was so aware of the marked differences between the organizations I despaired of ever seeing the similarities. Interestingly, the commonalities began to emerge with particular clarity when I began attending to the metaphors the women used to describe their goals, organizations, and approaches to leadership. "Voice," for instance, was the overriding metaphor they used to describe their organizations' most basic goal: to draw out the voices of an excluded group of people. They shared a conviction that all the voices must be heard if we are ever to build a more democratic and caring society (for a discussion of the importance of voice as an organizing metaphor for people at the margins see Reinhartz, 1994).

These organizations had many concrete structural features in common as well. All were initiated by women about twenty years ago with a very successful local project that seemed well worth developing as a model for bringing people into voice. Each group continued to work year after year to improve and extend its model, gathering more and more people as they went along. The groups' leaders became increasingly skilled at articulating the philosophy and practices that had enabled each of them to create nurturing public spaces. Each organization went on to build a national network providing a mutual support system for people around the country working on similar projects in their local communities. Members from each organizations now travel the world, establishing international networks with people doing similar work in Europe and the Third World.

By conventional standards, none of these organizations would be considered a success. They are small, in terms of the numbers of people involved. With the exception of the German Mother Centers, all are chronically starved for funds. (European governments—unlike ours—provide high levels of financial and program support for families, as it is assumed that the development of children is as important to the nation as the development of industry, roads, and the military.)

Although these organizations are well known within very limited circles, outside these circles they are largely ignored or misunderstood. There are many reasons why these organizations are largely invisible to traditional leaders, the media, funding agencies, and the general public. None of them has the clearly and narrowly defined objectives, target populations, and lines of authority that are the mark of organizational success in the minds of many. Organizations that are always evolving to meet the changing needs of developing people and communities can seem nebulous to anyone who does not appreciate a developmental perspective.

People discount the women when they say their organizations are run largely by grass-roots people. There are several causes of this disbelief. Organizations that successfully support people from the margins to develop a high level of competence are caught in a catch-22 situation. Social and economic status and intellectual performance are so strongly linked in our society, some do not think it is possible that people who function at a high level could have originated from the bottom rungs of society. Others assume that whatever a person's roots are, once a person does become educated and accomplished he or she is a part of the middle class, even if the person maintains an identity as a member of the poor and working classes. Upward social mobility is so highly valued in our society many find it hard to imagine that poor people would voluntarily maintain ties to their community of origin once they had acquired the skills that would able them to move onward and upward.

There is also a cultural blind spot that makes it difficult to see, name, and count any activities and values associated with women's traditional work of homemaking and promoting human development. When organizations like the Mothers' Centers movements adopt maternal metaphors and language they are likely to be dismissed outright. Some critics assume that anyone who uses the language of mothering is a member of the conservative right, trying to push all women back into the most traditional of social roles; others argue the language of mothers must be avoided or fathers will be discouraged from taking a more active role in parenting. Mostly, it seems, mothers are ignored because they are seen as irrelevant to public life. It is as if the society has focused its public life so intently on generating commerce and profits it has failed to develop a common language for articulating civic enterprises that generate human and community development.

When funding agencies do see the importance of the homeplace women's work they are likely to provide resources for "a new and innovative project." Once the project is "tried and true," the funders move on and the homeplace women find themselves again struggling with no or little institutional support.

Needless to say, all of these organizations are likely to become increasingly stressed as the gap between "the haves" and "the have-nots" continues to grow and the society continues to withdraw more and more of the resources that have been allocated in the past to support the growth and development of children, families, and communities.

Whether they were recognized and supported by others or not, it was clear to me that all of these organizations were highly successful in achieving their most basic goal: to nurture the development of voice among people silenced at the margins of society. Although organizations of this type are seldom studied and have no common name, observers concerned with the formation of a more democratic and caring society have long argued for just this kind of enterprise. These organizations are the kinds of places the educational philosopher Maxine Greene (1988) speaks of as authentic public spaces, places where people can appear before each other the best they know how to be. The political scientists Sara Evans and Harry Boyte (1986) call such organizations "free spaces." Free spaces, they argue, enable people to learn a new self-respect, a deeper and more assertive group identity, public skills, and values of cooperation and civic virtue (see also Lappe & Du Bois, 1994).

The developmental psychologists Ann Colby and Bill Damon (1992) were somewhat surprised to find that the moral leaders they studied depended on these kinds of communities for their own development and sustenance. Other developmental psychologists—Larry Daloz, James Keen, Cheryl Keen, and Sharon Parks (1996)—were well aware of the importance of such communities before they embarked on a study of people highly committed to the common good. Indeed, a major goal of their study was to describe in detail the qualities of environments that nurtured the development of the leaders they studied. They also described some of the communities these leaders went on to create to nurture the development of social commitment in others.

The political sociologist William Gamson (1992; 1995) looks more pointedly at the importance of these groups as communities of resistance for people cast as "Other" and excluded from society—sometimes through execution and genocide, sometimes through stereotyping that renders them invisible. Such communities have been essential to the survival of African Americans, people long subjected to the most subtle and the most extreme forms of Otherness. The cultural critic bell hooks (1990) calls such communities "homeplaces":

> We could not learn to love or respect ourselves in the culture of white supremacy, on the outside; it was there on the inside, in that "homeplace," more often created and kept by black women, that we had the opportunity to grow and develop, to nurture our spirits. .   408   408. . Failure to recognize . . . the remarkable revisioning of both women's role and the ideal of "home" that black women consciously exercised in practice, obscures the political commitment to racial uplift, to eradicating racism, which was the philosophical core of dedication to community and home., 42–44)

Ella Baker, a major figure in the civil rights movement and an adult adviser to the Student Non-Violent Coordinating Committee (SNCC), thought of the movement as "the beloved community" (See Payne, 1995; Zinn, 1964). She encouraged others to do the same. As a "beloved community" the movement became a model of the kind of world she and the students were trying to bring into being. Having a working model of a deeply moral society is of the utmost importance if a subordinated people are to transform rather then replicate an unjust society.

Evans and Boyte say "free spaces" (or Greene's "authentic public spaces," hooks's "homeplace," and Baker's "beloved community") bridge public and private life. They are places where ordinary citizens can act with dignity, independence, and vision. To emphasize this bridge we decided to modify hooks's term *homeplace*, we would call such communities "public homeplaces." We worried that without the additional designation as "public" those who draw a firm line between public and private life might think of homeplaces as serving only those with biological ties.

"Public homeplace" seemed a better metaphor than "invisible college" for naming public institutions dedicated to goals usually associated with private life—caring for and raising up the most vulnerable members of the communitiy. The mission of most degree-granting colleges is to educate the most successful so they can reach the apex of society. For the most part these highly competitive institutions have little concern for those struggling at the base. Conventional colleges are also more likely to focus on the students' acquisition of technical competence; invisible colleges emphasize individuals' development as full human beings.

Public homeplaces also seemed more appropriate than Listening Partners as a name for organizations that sponsor the development of a *public* voice among excluded and silenced people. Although the dyadic relationship implied by the title Listening Partners may be very empowering for an individual's personal development, participation in a larger conversation is undoubtedly a necessary condition for the development of a public voice and a commitment to the common good.

METAPHORS AND CIVIC VIRTUES

In a critique of a society that excludes values associated with home and domesticity from public life, the educational philosopher Jane Roland Martin (1992) argues for "schoolhomes." She joins "school" with the metaphor of "home" because she envisions schools organized around core values of care, concern, and connection. Schoolhomes, she argues, would cultivate the civic virtues needed to sustain a humane and democratic society. Martin places her plea for schools as "a moral equivalent of home" alongside an appeal made by William James in the celebrated essay "The Moral Equivalent of War." Because modern warfare is so destructive, James argued, we need to construct other opportunities that are "the moral equivalent of war," if youth (that is, boys) are to continue developing the "martial virtues." His example: "All young men [would] be conscripted into an army and sent out as railroad men and miners, tunnel makers and fisherman *to fight nature*" (Martin, 1992, p. 18, emphasis added). The "martial virtues" James wished to perpetuate include "intrepidity, contempt of softness, surrender of private interest, obedience to command" (Martin, 1992, p. 17).

The psycholinguists George Lakoff and Mark Johnson (1980) say that war metaphors like those venerated by James shape so much thinking in contemporary society that it is hard to imagine a culture premised on different notions:

> [For instance, it is hard for us] to imagine a culture where arguments are not
> viewed in terms of war, where no one wins or loses, where there is no sense
> of attacking or defending, gaining or losing ground. Imagine a culture where
> an argument is viewed as a dance, the participants are seen as performers,

and the goal is to perform in a balanced and aesthetically pleasing way. In such a culture, people would view arguments differently, experience them differently, carry them out differently, and talk about them differently., 4–5)

Although the homeplace women sometimes call themselves warriors, war making is not their major organizing metaphor. Instead, they have created a culture where everything is viewed in terms of families dedicated to promoting the welfare and development of human beings. On the deepest level, the homeplace women think of all human beings as belonging to a single family; the human family has an obligation to raise up all its members well. When the homeplace women speak of an injustice they are much more likely to describe "growth interrupted" than a right denied. Although the women are concerned to draw a particular group back into the circle and make the family whole again, their ultimate goal is to transform the social arrangements that led the human family to cast off its own kin.

You can hear all of this by pondering the metaphors of home and family the homeplace women use to describe their organizations. A few examples among hundreds: "We are like a family." "I am really at home here." "This is a place where I can be who I am." "You make friends here and they become part of your extended family, the family that you are actually living in." "It was like a constant coffee klatch, night and day. Before we got an office we just moved from one kitchen table to another. Actually we still do, even though the new office is quite nice." "We think of our center as a public living room." "In this family everyone has a say and every voice is important. This is not anything like the family I grew up in, that is for sure!" "We're like the kind of family where people can fight fearlessly but no one ever even thinks of leaving—well, hardly ever." "When we have differences we keep struggling until we find a way that is pretty much okay for everybody. Some people call this 'reaching consensus,' some call it a 'win/win' approach. We are just trying to see that everyone in the family has a voice in the way things are run." "People were here for me yesterday, they will be here for me tomorrow, next year, ten years from now, whatever." "When someone asks me, 'How can poor and working-class women build so many complex programs?' I invariably say something like 'We are a like a family, we have made a lifelong commitment to each other. People who know they are going to be together over the long haul can take on something that might take ten years or more to accomplish.'"

In public homeplaces even people well schooled in the "surrender of private interest" learn to voice their own needs, values, and perspectives. Those who once were highly "obedient to command" learn to take a critical stance toward the authorities that once kept them and others isolated and silenced. In other words, the public homeplaces are the moral equivalent of homes that teach people "to fight like hell" while rejecting all the other "martial virtues" praised by James.

NAMING PUBLIC LEADERS FOCUSED ON DEVELOPMENT

Just as "invisible college" came to seem inadequate as a metaphor for suggesting the nature of the organizations under study, "connected midwife teaching" was not quite right for depicting the homeplace women's leadership approach. At first, "connected midwife leaders" seemed a better metaphor. Although the homeplace women are teachers at heart, teaching is only one aspect of the work they do. It seemed especially important to emphasize the idea of leadership because these women bring the skills of connected knowing to a social role traditionally closed to women and their so-called ways.

It was not long before the term *midwife leader* itself began to seem somewhat misleading as a metaphor. It implies that these leaders pattern their work on a doctor–patient relationship. In reality many of the homeplace women reject this model vehemently. The typical doctor–patient relationship is characterized by an imbalance in power and knowledge that is unlikely to be overcome. The homeplace women are always trying to right such imbalances. The doctor–patient relationship is also focused on abnormality and disease, whereas the homeplace women center on wellness, strengths, and growth. Midwifery, in particular, refers to a momentary relationship that ends with a birth. The homeplace women liken themselves to mothers who take a lifespan perspective. This focus was made abundantly clear in the interviews in which the founders and the earliest members gave retrospective accounts of twenty years or more.

The metaphors, verbs, and adjectives the homeplace women actually use to describe themselves as public leaders almost always suggest activities that foster growth, development, and connection: "raising up," "nurturing," "growing," "caring," "uplifting," "lifting up," "drawing out," "drawing from," "bringing out," "connecting," "drawing in," "networking," and "bridging."

It seems that the homeplace women have developed themselves as public leaders by extending and elaborating women's traditional roles and women's ways to an extraordinary degre (see Howell, 1977, for a rare account linking women's public leadership to the approaches, skills, and values women have developed in private life). Most participants in these organizations would agree with this analysis. When members at large want to describe the people most responsible for bringing their organization into being they speak of the "Founding Mother(s)."

The Founding Mothers use this terminology. They also like to describe themselves as "bridge-persons." Looking through the transcripts for the many references to "bridge-person" the meaning seemed best summed up like this: "I am a person who is always trying to bring this unruly and divided human family back together." As one of the Founding Mothers put it, "I want everybody in the family to be all right. I want everybody to be included. I want this circle. I want a whole. But let me tell you, it's not easy."

In seeking a way to talk about the homeplace women's approach to leadership I tried at first to avoid metaphors suggesting the maternal. I was certain that any reference to "mother" would bring on more accusations of "essentialism." People would assume I was saying that women have a distinctive nature, separate from men's, rooted in biology and immutable. Worse still, I would be indicated for confining women to the most narrow and oppressive of social roles.

Try as I might, I could not think of a better label than "maternal leadership" for the approach shared by the Founding Mothers of public homeplaces. The raising of children can be seen as the paradigm that undergirds all of these organizations, if child raising is conceptualized in terms of drawing people who are unequal in terms of power, status, and abilities into relationships of full equality with others in society (Miller, 1987, 1988). The familylike structures created by the homeplace women model the kind of democratic society they seek: (1) a society that nurtures the development of all its citizens but most especially that of the most vulnerable and (2) a citizenry committed to the common good, responsible for the development of the community as a whole.

If leadership centered on promoting human development is more common among women than among men, it is because women have engaged themselves with the work involved in raising the young down through the ages. (For discussion of the relationship between a person's standpoint or social roles and his or her thinking, see Bem, 1993; Harding, 1986, and this volume; Ruddick, 1994, and this volume). A highly elaborated developmental approach can be realized by anyone—male or female—through engaged practice, mentoring, dialogue, and extensive reflection.

In our society, traditional leaders often think of themselves as patri-
archs, ruling over others—not raising them up. Some think of themselves
as warriors, battling to win out over their opponents, if not to destroy them
outright (Lakoff & Johnson, 1980). Even though the homeplace women
are engaged in many serious ongoing battles with oppressive systems and
peoples and sometimes call themselves "warriors," they are an unusual
bunch of fighters. They focus their energy on uplifting and empowering
the oppressed; they would transform, not destroy, the oppressor.

The black studies scholar Patricia Hill Collins (1991) says leaders
committed to uplifting the most vulnerable members of the community
have been crucial to the survival of African Americans. She calls them
"community othermothers."

> Community othermothers work on behalf of the Black community by
> expressing ethics of caring and personal accountability which embrace con-
> ceptions of power and mutuality. . . . Such power is transformative in that
> Black women's relationship with children and other vulnerable community
> members is not intended to dominate or control. Rather, its purpose is to
> bring people along, to—in the words of late-nineteenth-century Black femi-
> nists—"uplift the race" so that vulnerable members of the community will be
> able to attain the self-reliance and independence essential for resistance.,
> 131–132)

Collins says that the cultural traditions of community leaders who treat
biologically unrelated people as if they were members of one's own family provide a foundation for black women's political activism that is little
understood in the broader society.

The civil rights historian Charles Payne (1995) says leadership concerned with fostering people's development is one of two distinct leadership traditions long cultivated by black folk living in the rural South. It
is, he says, a tradition that is seldom named and discussed by historians
(or anyone else, I might add). The more commonly recognized leadership tradition is that of the articulate, charismatic leader who is likely to
head the church and other important institutions in a community.
Charismatic leaders, Payne says, are generally male, well educated, and
ministerial; they lean toward the authoritarian. In this tradition the
leader is a shepherd; the followers are gathered into the fold. The Rev-
erend Martin Luther King, Jr., is the outstanding example of a civil rights
leader operating out of this tradition.

Leaders from the less understood developmental tradition, Payne says, are more often women with less education, and little or no institutional support. They were not so interested in mobilizing followers as they were in supporting the oppressed to develop their own leadership capacities. He argues that developmental leaders like Ella Baker created the infrastructure that upheld the civil rights movement when it came to the deep South. Leaders like Ella Baker were so successful in reaching people in the most oppressed areas of the segregated South, he says, because they created environments where people and their thinking could grow. They made personal connections, cutting through stereotypes and seeing the people's human qualities and strengths. Rather than directing their "followers" as traditional leaders do, these leaders asked good questions and drew out the people's thinking so they could find their own direction. It was, Payne thought, the participatory process of thinking everything through for themselves that enabled the people to withstand the violence of the opposition they faced. Although leaders like Ella Baker were passionately centered in strong moral beliefs, they were always questioning and open to new learning. They encouraged people to look on their projects as experiments that could be studied and improved on. This "let's try it and see" attitude helped people feel free to make mistakes and try again. The people did keep on trying until they found themselves overcoming obstacles everyone in the nation had assumed were insurmountable.

The African American educator, activist, and writer Barbara Omolade calls herself one of Ella's daughters. She got most of her leadership training from Ella Baker when she left college, joined the Student Non-Violent Coordinating Committee (SNCC), and threw herself into the civil rights movement.

Omolade says developmentally oriented leadership is a tradition with "no name" even though it is an ancient tradition that originated in African tribal societies organized around democratic–consensus processes.

Under Ella Baker's guidance, Omolade says, SNCC provided a laboratory where participants could create ways of addressing social problems within a democratic organization of rich and poor.

Bringing white and Black college students into SNCC enabled Ella Baker to influence and train leaders who became part of [many] national movements promoting change . . . [in and beyond the Black community]. The white men she mothered brought the New Left Movement into being. The white women she mothered in the movement inspired others, creating second-

wave feminism. . . . Her Black daughters combined and took from feminism,
nationalism and the New Left, adding their own unique notions, to birth
womanism. (1994, p. 165)³

In short, Omolade says, contemporary feminism is rooted in the appren-
ticeships that she and so many other women (black and white) held in
the civil rights movement. They are all, she says, Ella's daughters. (For
extensive discussion of the link between the civil rights movements and
feminist movements see Evans, 1979.)

Maternal leadership devoted to promoting the development of the
most vulnerable members of society arises in many cultures and eras,
although its appearance outside the African American community is so
intermittent it may be a misnomer to call it a tradition. Jane Addams, the
Hull House women, and their allies in the neighborhood cultivated this
leadership approach in Chicago at the turn of the century. The Mothers
of the Plaza de Mayo reinvented the form more recently in Argentina.
With the "disappearance" (a euphemism for execution) of their politically active children, the Mothers turned their private despair into a public force. They created a free space that enabled poor and working-class
women to resist openly and successfully one of the more brutal dictatorships in our hemisphere in modern times. In an extensive study of the
Mothers' philosophy and practices, the poet Marguerite Guzman Bouvard (1994) says these women were able to mount such a powerful, persistent, and effective force against this brutal dictatorship precisely
because they infused their politics with maternal values. Their practice
of nurturing development, pacifism, cooperation, and mutual love
revealed the military values of hierarchy, obedience, and the unchecked
use of physical force in a way the Argentinean people could no longer
ignore.

The maternal approach to leadership in both public and private
homeplaces must be continually reinvented because it is a discipline
whose philosophy and practice are seldom acknowledged and articulated. This strange silence about mothering occurs because women's
caring work is seen as an activity *of* nature, rather than an interaction
with nature (Haste, 1994; Hirsch 1989; Martin, 1992; Ortner, 1974;
Ruddick, 1994, and this volume; Shiva, 1989). Mothers do not develop
their craft; it comes to them through intuition and biological inheritance. Because the mother is seen as exerting no agency, her caring work
is counted as doing nothing. In her study of early mothering, psychologist Amy Rossiter (1988, p. 19) sees these assumptions reflected in the
daily language of mothers: "'No. I'm not working now'; 'Dr. Ross deliv-

ered the baby'; 'I didn't do anything today.'" The New Zealand econo-
mist Marilyn Waring (1988) says this tendency to see women's caring
work (and nature) as nothing can be observed in the economic accounting systems used worldwide for assessing a nation's wealth. Whereas
women's traditional work is classified as "reproductive," waging war is
classified as "productive." The military is counted as adding to the
wealth of a nation in spite of the fact that military spending allocates
resources to unproductive and destructive endeavors. Even women who
spend most of every day gathering foodstuffs, firewood, fibers, and building materials from the forest for feeding, clothing, and housing themselves and their families are not recorded as contributing anything to the
nation. A beautiful river is accorded value only when it is polluted and
moneys are allocated to remove the dangerous contaminates. Undefiled,
the river has no worth according to the accounting systems used worldwide. Needless to say, these systems were devised to help nations understand how to pay for the wars they wage, not to provide for the development of their peoples. AND developed by men

Women's abilities to raise up others (whether in private or public
homeplaces) are cultivated through continuous reflection on highly valued work and the creation of a subculture where the ideas can be discussed, solidified, and taught to the next generation. The philosopher
Sara Ruddick (1994) calls the body of reflections women generate out of
engaged practice "maternal thinking." Maternal practice, she argues, is a
discipline associated with a body of knowledge — just like the disciplines
of law or medicine:

> The discipline of maternal thought, like other disciplines, establishes criteria
> for determining failure and success, sets priorities, and identifies virtues that
> the discipline requires.... Maternal thinking is one kind of disciplined
> reflection among many, each with identifying questions, methods, and aims.
> (p. 24)

Ruddick says it is a struggle for women to make their own viewpoint
heard, even to each other and to themselves. She says maternal thinking
is "a revolutionary discourse" that has been silenced. "As a central discourse," she says, "[it could] transform dominant, so-called normal ways
of thinking" (p. 269).

The study of the philosophy and practices common to the diverse
group of women who founded and lead the public homeplaces reveals
an approach to public leadership that is rooted in maternal practice and
maternal thought. The homeplace women have worked hard to cultivate

this approach because they feel a great urgency to transform the more "normal ways of thinking."

PHILOSOPHY AND PRACTICE OF MATERNAL LEADERS: DIALOGUE AND PRAXIS

Although the homeplace women share many commonalities in terms of their philosophy and practice, only two of their most fundamental tenets—dialogue and praxis—will be examined here. All of them see dialogue as the central activity promoting development and bringing people into voice. Even so, none is satisfied with "just talk." Each organization has sponsored an endless stream of hands-on action projects in which people work together actually testing out and implementing the ideas under discussion. Dialogue and praxis permeate all aspects of public homeplaces and can be well illustrated by the genesis story of each organization.

All of the public homeplaces began with an interview study that evolved into just the kinds of collaborative political projects that Sandra Harding (1987; this volume) advocates. All of the founders, concerned that a particular group of people were not being heard, decided they would listen in a sustained and systematic way. Although most of the interviews were initially conducted with the people in groups, the discussions continued in many forms—dyads, triads, whatever. One gets a vivid sense that the founders/researchers got a good sense of a whole community of people while seeing each individual in her own terms. Because they were concerned with exclusion, they listened with special care to the most tentative and halting voices.

The researchers wanted to hear what the excluded had to say; they would learn from what they had to contribute. And, most importantly, they would bring this voice into a dialogue with the larger society.

As researchers, all of the homeplace founders asked questions that demanded people think carefully about who they were, where they wanted to go, and what abilities they could cultivate to help them reach their goals (for discussions of the power of reflective interviews and conversations for individuals and groups see Mishler, 1986; Reinharz, 1994; Sanford, 1982; and Tarule, this volume).

The researchers were particularly interested in the people's strengths and visions for a better future; they found myriad ways to mirror what they found.

The U.S. Mothers' Center movement was founded when the social worker Patsy Turrini and others decided to listen to young suburban mothers isolated from society and one another. They put together an interview schedule covering all aspects of pregnancy, childbirth, and care of infants. When they placed an ad in a local newspaper requesting participants for a study on mothering they were swamped with calls. Lorri Slepian and other women with a good deal of experience with the women's conscious-raising (C-R) groups that were burgeoning at that time volunteered to help cope with the torrent of applications. They could see that Patsy and her friends were creating a conscious-raising experience much more intensely focused on women's mothering than most. Although Lorri disagreed with many critics who accused the women's movement of being "against motherhood," she believed it was a topic poorly explored in most C-R groups. She thought Patsy's approach had the potential of broadening the movement to include many women who were still standing on the sidelines. Lorri volunteered to lead one of the initial discussion groups. She and many others stayed on to help Patsy turn the research project into a permanent organization.

One of the women who answered the newspaper ad looks back on the experience some twenty years later:

> I was a mother. That's all I was. I had nothing else. I was isolated. No car. Husband going to school, husband going to work. When I read the ad, "young mothers to assist in a research project on women's needs during pregnancy, childbirth, and first experiences with an infant," I thought, "I was needed for a research project! Someone wanted to know about my experience." . . . It was wonderful. I intended to do it for 6 weeks. I lasted 7 years.

For six weeks the women met in small groups while their children played together in a nearby room. The researchers took notes and videotaped the sessions. After the six weeks the women decided to continue meeting. Not only had their conversations barely scratched the surface of what they had to say, they realized that many of the problems their conversations revealed were rooted in social arrangements that could be ameliorated if they worked together. For instance, the women could see that most of the difficulties they had experienced around childbirth were a function of hospital policies and practices that did not take into account the needs and perspectives of mothers. To confirm this impression, they polled other women about their experiences and documented widespread discontent of women with hospital maternity services. They also conducted an extensive study of the policies and practices of the hospitals in the area. Once they had collected data to back up their position, the women approached the hospitals with requests for reform.

Watching the videotapes they had made, the women were amazed by the quality of their thinking, the data they had collected, and their public presentations. They were also startled to discover how contemptuous the doctors and hospital administrators were of them and their arguments. As the women began to edit their films and present their case to other community groups, the hospital personnel began to see themselves through the eyes of the women they were supposed to be serving. It was not long before all the local hospitals had completely redesigned their maternity services. This original process—carefully designed interview questions, long thoughtful conversations, and community action projects—provided the basic model for the Mothers' Centers that have developed in communities across the United States.

The Mothers' Center movement in Germany also started with a research project. A sociologist, Monika Jaeckel, and a small group of feminists—all highly educated politically active professionals, most childless, some lesbian—had begun to notice how alienated mothers were from feminist politics. They questioned a feminist stance that excluded mothers. They also realized that they themselves knew next to nothing about ordinary women living traditional lives as housewives. To remedy the situation, Monika and her colleague Greta Tüllmann obtained a research grant to study mothers. The granting agency commissioned them to study why housewives avoided the standard educational programs available in their communities. The two women conducted extensive interviews with groups of young mothers. They found housewives disliked the educational programs because they felt teachers looked down on them; they did not teach things that seemed important; nor did they ask them what they were interested in learning. The young housewives also criticized programs and people who tried "to serve" them or "cure" them as patients or clients. They did not want "service" and they did not want "treatment." They simply wanted to be respected as competent adults with critical skills and values who could make important contributions to society.

In extended conversations the researchers and housewives began to envision the kinds of programs that could make a difference. One theme appeared again and again: There should be a meeting place where women could drop in with their children to carry on the same kind of highly reflective, hard-nosed conversations they had been holding with Monika and her colleagues. The place would be called a "Mothers' Center," because it would put mothers at the center—something few other public institutions do. It would be like a public living room where children could play and make friends while the mothers talked around a coffee table. Everyone would share responsibility for the organization, which would be run in a collaborative, democratic fashion. Although the women dreamed of many other possible facets a center might have, the coffee table was always the focal point. They were given ample funding to test out their plan by building centers in three different communities. By everyone's accounts all three were a great success. Although the grant stipulated that the project directors publish a report on the effort, it was decided that the mothers themselves would author the report in a form of a book (Jaeckel & Tüllman, 1988). The book was an instant best-seller among young mothers throughout Germany. As Monika said, "The women wrote a book so alive that the book itself created the Mothers' Center movement. Everywhere women who read the book said, 'We can do it too. What those women did, we can do in our town.'"

In both the United States and Germany researchers brought groups of mothers together, listened, and recorded what they heard with care. One group produced well-edited videotapes and the other a book, giving the women an opportunity to polish their ideas on mothering and society's treatment of mothers, and to share these ideas with a larger public. In both cases the women found the conversations and the collaborative projects so fruitful they decided to establish a public place where mothers could continue the process. Mothers in both countries created an institutional structure that supported them to change the conditions of their lives, their families, and their communities.

The National Congress of Neighborhood Women has a similar story. When Jan Peterson, a young activist, started creating an interracial, intercultural force for social change in a poor Brooklyn neighborhood, she had not begun to think about gender. That changed very quickly. It soon became clear that the traditional leaders of the community would not tolerate Jan or any other woman's asserting herself as a community leader; they were also scandalized that women from different ethnic and racial backgrounds might work together. An open war was declared when the neighborhood women announced they were seeking a building to house their programs. They would leave meetings to find their car tires slashed; their phones rang through the night. The ensuing silences were unsettling, the threats against them and their children terrifying.

Drawing on her college training as a history major, Jan helped the women document how the community was being run. When they saw that community women were systematically excluded from the formal governance structures they began looking at the informal structures women had created for themselves. Jan mirrored the strengths she found in the Neighborhood Women as politically committed leaders, as historian might:

> I'm very good on history. I am very good at tying together and articulating the kinds of political involvements that most women forget. Women are always saying, "I'm not political." You can see that they are actually the most political people in the world: they are out there speaking up, organizing, pressuring, and advocating!! And then they say, "I'm not political!!" I could just roar! They want to erase their own history! I keep track of the history because I am very big that women should know what they have done, that they should see the impact of their work. Women's lack of awareness of the way they impact public space is one of the major problems in terms of women's voice today.

Jan was particularly interested in the ways the many Italian and African American women in the neighborhood were drawing on their cultural and family traditions to recreate a sense of community in what could have been a very barren urban landscape. She apprenticed herself to these women, some she said, "old enough to be my mother," to learn more about these traditional ways. Together the women reinstated the best of these cultural variations as they sought methods to create a caring community. Immigrant women who might have felt ashamed of their newcomer status began to realize they had important knowledge to contribute to the neighborhood and the nation.

The neighborhood women themselves began to "do history." In a long series of conversations they articulated how things really *did* work in their neighborhood, how they *had* worked in other times and places, and how they *should* work. It wasn't long before the women were "making history." To bring the community more in line with the common visions they had articulated to each other, the women began developing one action project after another. As we have seen, the list of their projects is a long one.

Whenever a new project was successfully launched, the women would stage a community celebration, making sure that they were publicly recognized for their leadership, so, they said, the community "would get the history straight." The traditional leaders of the community, it seems, finally did learn to share the bandstand as well as the leadership roles. From the stories the women tell, it seems that the battle for recognition (being named as the community leaders they had become) was almost as difficult as the battle for some modicum of political power.

The neighborhood women learned to approach each project as an experiment. Before the celebrations were even over they would begin asking what had become their standard questions: "Which of our goals did we meet?" "What was left undone?" "What can we learn from this?" "How can we push the issues to the next level?" Essentially the neighborhood women established a community think tank where they could continue discussing their visions for the community and developing strategies for bringing those dreams into reality.

It was not long before Brooklyn women began to link themselves with other women leaders across the country struggling to improve the condition of their grass-roots communities. They named their expanded think tank the National Congress of Neighborhood Women. The newest endeavor of the group has been to establish Grassroots Organizations Operating Together in Sisterhood (GROOTS), an international network linking grass-roots women from developed and developing countries. Between the two organizations they support the leadership of women working at the grass-roots level in communities around the world.

The ideas that led to the Center for Cultural and Community Development began accumulating in Jane Sapp's mind in the 1960s as she studied African American folk traditions. An accomplished Gospel singer, Jane conducted a series of systematic studies of the music and the culture in two areas of the rural South where blacks were maintaining many of the ways of their African ancestors: the coastal Sea Islands and the black belt or cotton belt that cuts across the southern states. Calling herself a cultural worker, Jane describes her approach:

> As a cultural worker you hang out in the community. You have to walk around in the community, look, and listen. You are looking for the knowledge the people have created for themselves. It is always there. You have to walk and look. But you have always to keep looking with "new eyes" so that you see things beyond what people usually look for. If you see that the people care about quilting you might get them to help you give classes for young people on quilting. When you start from what is most important to people, it says, "I think you are important." To go to a woman who quilts and say, "Would you come share your quilting?" it says, "I honor you." And people respond to your coming to those things that are most precious to them. Cultural work is about how you nurture people, how you affirm people, how you help people to know what they know, how you help people to know that they have a culture and a knowledge base to build on, how you help people to know that they are creative and that they have a creative base upon which to build.

Jane encouraged the people to develop the community's arts as a way to make their personal and collective statements to the world. As a musician of enormous talent, Jane concentrated most on creating music groups, music schools, and folk festivals. Her projects almost always evolved into a public dialogue, albeit one often conducted largely in song. Jane says:

> My aim was not really to have, quote, "a music program," but to have a place where people could come and talk to each other and share their experiences through music. You teach them to sing. When you shake people out with the singing, they build a relationship between each other. Then you start talking about what you're singing about. You keep asking, "Why do you sing?" and "What's important about that?" and exploring the meaning of the songs in terms of their lives and their history. You want them to know why they're singing and what they're singing.

Like all the other homeplace women, Jane holds up a mirror that allows a community to see beyond demeaning stereotypes and behold the fullness of their humanity. In Jane's case the mirror is created by the art making.

> Cultural workers hold up a mirror for people to look at themselves, their lives and their communities. Our work as cultural workers is to show you what we see. The reflections help people inventory their culture, their history, their stories, and their social relationships. At our best we are your mirrors. Sometimes artists are the only people who can announce to you that you are okay.

Jane and the other cultural workers encourage people to participate in the art making, so the mirror that is held up will reflect their most passionate statements about them and the world they live in. The art making loosens the mind and opens the heart. People begin to imagine things could be otherwise. They dream of the world as it should be. They realize they share a common vision.

When the artwork is polished enough to reflect the fullness of the people's visions the cultural workers arrange to have it seen by a wide variety of audiences. By presenting themselves to the public in the most vivid terms of their own choosing, people cut through the stereotypes that had kept hidden the reality of themselves, the world, and visions of better ways to live (see Maxine Greene, 1988 & 1995 for a compelling descriptions of the role of the arts in unleashing the moral imagination).

One example gives the flavor of the process. In the late 1960s Jane helped Miles College in Birmingham, Alabama, establish the first college-level program for blacks living in and around Green County, Alabama, one of the poorest and most segregated places in the nation. Most residents at the area had never thought about a college education.

Jane and her colleagues built much of the curriculum around oral histories and the folk art they collected in the area with support of a major
grant from the National Endowment of the Arts. Seeing their culture
reflected in the mirrors that Jane erected, the students began to appreciate how able they and their people were, even if all other reports were to
the contrary. Mollie Gaines, a housing expert, looks back twenty years
later and assesses the impact Miles College had on her as a student:

> Now I am a thinker but I didn't start thinking till Miles College and Jane
> Sapp came to Green County. In those days your parents thought for you:
> "You do this, Mollie. You do that." We were farmers—essentially sharecrop-
> pers. My father had died. We had to work very hard. You would get up every
> day, you dressed, you went to school, you came home, you went to the field,
> you picked cotton, you came home. Your mom told you what chores you had
> to do and that's what you did. You didn't really have to think. You didn't have
> choices. Mrs. Sapp made me know that as a black person I could be proud of
> what I was, that I could be something, that I could stand for something.
> That's the image Jane pictured for me: a black African woman who was about
> doing things, who was moving forward. That's what I wanted to do—move
> forward. Jane gave me the courage to think for myself. Jane made me feel that
> I could think and make good decisions for myself; that I could decide what's
> best for me in my life. She was right, I did have choices.

The African American cultural workers build on ancient cultural traditions that place art making at the center of the daily life of ordinary people. The cultural workers understand that when a public dialogue is ele-
vated by an art form a chain of events is likely to begin. The community
is likely to broaden its perspective on the world as it is and as it could be,
to arrive at a new place of understanding, to find new possibilities for
growth and transformation. The improvised and evolving song itself
becomes a metaphor for the community dialogue the cultural workers
seek. The ability to compose one's own music becomes a metaphor for
the ability to compose a life for one's self and one's community.

Jane and many of the other African American cultural workers have
one practice that is not shared by the other homeplace women I studied.
Whatever else they are doing, these women always seem to have at least
one project directed toward art making with young people. They "rope"
multitudes of these kids into one musical event or theater production
after another. They are especially concerned to draw in the invisible and
silent children standing in the margins of their community. The children
find themselves members of a community where people talk together
and care for one another. Through the art making the young people

begin talking to one another in the most serious way; they develop their "statements" to the world through the songs and plays they write. The art can be so powerful that adults begin looking at their community through the eyes of the children and decide something must be done. (See Belenky, Bond, and Weinstock, in press, for a description of the role students played in dismantling the tracking system that had resegregated public schools in Selma, Alabama.)

The cultural workers try to pick from the throng of kids those who have the potential of "seeing beyond what others see" and becoming one of the next generation's community othermothers. They are especially interested in identifying potential leaders who will strengthen the whole community by supporting the development of the most vulnerable.

Once the potential leaders are identified, the cultural workers do what their grandmothers and neighborhood women did for them when they were chosen. They back up the young people, nudging them to take their leadership potential very seriously. They talk with them about the serious issues facing the community. They encourage them to apply for scholarships and the like. They give the young people so many tasks that benefit the community you could say the kids were being thrust into an apprenticeship program. The cultural workers also create summer camps and other programs where the skills of "community-focused" leadership are systematically taught. They are quite aware that most formal educational institutions teach only the skills of "self-focused" leadership and pay little attention to the development of silenced and vulnerable members of society.

Charles Payne and Barbara Omolade seem to be right. The African American cultural workers are clearly participants in a leadership tradition that is being passed down from one generation to the next—even if that tradition has no name. The cultural workers were trained by their grandmothers, mothers, and neighbor women to become community leaders; they take it upon themselves to draw out and develop the potential of the young people just coming up. Of course, with so little institutional backing, the cultural workers will only reach a few of the multitudes that ought to have such teachers.

THE GENESIS STORIES SUMMARIZED

In the process of conducting their research studies, all of the homeplace women "apprenticed" themselves to their so-called research subjects. The researchers were like students; their "subjects" were the authorities who would teach them what they needed to know. In the give and take of the two-way (no, the many-way) conversations that ensued, "the researched" soon began to ask questions of their own. All— researchers and research subjects—became collaborators, analyzing their situation and imaging alternatives. Discussions continued until a consensus was formed. Common dreams became a group's goal and a project was initiated. These projects proved so productive each group declared itself an organization so the work would be ongoing. While continuing to experiment with hands-on projects in their local communities, each organization began reaching out to others doing similar work in other cultural communities throughout the country. Finding common ground, each group created a national network as a mutual support process; all are in the process of establishing ties with people and groups around the world. The national and international networks of very dissimilar people engaged in similar projects enable participants to gain the broadest global perspectives without losing touch with the concrete realities of their particular experiences and goals.

When WWK first came out a number of people said to us something like "You have given words to things I have always known." At first we were taken aback by what seemed to be faint praise. As time went on, we came to understand that this was the highest of compliments: that the whole nature of the enterprise we had undertaken was to give names to traditions that have no names; to tell the untold stories.

The story the homeplace women tell is an old story. It is the story of the Dewey School I attended as a child.[4] It is the story of Addams's Hull House. It is the story of the Mothers of the Plaza de Mayo. It is the story of Ella Baker and her many daughters and sons.

The story needs to be well told again and again with all of its variations. The philosophy and practice of developmentally oriented leadership need to be well taught (with lots of hands-on experiences) in schools and communities on all levels of the society; its practitioners should be given strong institutional backing.

If all that were to come to pass, generations of young people—male and female—would begin weaving the story line into their life narratives (Heilbrun, 1988). We would finally begin to achieve the kind of democratic and caring society we long to have.

NOTES

1. In *WWK* we named this outlook "Silence." I have taken the liberty of changing the name to "Silenced." The added *d* helps distinguish this way of knowing from the approaches observed in several non-Western cultures described by Nancy Goldberger (this volume). Here silence gives rise to powerful modes of connecting with and apprehending the world that do not depend on language and are poorly understood by "word people" like us. I cling to our original definitions of Silence and Received Knowledge because I believe it is important to have distinct epistemological categories that clearly indicate how people's capacities for meaning making can be stifled. As the educator Paulo Freire (1970) has shown, the emancipation of the oppressed is a two-step process: the poor must become coconstructors of knowledge and take a critical stance toward those who would deny them the right to name the world as they see it. I worry that if the categories of Silenced and Received Knowing are redefined to include active means of constructing meaning, these categories will lose their value for those of us who are trying to tackle emancipatory projects.

2. Ann Stanton, a contributor to this book, spent a sabbatical year with us analyzing the data. As we worked together assessing what had been empowering to rural women Ann designed the program for college women she describes in her chapter, this volume.

3. Omolade and many other African American women use "womanist" to distinguish their approach from "feminist" visions more common among European Americans (see Walker, 1983).

4. The Park School of Buffalo, founded in 1912 by Helen Lewis, a colleague of John Dewey's. From her account of the school's founding (Lewis, 1985) it is clear that Lewis's vision of the school was completely intertwined with metaphors of family and home. As with the homeplace women, Lewis's notion of family was a deeply democratic one: everyone would have a voice in its its govenance. The aim was twofold: promoting the development of each particular individual and of the family as a whole. The Deweyites, like the homeplace women, understood that development flourishes when individual and the community are given equal consideration.

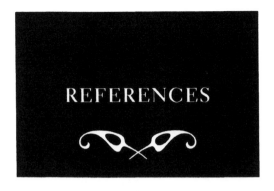

REFERENCES

Addams, J. (1910). *Twenty years at Hull House.* New York: Macmillan.

Belenky, M. F., Bond, L. A., & Weinstock, J. S. (in press). *A tradition that has no name: Public homeplaces and the development of people, families, and communities.* New York: Basic Books.

Belenky, M. F., Clinchy, B. M., Goldberger, N. R., & Tarule, J. M. (1986). *Women's ways of knowing: The development of self, voice, and mind.* New York: Basic Books.

Bem, S. (1993), *The lenses of gender: Transforming the debate on sexual inequality.* New Haven, CT: Yale University

Bond, L. A., Belenky, M. F., & Weinstock, J. S. (1991). *Listening partners: Psycho-social competence and prevention.* Final Report of Grant MCJ–500541 (10/86–6/91) to The Maternal and Child Health Bureau, Rockville, MD.

Bond, L. A., Belenky, M. F., Weinstock, J. S., & Cook, T. (1996). Imagining and engaging one's children: Lessons from poor, rural, New England mothers. In Sara Harkness, Charles Super, & Rebecca New (Eds.), *Parental ethnotheories: Their sociocultural origins and developmental consequences.* New York: Guilford.

Bouvard, M. G. (1994). *Revolutionizing motherhood: The mothers of the Plaza de Mayo.* Wilmington, DE: Scholarly Resources.

Colby, A., & Damon, W. (1992). *Some do care.* New York: Free Press.

Collins, P. H. (1991). The meaning of motherhood in black culture and black mother–daughter relationships. In P. Bell-Scott, B. Guy-Sheftall, J. J. Royster, M. DeCosta-Willis, & L. P. Fultz (Eds.), *Double stitch: Black women write about mothers and daughters,* 42–60. Boston: Beacon Press.

Collins, P. H. (1991). *Black feminist thought: knowledge, consciousness, and the politics of empowerment.* New York: Routledge.

Daloz, L., Keen, S., Keen, J., & Parks, S. (1996). *Common fire: Lives of commitment in a complex world.* Boston: Beacon Press.

Deegan, M. (1988). *Jane Addams and the men of the Chicago school, 1892–1918.* New Brunswick, NJ: Transaction Books.

Dewey, J. (1916). *Democracy and education.* New York: Macmillan.

Elbow, P. (1970). *Writing without teachers*. London: Oxford University Press.

Evans, S. (1979). *Personal politics: The roots of women's liberation in the civil rights movement and the new left*. New York: Vintage.

Evans, S., & Boyte, H. (1986). *Free spaces: The sources of democratic change in America*. New York: Harper & Row.

Freire, P. (1970). *Pedagogy of the oppressed*. New York: Herder & Herder.

Gamson, W. A. (1992). *Talking politics*. New York: Cambridge University Press.

Gamson, W. A. (1995). Hiroshima, the holocaust, and the politics of exclusion: 1994 Presidential Address, American Sociological Association. Reprinted *American Sociological Review, 60*, 1–20.

Greene, M. (1988). *The dialectic of freedom*. New York: Teachers College Press.

Greene, M. (1995). *Releasing the imagination: Essays on education, the arts, and social change*. San Francisco: Jossey-Bass.

Harding, S. (1986). *The science question in feminism*. Ithaca, NY: Cornell University Press.

Harding, S. (1987). Struggling for self-definition. *Women's Review of Books, 4* (6), 6–7.

Haste, H. (1994). *The sexual metaphor*. Cambridge, MA: Harvard University Press.

Heilbrun, C. (1988). *Writing a woman's life*. New York: Ballantine.

Hirsch, M. (1989). *The mother–daughter plot: Narrative, psychoanalyses, feminism*. Indianapolis: Indiana University Press.

hooks, b. (1990). *Yearnings: Race, gender, and cultural politics*. Boston: South End Press.

Howell, M. (1977, December). Just like a housewife: Delivering human services. *Radcliffe Alumnae Magazine*, 5–7.

Jaeckel, M., & Tüllman, G. (Eds.) (1988). *Mütter im zentrum/Mütterzentrum*, Munich; DJI Verlag Deutsche Jugendinstitut.

Lakoff, G., & Johnson, M. (1980). *Metaphors we live by*. Chicago: University of Chicago Press.

Lappe, F. M., & Du Bois, P. (1994). *The quickening of America*. San Francisco: Jossey-Bass.

Lewis, M. (1985). *An adventure with children*. Lanham, MD: University Press of America.

Martin, J. (1992). *The schoolhome: Rethinking schools for changing families*. Cambridge, MA: Harvard University Press.

Miller, J. B. (1987). *Towards a new psychology of women* (2nd ed.) Boston: Beacon Press.

Miller, J. B. (1988). Connections, disconnections, and violations. *Work in progress*, No. 33. Wellesley, MA: Stone Center Working Paper Series.

Mishler, E. (1986). *Research interviewing: Context and narrative*. Cambridge, MA: Harvard University Press.

Omolade, B. (1994). *The rising song of African American women.* New York: Routledge.

Ortner, S., (1974). Is female to male as nature is to culture? In M. Rosaldo & L. Lamphere (Eds.), *Women, culture, and society.* Stanford, CA: Stanford University Press.

Parks, S. D. (1989). Home and pilgrimage: Companion metaphors for personal and social transformation. *Soundings, 79,* Summer/Fall, 297–315.

Payne, C. M. (1995). *I've got the light of freedom: The organizing tradition and the Mississippi freedom struggle.* Berkeley: University of California Press.

Reinharz, S. (1994). Toward an ethnography of "voice" and "silence." In E. J. Trickett, R. Watts, & D. Briman (Eds.), *Human diversity: Perspective on people in context.* San Francisco: Jossey-Bass.

Rogoff, B. (1990). *Apprenticeship in thinking: Cognitive development in social context.* New York: Oxford University.

Rossiter, A. (1988). *From private to public: A feminist exploration of early mothering.* Toronto, Ontario: Women's Press.

Ruddick, S. (1994). *Maternal thinking: Towards a politics of peace.* Boston: Beacon Press.

Sanford, N. (1982). Social psychology: Its place in personology, *American Psychologist, 37,* 896–903.

Seigfried, C. H. (1996). *Pragmatism and feminism: Reweaving the social fabric.* Chicago: University of Chicago Press.

Shiva, V. (1989). *Staying alive: Women, ecology, and survival in India.* London: Zed Books.

Shure, M. B., & Spivack, G. (1978). *Problem solving techniques in childrearing.* San Francisco: Jossey-Bass.

Walker, A. (1983). *In search of our mother's gardens.* San Diego: Harcourt Brace and Jovanovich.

Waring, M. (1988). *If women counted: A new feminist economics.* New York: HarperCollins.

Zinn, H. (1964) SNCC: The new abolitionists. Boston: Beacon Press.

Gendered Ways of Knowing and the "Epistemological Crisis" of the West*

SANDRA HARDING

REREADING WOMEN'S WAYS OF KNOWING

REREADING WOMEN'S WAYS OF KNOWING (WWK) ten years after its publication left me with renewed appreciation for how carefully Mary Belenky, Blythe Clinchy, Nancy Goldberger, and Jill Tarule positioned their arguments within some of the most difficult and complex of contemporary epistemological controversies (Belenky, Clinchy, Goldberger, & Tarule, 1986). These controversies have been referred to as "the crisis in epistemology" or "the crisis of the West" since their topic is the increasing loss of legitimacy and authority for the kinds of justifications of knowledge claims that have been developed by the modern West.[1] This "crisis" has many origins, including the end of formal European colonial rule, the continued rapaciousness of capitalist economic relations, the obvious failures and disasters around the globe due to Western militarism, Third World development policies, wrong-headed environmental policies, and the long-recognized alienation that people in industrialized societies feel from their cultures, communities, and "true

*I thank the editors for comments that helped me strengthen this essay.

431

selves." The epistemology, ethics, and politics of Western sciences and technologies, apparently inseparable, are implicated in these failures. Recent histories have shown how modern European sciences and technologies have provided resources for these problematic projects and, in turn, have been advanced through them (as will be reviewed later). Such epistemological controversies are occurring in every discipline and public forum. They promise to remain lively for a long time to come.

Feminisms, too, have made their important contributions to this crisis. Their criticisms of the dominant Western paradigms of reason, knowledge, "human progress," ethics, and politics often have coincided with those arising from other victims of European modernity (Compare, for example, Harding, 1986, 1991; Keller, 1984; Lloyd, 1984; Merchant, 1980). However, Western feminisms also have been troubled by this epistemological turmoil. How can feminisms justify their knowledge claims when those epistemologies that they have helped to delegitimate are no longer available to do the job?

In light of these issues, three ways that the authors positioned their arguments were particularly striking to me on this rereading since I am rethinking them in the course of my current work, which is focused on "decolonizing" Western science studies, including its feminist projects. First, they kept a clear focus on the importance of locating women's ways of knowing in terms of not only the gender relations the title indicates but the differences between women—in the cases they studied, differences due, for example, to class resources and to experiences of family violence or other forms of family deprivation. They point out how both have effects on women's ways of knowing. Thus they resisted the "essentialist" ways of thinking about women as fundamentally all alike, a homogenous group with common life opportunities and experiences, already "known" to us before we actually see them or hear from them. Second, they showed how the conditions of women's lives that they charted provided both resources and limitations to the theories of knowledge that they would be able to develop, to their senses of self, voice, and mind; and, indeed, to what they could come to know. What women (and, presumably, men) do both enables and limits what they can know. Third, they kept in clear focus the links between power and knowledge and showed how less powerful positions nevertheless have distinctive epistemological resources. They charted the surprising epistemological "powers of the weak." In the case of gender relations, knowledge possibilities are shaped not only by the activities in which men and women characteristically engage, but by the positions they are assigned in power relations.

These three themes are centered in my current work also, although in ways that at first may seem irrelevant to the issues of WWK (Harding, 1993, 1994, 1995, in press, 1996a, 1996b, forthcoming; Harding & McGregor, 1996). I hope to show here that they are, indeed, relevant. I am a philosopher, not a psychologist. I am interested in issues about how different standards for scientific knowledge and, consequently, different knowledge emerge through the politics of historical and cultural knowledge-seeking projects. Historical conditions create different resources and limitations for the production of knowledge and for theories about knowledge, and especially for scientific knowledge. This interest I share with the mainstream of the last three decades of Northern social and cultural studies of science and technology.

However, these Northern studies focus primarily on historical and cultural differences within European/U.S. scientific and technological projects. What about the diversity in theories of knowledge favored by cultures other than European/U.S. ones? What about the different kinds of actual knowledge about nature that different cultures tend to produce? Different cultures know different things about nature and social relations, and they have different theories of what constitutes knowledge and how to get it. This is an interest that I share with postcolonial science and technology critics, including the gender and (Third World) development theorists (sometimes referred to as "Southern" science and technology studies).[2] These fields ask such questions as what are the social, natural, and epistemological conditions that made possible the development of modern sciences in Europe rather than in China, in spite of the latter's far more advanced scientific and technological tradition at the point when modern science emerged in Europe? Are there causal relations between the two great events marking the beginnings of modernity: European expansion and the emergence of modern sciences in Europe? What are the conditions, invisible from Northern perspectives, that make possible "European ways of knowing"? Do only the modern "high sciences"— physics, chemistry, abstract biology—deserve to be thought of as "real science"? Once they, too, are understood to be fully lodged in their historical eras and cultures, as the last three decades of Northern histories and social studies of science and technology argue, what distinguishes them from the "indigenous knowledge traditions" that are of interest to the gender and (Third World) development debates? What are the conditions that provide both resources and limitations for such "local knowledge systems" (LKS) in the cultures of Tahiti, premodern India, the Peruvian Andes, or high-energy physics at the Stanford linear accelerator?

Such issues may seem irrelevant to WWK's concerns. However, gendered ways of knowing are also kinds of LKS since, as the authors point out, they are not universally human. Women's ways of knowing are very much situated in the lives of the women the authors studied, and the contrasting dominant epistemologies are situated in the lives of men. Of course, the authors did not interview men or focus on "men's ways of knowing." However, they clearly attribute the fact that psychologist William K. Perry (and others) find reasonable the purported universality of the prevailing epistemological standards to the way such standards "fit" distinctive features of the lives of men in the dominant groups.

I think we can learn more about gendered ways of knowing by looking at what they share with other kinds of culturally distinctive ways of knowing. Here I shall briefly review how the three WWK themes mentioned earlier appear in the historical and cross-cultural studies of gender, science, and technology with which I have been working. These themes are the necessity of feminist analyses that can recognize differences as well as commonalities among women, the cultural differences that create both resources and limitations for women's ways of knowing, and the power/knowledge analyses that have been centered in the distinctive feminist standpoint epistemologies developed in the last two decades. Such a study of "other epistemologies" can clarify which features of women's and men's ways of knowing are unique to gender relations (and, possibly, to U.S. or Northern ones), and where they can be found also in other kinds of social relations, such as those of other cultural traditions or those due to colonialism and imperialism. Such analyses can also provide additional arguments for grasping how the strengths of women's ways of knowing promise to provide valuable resources for human social relations more generally. These resources are less visible when one uses only the lens of gender relations to examine epistemological multiplicity. Moreover, since the most "advanced" of the dominant epistemologies that Perry identifies are those structuring modern scientific and technological knowledge, the legitimacy and authority of which increasingly are questioned, such analyses point to fruitful strategies for simultaneously deepening and moving past the crisis of Western epistemology.

ANTIESSENTIALISM: RESOURCES PROVIDED BY DIFFERENCES BETWEEN WOMEN

One of the great achievements of late-twentieth-century feminist thought is the discovery that gender relations are fundamentally social and cultural relations (or, for constructivists, the invention of such a conceptual framework). This theoretical achievement has enabled thought to move away from the constraining assumptions of biological determinism. Moreover, the concept of gender was enriched by the analyses by "marginalized women"—working-class, African American, Asian American, Jewish, Native American, Chicana, lesbian, those in the Southern cultures, on so on—showing the diverse historical and cultural forms in which gender relations have appeared. It became clear that these historical and cultural relations are fundamentally structural and symbolic ones, not just properties of individuals, as earlier individualist philosophies, psychologies, and other social sciences had assumed. Of course, each of us experiences our gender as belonging to us, as individuals. But explanations of how particular cultural patterns of gender identity come into existence, change over time, and eventually decline require richer conceptual frameworks than the individualist approaches (not to mention the biological determinist ones) could provide. Residues of the older biological discourses and of simplistic and distorting individualist gender discourses are still all around us. But more useful possibilities that were not present even three decades ago now are also widely available. The analysis of WWK clearly is located on this kind of map of gender that was only emerging into clarity at the point when the study was conducted. This section reviews the major components of the shift from individualist to structural and symbolic concepts of gender relations.

Five shifts were made in theorizing gender. First, gender is now understood to be a *relationship* between women and men, womanliness and manliness, not a property that women and men have apart from the other gender. Thus to understand "women" (or "men"), one must always look at the relationship between women and men. Note that it thus distorts social relations to use *gender* simply as a more polite, or more fashionable, substitute for *women* or, often, *female*. In such a distorting usage, when women are discussed, gender relations appear as an appropriate topic; when all-male or mostly male groups are discussed (the Supreme Court, the board of trustees, the military), we are encouraged to think that we are considering human relations; it is implied that no gender relations are present. Gender issues arise only when Sandra Day O'Connor enters the Supreme Court, a woman is appointed to the board, or women try to gain entry to military careers.

Second, in this work, gender is produced primarily not by individual choices, but, more fundamentally, by social structures and their culturally distinctive meanings. Gender relations are fundamentally structural relations of the social order and symbolic meanings of "discourses" (religious, scientific, legal, and other institutions and their practices, cultures, and ways of thinking). They are not fundamentally matters of individuals' bad attitudes and false beliefs. Although it makes a difference when individuals can help more emancipatory discourses be circulated in powerful institutions (in religious, scientific, or legal circles), the causal effects of gender relations travel primarily from social structure and symbolic system to individuals, not in the opposite direction. Thus gendered identities are not "givens," prior to the structural and symbolic relations infants enter; they are created and continually maintained by the latter, and they change as structural and symbolic relations change over time.

Structual gender is achieved by assigning different social activities to what are claimed to be significantly different groups in a culture—for example, assigning rule or production of scientific claims to one group and responsibility for daily household maintenance and kin welfare to another. Symbolic gender is "totemic"; it uses a claimed relationship between males and females to give meaning to phenomena that have little or nothing to do with two-sex reproduction. Thus governing and doing science are taken to signify the distinctively human values and achievements. In contrast, satisfying the daily subsistence needs of household and kin is taken to be merely part of natural behaviors, or merely culturally local. Symbolic gender also gives meanings to hurricanes, nations, ships, and such concepts as objectivity, rationality, and moral virtue, which have even less to do with the kind of sex differences humans share with many other species. So individuals become gendered through the positions that they are assigned in culturally varying gendered structural and symbolic systems. What is regarded as womanly in one culture or historical moment—farming, market trading, typing, or secretarial work—has been gendered as distinctively manly in another.

Third, gender is always inextricably interlocked with class, race, ethnicity, religion, imperialism, and whatever other structural and symbolic systems organize cultures as distinctive. Thus what women do and what womanliness means are always culturally local, depending on how gendered social relations and their meanings are used to maintain, or struggle against, relations of class, caste, ethnicity, race, imperialism, heterosexism, or whatever other "macro-" social relations are in fact effective. Economically privileged white women also have racialized and class-specific positions in gender relations, not just poor women, or "ethnic women" (compare, for example, Anzaldúa, 1987; Bing & Reid, this volume; Collins, 1991; Enloe, 1989; Haraway, 1989; Harcourt, 1994; hooks, 1983; Mies, 1986; Trinh, 1989).

Fourth, consequently, gender relations are dynamic and historically changing, never fixed or transcultural. Any kind of social change can be, and usually is, a site of struggle over gender relations, as different classes, ethnicities, and "races" try to control the outcome of such changes through manipulating the meanings and social locations of their own and other groups' gender relations. For example, scientific and technological changes are frequently sites of such gender struggles: Who is to gain access to the new education such changes require? Whose educations are to become archaic? Who is to gain and who lose access to the applications and technologies such changes make possible? How are the "persons" who will be given credit for bringing about this change gendered? Is the change being justified in terms of national (that is, manly) identity? Economic (that is, manly) superiority? Consider the case of computers. Are computing skills to be for women, too? How are diverse new computer cultures gendered masculine or feminine for different class, "race," and ethnic groups in their characteristic work and play contexts (Cockburn, 1985; Wacjman, 1991)?

Last but not least, gender relations are always power relations. Changes in gender relations are always struggles over the distribution of scarce resources, be they material or symbolic. Of course, women and men have different kinds and degrees of power in different cultures, as historians and anthropologists point out. Thus strategies for improving women's situations must always address issues of power imbalance.

This now widely used conception of gender relations deeply challenges conventional Western philosophic assumptions since it denies the possibility of the kinds of abstract, rational humans that are the assumed "subjects" or agents of knowledge in conventional epistemologies: selfs, voices, and minds are always historically local. Here I shall pursue further two analytically distinct kinds of conditions that can both enable and limit the production of knowledge: those created by "mere" cultural differences, and those created by power differences—both of which were already signaled in WWK.[3] In actual social situations of women within "one culture" such as the contemporary United States, these two kinds of nonessentialist gendered "ways of knowing" often are difficult analytically to separate. Their different origins and effects are easier to see through the lenses of various fields of science studies that have been developed since World War II.

HOW CULTURAL DIFFERENCES CREATE RESOURCES AND LIMITATIONS FOR LOCAL KNOWLEDGE SYSTEMS—INCLUDING SCIENTIFIC ONES

Post–World War II science studies have developed in a number of different directions as different groups around the globe have inspected modern sciences and other scientific traditions from the perspectives of their different experiences of these sciences. Yet in important respects they converge to challenge conventional scientific epistemologies. In different ways, they all argue that all knowledge about the natural world is embedded in culturally local projects. All knowledge systems, including those of modern sciences, are local in ways that go far beyond conventional ways of thinking about the "historical origins of universal modern sciences." They all end up showing how cultures' different locations in nature's heterogeneous patterns, cultures' different interests, discursive resources, and ways of organizing the production of knowledge ensure that all "scientific" knowledge will be culturally local. Before turning to look at how gendered ways of knowing also can be illuminated by such a conceptual framework, I shall take the space briefly to characterize how these diverse science studies make their arguments. If modern sciences, too, are LKS in significant respects, then it is not the cultural specificity of women's ways of knowing that requires explanation but, rather, the illusions of transculturalism characteristic of androcentric and Eurocentric, conventional Northern epistemologies.

POST–WORLD WAR II SCIENCE STUDIES

During the 1960s, historians of Western science began providing accounts of the ways that different significant moments in modern science were fully a part of their own (European) historical moment, shaped by and shaping the social and cultural worlds within which they occurred. Studies of the invention of experimental method no less than the discovery of human evolution and of quarks revealed how fully these important advances in scientific knowledge were constituted by and in turn helped to constitute political and cultural projects of their time and place. One could refer to these as "post-Kuhnian" science studies simply to locate them for readers not familiar with this development, using historian of science Thomas S. Kuhn's work to mark this shift. Subsequently ethnographers joined the historians, producing studies of "laboratory life" and the culture of high-energy physics, for example, that revealed the local cultural assumptions, interests, and ways of organizing the production of scientific knowledge that have been responsible for high points in the history of modern sciences (Kuhn, 1970; Latour & Woolgar, 1979, Pickering, 1984; Shapin, 1994; Shapin & Schaffer, 1985; Traweek, 1988).

Meanwhile, there emerged also a shift in one part of the "comparative ethnoscience" movement that originally had focused only on non-Western belief systems (and still largely does so today). In the 1960s some of these anthropologists began to argue that modern science, too, was just one belief system among others. It could be studied with the same ethnographic methods developed to understand and explain Inca mathematical practices or Pacific Islanders' navigational skills (Watson-Verran & Turnbull, 1994). Modern science was no longer to be immune to the kind of objective, historical, and sociological gaze to which every other culture's knowledge systems had been subjected. There were to be no more accounts of European sciences only from the perspective of the "natives" in those sciences—that is, scientists and their governmental and coprorate sponsors, who had received such benefits from them.

Another direction in science studies was generated by what has come to be known as postcolonial science studies. With roots in the history of European imperialism and colonialism, these projects developed subfields of "science and empires" studies and critical studies of (Third World) development policies and their effects. Initiated primarily by science and technology intellectuals in the former European colonies, but commanding a far broader participation today, postcolonial science studies have been resolutely anti-Eurocentric. One important focus here has been to examine the causal relations between the development of modern sciences in Europe, European expansion from the fifthteenth century forward, and the decline of science and technology traditions in the cultures into which Europe expanded. Conventional historians had treated these three phenomena independently. In the conventional histories, European roots reaching back into ancient Greece and Rome were carefully delineated, but, with a few "anomolous" exceptions, all other scientific and technical traffic between Europe and other cultures was presented as having diffused outward from Europe. In other words, all of those magnificent, "human" achievements of "civilization" legitimately could be attributed to peoples of European descent.

In contrast, postcolonial science studies located scientific and technological activities in the "interactionist" history that had been developing in other areas since the 1940s—in economic, political, and cultural history, for example. This kind of science and technology history showed how European expansion turned the world into a laboratory for European sciences, in the process destroying the scientific and technological traditions of other cultures. Moreover, the success of European expansion depended on the knowledge that European scientific and technological projects provided. European expansion and the rise of modern science in Europe have been in a "codependency" relation from their beginnings (compare, for example, Bernal, 1987; Blaut, 1993; Goonatilake, 1992; Hess, 1995; Petitjean et al., 1992; Sardar, 1988). Power creates certain kinds of resources for the advance of socially situated scientific and technological knowledge and destroys other kinds of resources. It creates resources and limitations for the growth of knowledge.

The theorists of (Third World) development policies were already by the early 1960s beginning to have their doubts that the importation of Northern industrial models into the "developing countries" was going to have its intended effects of enabling these societies to catch up to Northern standards of living. Development projects frequently were, at best, unsuccessful. At their worst, they were delivering resources only to the already most advantaged, further disadvantaging the vast majority of already economically vulnerable peoples, and destroying the environments on which everyone's daily subsistence developed. Moreover, they invariably continued to shift resources and political power from the developing countries to the North. As critics expressed the point, so-called development was in fact a continuation of Northern imperialism and colonialism "by other means" (Braidotti et al., 1994; Harcourt, 1994; Sachs, 1992). Northern sciences and technologies, their epistemologies, ethics, and politics, have been deeply implicated in these development failures in ways detailed in the literature cited.

Feminist science and technology analyses have primarily been part of the first and last of these post–World War II science studies—the post-Kuhnian studies of European sciences and the development critiques. Within the "alternatives to development" movement, feminist analyses have gained increasing respect in the last decade as they have been able to make clear how bypassing women in the delivery of resources ensured the "dedevelopment" not only of the women bypassed, but also of all those dependent on them: children, the elderly, the rest of their households, and the communities maintained by their daily activities. This was especially obvious in the rural areas from which most adult men had migrated in search of work, but it was no less the case in urban areas. (Braidotti et al., 1994; Harcourt, 1994; Mies, 1986; Shiva, 1989). The analytic power of these arguments in the "alternatives to development" literature is another link between postcolonial studies and Northern feminist epistemologies.

These different "schools" of contemporary science and technology studies by no means are coherent with each other, or even all epistemologically or politically friendly. Most obviously, the Northern social studies of science and technology that were mentioned first for the most part remain firmly located on Eurocentric, "separate-stream history" maps of the history of European sciences and technologies. However, these diverse schools of science studies nevertheless share assumptions and concerns that put them firmly in opposition to the conventional histories and philosophies of science that have been devoted to legitimating the authority of Northern epistemologies. They all understand that scientific and technological knowledge, too, is "socially situated." Though it often can be valuable in cultures other than those that developed it, and far from the temporal or geographic site where the observations of nature were first made, it can never be completely culture-free. Its cognitive core, its representation of nature's regularities, is constituted by the distinctive resources and their limitations that different cultures bring to their knowledge projects about the natural world. My point here is that these diverse fields of science and technology studies are "on the same side" as the authors of WWK in their critique of dominant Northern epistemological models and their attempts to identify and develop further already existing alternatives.

LOCAL CONDITIONS FOR LOCAL SCIENCES

From such analyses one can identify four sources of these distinctive local resources and limitations, each of which we can use to think about distinctively gendered ways of knowing, also. First, different cultures are located in different parts of nature;[4] they are exposed to different regularities of heterogeneous nature. They are located in mountains or on fertile plains, bordering oceans or in deserts, in the Arctic or the tropics, in earthquake or hurricane territory, sharing their environments with the causes of Lyme disease, malaria, scurvy, or cancers. Second, they have different interests in observing and explaining even "the same" of nature's regularities. Cultures living on the borders of the Atlantic can be interested to fish it, use it as a highway for trade or emigration, desalinize it for drinking water, mine the oil and ores under it, harvest its seaweeds, or use it as a highway for military projects. Third, cultures can draw on different discursive traditions through which to observe and explain nature's regularities. They can "see" nature through the lens of Christian beliefs about how nature's order and human minds were both created in the image of God's mind, or through Chinese beliefs about nature's internal order to which humans should adjust their activities (compare Needham, 1969). They can see the Earth as Mother Nature; God's special gift to his chosen people; as a former Garden of Eden, or a former wilderness; as planet Earth, spaceship Earth, or lifeboat Earth. Fourth, they can give to their projects culturally different ways of organizing the production of scientific and technological knowledge. "Voyages of discovery" are one way to organize the production of knowledge; so are cooperative or competitive laboratory relations. Moreover, their epistemological standards are part and parcel of these other culturally distinctive resources, themselves shaped by different locations in nature, interests, discursive resources, and ways of organizing the production of knowledge, as they, in turn, shape them. Theories of knowledge are no different in these respects from theories about nature and social relations.

GENDERED LOCAL KNOWLEDGE SYSTEMS

Such an analysis can illuminate further what makes possible distinctively gendered ways of knowing also. We can treat the genders as distinctive cultures—as "gender cultures." Of course women and men occupy the same cultures in many familiar uses of this term; ethnic or religious or class cultures contain both genders. However, there are also more or less single-gender cultures within these other cultures. This is true in the sense that only women or men, or primarily women or men, are to be found in them; but it is also the case in the sense that many such subcultures are gender-coded in ways that don't necessarily reflect the proportion of women and men in them. Thus we talk of the masculine cultures of locker room, board rooms, and the military even when women are visible in them (or when only women are occupying a particular locker room, board room, or military group), and of the feminine cultures of elementary school classrooms, kitchens, the world of fashion, or the novel, even though plenty of men are to be found in all of them. It is in this latter sense that we can talk about the gender cultures of scientific and technological knowledge seeking. The more complex understanding of gender described earlier alerts us to such gender cultures.

Obviously, women and men are exposed to different elements of nature's regularities for biological as well as social reasons. A woman's concerns with contraception are different from her partner's since it is she who could become pregnant. Her physiological characteristics make her susceptible to different sports injuries and give her different physical resources than her brothers can call upon. Moreover, to the extent that gender social structures assign women and men to different activities, they will tend to interact with different parts of nature—for example, with babies or car motors, to take stereotypical examples.

Even when interacting with "the same" part of nature, men and women can have different interests in such interactions. Her interests in the local environme ͏ be a matter of finding resources for her work of providing daily subsistence, while his are for growing cash crops. Each has interests in the success of the other's projects, but their interests and, consequently, knowledge of the local environment can be different.

Furthermore, men and women can have different relations to the cultural discursive traditions that direct their practices and give them meaning. For example, a woman graduate student's interactions with a linear accelerator are not seamlessly embedded in developing models of manliness in the ways that a male physicist's similar interactions are, though she may have to "demonstrate manliness" in order to succeed as a physicist (Traweek, 1988).

Finally, men and women often have different, socially developed ways of organizing the production of knowledge. Japanese women primatologists evidently can recognize hundreds of primates individually; Japanese male primatologists report that they have no idea how the women do it (and it is not a genetically shaped skill) (Haraway, 1989). Anecdotal evidence suggests that women scientists tend to seek research "niches" of their own rather than joining the "hottest," most competitive new fields; that they tend to organize their research teams more around cooperation and less around competitive relations; and that their peer networks tend to have different kinds of resources than those used by their male colleagues (Barinaga, 1993).

One can identify traces of the distinctive resources, their strengths and limitations, that women bring to their knowledge projects in WWK, though such an explanation of the causes of gendered ways of knowing was not the major focus in the study. However, the authors noted how family violence, pedagogical and curriculum institutions and practices, and motherhood are sites where women's epistemologies are especially liable to enablement and/or restriction. Lack of opportunities to play and engage in dialogue removed resources from women's epistemological development projects. The necessity to balance the demands of the work world and public life with the responsibilities of family life provided valuable resources for such development. Thus we can see that some of the resources and limitations in women's ways of knowing are due to the "culturally" different content of their activities. The development of "self, voice, and mind" through theories about knowledge occurs in ways that bear similarities to how cultures other than the dominant European ones develop their distinctive senses of "self, voice, and mind."

Issues of how power relations shape systematic knowledge and systematic ignorance have been referred to here and there in the discussion so far. This theme that already appeared in WWK was independently elaborated into a distinctive feminist standpoint epistemology.

POWER AND KNOWLEDGE

Standpoint epistemologies, whether or not articulated in such terms, have been the main approach in both feminist and postcolonial science studies to understanding relations between knowledge and power.[5] Standpoint epistemologies add a second kind of "difference" to the "mere cultural difference" that enables cultures to generate distinctive epistemologies and corresponding bodies of knowledge.

In the last two sections we saw that all knowledge is local—modern Northern scientific knowledge no less than the "ethnosciences" of other cultures. However, obviously not all such LKS are equally powerful. Some can explain a great deal more than others because, for example, they have access to or control more of nature and social relations, and so can gather and reflect on information from a greater diversity of sources. Some LKS are powerful enough to be able systematically to siphon knowledge from other LKS, giving nothing in return, leaving the other LKS mere empty husks of their former selves. We could think of these as positional rather than substantive epistemological and scientific resources to mark how it is a position in power relations with respect to other cultures that generate such resources.

However, there are always also accompanying limitations and losses to these power positions no less than to any "merely cultural" difference in knowledge production. That is, culturally local knowledge-seeking projects, including those with immense power over others' such projects, always also create distinctive patterns of ignorance. Standpoint theory articulates the surprising epistemological resources created by the positional "powers of the weak." Postcolonial critics point out that it is only by standing "outside" the dominant European epistemology that one can detect strengths and limitations of it that are invisible from "inside it." For example, pursuing the question of why it was that modern sciences developed in Europe rather than in some other culture from the perspective of the cultures into which Europe expanded as its sciences developed enables one to detect the Eurocentrism of Northern sciences, philosophies, and histories of science. From such a marginal, outsider, or borderlands standpoint one can detect, for example, that the epistmological dominance of Northern thought was in fact not established through the purportedly uniquely admirable "internal" properties of European scientific and epistemological methods that conventional epistemologies claim. Instead, it developed through European expansion's power to test scientific hypotheses across extremely diverse ranges of natural conditions; through European expansion's interests in better navigation, oceanography, climatology, mining of precious ores, farming, disease control, cartography, and so on; and through European expansion's spread of this thought and simultaneous destruction of other competing bodies of knowledge and thought processes. Thus European history and philosophy of science suffer from the excessive dominance of Eurocentric perspectives that hide how European expansion and the growth of modern sciences in Europe were dependent on each other.

Moreover, the picture of nature that emerges from Northern sciences contains what those who fund and support modern sciences have wanted to know about nature and excludes what has not interested them and what they positively have wanted "not to know." For example, they have wanted to know about how to farm lands in the South for Northern profit rather than how to keep fragile environments productive for the peoples whose local daily subsistence depends on them. They have wanted to know the "causes" of cancer that are to be found within individuals' biological makeup and their "life-styles" much more than the causes to be found within their environments, or, as some critics have pointed out, in governmental and military policies that tolerate environmental toxicity, especially for the already most politically and economically vulnerable. The production of systematic ignorance has accompanied the production of systematic knowledge in these most powerful of knowledge systems no less than in less powerful ones.

Thus starting off thought from outside such dominant conceptual frameworks or discourses can generate more accurate and comprehensive accounts of nature's regularities and their causes. It can maximize objectivity in ways that thought contained within one dominant framework can not. Such epistemological and scientific resources are not dependent on the particular social activities in which one engages, but on one's position, and one's culture's position, in power relations. The point here is not that every poor or otherwise marginalized person already can or does "see the truth," but rather that discourses oppositional to the dominant ones can arise as marginalized groups begin to articulate their histories, needs, and desires "for themselves" instead of only in the ways encouraged by their "masters'" favored conceptual frameworks.

Feminists have most clearly articulated this epistemology as such. Feminist standpoint theories link political struggles by "outsiders" to especially valuable ways of knowing (compare Harding, 1986; 1991; Hartsock, 1983; Jaggar, 1983; Rose, 1993; Smith, 1987; 1990). Such arguments appear in appeals that feminist theory be constructed "from margin to center," by "outsiders within," from "borderlands," in the "lines of fault" that create "bifurcated consciousnesses," and through "situated knowledge" that is located outside dominant power structures (hooks, 1983; Collins, 1991; Anzaldua, 1987; Smith, 1987; 1990; Haraway, 1991). For these thinkers, Northern feminists and postcolonial science critics alike, gaining this kind of knowledge always requires political struggles since it reveals exactly what is "not supposed to exist"—the interested, "subjective," local, ethnocentric character of dominant knowledge systems that claim to be disinterested, maximally objective, universally valid, and speaking from no particular social location at all. It reveals, for example, that modern European science, too, is an "ethnoscience."

The authors of WWK clearly linked the resources available to the women they studied to the gendered power relations within which women work to gain enabling selves, voices, and minds. However, here I must note that two features of their research design seemed to me to limit the picture they could present of how women come to gain this politicized sense of the project of gaining self, voice, and mind. I am sure their thought has developed in the last decade in ways that may well dissolve such limits, so my comments here are restricted to the text of a decade ago. The "constructivism" they identify can result in either relativist or (antiabsolutist and antirelativist) standpoint epistemologies. All knowledge claims are socially situated; historically local; shaped by culturally distinctive locations in nature, interests, discursive resources, and ways of organizing the production of knowledge. They are sociologically or historically relative in this sense. But such a position does not commit one to epistemological relativism, for we can still present rational evidence and arguments to show (provisionally) that, for example, European expansion generated far more powerful scientific claims than could those social situations that restricted observers to exposure to a smaller proportion of nature's regularities. To take another example, one where we can see the "epistemological powers of the weak," women's experiences of their own bodies, and the interests, discursive resources, and ways of organizing the production of knowledge about women's bodies (really listening to what women say, not devaluing what they say, and so on), have enabled the women's health movement to identify patterns of systematic ignorance in the dominant biomedical knowledge system. Sometimes the authors seem to imply that there is no reasonable way to judge whether one knowledge strategy or knowledge claim is better or more powerful than another. At other times they appear clear that the constructivist epistemologies they identify are especially powerful and lead to more reliable knowledge claims than the claims of those constrained by the other epistemologies. Thus I find their account ambivalent here.

I was also struck by the fact that the voices of women political activists, women engaged in collective political projects, could not be heard in the project. Interviewing women community activists, union organizers, and the like, or, perhaps, asking questions to elicit these collective and politicized processes of knowing, would bring into hearing many women's awareness of how political struggle is a "way of knowing." It would also present an epistemological stance that moves beyond the sociological and historical relativism sometimes implied as ultimately desirable by the authors. Moreover, relatedly, interviewing individuals, rather than groups who, like the authors themselves, work together, tended to silence such collective ways of knowing, I suspect. Do U.S. women lack the collective sense of "we" that could be heard in the voices of Russian peasants? The women in the study appear isolated from other women and from the resources that such collective struggles provide. They still appear as the apolitical individuals centered in the dominant epistemologies that the authors otherwise find so limited. Might union women evidence a different and useful way of knowing that we could not hear in the voices even of those thoughtful highly educated individuals in the study? Might their "way of knowing" in fact reveal more about the epistemologies of marginalized groups around the world as they become groups "for themselves" rather than primarily only "in themselves," as women appear in WWK? Hasn't this study itself helped to turn women from a group "in itself" endlessly acted on and observed from outside to a politically mobilized gender "for itself," capable of becoming subjects of history and knowledge? (However, see the chapters by Tarule and Goldberger, this volume.)

CONCLUSION

I have been reflecting on three different issues raised in WWK that have gained added significance since its publication. First, the development of antiessentialist ways of understanding gender relations has provided rich resources for understanding how gender is shaped by and, in turn, shapes other structural features of societies and their meanings. Moreover, the (antiessentialist) differences in women's ways of knowing have two distinguishable sources. Their conflation has sometimes led to misreadings of feminist epistemological studies. There are gender differences in theories of knowledge that arise from the substantive cultural or historical differences in people's lives. To the extent that women and men are assigned different activities and experiences, those activities and experiences will provide resources and limitations for developing knowledge about different aspects of nature and social relations with which they interact, and this would be so even if there were no power relations between women and men. Since our theories of knowledge tend to vary according to the kinds of knowledge projects in which we engage, it should not surprise us that parenting, juggling work and family obligations, or experiencing family violence or little opportunity for play or dialogue should affect the theories of knowledge of those who have such experiences.

However, we can at least analytically distinguish differences in knowledge and theories of knowledge that arise from how people are positioned in power relations. Some resources for generating knowledge clearly are available primarily for those in powerful positions in a culture. But other resources are generated on the margins of any knowledge system, and on the borderlands between competing knowledge systems. Such resources are not available in the power positions. So our positions in social hierarchies, as well as the content of what we do, enable and limit what we can know and the theories of knowledge we will be likely to develop.

Moreover, both of these features of women's ways of knowing—themselves developed on the margins of the dominant knowledge system— offer valuable alternative resources to those available in the prevailing androcentric and Eurocentric epistemological frameworks. The limitations of androcentric epistemologies are also the limitations of the epistemologies of the modern West. Both sources of resources for women's ways of knowing show how legitimating and exploring diversely socially situated knowledges can expand human knowledge while also advancing recognition of the richness and diversity of human cultural traditions.

With such a culturally respectful epistemological program, advancing knowledge can be more firmly linked to advancing democratic social relations than is possible in societies under the illusion that the dominant groups have the one true story about themselves and the natural and social worlds around them.

NOTES

1. A good review of the origins and progress of this developing "crisis" can be found in chapter 15, "The center does not hold," of historian Peter Novick's *That noble dream* (1988). See also the introduction to philosopher Richard Bernstein (1983), and the various postcolonial writings cited later.

2. It is a problem in an essay reflecting on a book about "the development of self, voice, and mind" that the literature to which I wish to refer here is commonly referred to as about "development"—by which is meant the post–World War II projects to "help" the "undeveloped" Third World societies by transferring to them the models of modernization and, thus, industrialization that are assumed to be responsible for the North's high living standards. I shall insert *Third World* before *development* wherever clarification appears necessary.

   Another issue about the terms used here should be noted. In the postcolonial parlance adopted here, *Northern* and *Southern* refer to theoretical and political standpoints or discourses, not to ethnicities, citizenship, or places of residence. Some Northern science theorists, who adhere to the standard Enlightenment perceptions of science and the nature it studies, are Brazilian, Nigerian, Indian, and Japanese nationals living in their homelands. Some Southern science theorists who criticize the Eurocentrism of such representations of science and nature are French, Brits, Swedes, and Americans living in their countries. A Northern discourse starts thinking from within conventional Northern conceptual frameworks and their assumptions. A Southern discourse starts outside it. My impression is that the terms *Northern* and *Southern* began to gain international currency after the 1992 Rio Environmental conference, replacing Western–Non-Western, First World–Third World, and other older contrasts presumably carrying more residues of Eurocentrism.

3. The authors' discussion of Russian psychologist L. S. Vygotsky's studies of Russian peasants' ways of knowing (32–33), for example, already hints at this matter of how gendered ways of knowing involve both "mere" cultural differences and power differences. The authors report

that Russian peasants' ways of knowing are similar to those of some contemporary U.S. women because in both cases their cultures deprive them of opportunities for play and for dialogue. Yet, powerless though the Russian peasants were in some respects, in others the conditions of their lives gave them a firm sense of the authority of their experiences, and a collective sense of self, voice, and mind, both of which were denied to the U.S. women by their low positions in gendered power relations.

4. See Harding (in press) for a fuller discussion of these issues.

5. Standpoint epistemologies became useful precisely because they centered the relations between knowledge and power, refusing to assume the apolitical ideal of conventional Enlightenment epistemologies of science and knowledge seeking more generally. However, poststructuralist approaches have been especially helpful in enabling standpoint theories systematically to examine critically pluralities of power relations, of the sort indicated in the earlier discussion of gender as shaped by class, race, and other historical cultural forces, and how these are disseminated through "discourses" that are both structural and symbolic. I set aside further discussion of the complex relations between the originally oppositional but increasingly converging histories of standpoint and poststructuralist epistemologies.

REFERENCES

Anzaldúa, G. (1987). *Borderlands/La frontera*. San Francisco: Spinsters/Aunt Lute.

Barinaga, M. (1993, April). Is there a "female style" in science? *Science 260*, 384–391.

Belenky, M. F., Clinchy, B. M., Goldberger, N. R., & Tarule, J. M. (1986). *Women's ways of knowing: The development of self, voice, and mind*. New York: Basic Books.

Bernal, M. (1987). *Black Athena: The Afroasiatic roots of classical civilization* (Vol. 1). New Brunswick, NJ: Rutgers University Press.

Bernstein, R. (1983). *Beyond objectivism and relativism*. Philadelphia: University of Pennsylvania Press.

Blaut, J. M. (1993). *The colonizer's model of the world: Geographical diffusionism and Eurocentric history*. New York: Guilford Press.

Braidotti, Rosi, et al. (1994). *Women, the environment, and sustainable development*. London: Zed Books.

Cockburn, C. (1985). *Machinery of dominance: Women, men and technical know-how*. London: Pluto Press.

Collins, P. H. (1991). *Black feminist thought: Knowledge consciousness, and the politics of empowerment*. New York: Routledge.

Enloe, C. (1989). *Bananas, beaches and bases: Making feminist sense of international politics*. Berkeley: University of California Press.

Goonatilake, S. (1992). The voyages of discovery and the loss and rediscovery of the "Other's" knowledge. *Impact of Science on Society, 167*.

Haraway, D. (1989). *Primate visions: Gender, race and nature in the world of modern science*. New York: Routledge.

Haraway, D. (1991). Situated knowledges: The science question in feminism and the privilege of partial perspectives. In her *Simians, cyborgs, and women*. New York: Routledge.

Harcourt, W. (1994). *Feminist perspectives on sustainable development*. London: Zed Press.

Harding, S. (1986). *The science question in feminism*. Ithaca, NY: Cornell University Press.

Harding, S. (1991). *Whose science? Whose knowledge?* Ithaca, NY: Cornell University Press.

Harding, S, (Ed.) (1993). *The "racial" economy of science: Toward a democratic future.* Bloomington: Indiana University Press.

Harding, S. (1994). Is science multicultural? Challenges, resources, opportunities, uncertainties. In *Configurations 2* (2) and in D. T. Goldberg (Ed.), *Multiculturalism: A reader.* London: Blackwell's.

Harding, S. (1995). "Strong objectivity": A response to the new objectivity question. *Synthese, 104*(3), 1–19.

Harding, S. (in press). What makes possible women's standpoints on nature? *Osiris 2.*

Harding, S. (1996a). Is modern science an ethnoscience? In J. Spaapen & T. Shin (Eds.), *Sociology of the Sciences Yearbook 1996.* Dordrecht: Kluwer.

Harding, S. (1996b). *Is science multicultural? Feminist and postcolonial perspectives.* Bloomington: Indiana University Press.

Harding, S. & McGregor, E. (1996). The gender dimension of science and technology. In H. Moore (Ed.), *World science report 1996.* Paris: UNESCO.

Hartsock, N. (1983). The feminist standpoint. In S. Harding & M. Hintikka (Eds.), *Discovering reality.* Dordrecht: Reidel/Kluwer.

Hess, D. J. (1995). *Science and technology in a multicultural world: The cultural politics of facts and artifacts.* New York: Columbia University Press.

hooks, b. (1983). *Feminist theory from margin to center.* Boston: South End Press.

Jaggar, A. (1983). *Feminist politics and human nature.* Totowa, NJ: Rowman & Allenheld.

Joseph, G. G. (1991). *The crest of the peacock: Non-european roots of mathematics.* New York: I. B. Tauris.

Keller, E. F. (1984). *Reflections on gender and science.* New Haven, CT: Yale University Press.

Kuhn, T. S. (1962). *The structure of scientific revolutions.* Chicago: University of Chicago Press.

Latour, B., & Woolgar, S. (1979). *Laboratory life: The social construction of scientific facts.* Beverley Hills, CA: Sage.

Lloyd, G. (1984). *The man of reason: "Male" and "Female" in Western philosophy.* London: Methuen.

Merchant, C. (1980). *The death of nature: Women, ecology and the scientific revolution.* New York: Harper & Row.

Mies, M. (1986). *Patriarchy and accumulation on a world scale: Women in the international division of labor.* Atlantic Highlands, NJ: Zed Press.

Needham, J. (1969). *The grand titration: Science and society in East and West.* Toronto: University of Toronto Press.

Novick, P. (1988). *That noble dream: The "objectivity question" and the American historical profession.* Cambridge: Cambridge University Press.

Petitjean, P., et al., (Eds.) (1992). *Science and empires: Historical studies about scientific development and european expansion.* Dordrecht: Kluwer.

Pickering, A. (1984). *Constructing quarks.* Chicago: University of Chicago Press.

Pickering, A. (Ed.) (1992). *Science as practice and culture.* Chicago: University of Chicago Press.

Rose, H. (1993). Hand, brain, and heart: A feminist epistemology for the natural sciences. In S. Harding and J. F. O'Barr (Eds.), *Sex and scientific inquiry,* Chicago: University of Chicago Press.

Ruddick, S. (1989). *Maternal thinking: Towards a politics of peace.* Boston: Beacon.

Sachs, W. (Ed.) (1992). *The development dictionary: A guide to knowledge as power.* Atlantic Highlands, NJ: Zed Books.

Sardar, Z. (Ed.) (1988). *The revenge of Athena: Science, exploitation and the Third World.* London: Mansell.

Shiva, V. (1989). *Staying alive: Women, ecology and development.* London: Zed Books.

Smith, D. E. (1987). *The everyday world as problematic: A feminist sociology.* Boston: Northeastern University Press.

Smith, D. E. (1990). *The conceptual practices of power: A feminist sociology of knowledge.* Boston: Northeastern University Press.

Todorov, T. (1984). *The conquest of America: The question of the other.* (Richard Howard, Trans.). New York: Harper & Row.

Traweek, S. (1988). *Beamtimes and life times.* Cambridge, MA: MIT Press.

Trinh, M. (1989). *Woman/Native/Other: Writing postcoloniality and feminism.* Bloomington: Indiana University Press.

Wacjman, J. (1991). *Feminism confronts technology.* University Park, PA: Penn State Press.

Watson-Verran, H., & Turnbull, R. (1994). Science and other indigenous knowledge systems. In *Science and technology handbook.* Berkeley, CA: Sage.

CONTRIBUTORS

MARY FIELD BELENKY, ED.D., is a coauthor of *Women's Ways of Knowing* and a coeditor of *Knowledge, Difference, and Power*. She is associated with the Department of Psychology at the University of Vermont. Her professional work has centered on educational and social programs that support women's intellectual and ethical development. She co-directed The Listening Partners, a project that sponsored isolated, poor, rural mothers to gain a voice and claim the power of mind. She has also recently studied a series of organizations—public homeplaces—created by women to empower women living at the margins of society. These studies will be published in 1997 in *A Tradition That Has No Name: Public Homeplaces and the Development of People, Families, and Communities*, coauthored with Lynne Bond and Jackie Weinstock.

VANESSA MARIE BING, PH.D., is staff therapist at the Postgraduate Center for Mental Health in New York City, a faculty member at the College of New Rochelle, and a project consultant for an Early Intervention Program at Edwin Gould Services for Children. She is a past recipient of an APA Minority Fellowship. Her current research interests include coping behaviors in African American women and children, racial identity formation in children, and racial and cultural barriers to effective psychotherapy. Dr. Bing served on the board of directors for the New York Association of Black Psychologists and conducts workshops addressing cultural diversity in academia and the workplace.

LYN MIKEL BROWN, ED.D., is assistant professor and cochair of the Education and Human Development Program at Colby College, Waterville, Maine. She is coauthor (with Carol Gilligan) of *Meeting at the Crossroads: Womens Psychology and Girls' Development* (1992) and has written numerous articles on girls' and women's psychological development, girls' education, and feminist methods. She is currently working on a new book, *Stones in the Road: Anger, Class, and Adolescent Girls*, to be published by Harvard University Press.

BLYTHE MCVICKER CLINCHY, PH.D., a coauthor of *Women's Ways of Knowing* (1986) and a coeditor of this volume, is a professor at Wellesley College, where she teaches courses in research methodology and in child and adult development. She received her A.B. from Smith College, her M.A. from the New School for Social Research, and her Ph.D. from Harvard University. Her research focuses on the evolution of conceptions of knowledge, truth, and value in males and females from early childhood through adulthood and the implications of this development for the practice of education from nursery school through college. With Julie Norem, she is editing *Readings in Psychology and Gender*, to be published in 1997 by New York University Press.

ELIZABETH DEBOLD, ED.D., a consultant and activist, is coauthor (with Marie Wilson and Idelisse Malave), of *Mother Daughter Revolution: From Good Girls to Great Women* (1994). She was a founding member of the Harvard Project on Women's Psychology and Girls' Development. Dr. Debold is currently director of evaluation of the Ms. Foundation for Women's Healthy Girls/Healthy Women Collaborative Fund and is working on a new book on embodiment and gender.

NANCY RULE GOLDBERGER, PH.D., is a member of the clinical psychology faculty of the Fielding Institute in Santa Barbara, California, and visiting scholar at New York University. In addition to *Women's Ways of Knowing* (1986), which she coauthored, and *Knowledge, Difference, and Power*, which she coedited, she is coeditor of *The Culture and Psychology Reader* (1995) with Jody Veroff. She has written extensively in the areas of women's development and epistemology, innovative education, adolescent development, cognitive style, and the implications of ways of knowing theory in psychotherapy and clinical practice. She is currently codirecting a longitudinal research project on adult midlife graduate education, called Constructing an Education.

SANDRA HARDING, PH.D., is professor of philosophy at the University of Delaware and adjunct professor of philosophy and women's studies at UCLA. She is author or editor of seven books, including *Discovering Reality: Feminist Perspectives on Epistemology, Metaphysics, Methodol-*

ogy, and Philosophy of Science (1983), *The Science Question in Feminism* (1986), *Sex and Scientific Inquiry* (1987), *Feminism and Methodology* (1987), *Whose Science? Whose Knowledge? Thinking from Women's Lives* (1991), and *The "Racial" Economy of Science: Toward a Democratic Future* (1993). She is coauthor of a chapter in UNESCO's *World Science Report 1997*, "The Gender Dimension of Science and Technology." Her most recent book, *Is Science Multicultural? Feminist and Postcolonial Perspectives*, will be published in 1997.

AÍDA HURTADO, PH.D., is associate professor at the University of California, Santa Cruz. Dr. Hurtado's research focuses on the effects of subordination on social identity. She is especially interested in group memberships such as ethnicity, race, class, and gender that are used to legitimize unequal distributions of power between groups. Her expertise is in survey methods with bilingual–bicultural populations. She has published extensively on issues of language and social identity for the Mexican-origin population in the United States. Dr. Hurtado received her B.A. in psychology and sociology from Pan American University in Edinburg, Texas, and her M.A. and Ph.D. in social psychology from the University of Michigan.

FRANCES A. MAHER, ED.D, is coauthor with Mary Kay Tetreault of *The Feminist Classroom: An Inside Look at How Professors and Students Are Transforming Higher Education for a Diverse Society* (1994), an in-depth study of seventeen feminist college teachers nationwide over the period 1987–1993. She is professor and chair of the Education Department at Wheaton College, where she also coordinated the Wheaton's Balanced Curriculum Project to integrate the study of women into introductory courses. She has published widely in the field of feminist pedagogy and has taught courses in feminist theory and introduction to women's studies as well as in education.

MICHAEL J. MAHONEY, PH.D., earned his doctorate in 1972 at Stanford University. He was elected to fellow status in the American Association for the Advancement of Science in 1989 "for significant theoretical and empirical contributions to the understanding of basic processes in human psychological development and psychotherapy." He is the author or editor of fifteen books, the most recent being *Human Change Processes* (1991), *Cognitive and Constructive Psychotherapies* (1995), and (with R. A. Neimeyer) *Constructivism in Psychotherapy* (1995).

CARRIE MENKEL-MEADOW, J.D., is professor of law at UCLA and Georgetown University and is codirector of the UCLA Center for Inter-Racial/Inter-Ethnic Conflict Resolution. She formerly served as director of the UCLA Center for the Study of Women and she teaches in the Women's Studies program at UCLA. Professor Menkel-Meadow has written extensively in the fields of feminist legal theory and jurisprudence, women in the legal profession, legal ethics, legal education, sociology of the profession, delivery of legal services, and dispute resolution (negotiation, mediation, and litigation). She is the author of "Portia in a different voice: Speculations on a woman's lawyering practice" and "Portia redux: Another look at feminism, gender, and legal ethics," among other articles and books.

PAMELA TROTMAN REID, PH.D., professor of psychology, serves as associate provost and dean for academic affairs at the Graduate School and University Center of the City University of New York. Her research combines feminist theory with developmental psychology methodologies to confront issues of gender, class, and ethnicity. She is a former president of the American Psychological Associations's Division of Psychology of Women and a recipient of the Association of Women in Psychology's Outstanding Publication Award.

SARA RUDDICK, PH.D., teaches philosophy and feminist studies at the New School for Social Research. She coedited two feminist collections of personal essays: Working It Out (1977) and Between Women (1984). Her most recent book is Maternal Thinking: Toward a Politics of Peace (1989). With Julia Hanigsberg she is coediting a collection of essays by legal theorists, philosophers, and theologians on difficult issues in mothering. She is also finishing a book in feminist ethics.

PATROCINIO P. SCHWEICKART, PH.D., professor of English at the University of New Hampshire, is widely published in the area of feminist theory, as well as feminist literary criticism. She is coeditor, with Elizabeth A. Flynn, of Gender and Reading: Essays on Readers, Texts, and Contexts (1986). Her publications include "Engendering Critical Discourse" (1987), "Reading, Teaching, and the Ethic of Care" (1990), and "What Are We Doing? What Do We Want? Comprehending the Subject of Feminism" (1995). Her essay "Reading Ourselves: Toward a Feminist Theory of Reading" won the Florence Howe Award in 1984. She is editor of the National Women's Studies Association Journal.

ANN STANTON, PH.D., is an associate professor of liberal studies in the Adult Degree Program, Vermont College of Norwich University, in Montpelier. Her longtime interest in innovative education began as a charter member of Pitzer College, where faculty and students held weekly town meetings to debate philosophies of education and devised the governance structure of the college. She worked in community-based education for three years in Peru and El Salvador with the Peace Corps and spent another year in rural Mexico conducting research. Since 1980, she has been actively involved in research and teaching in the area of education for women's development.

JILL MATTUCK TARULE, ED.D., is coauthor of *Women's Ways of Knowing* (1986) and coeditor of *Knowledge, Difference, and Power.* She is currently dean of the University of Vermont College of Education and Social Services, having previously been a faculty member or administrator at Goddard College, Lesley College, and the Vermont State Department of Education. She holds a doctorate from the Harvard Graduate School of Education and an honorary degree from the University of New Hampshire. Her research has focused on adult and women's education and collaborative learning.

MARY KAY TETRAULT, ED.D., vice president for academic affairs at California State University, is the coauthor of *The Feminist Classroom* and the author of *Women in America: Half of History* (1979), a collection of primary source materials. In 1984 she received the Women Educators' Research Award of the American Educational Research Association for her study of the treatment of women in high school textbooks on U.S. history. She is also the author of numerous articles on feminist phase theory and curriculum integration.

DEBORAH L. TOLMAN, ED.D., is a research associate and director of the Adolescent Sexuality Project at the Center for Research on Women at Wellesley College. She is currently studying how femininity ideology may relate to a range of risks and resiliences embedded in sexual and intimate relationships for culturally and socioeconomically diverse girls as they move through adolescence. She is the author of numerous journal articles and book chapters addressing female adolescent sexuality. She is writing a book based on her research about adolescent girls' experience of their sexuality, *Dilemma of Desire*, to be published by Harvard University Press.

SUBJECT INDEX

AUTHOR INDEX